Human Resource Development

Human Resource Development

Strategy and tactics

**Juani Swart, Clare Mann, Steve Brown and
Alan Price**

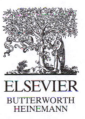

ELSEVIER
BUTTERWORTH
HEINEMANN

AMSTERDAM BOSTON HEIDELBERG LONDON NEW YORK OXFORD
PARIS SAN DIEGO SAN FRANCISCO SINGAPORE SYDNEY TOKYO

Elsevier Butterworth-Heinemann
Linacre House, Jordan Hill, Oxford OX2 8DP
30 Corporate Drive, Burlington, MA 01803

First published 2005

British Library Cataloguing in Publication Data
A catalogue record for this book is available from the British Library

Library of Congress Cataloguing in Publication Data
A catalogue record for this book is available from the Library of Congress

ISBN 0 7506 6250 6

For information on all Elsevier Butterworth-Heinemann publications
visit our website at http://books.elsevier.com

Typeset by Charon Tec Pvt. Ltd, Chennai, India
www.charontec.com
Printed and bound in Great Britain

Working together to grow
libraries in developing countries

www.elsevier.com | www.bookaid.org | www.sabre.org

ELSEVIER   BOOK AID International   Sabre Foundation

Contents

Chapter 1

The strategic importance of human resource development

Introduction

We start this chapter by examining the reasons why human resource development has become a critical part of an organization's competitive capabilities, and explaining why people are important in organizations. We will also discuss how human resource development has changed over time, and why it is important in the modern competitive arena.

The next section explores how human resource management has been modified to reflect the step changes in markets and production requirements over time. We will describe the nature of the changes to major business eras, leading to an appreciation of how skills requirements have reflected these major changes.

After explaining what is meant by strategy, the third section develops key strategic issues in human resource development. We will also investigate how human resources can play a profoundly important part in developing and implementing strategy within an organization.

Next, the emergence of human resources as a strategic issue is explored in greater depth. This section explains the critical differences between many Western firms' and Japanese approaches to human resource development. We will show that human resource development needs to be in place alongside other important human resource issues, including industrial relations, and describe how human resources can become part of the core competence of an organization.

The final section looks at how some firms have developed a set of best practices, thus enabling reconfiguration in order to improve performance in innovation, quality and other important competitive variables. We will explain some of the key requirements in developing best practice in human resource development, and how firms have had to reconfigure themselves – which can only be done as part of wider human resource development.

Objectives

By the end of this chapter you will be able to:

- Appreciate why human resource development is of strategic importance in the current business world
- Realize how human resource development has changed over time
- Understand why some firms have problems in viewing human resources in a strategic manner
- Have a basic insight in the key areas that will then be explored further in subsequent chapters.

The strategic importance of human resource development

Why people are important in organizations

It should be self-evident: organizations consist of people, and so the development of these people should be a key task for organizations. If you were to speak to senior-level managers within firms they would, typically, state how important their staff are. Sadly, however, these same senior-level managers will often concentrate on slashing budgets related to human resource development. They may also have no qualms about downsizing the number of employees at the same time. What is sometimes not clear, though, is that people really do matter in organizations. People matter because in the highly competitive environment which firms now face, human capital has become a precious commodity in gaining any sort of advantage over other firms. The following states it succinctly:

> A culture that values curiosity is inventive and exciting. Walk into the headquarters of USA in San Antonio, Texas, 3M in St Paul, Minnesota, or Lockheed Martin in Fort Worth, Texas, and you can feel the heat of originality cooking in the organizational oven. What you later learn is that you're in a place with an ever-lasting focus on perpetual growth. The popular label for such an environment is a learning organization. A more accurate description is a discovering organization. The term learning can imply the act of adding to or increasing what's already there; discovering means uncovering or finding. Learning can happen through osmosis, in which you're passively the recipient of growth, without much effort. Discovering suggests an active search and a deliberate exploration.
>
> (Bell and Bell, 2003: 57)

Human Resource Development is a vital area for firms because ideas for innovation, quality and continuous improvement, as well as other critically important inputs needed to compete in the modern, highly competitive business world, come from people and not from machines. The extent to which people will provide suggestions for improvements – in all forms – will depend, to a large extent, on human resource development strategies within firms. The need to develop human resources on an ongoing basis has not always been so prominent. For example, the eminent management writer, Peter Drucker described how 'My ancestors were printers in Amsterdam from 1510 or so until 1750 … and during that entire time they didn't have to learn anything new' (*Business 2.0*, 22 August 2000).

Drucker is not being critical of his ancestors, nor is he accusing them of not caring about their employers or stating that such an approach was 'wrong'. Indeed, it might well be argued that in previous times such an approach would have been entirely appropriate. The issue is: in today's competitive arena it is not appropriate.

The need for both the employer and employee to understand the role of human resource development is important. For the employer, the following is pertinent:

> 'Survival isn't just a matter of smart machines. Workers have to get smarter as well, and show a willingness to learn new technologies', says John A. McFarland, CEO of Baldor Electric Co., the largest

maker of industrial electric motors in the US. A versatile corps of workers has helped Baldor ride out the manufacturing recession without a layoff.

(*Business Week*, 5 May 2003)

For the employee, it has become eminently clear that the notion of a 'job for life' is now an outdated and unsustainable proposition. Thus the terms of engagement have to change when a new employee applies for a job opportunity, and this was captured by Davis and Meyer (2000: 12):

> You must realize that how you invest your human capital matters as much as how you invest your financial capital. Its rate of return determines your future options. Take a job for what it teaches you, not for what it pays. Instead of a potential employer asking, 'Where do you see yourself in 5 years?' you'll ask, 'If I invest my mental assets with you for 5 years, how much will they appreciate? How much will my portfolio of career options grow?'

However, the overwhelming evidence seems to be that organizations do not fully understand the strategic importance of human resource development. Many firms are too quick to downsize or 'rightsize' in the pursuit of cost-cutting initiatives. Other strategic decisions, including mergers and acquisitions, may threaten the culture that had human resource development as part of its core capabilities:

> Many of us Hewlett-Packard retirees and former employees agreed with Walter Hewlett when he opposed the acquisition of Compaq. He wisely anticipated the questionable value and performance described in Adam Lashinsky's 'Wall Street to Carly: Prove It!' (First, Jan. 12). But of equal significance was the sad absence of Hewlett-Packard from the 100 Best Companies to Work For list in the same issue. We also remember when HP was at or near the top of that list because of our proud adherence to the culture called 'the HP Way'. That culture, perhaps HP's greatest invention, continues to thrive in Silicon Valley and beyond, but not, regrettably, at HP.

(*Fortune*, 9 February 2004)

There may well have been good reasons for the merger between HP and Compaq; what is important here, though, is that this threatened the very culture of the organization that had served HP in the past, and a key element of this was commitment to human resource development.

Academics, researchers and practitioners alike do not urge the need for human resource development strategies within firms because they think it is a 'nice thing to do'. Rather, they advocate human resource development because they recognize the vital role that humans can play within organizations. For example, back in 1978 Peter Drucker, whom we cited earlier, wrote, prophetically: 'To make knowledge work productive will be the great management task of this century, just as to make manual work productive was the great management task of the last century'.

Firms are becomingly increasingly dependent on their human resource capabilities. This is because much of the tacit, as well as coded, formal or documented, knowledge that a firm possesses centres on human resources. A firm can accumulate this knowledge and general know-how, related to processes, over time. However, such development does not come about by chance; instead it comes from having a strategy for such development. A motivated, highly trained, workforce must form the backbone of any would-be world-class firms. As Grindley (1991) observes:

> The skills base is one of the firm's main assets. It is hard for competitors to imitate … this calls for an attitude to encourage learning and to reward efforts which add to the firm's knowledge. Skills go out of date and need constant replenishment. In the long term what is most important may not be the particular skills, but the ability to keep learning new ones.

The vital importance of human resources is indicated in a telling quotation from the Managing Director of British Chrome and Steel who, in 1998, stated: 'There is no other source of competitive advantage! Others can copy our investment, technology and scale – but NOT the quality of our people …' (in Brown *et al.*, 2000).

Chief Executive Officers (CEOs) will often go on record stating how important their people are for the success of their firms. For example, General Electric's former CEO, Jack Welch, mentioned in an interview in *Fortune* how: 'We spend all our time on people … The day we screw up the people thing, this company is over' (*Fortune*, 21 June 1999).

Clearly this is an over-simplification of what human resource development is about, but it does serve to illustrate how CEOs will go on record regarding the importance of their staff. A motivated, highly trained workforce must form the backbone of any would-be world-class company. The need for innovation, new idea generation, flexibility and inventiveness comes, essentially, via the human input, not via 'machinery' and, as Lazonick (1991: 78) observes: '… the enterprise must plan its human resource needs not only to facilitate the production and distribution of existing products, but also to generate new processes [and] … new products that will permit the *long-term stability and growth of the enterprise*' (italics added).

The fact is that people matter. This apparently obvious statement underpins one of the key lessons that firms aspiring to be world-class learned in the latter part of the twentieth century, and are continuing to do so today. From a position in which people were seen simply as factors of production, as 'hands' to work in factories and offices, there has been a change to recognition of the enormous potential contribution that human resources can offer. Whether in systematic and widespread problem-solving (such as helped the Japanese manufacturing miracle), in the flexibility of teamworking or in the emerging role of 'knowledge workers', the distinctive capabilities of human beings are now being recognized. In the 'resource-based' view of strategy, organizations are encouraged to identify and build upon their core competencies; what is now clear is that a major (but still often under-utilized) resource is the people involved in the organization – the development of 'human resources'.

Why people are important: the evidence

If any of us had been asked to predict the stocks that would perform best in the USA between 1972 and 1992, it is unlikely that we would have chosen a small regional airline, a small publisher, an unknown retailer, a poultry farmer or a video rental business. Yet each of these outperformed the rest of the stock market, including some of the most glamorous and high technology stocks (Pfeffer, 1994). The scale of expansion is shown in Table 1.1.

Activity 1.1

- Why might we be surprised by the types of firms listed in Table 1.1?
- Why are people vitally important in organizations which provide services – such as Wal-Mart and South West Airlines – two firms that appear in Table 1.1?
- Why do human resource capabilities need to be developed and not simply 'bought in' for temporary periods?

Table 1.1
High-performing firms and the increase in their stocks between 1972 and 1992

Company	Increase (%)
Plenum Publishing	15 689
Circuit City	16 410
Tyson Foods	18 118
Wal-Mart	19 807
SouthWest Airlines	21 775

Source: Brown *et al.*, 2000.

The performances of the firms listed in Table 1.1 are significant achievements, but this takes on even more importance when set against the performance of the rest of the sectors in which these firms operate. They do not compete within niche businesses; the industries are highly competitive and overcrowded – with the result that many firms in these fields have gone bankrupt, and all face serious challenges. Perhaps the greatest single challenge for these firms is how best to develop human resources in a way that will enable them to out-perform other firms. To perform well under these highly competitive conditions takes a particular kind of competitive advantage – one that is highly firm-specific and difficult to imitate. In doing so such firms have a 'distinctive' capability or competence, and much of this depends on human resources (Kay, 1993).

The vital role of human resource development

In the firms listed in Table 1.1, it was not the possession of specific assets or market share or their size or advanced technology that accounted for their success. They achieved (and more to the point, they attribute) their growth through the ways in which they managed to organize and work with their people to produce competitive advantage. This is evident in both manufacturing and service sectors. Example 1.1 provides an illustration.

Although SouthWest Airlines is outstanding, it is not an isolated example. There are other studies that point to the same important message. For example, research on the global automobile industry in the 1980s showed that there were very significant performance

Example 1.1: The case of South West Airlines

In his research on outstanding firms that develop human resources, Pfeffer (1994) quotes the case of SouthWest Airlines. This firm did not have specially designed aircraft, but used industry standard equipment. It did not have access to major international reservation systems, and for many years its aircraft were unable to fly in and out of its primary regional airport – Dallas-FortWorth – for a long time having to make do with smaller local airports. Their chosen market segment was not in a small niche but in the mainstream business of trying to sell a commodity product – low price, no frills air travel. Yet SouthWest achieved significantly better productivity than the industry average (79 employees vs 131 average per aircraft in 1991), more passengers per employee (2318 vs 848) and more seat miles per employee (1 891 082 vs 1 339 995). One of its most significant achievements was to slash the turnaround time at airports, getting its planes back in the air faster than others. In 1992, 80 per cent of its flights were turned around in only 15 minutes against the industry average of 45; even now the best the industry can manage is around 30 minutes. All of this is not at a cost to service quality; SWA is one of the only airlines to have achieved the industry's 'triple' crown (fewest lost bags, least passenger complaints and best on time performance in the same month). No other airline has managed the 'triple', yet SWA has done it nine times!

Activity 1.2

- What specific human resource developments do you think need to take place within firms in order to achieve the sort of success evident at SouthWest Airlines?
- Why do firms often ignore the importance of human resources and, consequently, fail to invest in developing them?

differences between the best plants in the world (almost entirely Japanese-operated at that time) and the rest. The gaps were not trivial: on average the best plants were twice as productive (based on labour hour per car), used half the materials and space, and the cars produced had half the number of defects. Not surprisingly, this triggered a search for explanations of this huge difference, and people began looking to see if scale of operations, specialized automation equipment or government subsidy might be behind it. What they found was that there were few differences in areas like automation – indeed, in many cases non-Japanese plants had higher levels of automation and use of robots – but there were major differences in the way work was organized and in the approach taken to develop human resources (Womack *et al.*, 1990).

In a major Department of Trade and Industry Report in the UK, published in 1997, of a study of high performance organizations (by that it is meant those organizations which scored in the

Table 1.2
Key findings of the 1997 DTI Report on UK firms

- 90% said that management of people had become a higher priority in the past 3 years
- 90% have a formal training policy linked to the business plan
- 97% thought training was critical to the success of the business
- 100% had a team structure
- 60% formally train team leaders so the team system becomes effective more quickly
- 65% train their employees to work in teams – this is a skill that has to be learned; it does not come about by chance

upper quartile on various financial and business measures), similar conclusions were made. Factors such as size, advanced technology and other variables were not listed as particularly significant, but 'partnerships with people' were. Of the sample of around 70 firms, the details listed in Table 1.2 came to light.

A telling quotation came from one manager in the DTI study:

> Our operating costs are reducing year on year due to improved efficiencies. We have seen a 35% reduction in costs within two and a half years by improving quality. There is an average of 21 ideas per employee today compared to nil in 1990. Our people have accomplished this.
>
> (Chief Executive, Leyland Trucks; in Brown *et al.*, 2000)

From these and from other evidence that we will provide throughout the book it will become clear that competitive advantage is occurring not through scale of operations, or special market position, or the deployment of major new technologies, but rather from what these organizations do with their people. Teamworking, employee involvement, decentralization of many decisions, training, flexibility – all of these become meshed into a pattern of behaving ('the way we do things around here') and then become ingrained within the company culture. Although 'soft' and intangible, the evidence is clear that possessing such a culture is as powerful a strategic resource as a major patent or an advantageous location. However, such cultures do not emerge by accident; they must be built, maintained and developed.

We have already cited a number of studies that have demonstrated the importance of human resources on subsequent performance within the firm but, as the *Economist* (28 September 1996) has rightly pointed out, human resources are important on a national level as well as being of significance for individual firms:

> The rich economies are coming to depend increasingly on the creation, distribution and use of information and knowledge involving both technology and human capital. The most distinctive feature of the knowledge-based economy is not that it churns out lots of information for consumers though it does that too but that it uses knowledge pervasively as both an input and an output throughout the economy.

How human resource management has changed over time

The three major eras in production

One of the major reasons behind the importance of human resources development in the current competitive arena comes to light when we see how human resources have changed over time. The major changes over time are shown in Figure 1.1, and we shall discuss each in turn.

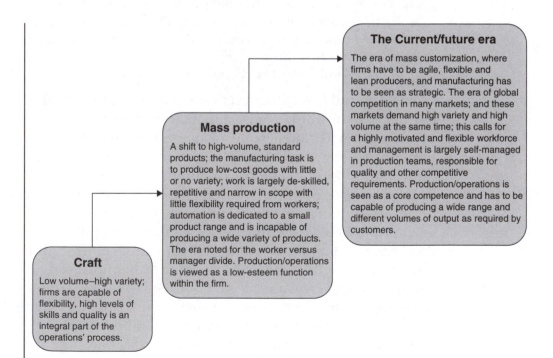

Figure 1.1
The change of requirements from human resources over time (from: Brown *et al.,* 2000).

The craft era

The first major era is now referred to as 'craft' manufacturing. This system was European in origin, and was linked to the way in which specific skills were developed. The apprentice–journeyman–master progression led to the creation of guilds of skilled people who sought to control the supply of their speciality, and the consolidation of skill within a particular sub-sector of society (as, for example, skills were passed on from father to son). Human resource development was largely a 'lock-in' process so that, having completed an apprenticeship or other qualification that indicated a level of expertise, a person would remain closely tied to a particular firm and, in turn, an industry. The craft era was noted for low-volume, high-variety products, where workers tended to be highly skilled and quality was built into the very process of operations. It was also appropriate for largely national markets, supplied internally with minimal imports and exports. Some craft manufacturing still remains today, in markets where exotic products and services can control demand through some unique feature or high level of desirability. For instance, some house building, furniture making, clock and watch making is still carried out by skilled craftsmen/women working on a single or few items of output at a time.

Activity 1.3

Although it is a very small part of the modern economy, craft production still takes place today.

- Give three examples of where craft production takes place today.
- What are the key areas of human resource development that need to take place in craft production today?

The craft era has been largely replaced by subsequent changes related to mass production and other processes that are discussed later in this chapter. In the craft era, the need for human resource development was clearly apparent. However, under mass production the need for developing human resources appeared to diminish.

The mass production era

The second major era is that of mass production. This system developed in North America and is often associated with two major figures in production: F.W. Taylor and Henry Ford. Both of these were able to deal successfully with three major challenges of the USA, which were:

1 The need to export
2 The need to become established as a world player, which meant infiltrating other regions with ideas clearly associated with the USA
3 The need to provide employment for a massive, but largely unskilled, workforce.

In short, the Americans could not play by the European rules, so they reinvented the game. In essence, standardization was the key issue: standardized products were made by standardized operations practices, mass produced in order to standardize the market requirements, too. Fortunately, the market was immature and would do what it was told. Thus, mass production reversed the paradigm of craft production: volume was high with little variety. The system was massively successful and changed the working and buying practices of the world in the first few decades of the twentieth century. The marketing ploy was exemplified by Henry Ford's famous declaration, from now on: 'a customer can have a car painted any colour he likes, as long as it is black!' In mass production, workers were typically unskilled. This was the era that owed a great deal to the contribution of F.W. Taylor's *Scientific Management*, whereby workers had very narrowly defined jobs, involving repetitive tasks, and quality was left to 'quality experts' at the final stage of the overall process rather than being an integral part of operations at each step.

Taylor enabled firms, for the first time, to control costs, times and resources, rather than relying on skilled craftsmen and women to decide what was appropriate. Coupled with the developments made in mechanization and employee co-ordination during the European industrial revolutions, Taylor's ideas provided an entirely different way of operating. Although our text focuses on the need for ongoing human resource development and this was not part of Taylor's system, we should not be overly critical of Taylor's approach – he did, after all, inherit a largely unskilled workforce, and his main task was to make the best possible use of this largely unskilled group. However, time caught up with the Taylor system and this was brought to light by the following speech to a group of US executives, where Konosuke Matsushita stated the following:

> We will win, and you will lose … Your companies are based on Taylor's principles … You firmly believe that good management

means executives on one side and workers on the other; on one side men who think, and on the other side men who can only work. For you, management is the art of smoothly transferring the executive's ideas to the workers' hands … For us, management is the entire workforce's intellectual commitment at the service of the company.

(Shores, 1990: 270)

This highlighted the key differences between the Japanese (who were disciples of human resource development) and the majority of Western firms (who clearly were not so committed to human resource development).

Activity 1.4

- What would be the extent of human resource development under mass production?
- What possible problems might this approach provide for managers and workers alike?

In 1926 *Encyclopaedia Britannica* asked Henry Ford to christen his system, and he called it mass production. He meant 'mass' in the sense of large-volume production. Perhaps he did not see the other meaning of mass as 'heavy, cumbersome', which is what the system turned out to be (in terms of management systems and superstructure), once the market no longer bought what it was told.

The modern era

The third era (the current and, for the foreseeable future at least, the likely scenario) is more difficult to name, and has been called various things. The terms used to describe the current era are listed in Table 1.3.

Whatever it is called, the paradigm for the current era addresses the need to combine high volume and variety, together with high levels of quality as the norm, and rapid, ongoing innovation in many markets. It is, as mass production was a hundred years ago, an innovation that makes the system it replaces largely redundant.

Table 1.3
Paradigms of the modern business environment

Name	Reference	Description
Mass customization	Pine *et al.* (1993)	Reflecting the need for volume combined with recognition of customers' (or consumers') wishes
Flexible specialization	Piore and Sabel (1984)	Related to the manufacturing strategy of firms (especially small firms) to focus on parts of the value-adding process and collaborate within networks to produce whole products
Lean production	Womack *et al.* (1990)	Developed from the massively successful Toyota Production System, focusing on the removal of all forms of waste from a system
Agile	Kidd (1994)	Emphasizing the need for an organization to be able to switch frequently from one market-driven objective to another
Strategic	Hill (1995), Brown (1996)	In which the need for the operations to be framed in a strategy is brought to the fore

Activity 1.5

- Looking at the list of paradigms in Table 1.3, why do you think human resource development has become a central feature in modern production/operations management?
- In what ways do humans need to be developed if firms are to compete in the modern competitive world?

As each era appeared, however, it did not entirely replace the former one. As we have seen, a few pockets of craft manufacture still exist. Mass production is still apparent in chemical plants and refineries and other high-volume/low-variety environments.

However, many are changing fundamentally as existing economies of scale are questioned – thus steel manufacturers face variety requirements and have to develop 'mini-mills' to lower economic batch sizes, and the same is true for brewers and pharmaceutical companies.

A telling example of the need to equip the workforce via human resource development comes from Compaq's fortunes in the 1990s. Compaq's problems began in 1994 when its former CEO, Pfeiffer, announced that Compaq would make all its PCs on a 'build to order' basis by 1996. At the time of the 'build to order' statement from Pfeiffer, Compaq built less than 5 per cent of its machines to order. By the beginning of the new millennium, Compaq was way behind Dell in build-to-order capabilities, and Dell had surpassed Compaq in desktop PC sales to US businesses for the first time. Perhaps more than any other single factor, it was the absence of customer-focused operations strategies that cost Compaq's Pfeiffer his job. The reason why Compaq had failed to deliver on their customer promises was that no human resource development strategy was in place to enable workers to understand the shift from low-cost, high-volume production to a more customized approach.

The ability to achieve the wide-ranging requirements of the current era does not come about by chance: it is derived from accumulated learning and know-how gained by the firm over time. At the core of the current era is a view of human resource development as a *strategic* factor. While having a strategic view of human resources may not guarantee that firms succeed, treating human capabilities as a side issue to strategic areas is likely to mean the firm will suffer in the current era of rapid change and volatility.

Human resource development and business strategy

Defining strategy, and the importance of human resources in its formulation and implementation

Strategy is a complex issue (Mintzberg *et al.*, 2000; Whittington, 2002), but we suggest it is essentially about three things:

1   Satisfying and, where possible, delighting customers
2   Making the best use of limited resources, and leveraging these resources either alone or with partners

3   Developing capabilities that are superior to those of other competitors, and which other competitors either cannot, or will find it extremely difficult to, copy.

It is this third factor where human resource development can play a vital and central role. For example, Dell's 'secret' of its phenomenal success is not a secret at all, but no other competitor can quite emulate what Dell does via its operations capabilities.

The term 'strategy', as used in the 'corporate' or 'business' strategy sense, clearly has strong associations with (and owes its origins to) military terminology. Strategy in the military includes devising plans in order to outmanoeuvre the opposition.

Human resource development is vitally important in the strategy process. First, an obvious – but often overlooked – point is that strategy formulation and planning are devised by human imagination and planning. Second, strategy implementation is dependent upon humans within the organization who need to own and manage the change process. Third, as we saw above, human resource capabilities can be a source of advantage for firms. The latest process technology can be bought and accumulated, but human-skills are more complex. In any event, an important ingredient in successfully managing technology is having appropriate skills levels in place.

Activity 1.6

Look at business journals such as *Fortune, Business Week* and the *Economist,* and search for five articles that are concerned with business strategy.

- Are human resources – in particular training and development – mentioned in the articles?
- If they are, in what context are they mentioned and how are they linked to the firm's stated strategy?
- If human resource development issues are not mentioned, what does this say about how some firms devise their business strategies?

Very often you will find that companies look retrospectively at the organization's success and then state how dependent this was on managing human resources. Very few, however, seem to go on record stating what their human resource strategy is and how it helps them to realize their overall business strategy.

Strategic human resource development in the firm's human resource audit

There are several key developments that have taken place in recent years, and these all have relevance to human resource development. These key changes include:

1   *Downsizing within the workforce.* Clearly, this can be at odds with any notion of human resource development. This was a major factor that had an effect on many firms, especially in the USA during the 1980s and 1990s. Downsizing may be seen (in a cynical sense) as simply 'getting more for less'. Alternatively, it may be seen as a necessary requirement to compete in highly volatile industries where rapidity, innovation and costs are requirements. What it must not be, though, is a short-term mechanism or excuse to cut costs – such short-sightedness seems to have become common in many firms, in the name of 're-engineering' (Grint and Case, 1998). Human resource development is still a critical issue because the challenge for managers is how best to manage, nurture and develop those who remain in the organization. This is a difficult task, and calls for the best of managerial skills in knowing how to develop the staff who remain after downsizing has taken place.

2   *Reducing the number of levels of the management hierarchy.* This puts greater responsibility on operators to be more 'managerial' in their approach. Human resource development is important here because such reduction puts greater responsibilities on those managers who formerly might have been 'hidden' in very hierarchical organizations. In flatter hierarchical structures, managers' contributions become more visible and more easily accountable than in organizations that have many layers of management (Cho, 1996).

3   *Empowering operators in order to elicit process and productivity improvements from the workforce.* A major development in recent times has been in developing and training operators so that instead of simply 'doing' operations they look at how they might improve processes. Again, this is a particularly difficult task in the light of any downsizing that may be taking place simultaneously with the

'empowerment' of those who remain in the workforce (Kendall, 2003; Bassi and McMurrer, 2004). Training the workforce is obviously a key factor here, and is discussed in depth later in the book.

4   *Changing the role of managers from 'policing' to 'facilitating'.* This clearly changes traditional approaches – the 'us and them' mentality between workers and managers that we cited earlier under the Taylorist system – and calls for expert managerial skills in areas such as communication, motivation and leadership. Such skills need to be accrued and developed over time (Herzberg, 2003).

5   *Organizational learning becoming a major feature.* There is a number of ways in which a firm might learn (Burnes *et al.*, 2003), and these are discussed later in this chapter.

Activity 1.7

Again, look at business journals such as *Fortune*, *Business Week* and the *Economist,* and search for articles on downsizing.

• What is the rationale given for downsizing?
• Is any reason given, other than cost?
• Is there any mention of how remaining staff will be developed?

The enigma of human resources and the 'quick-fix' solution

We mentioned earlier how downsizing can be part of the audit for strategic human resource management and development. One of the strange enigmas of the traditional behaviour of many firms is the ease and readiness with which they will downsize the workforce. This provides insight into the lack of strategic human resource development within firms, because direct labour costs typically amount to only 10 per cent of costs in key industries such as the cars, telecommunications and computers. This cost is a fraction of the total – far less than the huge costs associated with inventories and bought-in components for these products. This provides one of the biggest clues to traditional manufacturing: firing people takes little or no skill, and can be demoralizing both for the 'fired' employee and for those who remain in the workforce (Kanter, 1995). Admittedly, there are those firms who have 'job clubs' and other supportive ideas in order to help the staff who are exiting to find new jobs; however, firing is, essentially, a 'quick-fix' solution. In contrast, Japanese firms have been loath to fire personnel – and this includes Japanese transplants in the West.

How downsizing can damage human resource development

We noted that in high-volume manufacturing, labour costs would account for less than 10 per cent of production costs. Even so, human resources are the first target under threat when cost reductions are to be made. Why is this? The answer must be because it is the easy, instant-solution approach to management. Firing people takes little or no skill. However, enormous damage can be done to the firm when it reduces staff (Sahdev, 2003). The organization has been likened to the brain, and in radical down-sizing part of this 'brain' can suffer a 'corporate lobotomy' and entire firms (or specific plants within firms) can forget how to perform to world-class standards. There will be occasions when a firm *has* to reduce numbers: it must avoid becoming bloated, particularly in terms of hierarchy. However, it is the rationale behind and the motives for downsizing – together with how it is handled – that provide clues to how firms manage their most important asset: human resources. The reality is that frequently human resource development will be the first target in cost-cutting, and this was clearly evident in the epidemic levels of downsizing that took place in the early 1990s. As Hamel and Prahalad (1994) wrote:

> In 1993, large US firms announced nearly 600 000 layoffs – 25% more than had been announced in a similar period in 1992 and nearly 10% above the levels of 1991, which was technically the bottom of the recession in the United States.

At the same time, *Business Week* (9 May 1994) put the situation in a more dramatic fashion:

> The sight of so many bodies on the corporate scrap heap is spark-ing a corporate debate – about profits and loyalty, and about the benefits and unforeseen consequences of layoffs. Critics believe

massive downsizing has become a fad, a bone to throw Wall Street when investors begin baying for cost-cuts.

A sad example of downsizing came with GM's closure of its Tarrytown, New York plant:

> When Bob Stempel announced in early 1992 that Tarrytown would be among the plants scheduled for closing, there was stunned disbelief among the workers, followed by outrage. It was at least the fourth time in GM's recent history that a particularly motivated group of workers tried to save their jobs by doing exactly what management asked, only to see the company fail them.
>
> (Keller, 1993: 186)

There may well be occasions when a firm might have to make reductions. However, the rush to downsize that took place in the 1990s in many US and UK firms, and which continues to take place in the new millennium, highlights one of the major distinctions between Japanese and traditional Western approaches to manufacturing. In short, Western firms have often seen staffing as the first area in which to reduce costs: in doing so these firms reveal short-sightedness and tactical approaches rather than having a strategic vision of human resources in manufacturing.

Fortune (21 June 1999) stated how its CEO, Lou Gerstner, changed life at IBM:

> When Lou Gerstner parachuted in to fix the shambles John Ackers had left of IBM, he focused on execution, decisiveness, simplifying the organization for speed, and breaking the gridlock. Many expected heads to roll, yet initially Gerstner changed only the CEO, the HR chief, and three key line executives – and he has multiplied the stock's tenfold.

What *Fortune* omitted to say here, though, was that Gerstner *did* fire staff at IBM – over 100 000 of them, in fact. In an earlier article, *Fortune* (14 April 1997) stated:

> … Gerstner became CEO of IBM in 1993 … Within 90 days, he made fundamental decisions about the company's future course, completing the reduction of its workforce from 406 000 to 219 000 …

Interestingly, the degree of downsizing was not mentioned or explored to any great degree in Gerstner's (2002) autobiography. No doubt the strategy worked in terms of making IBM prosperous again, but it fundamentally changed the culture of IBM forever.

IBM, once the firm that prided itself on never firing anybody, has now shown itself capable of downsizing like other firms. For sure, IBM's culture *had* to change. It had become a victim of its own success in the mid-1980s, when extraordinary profits deflected attention from a new breed of aggressive entrants into the PC industry whose capabilities were superior to those of IBM. Part of the problem was also with not confronting issues:

> Our culture was very congenial, so congenial you never knew where you stood … Meetings would always go fine. You'd go in, and everyone would be very proper and well-dressed, and a bunch of people would sit around and have a nice chat. The results might be good, and people would say, 'Thank you very much.' Or the results might be awful, and it would still be, 'Thank you very much; we know you tried your best.'
>
> (*Fortune*, 14 April 1997)

IBM slimmed itself down from 406 000 employees in 1987 to 202 000 in 1995 – one of the most dramatic workforce reductions ever. Other developments were disturbing. For example, only 15 months after opening its plant in Tyneside in the north of England, Siemens of Germany closed the plant at a cost of around DM1 billion ($564 m). In 1995, AT&T announced that it was sacking 40 000 people – it shed 140 000 in the 10 years following deregulation in 1984. However, the announcement in 1995 was particularly painful for AT&T's employees because it came at the very time when AT&T was prospering. What made matters worse was that at the very time of the downsizing announcement, AT&T's CEO, Bob Allen, saw his salary increase to $5 million a year – although he was later ousted from AT&T in 1997 (Brown, 2000). In addition, just to complete the picture, Wall Street responded to the dismal news of AT&T's downsizing by boosting the value of the company's shares. Other headlines in the mid-1990s were equally alarming: 50 000 reductions at Sears, 10 000 at Xerox, 18 000 at Delta, 16 800 at Eastman Kodak, and a further 35 000 at IBM (Brown, 2000). The downsizing trend had not finished by the end of the decade either. In 1998, Motorola announced that it would lay off 15 000 staff and consolidate its manufacturing. The reason for this was that second-quarter earnings were expected to fall 'well below expectations'. More alarmingly, Motorola did not say more specifically where the staff cuts and facilities consolidations would take place, and uncertainty was rife. It remains to be seen what impact such an announcement will have on Motorola's world-class quality performance, where six sigma quality has been touted as the norm within its plants.

In 1998, General Motors announced it would close a number of domestic factories, shed jobs and eliminate models in an effort to become more competitive. GM's North American sales and marketing operations would be reduced to a single division, thereby reducing bureaucracy, costs … and jobs.

High-tech firms were ravaged by downsizing at the beginning of the new millennium, and even those companies listed by *Fortune* as the '100 Best Companies to Work For' were busy reducing headcount, as *Fortune* (9 February 2004) noted: 'The tech downturn hasn't left Cisco unscathed – it laid off 6,000 employees in 2001, and some stock options are still underwater'. Downsizing has been evident within more traditional sectors, and has impacted those firms which were previously against downsizing:

> Schwab has a policy of giving news to employees almost instantaneously, sort of an internal transparency. So it was with the decision to downsize. It occurred at 8:45 on Jody Bilney's very first morning last year. By noon the new marketing executive VP watched incredulously as Pottruck broadcast the news to the entire workforce. 'Wow,' she recalls thinking, 'we are so forthcoming. We absolutely wear it on our sleeves.'
>
> But the details would take weeks to work out, and that caused tremendous disruption and fear. 'It became very hard for people to focus,' says Eleccion, the broker, who is now at another firm. 'With each successive layoff, you had to say goodbye to friends. This was a place where the jerks were few and far between.' Donna Stapleton, a program manager, packed up her belongings and waited. 'There were days when I thought I read signals that I would be laid off, and then days when it was obvious that I would not,' she recalls. She did lose her job in October of last year. (This October, though, she became one of the few employees to be hired back.) Schwab soon found itself trapped in its own largesse. Last year's $97 million in severance costs, along with other charges, wiped out the company's fourth-quarter $86 million operating net, plunging the company into the red.
>
> (*Fortune*, 8 December 2003)

Fortune provided interesting insight into how many US firms have simply downsized and outsourced much of their human resources:

> The standard history of modern American manufacturing reads like a *Rocky* script. Pummeled by foreign competitors, out-of-shape American manufacturers rehabilitated themselves with massive

job sacrifices and clever technology. Today (cue the triumphant music), American factories are lean (with 12% fewer employees than at the 1979 peak), strong (producing 51% more stuff), and fast (increasing productivity at a torrid 3.5% annual rate). Dramatic, yes. If only it were true. Sure, American factories have cut costs and are making more widgets with fewer hands. But the manufacturing job outlook is nowhere near as grim – and productivity growth isn't quite as marvellous – as is generally believed. How could this be? Simple. Many factory layoffs have really been 'outsourcings' in which workers returned as (not always cheaper) vendors or contractors. And many newly resurgent factories, loath to increase permanent payrolls, are paying temp agencies instead.

(*Fortune*, 10 November 1997)

The concern is that not only does it make a nonsense of workforce figures, but that these firms then have dependence upon those very people who have been downsized and outsourced. The only difference can be that these ex-staff then have little or no loyalty towards the firms that have just fired them.

Activity 1.8

- Under what conditions might a firm be forced into downsizing?
- How does this impact on human resource development strategies?

The emergence of strategic human resource development

The failure of past approaches to human resource management

In the 1980s a number of Western manufacturing firms invested vast sums of money in technology, one aim of which was to reduce or replace labour costs. We need only look at the limited, or sometimes non-existent, improvements in the performance of the plants in which vast amounts of expenditure took place to realize that automation, by itself, is not the road to everlasting manufacturing success. Instead, massive reorganization is the only solution for many manufacturing firms whose structures and methods are now obsolete in comparison with world-class organizations. The reorganization includes recognition of the importance of human resources as a key input to world-class, strategic manufacturing, as well as the abandonment of traditional 'top down' approaches to management. This is summarized by Hayes and Jaikumar (1988:79) when they talk about the importance of human resources in new technology:

> Traditional managerial attitudes, manifested in top-down decision making, piece-meal changes and a 'bottom-line' mentality, are incompatible with the requirements and unique capabilities of advanced manufacturing systems. Until their attitudes change, companies will be slow to adopt the new technologies, and those that do will run a high risk of failure.

Activity 1.9

Search in business journals such as *Fortune, Business Week* and the *Economist,* and investigate a firm that has recently invested in technology.

- What has been the stated rationale for the investment?
- What costs were involved in the downsizing process?

Learning from Japanese human resource management

Kanter (1990) highlights the 'rediscovery' of the importance of human resource development to world-class manufacturing: '… the speed of workplace reform in the United States was significantly increased after the discovery of the importance of certain human resource management practices in Japanese firms' (Kanter, 1990, in Erikson and Vallas, 1990: 381).

The difference between Japanese and Western manufacturing was highlighted by Keller (1993: 162):

> One of the main factors that distinguished the Toyota Production System from Fordism was the amount of responsibility and individual control given to workers. In the West the assembly-line worker was a cog in a large machine … At Toyota … each worker was trained for a variety of jobs which they performed in teams. They were expected to think about how the tasks, parts, or equipment could be improved.

Clearly training was a major factor here, but it was not the only one: a culture of worker–manager respect and trust was also a requirement for the 'enlightened' approach to succeed. Gleave and Oliver (1990: 55) point out how Japanese manufacturers have seen human resources as a core area that helps to shape their manufacturing strategy:

> The major Japanese corporations appear to have succeeded in engineering a good 'fit' between their manufacturing strategy and their human resources strategy. They have manufacturing systems which are highly efficient but which require highly supportive employee attitudes and behaviour.

Hutchins (1988: 131) observes how this employee involvement is something that has been learned by the Japanese – the challenge for Western firms, then, is that they need to learn lessons, or 're-learn' lessons that have not been adopted:

> ... it is obvious from [Toyota] that near total harmony has been achieved between workers and management, managers and other managers, workers and other workers. Contrary to popular opinion, this harmony is not the result of some genealogical feature inherited by the Japanese ...

As we saw above, in the past manufacturing has often had an association with repetitive, low-motivation tasks. However, this has changed to some degree. The change is due largely to learning about Japanese manufacturing practices both within Japan itself and in the Japanese transplants in the West. Workers are far more involved in the *management* of production/operations – both within Japan itself and in Japanese transplants in the West – which is in contrast to the more traditional Western approaches. Part of the reason behind the Japanese plants' accumulation of skills has to do with the ongoing investment in training; another factor is learning gained within teamwork approaches. According to Gowen and Pecenka (1992), 'Japanese compensation strategy for high technology firms has historically been more team oriented than most American systems', and 'Another Japanese human resource strategy implemented in high technological firms is the consultative decision-making process called *nemawashi* ... The process involves the accommodation of employee input in middle-down-up collaborative style'.

The Nissan plant in Smyrna, Tennessee, provides vital insight into the important contributions of humans in manufacturing. Nissan in Smyrna uses only 2.23 workers to build its vehicles, in contrast to the 3, 4 or sometimes more workers per vehicle at typical auto plants operated by the Big Three automakers. However, the fact is that Nissan's workers do not work harder; they seem to work more efficiently than their US counterparts:

> There is little evidence to support UAW's contention that Smyrna employees work harder than their counterparts at less-productive plants … [Nissan] doesn't run shifts longer than nine hours, and it rarely asks employees to work more than one Saturday per month. Many unionized – and less productive – plants work longer shifts and far more weekends.
>
> (*Ward's Automotive Yearbook*, July 1999)

The key difference seems to be in the ongoing investment in developing skills and encouraging learning.

Activity 1.10

- Why might there be a conception that unions might be opposed to human resource development?
- In contrast, why do you think that unions might actually support human resource development initiatives within the organization?

Human resource development as part of the organizations' core competence

Human resources can be closely linked with the firm's core competencies, as described by Garavan *et al.* (2001: 48):

> This perspective on human capital takes as its starting point, the view that human competencies are one of the resources available to organizations. The origins of this notion of human capital can be attributed to the work of Prahalad and Hamel (1990) who analysed the competitiveness of organizations and attributed it to the possession of core competencies. They postulated that an organization can possess unique clusters of factors that allows it to be competitive and human capital is one of these. This resource-based view represents a current paradigm on firm competitiveness and conceptualizes the organization as a collection of competencies and draws attention to issues of learning, HRD investment, knowledge accumulation and experience.

Hamel and Prahalad (1994) describe core competencies as 'a bundle of skills and technologies rather than a single discrete skill or technology'. Although we cannot limit core competencies to human resources only, it is clear that human resource development must form at least part of the organization's core competence because 'skills' are grounded in human capabilities. These skills can be developed and nurtured over time in order to create a set of capabilities which other firms will find difficult to match or copy. Human resource management must be a key core competence for any world-class manufacturing firm. New ideas for innovation, new products, continuous improvement and so on, come from harnessing this creativity from humans, not via machines or 'technology'.

The case described in Example 1.2 provides useful insight into one Chief Executive Officer's view of strategic human resource development.

Example 1.2: The strategic importance of human resources at Nucor – the views of CEO Ken Iverson

I get calls from students at prestigious business schools all the time … The first thing they ask is, 'May I have a copy of your mission statement?' And I say, 'We don't have a mission statement.' Then they ask, 'Well, can we have a copy of your job descriptions?' And I say, 'We don't have any job descriptions….' If there is a Nucor success formula, the primary ingredients include:

Maintaining a lean management structure – the corporate headquarters office in Charlotte has a staff of just 25 people, and there are just four management layers between the CEO and front-line workers.

Pushing decision-making down to the lowest possible level – which means that the firm's business-unit managers have a high degree of autonomy, and production workers are extensively involved in devising methods to improve operations.

Encouraging experimentation and risk-taking – Nucor accepts that roughly half of its investments in new ideas and new technologies 'will yield no usable results' [Iverson says].

A performance-based bonus system – one that rewards managers and other employees for improving return on assets, and production crews for increasing productivity. [Last year, the company generated a record $623 000 in sales per employee.]

A commitment to fostering two-way loyalty – by cultivating a sense of 'shared purpose' among managers and workers. Not only do employees at all levels share in the financial success of their work groups or business units, but a 'share the pain' philosophy also dictates that everyone bears part of the burden during difficult times. [Although it has gone to reduced workweeks in slow periods, Nucor has never laid off an employee or shut down a facility for lack of work.]

Cultivation of an egalitarian atmosphere – with few, if any, of the management perks common at many other firms. Everyone, including senior executives, flies coach on business trips. And there are no company cars, no reserved parking spaces, and no executive dining rooms.

(Source: *Industry Week*, 8 June 1998)

The Nucor story is almost textbook in terms of what can be done. The issue is that there aren't many firms who have such policies in place.

Activity 1.11

- Read the Nucor case.
- Given that Nucor operates in an environment where labour costs are a relatively small part of operating costs, why do you think the company is so committed to human resource management and development?

Current 'good practice' in strategic human resource development

Towards best practice

A number of researchers have found compelling evidence which shows the benefits of human resource development strategies within organizations. Pfeffer (1998) and Pfeffer and Veiga (1999) report on a study of high performance work practices of 968 US firms representing all major industries. The study found that a one standard deviation increase in the use of such practices was associated with a 7.05 per cent decrease in staff turnover and, on a per employee basis, a $27 044 increase in sales per employee, a $18 641 increase in stock market valuation, and a $3814 increase in profits. It is important to note two points in such studies. First, they are not saying that a single practice will change things overnight; rather, success comes through a systematic and integrated approach carried through over a sustained period of time. Changing the way an organization behaves is a matter of consistent reinforcement and the establishment of a different set of values.

The second point is that we can see a high degree of convergence in different studies around the key dimensions of high performance HR management. For example, Pfeffer (1994) lists seven key practices of successful organizations, whilst the UK 'Competitiveness through partnerships with people' study highlights five key areas for change. We can group the key factors into a simple model (Figure 1.2) that provides an overview of the challenges for strategic operations management in this field.

Under each of these headings there is a number of factors: Table 1.4 lists the key elements.

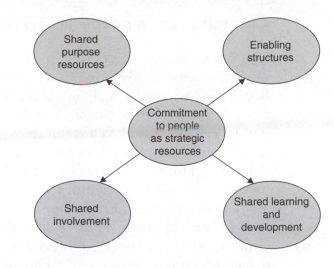

Figure 1.2
Strategic human resource development (from: Brown *et al.*, 2000).

Table 1.4
Elements of strategic human resource development

Area	Key elements
Commitment to people as strategic resources	Employment security Choosing the right people Valuing and rewarding them Wage compression Symbolic egalitarianism
Shared purpose	Strategic leadership Shared planning processes Policy deployment Information sharing Employee ownership
Enabling structures	Appropriate organization design Job and work organization design Devolved decision-making Supportive communications
Shared learning and development	Commitment to training and development Embedding a learning cycle Measurement Continuous improvement culture
Shared involvement	Teamworking Cross-boundary working Participation and involvement mechanisms Stakeholder focus and involvement

Commitment to people as strategic resources

There is no 'magic ingredient' in the recipe for developing high performance organizations of this kind, but there is a need to develop some basic principles. At the heart of such organizations lies a belief in the importance and potential contribution that employees can make. As a result there is the belief in and, more to the point, the practice of human resource development strategies. From these a series of practices follow which reinforce the message and enable sometimes 'extraordinary efforts from ordinary people' (Joynson, 1994). One of the basic human needs is for security and, in an uncertain world, providing some measure of employment security is a powerful way of signalling the value placed on human resources. Of course this is not something that can be guaranteed, and there is a risk of 'feather-bedding' employees – but providing some form of contract that shares the risks and the benefits is strongly correlated with success. For example, one of the most successful US firms is Lincoln Electric, which operates on this basis:

> ... Our guarantee of employment states that no employee with 3 years or more of service will be laid off for lack of work ... this policy does not protect any employee who fails to perform his or her job properly, it does emphasize that management is responsible for maintaining a level of business that will keep every employee working productively. The institution of guaranteed employment sprang from our belief that fear is an ineffective motivator ... relief from anxiety frees people to do their best work ...
>
> (cited in Pfeffer, 1994)

However, on occasions firms will commit to such policies and subsequently things will change. For example, the UK car maker Rover pioneered an agreement in 1992 which promised no redundancies in return for commitment to change. This scheme proved critical in introducing new and flexible approaches to problem-solving and improvement across the company's plants. It then came under threat with the takeover of the firm by BMW – an indicator that 'cast-iron' guarantees of this kind can never be made.

The converse of this is also true; if people feel their efforts are likely to have a negative impact on their employment security, they will not make them. So introducing programmes that engage employees in development activities that raise productivity will only work if there is some form of reassurance that these employees are not improving themselves out of a job!

Much depends on ensuring that the right people are involved in the first place, and there is a clear trend towards more selective and careful recruitment practices within organizations – for example, SouthWest Airlines received nearly 100 000 job applications in 1993; 16 000 were interviewed and only 2700 people were actually employed (Pfeffer and Veiga, 1999). Given the flexibility and creativity required and the increasing emphasis on teamworking in the competitive environment, a broad range of social skills has become an important part of the skills mix firms are seeking.

Reorganizing human resources

On occasions, firms *have* to entirely reinvent and reconfigure themselves. Such change often comes about by necessity rather than choice and, as we saw earlier with IBM, such reconfigurations can be dramatic, including a large degree of downsizing. However, this does not always have to be so. For example, before its merger with Daimler, Chrysler underwent change that was fundamental and company-wide. Chrysler embarked on a dramatic cultural change from a traditional, bureaucratic, vertically structured organization to one organized into four nimble, cross-functional platform teams – one for small cars, one for large cars, one for minivans, and one for Jeep vehicles and trucks. Teamwork was the pivotal issue here, and at Chrysler everyone focuses not on just pieces of the car, but on the total vehicle. Communication flows are simultaneous and two-way, rather than sequential and one-way. This change enabled Chrysler to be very innovative. Between 1992 and 1995, Chrysler introduced more models than it had done in the previous twenty years (Brown, 1996). The reorganization resulted in development times that matched those of the Japanese.

Activity 1.12

- Why is it that human resource development is an important issue in firms that wish to be faster in innovation?
- What *specific* skills need to be enhanced by such development strategies?

One of the major areas of learning from Japanese styles of organization is in the lack of levels of hierarchy within Japanese firms:

> In contrast with their Japanese competitors, American firms have several extra layers of hierarchy arranged as an organizational tree. To communicate with one another, people working in different departments often have to go up the tree to their lowest-level common superior and then back down. In Japanese firms the hierarchy has fewer levels and it is layered rather than strictly treelike: people in one layer generally know and can easily communicate with people in the next-higher and next-lower layers, regardless of departmental boundaries.
>
> (Dertouzos *et al.*, 1989)

At one time, General Motors had 22 layers of management and Ford had 17, in contrast to Toyota, which had only 7. A number of Western firms have undoubtedly recognized the importance of reducing levels of hierarchy and promoting cross-functional teamwork. However, at NUMMI, the GM/Toyota joint venture, there are only four job classifications and workers enjoy frequent job rotation. Production is based largely on teamwork and other organizational initiatives, which GM has learned from the Toyota Production System. There have been no forced redundancies at NUMMI. Workers are called 'Associates' and regular meetings take place in order to review production processes and to make improvements. Staffing and materials sourcing decisions are made by teams, rather than by a personnel or purchasing function. There are indications that there is progress at other GM plants, although not as impressive as the NUMMI plants: GM's Cadillac division has reduced job classifications from 18 to 7, each with its own pay scale, and teams of workers are evident throughout the plant, responsible for their own training.

Ford has undergone major change. Ford *had* to change in order to compete. Its Ford 2000 approach linked together the company's European business with its North American one. This almost amounted to a merger, since Ford has separate management structures, products, factories and processes in the US and Europe.

Summary

Human resources are often seen as a core capability within firms. However, if this is the case it should be straightforward to think that all firms will nurture and develop such a key asset. As we have seen in this chapter, not all firms remain committed to developing human resources. One of the reasons for neglect of human resource development is the way in which management has changed over time.

The three major eras provide major clues as to how human resources development has progressed over time. The problem for some firms is that they have remained 'stuck' in the mass production era in terms of how they manage staff. The mass production era was entirely appropriate for its time; however, in the current business era it is vital that human resources are properly developed. This is because the firm is dependent upon human resources for ideas for innovation, and for continuous improvement in all areas.

Strategy is concerned with long-term planning and implementation for the organization. Human resource development should form part of this planning process, and in world-class firms this is exactly what happens. For example, every new Japanese transplant in the West has staff who have been trained and developed, thus enabling the plant to compete on key variables such as delivery speed and reliability, quality and low cost. Downsizing is often a quick-fix solution to a firm's current problem. There are major negative repercussions in firms that downsize radically. First, many firms attempt to be lean but end up becoming anorexic in the process (Brown, 2000). Second, the 'brain of the firm' – which is focused on human resource know-how – can suffer from what might be called a corporate lobotomy – i.e. the firm forgets how to do things. Third, getting rid of staff is easy, but dealing with the survivors is immensely difficult. It is remarkably difficult to motivate people in continuous improvement initiatives when staff are leaving and surviving personnel are in fear of losing their jobs.

Human resource development has emerged as a strategic factor within firms. One of the reasons for this is that firms have benchmarked against Japanese practices in human resources and have found that it is this factor – and not technology – that is central to their success. However, other important factors need to be in place. For example, the firm needs to rid itself of worker/manager problems. Once these and other issues have been dealt with, a firm can really begin to manage and develop human resources in a way that will allow it to utilize a key competitive component – its human resources.

There are tangible/financial benefits from developing 'best practices' in human resources. In addition, once a range of skills has been developed this enables the firm to be more flexible and to reconfigure the way in which it is organized. These reorganizations then enable the firm to be more focused and, in turn, can allow it to exploit what it does best.

References

Aston, A. and Arndt, M. (2003). The flexible factory. *Business Week*, **3831,** 90, 5 May.

Bassi, L. and McMurrer, D. (2004). How's your return on people? *Harvard Business Review*, **82(3),** 18.

Bell, C.R. and Bell, B. (2003). Great training leaders learn out loud. *Training and Development*, **57(9),** 52–7.

Brown, S. (1996). *Strategic Manufacturing for Competitive Advantage*. Prentice-Hall.

Brown, S. (2000). *Manufacturing the Future*. Financial Times Books.

Brown, S., Lamming, R., Bessant, J. and Jones, P. (2000). *Strategic Operations Management*. Butterworth-Heinemann.

Burnes, B., Cooper, C. and West, P. (2003). Organizational learning: the new management paradigm? *Management Decision*, **41(5),** 452–65.

Byrne, J. (1994). The pain of downsizing. *Business Week*, **3370,** 60–62, 9 May.

Charan, R. and Colvin, G. (1999). Why CEOs fail. *Fortune*, **139(12),** 68–76, 21 June.

Cho, N. (1996). How Samsung organized for innovation. *Long Range Planning*, **29(6),** 783–97.

Clark, K. (1997). Temp worker. *Fortune*, **136(9),** 25–30, 10 November.

Corenson, S. (2004). The end of the HP way. *Fortune*, **149(3),** 16–18, 9 February.

Daly, J. (2000). Interview with Peter Drucker. *Business 20*, **5(14),** 134–42, 22 August.

Davis, S. and Meyer, C. (2000). *Future Wealth*. Harvard Business School Press.

Dertouzos, M., Lester, R. and Solow, R. (1989). *Made In America*. MIT Press.

Drucker, P.F. (1978). *The Age of Discontinuity*. Harper & Row.

Erikson, K. and Vallas, S. (1990). *The Nature of Work*. Yale University Press.

Garavan, T., Morley, M., Gunnigle, P. and Collins, E. (2001). Human capital accumulation: the role of human resource development. *Journal of European Industrial Training*, **25(2),** 48–68.

Gerstner, L. (2002). *Who Says Elephants Can't Dance?: Inside IBM's Historic Turnaround*. HarperCollins.

Gleave, S. and Oliver, N. (1990). Human resources management in Japanese manufacturing companies in the UK: 5 case studies. *Journal of General Management*, **16(1),** 54–68.

Gowen, C. and Pecenka, J. (1992). Impact of technological leadership on American and Japanese turnaround strategies. *Journal of High Technology Management Research*, **3(2),** 263–87.

Grindley, P. (1991). Turning technology into competitive advantage. *Business Strategy Review*, **Spring,** 35–47.

Grint, K. and Case, P. (1998). The violent rhetoric of re-engineering: management consultancy on the offensive. *Journal of Management Studies*, **35(5),** 557–78.

Hamel, G. and Prahalad, C. (1994). *Competing For The Future*. Harvard Business School Press.

Hayes, R. and Jaikumar, R. (1988). Manufacturing's crisis: new technologies, obsolete organizations. *Harvard Business Review*, **66(5)**, 77–85.

Herzberg, F. (2003). One more time: how do you motivate employees? *Harvard Business Review*, **81(1)**, 87–97.

Hill, T. (1995). *Manufacturing Strategy*. Macmillan.

Hutchins, D. (1988). *Just in Time*. Gower Books.

Industry Week (1998). Tale of a 'maverick'. *Industry Week*, 8 June, **247(11)**, 22.

Joynson, S. (1994). Sid's heroes: uplifting business performance and the human spirit. BBC Books.

Kanter, R. (1995). *World Class Touchstone*. Simon & Schuster.

Kay, J. (1993). *Foundations of Corporate Success*. Oxford University Press.

Keller, M. (1993). *Collision Currency*. Doubleday.

Kendall, R. (2003). Beyond empowerment: building a company of citizens. *Harvard Business Review*, **81(4)**, 119–22.

Kidd, P. (1994). *Agile Manufacturing – Forging New Frontiers*. Addison Wesley.

Lazonick, W. (1991). *Business Organization and the Myth of the Market Economy*. Harvard University Press.

Levering, R. and Moskowitz, M. (2004). The 100 best companies to work for in the United States. *Fortune*, **149(1)**, 50–52, 26 January.

Mintzberg, H., Ahlstrand, B. and Lamprel, J. (2000). *Strategy Safari: A Guided Tour through the Wilds of Strategic Management*. Financial Times Books.

Morris, B. and McGowan, J. (1997). Big blue. *Fortune*, **135(7)**, 68–79, 14 April.

Morris, B. and Neering, P. (2003). When bad things happen to good companies. *Fortune*, **148(12)**, 78–85, 8 December.

Pfeffer, J. (1994). *Competitive Advantage Through People*. Harvard Business School Press.

Pfeffer, J. and Veiga, J. (1999). Putting people first for organizational success. *Academy of Management Executive*, **13(2)**, 37–49.

Pine, B., Bart, V. and Boynton, A. (1993). Making mass customization work. *Harvard Business Review*, **71(5)**, 108–19.

Piore, M. and Sabel, C. (1984). *The Second Industrial Divide: Possibilities For Prosperity*. Basic Books.

Sahdev, K. (2003). Survivors' reactions to downsizing: the importance of contextual factors. *Human Resource Management Journal*, **13(4)**, 56–75.

Shores, A. (1990). *A TQM Approach to Achieving Manufacturing Excellence*. ASQC Press.

The Economist (1996). 28 September.

Ward's Automotive Yearbook (1999).Wards Communications Primedia Business Overland Park, KS.

Whittington, R. (2002). *What Is Strategy – And Does it Matter?* Routledge.

Womack, J., Jones, D. and Roos, D. (1990). *The Machine That Changed the World*. Rawson Associates.

Chapter 2

Conceptual issues impacting on the contribution of HRD at strategic and operational levels

Introduction

The knowledge-based view of the firm provides a unique backdrop for strategic human resource development (SHRD) because it places the knowledge and skills that are embedded in the routines of the organization at the heart of sustainable competitive advantage (Nelson and Winter, 1982; Grant, 1991). Central to understanding how knowledge is created and embedded in an organization is the theoretical concept of the learning organization and the process of organizational learning.

This chapter starts by asking whether organizations can learn, and reviews some of the learning processes at a collective level. Here it is argued that the role of SHRD is to facilitate learning of the organization as a whole, and not just training at the individual level. It then contrasts organizational learning with the learning organization itself. SHRD strategies for developing the learning organization are explored. The juxtaposition of organizational learning and the learning organization highlights the notion that knowledge sits at the core of both these theoretical constructs. Next, the origins and process of knowledge management are examined and HRD practitioners are urged to realign the developmental process in such a way as to enable the creation and sharing of knowledge. The chapter finally points to the importance of informal learning in the overall knowledge management agenda.

Objectives

By the end of this chapter you will be able to:

- Define and describe the process of organizational learning
- Define and describe the notion of the learning organization
- Differentiate between organizational learning and the learning organization
- Explain why SHRD sits at the heart of the learning organization
- Define the concept of knowledge management
- Describe how SHRD can enable the creation and sharing of knowledge.

Organizational learning

Key perspectives on organizational learning

With the diminishing competitive power of many companies in a burgeoning world market, and the need for organizational renewal and transformation, organizational learning has become the focus of organizational survival. The ability of organizations to learn is regarded as a core organizational competence (Prahalad and Hamel, 1990) and the only sustainable source of competitive advantage, especially in knowledge-intensive businesses (Stata, 1989). Moss-Kanter (1989) echoes this view by stating that for companies to be effective in an uncertain environment, application of existing knowledge is required, and new knowledge needs to be created at a rapid rate. The process of organizational learning is therefore intertwined with knowledge management in the development of a sustainable competitive advantage. In this section, the concept of organizational learning is explored and various viewpoints on organizational learning are examined. This builds a foundation for a closer look at the role of SHRD in the knowledge management process.

A plethora of research has been conducted since the pioneering empirical study of the phenomenon of organizational learning (OL) was performed by Cangelosi and Dill in 1965. Easterby-Smith (1997: 1085) states that the literature on OL has grown very rapidly between 1997 and 2002. Furthermore, as many academic papers on the subject were published in 1993 as in the whole decade of the 1980s (Crossan and Guatto, 1996). Unfortunately, most of

Table 2.1

Definitions of organizational learning

Definition	References
Organizational learning means the process of improving actions through better knowledge and understanding	Fiol and Lyles (1985)
Organizations are seen as learning by encoding inferences from history into routines that guide behaviour	Levitt and March (1988)
Organizational learning occurs through shared insights, knowledge and mental models ... and builds on past experience – that is, on memory	Stata (1989)
An entity learns if, through its processing of information, the range of its potential behaviours is changed	Huber (1991)

these studies sought to redefine the concept of OL or to draw from different perspectives in order to explain the phenomenon, and this led to fragmentation of the existing body of literature. Some of these differences can be illustrated by a small selection of diverse definitions on organizational learning (see Table 2.1).

These deep ingrained divisions in the literature motivated several authors (Hedberg, 1981; Shrivastava, 1983; Fiol and Lyles, 1985; Levitt and March, 1988; Dixon, 1990; Huber, 1991; Weick, 1991; Crossan *et al.*, 1995; Easterby-Smith, 1997; Tsang, 1997) to develop a framework for integration. However, even these attempts caused greater confusion given that they originate from vastly different perspectives. To illustrate, Huber (1991) uses a cognitive process as a theoretical framework to integrate the various OL perspectives, Fiol and Lyles (1985) focus on the main distinction between cognition and behaviour in their integration attempt, and Easterby-Smith (1997) accentuates the influence of different theoretical disciplines in his framework of contributions. It is therefore clear that many of these integration attempts have failed in their original purpose – i.e. the formulation of an integrated and comprehensive perspective on OL.

Activity 2.1

- Why have many authors failed to develop a comprehensive and integrated definition of organizational learning?

A possible explanation for the above failed attempts could be that the actions of categorization, unification and clinical isolation that are involved in the theoretical integration process are diametrically opposed to the nature of the phenomenon of OL. The possibility that OL (i) encompasses both cognition and behaviour; (ii) includes individual, group and organizational levels of aggregation; and (iii) applies to various disciplines, needs to be entertained and the ambiguity accepted. It could be argued that the very nature of the lack of integration and the existence of 'sub-realities' (different realities within the larger OL context) is a reflection of how learning takes place in organizational systems. It is therefore important to understand the current perspectives on OL before it can be defined.

Table 2.2 summarizes the various perspectives on OL by presenting some selected studies along the following dimensions:

1 Level(s) of aggregation – i.e. whether the individual, group or organization can learn
2 Orientation – i.e. emphasis on actual or potential behavioural or cognitive elements
3 Learning outcome.

(Key contributions to OL comprise studies with 20 or more citations or papers with more than 5 citations in 1 year, according to the Social Sciences Citation Index (SSCI); as advocated by Crossan *et al.*, 1995.)

This is not done in an attempt to integrate the perspectives, but merely displays the possible definitions of and approaches to the concept. It can therefore be seen as a summary of the state of affairs in the field of OL.

A comparison of these key perspectives on OL highlights a few key differences and questions that need to be answered:

1 Can an organization learn, or should SHRD focus mainly on individual and group learning?
2 Should we approach OL as a behavioural or an intellectual/cognitive process?
3 How do we know when organizational learning has taken place – that is, what is the outcome of the OL process?

Each of these questions will be discussed and answered below.

Table 2.2
Summary of influential papers

Author	Level of aggregation	Orientation	Learning outcome
Argyris (1967, 1976, 1977, 1996)	Organizations learn through individuals acting as agents for them	Error detection (cognition) and correction (behaviour)	Single or double loop. Performance is the outcome of learning
Cangelosi and Dill (1965)	'Organizational learning must be viewed as a series of interactions between adaptation at the individual or subgroup level'	Learning is adaptation or change in behaviour	Learning is improved performance in order to reduce divergence and conflict in goals and in outcomes of activity
Daft and Weick (1984)	Individuals carry out the interpretation process, but organizations preserve knowledge, behaviours, mental maps, norms and values over time	Strong behaviour/action emphasis, but cognition forms critical part in the interpretation process	Based on interpretation
Duncan and Weiss (1979)	Emphasis on group and organizational process, where the dominant coalition acquires knowledge	Both cognition and behaviour	Growth and change of organizational knowledge
Fiol and Lyles (1985)	OL is not simply the sum of each member's learning. Organizations develop and maintain learning systems, and learning is influenced by contextual factors. Group learning is not addressed	'OL means the process of improving through better knowledge and understanding'. Emphasis on cognition but including observable behavioural components	Lower level learning = behaviourally oriented; higher level learning = cognitively orientated
Garvin (1993)	Defines five main individual learning activities, but does suggest that organizations do learn	Focus on changes in behaviour, but states that ideas are essential for learning	Learning audit of cognitive and behavioural changes
Herriot *et al.* (1985)	Individual models of experiential learning	Experiential learning is a form of adaptive intelligence and the authors have modelled a collection of behavioural observations	Adaptive intelligence
Huber (1991)	Information processing perspective applied at individual, group, industry, or society level of analysis	'An entity learns if, through its processing of information, the range of its potential behaviour is changed'; focus on cognition and potential behavioural change	Could be conscious or unconscious, effective or ineffective; 'Entities can incorrectly learn and learn correctly things which are incorrect'

Author	Level of aggregation	Orientation	Learning outcome
Levitt and March (1988)	Emphasis on organizational level and the 'encoding of inferences from history into routines that guide behaviour'. Routines = forms, rules, procedures, conventions, strategies and technologies	Cognition will guide change in behaviour after encoding into organizational routines	Change in behaviour, but could be destructive, i.e. competency traps
March and Olsen (1975)	Individuals and organizations learn from experience. Focus on organizational participant (individual)	Cognition influences future behaviour, but past behaviour influences cognition	Acting, observing consequences, making inferences and drawing implications for future actions. Not all learning is positive
Parkhe (1991)	Inter-organizational = global strategies and alliances	Cognition; using a combination of Fiol and Lyles, and Argyris	Dependent on inter-firm diversity. Low level of diversity = single loop learning; high level of diversity = double loop learning
Senge (1990)	Focus heavily on individual level. Management teams are referred to	Strong cognitive element in five learning disciplines (team learning, shared vision, mental models, personal mastery, and systems thinking)	Superior performance in the long term
Shrivastava (1983)	'Organizational process rather than an individual process'	Action/behaviour orientated. Mention is made of changes in theories-in-use and worldviews, but this dimension is not developed	Integrated system of action outcome heuristics
Stata (1989)	Group focus (shared insights, knowledge and mental models). Dependent on institutional mechanisms to provide organizational and individual memories	Emphasis on behaviour: change, quality, improvement, innovation	Innovation and increased competitiveness

Source: adapted from Crossan *et al.* (1995: 340–43).

Can an organization learn? Comparing the individual and the organization

Early writers on the topic of organizational learning argued that if the term 'organizational learning' means anything, it means learning of the individuals who happen to function in an organizational setting (Vickers, 1968). From this perspective, to hold the view that an organization learns is to commit what the philosopher Gilbert Ryle called a category mistake (Argyris and Schön, 1996: 189).

Gradually researchers started to refer to organizational agents, which suggests a move away from viewing individuals as the only possible source of learning. This view was popular in the mid-1980s, and can be seen as bridging the gap between the individual and the organizational levels of learning. It is clear, however, that at this time the organization was not yet seen as having distinct learning capabilities. For example, Fiol and Lyles (1985) are of the opinion that learning is the process of improving actions through better knowledge and understanding, whether undertaken by individual or organizational agents. Inherent learning qualities were therefore not yet ascribed to the organization as a unit.

In the late 1980s and early 1990s, researchers became more comfortable with ascribing human qualities to organizational systems. Levitt and March (1988: 319) suggested that organizations learn when they encode inferences from history into the routines that guide their behaviour, and Huber (1991: 89) stated that an organization has learned if any of its components have acquired information available for use, either by other components or by itself, on behalf of the organization. In more recent work, Nevis *et al.* (1995) have given an account of organizations as learning systems.

It can therefore be said that researchers over the years have increasingly viewed organizations as entities with qualities that promote and enable learning. The vehicle for learning can accordingly be seen as the organization (and not only individuals as agents for the organization), and the intricate learning processes can be seen to be located within the fibre of the organization (organizational memory, routines, systems of belief and patterns of behaviour).

Activity 2.2

- Can an organization learn, or is it merely individuals that learn on behalf of the organization?
- In your discussion, think of how you would view an organization – that is, what is your organizational paradigm?
- How would this influence your view of SHRD?

The notion of an organization that learns or, an alternative vantage point, that it is the members of the organization that learn, depends on how we view an organization. That is the organizational paradigm that we hold. One extreme view is that organizations are *collectives made up of individuals*, therefore they learn when their individual members (or a substantial proportion of them) learn. As referred to earlier, this paradigm fits well into the early work on OL (Vickers, 1968). Along similar lines, the *individual cognitive aspect of organizations* is often emphasized – for example, Gioia and Sims (1986: 1) conceptualize organizations as 'the product of thought and action of their members'. Within this paradigm, learning is seen to have taken place if the thought structures change (Nicolini and Meznar, 1995: 739). The problem with this view is that in many cases an organization may know or learn less than its individual members, or in some cases due to organizational memory it may know more than all of its members put together. Alternative paradigms therefore need to be evaluated.

Another possibility is to view clusters of individual members as the agents who learn and act on behalf of the organization. The 'communities of practice' approach to learning (Seely Brown and Duguid, 1991; Wenger, 2000) falls within these parameters. A community of practice can be defined as 'a naturally occurring and evolving collection of people who together engage in particular kinds of activity, and who come to develop and share ways of doing things – ways of talking, beliefs, values, and practices – as a result of their joint involvement in that activity' (McGlagan, 1993: 33). Yet the learning outcomes generated by such a cluster may not be diffused through the larger organization, and even they are diffused, they may not enter into the stream of debates and deliberations that affect an organization's policies, programmes or practices (Argyris and Schön, 1996: 7).

Finally, organizations can be conceptualized as living organisms with personalities, histories and memories. These organizations are characterized by channels of communication, information systems, procedures and routines, systems of incentives, and common patterns of behaviour. The Darwinian language of evolution that some researchers use (Nelson and Winter, 1982; Kim, 1993; Nevis *et al.*, 1995) is representative of this paradigm. Kim (1993: 12) states that:

> ... although the meaning of the term 'learning' remains essentially the same as in the individual case, the learning process is fundamentally different at the organizational level. A model of organizational learning has to resolve somehow the dilemma of imparting intelligence and learning capabilities to a non-human entity without anthropomorphizing it.

Furthermore, Nevis *et al.* (1995: 4) refer to organizational learning orientations as values and practices that reflect where learning takes place and what is learned. Tsoukas (1996) is of the opinion that within this organizational paradigm information needs to be transferred from the relatively familiar domain of individual learning (the source domain) to a lesser-known phenomenon in organizations (target domain).

From this perspective, it is clear that the organization is a separate entity with its own capabilities, actions and memories. Yet it is a known fact that organizations cannot exist without individuals or clusters of individuals. The role of SHRD is therefore to go beyond what is traditionally known as the training of individuals, and should encompass larger-scale change that has an impact on the core competence of the organization. The aim of the HRD practitioner therefore needs to be to understand the wider organizational challenges and the capabilities needed to compete in the future. Organization-wide processes then need to be established that will enable the organization, as well as its members, to learn. Here, the organizational paradigm will influence the organizational development interventions and indeed the success of the organizational learning processes.

Once the view of an organization is clearly defined, it is important to ask whether we would approach the learning process as a change in behaviour or whether we view it as something that takes place in the heads of individuals.

Activity 2.3

- Is the learning process merely a change in behaviour, or would you say that a change in cognition (knowledge, understanding and insights) is an important indication that we have learnt? Outline the reasons for your answer.

Perspectives on organizational learning: cognition or behaviour?

Tsang (1997: 75) argues that most definitions of OL entail aspects of both cognitive and behavioural changes. Cognition in this context refers to knowledge, understanding and insights. Behavioural changes could be potential (lessons learned may have an impact on future behaviour) or actual (observable behavioural change). Fiol and Lyles (1985) are of the opinion that behavioural developments must be separated from cognitive developments, and OL must refer only to the latter. According to these authors, behavioural adaptation constitutes incremental adjustments, which they do not view as learning, and cognitive learning should be divided into low-level and high-level learning (as quoted by Nicolini and Meznar, 1995: 737; see Table 2.3).

Table 2.3

Behaviour vs cognition

Behaviour	Cognition
The ability to make incremental adjustments as a result of environmental changes, goal structure change or other change	The development of insights, knowledge and associations between past action, the effectiveness of those actions, and future actions
Not learning	Low-level learning: Short-term, temporary but with associations being formed (single-loop learning)
	High-level learning: Development of complex rules and associations regarding new actions. Understanding of causation. Learning that affects the entire organization (double-loop learning)
Source: adapted from Nicolini and Meznar (1985).	

From a review of the above dimensions (organizational paradigm and learning perspective) it is possible to present the following comprehensive definition of organizational learning:

> Organizational learning (OL) refers to the process through which an entity (whether it be an individual, group of individuals that act on behalf of the organization, or the organization itself) employs enabling abilities to create permanent cognitive and behavioural change within a system. The changed behaviour or cognition needs to be embedded in the fabric of the organization and be evident in the organizational memory.

Given this definition of organizational learning, we are still left with the question as to whether we will know that an organization has indeed learnt – in other words, what is the outcome of the learning process? It may indeed be the case that there is no clear outcome due to the continuous nature of the learning process. These criteria of learning outcomes at the organizational level will be explored in the below.

Activity 2.4

- Using a case organization that you are familiar with, or a team that you have worked in, list the outcomes that gave you an indication that the learning process had taken place.
- Discuss with your colleague or fellow student which changes were most important to you, and an indication that learning occurred.

The outcome of the organizational learning process

A learning outcome will be an indication that learning has occurred. This dimension is critical in evaluating the learning process within a system. As might be expected, this 'indication of learning' will be guided by the organizational paradigm and the cognitive–behavioural orientation.

A learning outcome can therefore differ according to:

1 *Level of outcome.* Can the outcome be identified at the individual, group, organizational or inter-organizational levels? It is possible that a view of organizational learning can include outcomes at all of these levels.

2   *Behavioural change.* Is it possible to see a definitive change in behaviour on behalf of the individual, which can be regarded as evidence that learning has taken place? It is important to include both visible and potential behavioural changes in this outcome category.

3   *Change in cognitive structures.* Do individuals or groups of individuals have changed knowledge, understandings and insights?

4   *Type of learning.* Distinctions can be made here between single-loop and double-loop learning. Single-loop learning is associated with incremental changes that result mainly from error detection and correction (Argyris and Schön, 1996), whilst double-loop learning relates to more transformational changes. The latter may take place when individuals in an organization ask: why do we do this? And, what if? This type of learning may be counter-cultural and resisted in many organizations. Gregory Bateson (1979) also identified a further form of learning, namely deuterolearning or the phenomenon of 'learning how to learn'. Organizational deuterolearning is critically dependent on individual deuterolearning (Argyris and Schön, 1996: 29).

5   *Continuity or discontinuity of the learning process.* Would it be possible to measure the outcome of learning after a learning intervention, or is organizational learning seen as a process without a clear start and finish? The latter view will pay much more attention to the enablers of learning within a system, and may ask 'can organizations ever "not learn"?' (Nicolini and Meznar, 1995: 738).

(For further information, see Fiol and Lyles, 1985; Kim, 1993; Nevis *et al.*, 1995; Nicolini and Meznar, 1995; Argyris and Schön, 1996; Tsang, 1997.)

The chronological development of the organizational learning research, described above, does not suggest that researchers solely focus on the organization as the unit for analysis (see Table 2.2), but it does point out that referring to the organization as the learning entity has become more acceptable in recent studies of the phenomenon of OL. This development formed the building blocks for a new stream of research with a more practical focus, which is normally labelled 'the learning organization'.

Organizational learning and the learning organization

Most writings on the learning organization have a different purpose to those on OL. They are more committed to the achievement of a desirable end state; they are eclectic in evaluating ideas according to their applicability; and they usually derive from an action research agenda, where there is a close link between generating change and studying the nature of that change (Easterby-Smith, 1997: 1103). Tsang (1997: 74) is of the opinion that this body of research adopts a more prescriptive stance and teaches managers the way that a company should learn. The main differences between OL and the learning organization are presented in Table 2.4.

Garvin (1993: 79) is of the opinion that a learning organization is an organization skilled at creating, acquiring and transferring

Table 2.4

Main differences between OL and the learning organization

Organizational learning	The learning organization
Descriptive	Prescriptive
Asks: 'How does an organization learn?'	Asks: 'How should an organization learn?'
Draws from: psychology and OD; management sciences; sociology and organization theory; strategy; production management; cultural anthropology. Each of these disciplines represents its own ontology and problematics	Originates from mainly management science and OD disciplines. First tradition (Senge, 1990; Garvin, 1993; Nevis *et al.*, 1995) starts from management science perspective and then adds insights from organizational development. Second tradition (Dixon, 1994; Hawkins, 1994; Nonaka, 1994; Torbert, 1994; Swieringa and Wierdsma, 1994) takes, as a starting point, models of human development and emancipation, and then distinguishes between cyclical and evolutionary models of learning
Authors focus on conceptualization and answering the questions such as: What does OL mean? How is OL at all feasible? What kinds of OL are desirable, and for whom and with what chance of actual occurrence? Literature is intentionally distant from practice and value-neutral	Authors (e.g. Garvin, 1993; Ulrich *et al.*, 1993) focus on continuous improvement, competence acquisition, experimentation and boundary spanning. They stress the need for visible commitment from managers to learning by incorporating it in strategic intent, measuring it, investing in it, and giving it symbolic expression
Source: adapted from Argyris and Schön (1996: 181–8); Easterby-Smith (1997: 1087–1107); Tsang (1997: 74–6).	

knowledge, and at modifying its behaviour to reflect new knowledge and insights. The process of knowledge creation can therefore be seen as the foundation upon which the learning organization is built.

Activity 2.5

- Which activities would an organization need to be skilled at if it aims to become a learning organization?

Learning organizations need to be skilled at the following processes (Garvin, 1993):

1 *Systemic problem-solving.* This involves less guesswork and more controlled testing (hypothesis testing and hypothesis generating). Accuracy and precision are essential for learning. However, it also refers to a wider perspective. Senge (1990) referred to this as systems thinking, which means that systems need to be viewed holistically rather than being broken down into smaller parts. Individuals in the learning organization therefore need to understand the dynamic linkages between separate sub-sections of a larger system. Essentially, the learning organization is able to balance scientific problem-solving with a more creative and holistic approach to *seeing* a problem.

2 *Experimentation with new approaches.* This involves the systematic searching and testing of new knowledge (Garvin, 1993: 82), and relates to the learning philosophy of the organization. In the learning organization, experimentation is not an accident but part of an underlying philosophy of embracing knowledge creation. For example, a software design organization based in the southwest of England has, as part of its performance management system, an allowance for experimentation during redundant time. Even though time is money in this organization, time is also set aside for creative thinking and experimentation. Interestingly, the CEO of this organization did ascribe their success in the marketplace to the culture of experimentation that was created in this small software house.

3   *Learning from their own experience and past history.* Mistakes should be noticed and reflected upon. Many organizations repeat mistakes without even noticing it. Burgelman (1994) refers to this as skilled incompetence. That is, the skills of the past are no longer relevant for the future competition, but the organization continues to practice irrelevant skills in a competent manner. In this sense experience and the building-on experience in a non-reflective manner may even lead to failure. Experience, whether it relates to success or failure, therefore needs to be linked to reflecting, and a great deal of understanding of future market conditions.

4   *Learning from the experience and best practice of others.* Skilled learning organizations often belong to knowledge networks, or groups of companies that share best practice. Even organizations in different sectors may be able to shed light on problem solutions. However, this can only be beneficial if received by open, attentive listening managers.

5   *Transferring knowledge quickly and efficiently throughout the organization.* During the last decade this has become one of the single largest areas of strategic concern. After de-layering and the experience of mergers and acquisitions, many organizations found that they were reinventing the wheel across several high-investment projects. Attention was therefore focused not only on knowledge-creating but also on the sharing of knowledge within and across organizations (Swart and Kinnie, 2003).

A review of some of the strategies for becoming a learning organization points to one central fact: knowledge, both its creating and transfer or sharing, sits at the heart of transforming an organization into a learning organization. Due to the pivotal role that knowledge plays in these strategies, as well as its importance to the HRD profession, the following section is dedicated to the concepts of knowledge and knowledge management.

As a key building block, it is important to view knowledge as part of the input and central to the organizational learning process, as well as the most significant output of the learning organization (see Figure 2.1). It is therefore *the* key form of capital of the learning organization.

Figure 2.1
Knowledge as input, process and output to organizational learning and the *learning* organization.

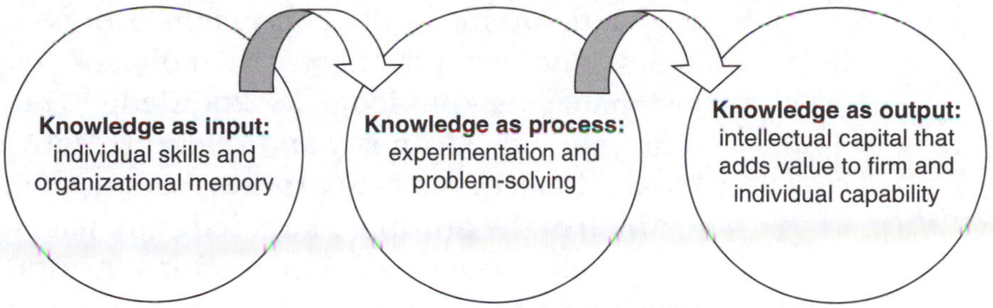

Knowledge as input: individual skills and organizational memory

Knowledge as process: experimentation and problem-solving

Knowledge as output: intellectual capital that adds value to firm and individual capability

Knowledge management

Peter Drucker claimed in 1993 that knowledge will become the only key to sustainable competitive advantage. This statement is founded upon the resource-based view of the firm (RBV), which views knowledge as a unique resource that cannot be copied by competitors. Firms will therefore rely on their knowledge base or their human capital to create unique and differentiated products and services (Swart *et al.*, 2003). From the knowledge-based perspective, the core business model is focused on the conversion of human capital (knowledge, skills and experience) into intellectual capital (tangible, knowledge-intensive products and services).

Knowledge management defined

It is therefore not surprising that the last decade has witnessed a growing interest in the field of knowledge management, with 320 articles written between 1994 and 1995, 30 conferences held on the topic in 1996 alone, and $US 1.5 billion spent on consulting in 1997. In a recent survey of UK and European business leaders, 85 per cent of the 1000 respondents described knowledge as the key business power (Ruggles, 1998). There is also agreement that knowledge management has now moved on beyond its fad status (Scarborough and Swan, 2001) and should be central to the HRD practitioner's agenda.

But what is knowledge management? O'Dell and Grayson (1998) define knowledge management as a conscious strategy of getting the right knowledge to the right people at the right time, and helping to share and put information into action in ways that strive to improve organizational performance. At the heart of this definition is the conversion process of information into action, and secondly there is the efficiency element – that is, not just managing knowledge for knowledge's sake, but making sure that knowledge is timely and relevant. Many organizations have looked to technology to provide this solution.

Much of the growth in knowledge management has been technologically focused, with many firms investing vast sums on the development of information technology and databases to manage their organization-wide knowledge base. Scarborough *et al.* (1999: 21) state that contributions from information technology have no doubt dominated the area, with 70 per cent of published articles currently originating from this discipline. This has, however, led to a sense of disillusionment and a realization that the management of *knowledge* in itself may be more complex than *information* management, and that complementary interventions therefore need to be put into place.

Interest has consequently been generated in the development of an understanding of how to manage knowledge workers, as well as the particular role that human resource management and SHRD in particular can play in this regard. In order to gain a clearer understanding of this contribution, it is important to develop a definition of knowledge.

What is knowledge that it may be managed?

Alvesson and Karreman (2001) refer to the concept of knowledge management as the 'odd couple'; knowledge to them is something that is fluid and personal and cannot be forced, structured or managed wilfully. Knowledge management can be regarded as an oxymoron. The prevailing notion in many knowledge management models is that knowledge is made up of 'separate units' that can be added to an extant heap of knowledge and transformed from one knowledge type into the next. Other knowledge management models regard information technology tools such as e-mail as the key to the assimilation of knowledge. Metaphors of mining, tapping into and transferring knowledge together with the view of knowledge as intellectual assets (the resource-based view) are often found within the technology approach. However, if knowledge is not open to manipulation and packaging, it may therefore not inherently be regarded as some*thing* that can be managed.

In order to develop a workable definition of this complex concept that has theoretical roots in philosophy, sociology, psychology and education, we begin by differentiating between data, information and knowledge – that is, we answer the question *what is knowledge not?*

Spender (1996: 65) postulates two radically different kinds of organizational knowledge – i.e. data and meaning – each generated, stored and applied in completely different ways, while intelligence shapes (and is shaped by) their interaction. Data can be regarded as the cellular level of an information system that may or may not contribute to a wider understanding (Allee, 1997: 115) or in organizational terms as structured records of transactions (Davenport and Prusak, 1998: 2) – for example, a spreadsheet with numerical input.

Information can be associated with data that have been contextualized and categorized. For example, I may obtain information about a holiday in the Caribbean in a travel agent's brochure. These are data that have been contextualized (my holiday being the context). However, if I have not been on a holiday in the Caribbean and have had no experience of the heat or the culture the beaches, then I cannot say that I have knowledge of a holiday in the Caribbean; I merely have information about what the experience may be like.

Whilst information establishes itself in the sphere of common understanding, knowledge derived from it is subjective in nature, and is intimately linked to the group of individuals generating it. For example, a folder filled with articles that have never been read and which may be from various disciplines may be regarded as data. Once the articles are read they become information. If the information is then compared and contrasted, further searching strengthens particular understandings and these understandings are then acted upon (through conversation, writing or searching), it could be said that one knows something about the 'topic' that has been read.

Data and information are not regarded as knowledge, mainly due to the lack of interaction and dialogue involved in communicating either. A definition of knowledge consequently needs to take into account the experience-based and personal nature of knowledge. Davenport and Prusak's (1997) definition adheres to these criteria, and they view knowledge as:

> A fluid mix of framed experiences, values, contextual information, and expert insight that provides a framework for evaluating

and incorporating new experiences and information. It originates and is applied in the minds of knowers. In organizations, it often becomes embedded not only in documents or repositories but also in organizational routines, processes, practices and norms.

This definition gives an indication that various knowledge types may be found in organizations, raging from individual and organizational knowledge to forms of knowledge that may be easier to put into words, and other forms that would probably be very difficult to explain to a colleague. Below, we take a closer look at the various categorizations of knowledge.

Categorizations of knowledge

One of the most frequently cited categorizations of knowledge is that of tacit and explicit knowledge. This categorization originates from the philosopher Michael Polanyi's work on the tacit dimension. Polanyi (1966: 4) was of the opinion that we will always know more than we can tell – that is to say, there will always be a part of the knowledge that we have that we cannot express. The tacit dimensions of knowledge relate mainly to embodied skills, where we may know how to ride a horse or be excellent at playing tennis, but we cannot translate all our skills into words for our colleagues/competitors to learn. It is for this reason that this form of knowledge is regarded as *the* key to sustainable competitive advantage, and sits at the heart of the knowledge-creation process.

Tacit and explicit knowledge

Nonaka and Takeuchi (1995) built upon Polanyi's notion of the tacit dimension of knowledge being differentiated clearly from explicit knowledge. According to these authors, the Western perspective on knowledge is formal and systemic; something that can be expressed in words and numbers. This is referred to as explicit knowledge. The Japanese, however, realize that explicit knowledge represents only a fragment of the collective knowledge. They therefore view knowledge as highly personal, and difficult to formalize and communicate. This category of knowledge is defined as tacit knowledge. 'Subjective insights, intuitions, and

Table 2.5
Types of knowledge

Tacit knowledge (Subjective)	Explicit knowledge (Objective)
Knowledge of experience (body)	Knowledge of rationality (mind)
Know-how	Know-what
An element of a system	Independent
Simultaneous knowledge (here and now)	Sequential knowledge (there and then)
Complex	Simple
Analogue knowledge (practice)	Digital knowledge (theory)
Not observable, in use	Observable, in use

Source: adapted from Nonaka and Takeuchi (1995: 61) and Winter (1987: 170).

hunches fall into this category' (Nonaka and Takeuchi, 1995: 8).
Table 2.5 provides a summary of the types of knowledge.

It is within the dynamic interplay between these two types of
knowledge, as well as the individual and collective levels, that
knowledge is created. A 'stock of knowledge' would therefore
evolve on the social level when individuals share their subjective
elements of knowledge. According to Nonaka and Takeuchi
(1995), four modes of knowledge conversion, known as the SECI
model, exist between individual and collective (shared) and tacit
and explicit knowledge:

- Individual tacit knowledge to shared tacit knowledge =
  Socialization
- Shared tacit knowledge to individual explicit knowledge =
  Externalization
- Individual explicit knowledge to shared explicit know-
  ledge = **C**ombination
- Shared explicit knowledge to individual tacit knowledge =
  Internalization.

These four modes of knowledge would subsequently integrate
via certain processes to form what is known as the 'spiral of
knowledge creation' (Nonaka and Takeuchi, 1995). Dixon
(1990) advocates that this knowledge spiral will have the following characteristics:

1   Discussion will be generated
2   All participants will be viewed as equal in the discussion

3   Knowledge-creating discussions will generate new meaning
4   Many alternatives in a particular situation will be generated
5   The need for the sharing and collection of facts will be discussed
6   Subjective experiences will be shared to create organizational meaning.

Activity 2.6

- Outline the HRD strategies that you believe can support or facilitate the characteristics of the knowledge-creating spiral.

Moss-Kanter (1989: 206) emphasizes the importance of teamwork and interactive learning in the process of creating new knowledge, and making tacit knowledge explicit. She states that:

> The creator's knowledge is not always codified – put into a form in which it can be transferred to others. Sometimes it is not even codifiable because it is elusive; it is a matter of 'feel' based on experience that is piling up. And whenever a group work together on a development task, their ability to share this rapidly accumulating knowledge makes a difference in how effectively they can work toward a common goal.

Venzin *et al.* (1998) are of the opinion that the above process will make use of at least three channels in organizations. These include, but are not limited to:

1   Language and signs
2   Tools
3   Marks.

In using language, individuals must be *aware* of their knowledge and have an appropriate repertoire of words to express their knowledge and feelings. If this is lacking, gesturing, playing and drawing can be used. Second, subjective knowledge may be shared in the knowledge-creation process by creating or applying tools to solve tasks. Lastly, marks are 'the results of acts established by the one acting in order to hold onto a definite element of knowledge and to remind one of this' (Venzin *et al.*, 1998: 64).

Organizational knowledge creation should therefore be understood as a process that 'organizationally' amplifies the knowledge created by individuals and crystallizes it as a part of the knowledge network of the organization. This process takes place within an expanding 'community of interaction', which crosses intra- and inter-organizational levels and boundaries (Nonaka and Takeuchi, 1995: 59).

Cook and Seely Brown (1999: 386) focus on the interactive and indeed the action-orientated aspects of knowledge, and prefer to refer to the act of knowing, when categorizing knowledge and understanding the process of knowledge creation. According to these authors, Western traditions have favoured the epistemology of possession over the epistemology of practice. It is therefore important to combine both knowledge and knowing when generating new knowledge. For example, you may hold explicit knowledge about cooking a meal (a recipe in a book), you may also have tacit knowledge about the process of cooking (the last time you cooked your favourite meal, you just seemed to stir it differently; there's nothing that you can express, but you 'just know' that it worked better that way). The actual act of preparing a meal for your guests will include both explicit knowing (i.e. action-orientated knowledge that can be expressed whilst engaging in the action, such as the chef explaining a process whilst cooking) and tacit knowing (embedded tacit skills that are used at that particular moment). By combining our explicit and tacit knowledge and knowing, we are able to generate new knowledge. That is to say, we learn something new by, for example, reading how to do it, then by practising and finally by sharing our newly learnt skills with others in our community of practice.

The bridging of the epistemology of possession (to own knowledge) and the epistemology of practice (to feel a sense of knowing whilst you are doing) makes an important contribution to the categorization of knowledge in so far as it enables HRD practitioners to include both knowledge transfer and the sharing of knowing in their intervention designs. In other words, experience-based learning will enable both knowledge and knowing to combine in the overarching learning experience.

The Cook and Seely Brown (1999) model does, however, still separate tacit and explicit knowledge. If we refer back to the originator of tacit knowing (Polanyi, 1966), though, it becomes evident that there is no knowledge other than tacit knowledge. In other words, Polanyi views explicit knowledge and explicit knowing as *information* and not knowledge. If we accept that the recipe for chocolate cake is merely information and not knowledge – i.e. it is only knowledge once I have baked the chocolate cake and then the locus of the knowledge is my experience of baking the cake – then we have to create a clearer understanding of tacit knowing. This is of particular relevance if we need to design HRD interventions that are based on the principles of tacit knowing.

Swart and Pye (2002) have developed a model that investigates the nature of tacit knowing (see Figure 2.2) – that is, it gives an illustration of how tacit knowing operates in organizations. The foundation of the model is three strands that work together in any given situation. The first of these is known as representation, which in essence is the picture that we have in our minds of how a system will work. For example, you may have a map in your mind of what the impact of a merger will be on your business unit – i.e. you have a rich understanding of all the interconnections in a system that has been built up through your experience in that system.

The second strand of the model refers to reflection and dialogue. In other words, we use the map of our system to guide our behaviour, but at times we may feel some inconsistencies in our map and reflect on where we may need to adjust our 'picture of the system'. In this situation, our experience will shape and re-shape the representations (strand 1) that we hold.

Finally, our picture of the system in which we operate (strand 1) and the reflection on this map (strand 2) will guide and inform our behaviour. The third strand is therefore labelled: practice and participation. It is important to understand that all three strands are intertwined and take place at the same time.

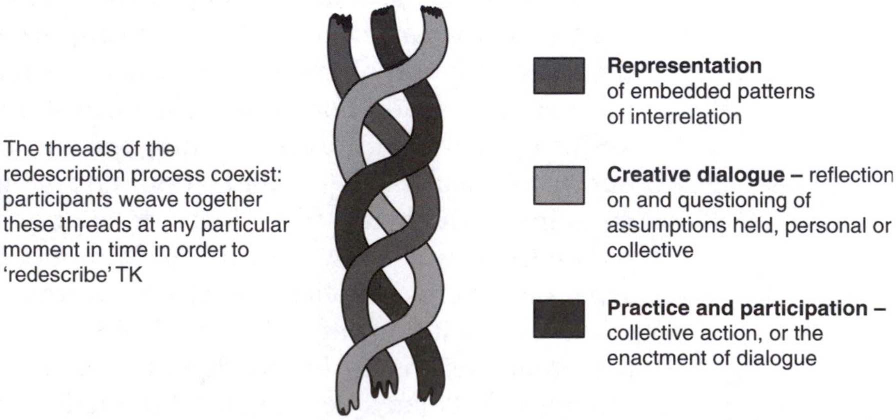

The threads of the redescription process coexist: participants weave together these threads at any particular moment in time in order to 'redescribe' TK

Figure 2.2
The nature of tacit knowing: a redescription process.

Representation of embedded patterns of interrelation

Creative dialogue – reflection on and questioning of assumptions held, personal or collective

Practice and participation – collective action, or the enactment of dialogue

Your practice (experience and participation in your project team, department or business unit) will shape your picture of how that particular system works; however, this shaping is combined with an internal or external dialogue in which you reflect on your current map and the pictures that would have influenced your action.

Activity 2.7

- How could you include all three aspects of tacit knowing (representation, reflection and dialogue and practice) in your HRD strategy?

Knowledge types

Reason and Heron (1995: 2) identify four types of knowledge – *experiential* knowledge, that is gained through direct encounter face-to-face with persons, places or things; *practical* knowledge, which means knowing how to do something demonstrated in a skill or a competence; *propositional* knowledge, which is knowledge about something expressed in statements and theories; and *presentational* knowledge, by which we first order our tacit experiential knowledge of the world into spatiotemporal patterns of imagery. According to Reason and Heron, propositional knowledge needs to be grounded in the experiential and practical of the subjects in the inquiry.

Along similar lines Blackler (1995: 1036) defines knowledge as an active process that is mediated, situated, provisional, pragmatic and contested. He differentiates between the following forms of knowledge:

1 Embrained knowledge – knowledge that is dependent upon conceptual skills and cognitive abilities
2 Embodied knowledge – action-orientated and only partially explicit knowledge
3 Encultured knowledge – achieving shared understandings
4 Embedded knowledge – this resides in systemic routines
5 Encoded knowledge – information conveyed in signs and symbols.

It is possible that some of these distinctions are somewhat oblique. For instance, embodied knowledge could not be constructed without encultured and embedded knowledge. Blackler's knowledge types, although essentially action-orientated, originate from different culturally located systems through which people achieve their knowing (Blackler, 1995). This view may lead to an approach that supports the management of knowledge together with a control of meaning (Spender, 1996: 66). In order to maximize our HRD strategy, we may need to seek integration of knowledge-construction processes (how the above forms fit into one another) rather than a classification of knowledge types.

The above definitions and categorizations of knowledge give us a clear indication that knowledge is a complex, fluid and situational construct that cannot be *managed* in the strict sense of the word. What is important, though, is that the creation, transfer and retention of knowledge are facilitated through the HRD processes and practices. In order for the organization to be competent at these processes, certain enablers need to be in place. Next, we will take a closer look at how we can facilitate these critical knowledge processes.

Activity 2.8

- Imagine that you are working in an organization that competes in a knowledge-based market and the creation, transfer and retention of knowledge is therefore critical if the organization is to establish competitive advantage. Which enablers would need to be in place to ensure that knowledge is created, shared and retained?

Knowledge management enablers

The HRD strategy for facilitating knowledge creation, sharing and retention needs to be sensitive to the *culture* and *structure* of the organization. It is essential to establish a fit between these knowledge requirements and the informal processes that are already taking place across the formal organizational structures. A small chemical research organization that employs mainly PhD chemists and has a culture of sharing ideas and working together on solving complex chemical problems may therefore not benefit from a more formal knowledge-sharing strategy. In essence, it is necessary to analyse the current organizational culture and ascertain to what extent it facilitates knowledge creation and sharing.

Culture can be defined as the combination of shared history, expectations, unwritten rules and social norms that affect the behaviour of everyone, from managers to mailroom clerks. It is the set of underlying beliefs that, while never exactly articulated, are always there to colour the perception of actions and communications (O'Dell and Grayson, 1998: 71). The culture of an organization will therefore dictate how successful and formal the knowledge-sharing process is. A naturally collaborative culture will most likely encourage knowledge sharing as a natural process that is 'part of the way we do things around here', whereas a more bureaucratic culture may hinder knowledge creation and sharing principally due to the subdivisions and conflicting interests that are created within this system.

Many authors regard culture as the single most important influencer of successful knowledge management. In a recent survey, 54 per cent of the respondents ranked culture as the number one barrier to knowledge transfer in their firm (Ernst & Young Centre for Business Innovation, 1998). It may therefore mean that knowledge management strategies, and by implication HRD strategies, do not only need to fit with the organizational culture; cultural change may also be necessary before knowledge management strategy can be effective.

Cultural barriers to knowledge creation, transfer and retention may include fragmentation based on individuality, a 'time is money' mindset and lack of incentives. First, fragmentation can be caused either by a very strong professional identity in the organization (Swart and Kinnie, 2003) or by departmentalization. Many professional service firms encounter the force of individuality where the doctor, lawyer, software engineer would prefer to work alone and not as part of a team. A very real barrier in this context is the diversity of professional 'languages', where each profession has built up a specific way of describing a problem and feels that it will not be time efficient to translate their 'expert language' into the team context. Fragmentation can also be caused by a culture that separates functions, disciples or business units. If multidisciplinary teams do not work together, a culture of 'them and us' is often created. If marketing and finance have different objectives, and once again speak different languages, then it would be nearly impossible to establish the mutual goal of knowledge sharing.

Second, a 'time is money' mindset could destroy the processes that sit at the heart of knowledge creation and sharing. The very process of creating knowledge may be time intensive, as individuals from differing points of view debate a problem or indeed try different solutions. It may also involve a team that has worked together for a considerable period of time, dedicated to applying their highly specialized knowledge to a novel situation. Other possibilities include an intuitive solution that needs to be reiterated in order to work, or solutions from one context that need to be adapted to fit into another. The bottom line is that all knowledge activities take time, especially in the initial phases – for instance, when the team works together for the first time. A tendency to rush the process or not engage in it at all because 'it may waste time' would therefore be counterproductive and fatal to the knowledge-based firm.

Third, individuals may not want to share knowledge if they feel that there is 'little in it for me'. This cultural dimension stems mainly from the 'knowledge is power' mindset. In this culture, a sense of insecurity or mistrust may encourage individuals to hoard their knowledge in order to secure a better position for themselves. This is often the case in organizations that thrive on innovations and knowledge creation. For example, teams of research scientist may compete to develop a solution and would therefore resist the knowledge-sharing process. In this situation, the incentives that result from not sharing knowledge are greater than those that are attached to sharing knowledge. A culture that works toward a common objective and thrives on reaching a solution together needs to be established if the knowledge-creation and -sharing process is to be effective. In this type of culture, the act of knowledge sharing itself will become the incentive, and formal incentives (financial or recognition) cannot be used to create a knowledge-sharing culture.

Besides a culture that supports and certainly drives the informal knowledge creation, sharing and retention processes, it is critical that a firm develops an infrastructure that enhances these knowledge-facilitation processes. O'Dell and Grayson (1998) identify three levels of knowledge infrastructure. The first is self-directed transfer, and refers to a system where individuals are provided with tools to search for the knowledge in their firm. Examples include knowledge databases or e-mail systems. The more advanced infrastructure includes knowledge services and networks. This structure would have knowledge managers who are responsible on a part-time basis for the sharing of knowledge (almost like company librarians). The firm would also have communities-of-practice or vocational teams who are dedicated to the development of skills and the sharing of knowledge.

The most advanced infrastructure is the facilitated transfer structure: here there is a dedicated group of employees who will focus on knowledge creation and sharing on a full-time basis. A key characteristic of this infrastructure is the presence of boundary spanners. These are groups of individuals (or indeed individuals) who span boundaries between projects, and whose role it is to translate knowledge from one context into another and to ensure that the knowledge becomes embedded in more than one project team. Many of the science and technology firms based in the southwest of the UK work on this basis, having dedicated engineers who work on various project teams and whose sole responsibility is the transfer of knowledge. Here, the performance management system and key responsibility areas of these roles need to reflect the dedication to knowledge sharing – i.e. the knowledge manager's key output will be knowledge sharing, and not product development.

Technology is the final and important enabler of knowledge creation, sharing and retention. It could, however, be regarded as a key knowledge management strategy. The reason for this is that many organizations embarked on a technology-driven strategy at the start of the 1990s and have since experienced both its benefits and disadvantages. The role of technology in knowledge management will therefore be discussed next.

Knowledge management strategies

With the burgeoning interest and highly sophisticated application of knowledge management, firms have had to face the possibility of implementing a vast array of strategies. Given the growth of the consulting interest in this area, their choices have not been made any easier. A closer analysis does however, highlight that all of these strategies can be grouped into two main categories (Hansen *et al.*, 1999):

1 Personalization strategies
2 Codification strategies.

Personalization strategies are highly applicable to environments where individuals work with novel complex problems and, by implication, organizations that need to innovate to compete. The emphasis of this knowledge management strategy is therefore on knowledge creation, rather than knowledge re-use.

The focus of this strategy is to establish as much high quality face-to-face interaction as possible. It also ascribes to the personal qualities of knowledge, and believes that knowledge can only be shared if the person who owns the knowledge is involved in the sharing process. In these situations, a firm mainly tries to share knowledge that is highly complex and tacit – i.e. individuals may find it difficult to put all their knowledge into words (they will know more than they can say; Polanyi, 1966) and the main vehicle of the strategy needs to be the shared practice or learning from one another through action. Key characteristics or dominant practices of the personalization strategy include:

- The establishment of interpersonal networks
- Multidisciplinary teams that work together on one novel problem
- Cross-boundary and cross-organization networks
- Open-plan working spaces that allow frequent interaction
- A culture that fits the 'family feel' description; this brings individuals from various disciplines together and creates a shared language and mindset, which in turn enables personalized knowledge-sharing.

Codification strategies, on the other hand, are suitable for firms who need to focus more on the use and re-use of explicit knowledge or information. This may involve the codification of knowledge in databases that can be used and accessed by all the individuals employed by the organization. The cost of this strategy may be higher during the initial phases because of the time invested in codifying and recording the knowledge. However, it is estimated that with this initial investment the strategy could be highly effective with minimum maintenance. It is critical that firms that adopt this strategy do not have innovation as their key competitive strategy, because although the codification strategy enables a firm to get to past information in a more time-efficient manner, it does not enable the development of fresh or new knowledge solutions. Key practices that would support this strategy include:

- Company·databases
- Specification records

- Procedure manuals
- Error detection and correction records
- Standardized formats for communication
- Detailed post-project reports.

Both strategies could, of course, be used in one organization – for instance, a firm that has innovation as its key focus may predominantly use the personalization strategy, and rely on some of the technological and codified systems to support their personalized strategy. For example, they may use technology to locate the expert, and electronic skills matrices to facilitate the face-to-face contact. The key advice here is to establish the firm's focus and plough most of the knowledge management resources into the dominant strategy, then use the complementary strategy as support. O'Dell and Grayson (1998) also provide a useful rule of thumb when balancing the personalization and codification strategies: when knowledge is complex, simple technology should facilitate personalized knowledge sharing; when knowledge is simple, complex technology may facilitate the technological knowledge sharing.

If the HRD policies and practices are to contribute to the competitive advantage of the firm, then the HRD practitioner needs to be familiar with why knowledge is important, and know exactly what knowledge is. This underpinning knowledge subsequently needs to be combined with establishing the correct knowledge management enablers, and creating and implementing a suitable knowledge management strategy (see above). The following summary section clarifies the role of SHRD and the knowledge management paradigm.

Summary

According to the knowledge-based view of the firm (Grant, 1991), a firm competes on the basis of its knowledge assets. It is therefore in the interest of the firm to create and develop both individual and collective knowledge assets. At the heart of this process is the facilitation of knowledge creation, sharing and retention. HRD practitioners need to use this three-pronged process as the blueprint of their training and development design.

First, HRD interventions need to be aimed at the collective level – that is, organization-wide development should be the focus rather than sporadic individual training interventions.

What is important here is that the systemic view is maintained and that the HRD practices create linkages in the organizational system that can improve organization-wide effectiveness. The HRD practices therefore need to work at the individual, team and organization levels, and specific interventions must establish careful linkages between the various levels. For example, individual skills development should feed into the knowledge-sharing processes of a vocational community-of-practice, which in turn needs to fit with the organizational knowledge-creation focus.

Once the level of contribution is established, the focus of knowledge creation, sharing and retention needs to be retained. Within this context, it is important for the HRD practitioner to conduct an analysis of current successful practices that facilitate these knowledge processes. It is often the case that informal practices are powerful facilitators of knowledge management. The HRD practices therefore need to embrace the autopoetic nature of an organization and recognize that the unfolding way in which individuals interrelate can often do the work of knowledge management. That is to say, a state of the art knowledge management strategy may destroy the collaborative culture and the learning-in-action processes that are already embedded in the organization. The golden rule when facilitating knowledge creation, sharing and retention is to detect and enhance informal learning processes.

Finally, internal fit or consistency needs to be established with the HRD strategy and the wider competitive strategy. This issue will be discussed in greater depth in Chapter 3, but it is important to mention consistency in the context of knowledge management. If the HRD practices are to have an impact on the organization as a whole, and on its ability to create, share and retain knowledge, then there needs to be an internal alignment, in the first instance, with HRM practices. For example, an HRD strategy that is focused on team-based knowledge creation, or informal learning in a project team, needs to go hand in hand with a performance management system that recognizes team-based performance. If you were to be rewarded for your individual innovative output, then you would probably not want to share knowledge and learning with your team. In this case the HRM strategy can destroy the HRD strategy and *vice versa*. As mentioned above, the HRD strategy also need to fit with the wider organization strategy if it is to generate the necessary investment to be implemented, and subsequently achieve the desired outcomes.

References

Allee, V. (1997). *The Knowledge Evolution: Expanding Organizational Intelligence.* Butterworth-Heinemann.

Alvesson, M. and Karreman, D. (2001). Odd couple: making sense of the curious concept of knowledge management. *Journal of Management Studies*, **38(7)**, 995–1018.

Argyris, C. and Schön, D.A. (1996). *Organizational Learning II: Theory, Method and Practice.* Addison-Wesley.

Bateson, G. (1979). *Mind and Nature.* London: Bantam.

Blackler, F. (1995). Knowledge, knowledge work and organizations: an overview. *Organization Studies*, **16(6)**, 1021–46.

Burgelman, R.A. (1994). Fading memories: a process theory of strategic business exit in dynamic environments. *Administrative Science Quarterly*, **39,** 24–56.

Cangelosi, V.E. and Dill, W.R. (1965). Organizational learning: observations toward a theory. *Administrative Science Quarterly*, **10,** 175–203.

Cook, S.D.N. and Seely Brown, J. (1999). Bridging epistemologies: the generative dance between organizational knowledge and organizational knowing. *Organization Science*, **10(4),** 381–400.

Crossan, M. and Guatto, T. (1996). Organizational learning research profile. *Journal of Organizational Change*, **9(1),** 107–12.

Crossan, M.M., Lane, H.W., White, R.E. and Djurfeldt, L. (1995). Organizational learning: dimensions for a theory. *International Journal of Organizational Analysis*, **3(4),** 337–60.

Davenport, T.H. and Prusak, L. (1998). *Working Knowledge: How Organizations Manage What They Know.* Harvard Business School Press.

Dixon, N. (1990). Organizational learning: a review of the literature with implications for HRD professionals. *Human Resource Development Quarterly*, **3(1),** 29–49.

Drucker, P. (1993). *Post-capitalist Society*. Butterworth-Heinemann.

Easterby-Smith, M. (1997). Disciplines of organizational learning: contributions and critiques. *Human Relations*, **50(9),** 1085–113.

Ernst & Young (1997). The Ernst & Young Centre for Business Innovation and Business Intelligence as 'Executive Perspectives on Knowledge in the Organization'.

Fiol, C.M. and Lyles, M.A. (1985). Organizational learning. *Academy of Management Review*, **10(4),** 803–13.

Garvin, D.A. (1993). Building a learning organization. *Harvard Business Review*, **71(4),** 78–91.

Gioia, D.A. and Sims, H.P. (1986). *The Thinking Organization.* Jossey-Bass.

Grant, R (1991). The resource-based theory of competitive advantage: implications for strategy formulation. *California Management Review*, **33(2),** 114–35.

Hansen, M.T., Nohria, N. and Tierney, T. (1999). What is your strategy for managing knowledge? *Harvard Business Review*, **Mar/Apr,** 106–16.

Hedberg, B. (1981). How organizations learn and unlearn. In P.C. Nystrom and W.H. Starbuck (eds), *Handbook of Organizational Design*, Vol. 1. Oxford University Press, pp. 3–27.

Huber, G.P. (1991). Organizational learning: the contributing processes and the literatures. *Organization Science*, **2(1),** 88–115.

Kim, D.H. (1993). The link between individual and organizational learning. *Sloan Management Review*, **Fall,** 37–50.

Levitt, B. and March, J.G. (1988). Organizational learning. *Annual Review of Sociology*, **14,** 319–40.

McGlagan, P. (1993). The search for poetry of work. *Training and Development*, **47(10),** 33–35.

Moss-Kanter, R. (1989). *When Giants Learn to Dance: Mastering the Challenges of Strategy, Management and Careers in the 1990s.* Simon & Schuster.

Nelson, R. and Winter, S.G. (1982). *An Evolutionary Theory of Economic Change.* Harvard University Press.

Nevis, E.C., DiBella, A.J. and Gould, J.M. (1995). Understanding organizations as learning systems. *Sloan Management Review*, **Winter,** 73–85.

Nicolini, D. and Meznar, M.B. (1995). The social construction of organizational learning: conceptual and practical issues in the field. *Human Relations*, **48(7),** 727–46.

Nonaka, I. and Takeuchi, H. (1995). *The Knowledge Creating Company.* Oxford University Press.

O'Dell, C. and Grayson, C.J. (1998). *If Only We Knew What We Know.* The Free Press.

Pedler, M., Boydell, T. and Burgoyne, J. (1988). *Learning Company Project Report.* Manpower Services Commission.

Polanyi, M. (1966). *The Tacit Dimension.* Routledge and Kegan Paul.

Prahalad, C.K. and Hamel, G. (1990). The core competence of the corporation. *Harvard Business Review*, **68(3),** 79–93.

Reason, P. and Heron, J. (1995). Co-operative inquiry. In J. Smith, R. Harré and L. Van Langehove (eds), *Rethinking Methods in Psychology.* Sage.

Ruggles, R. (1998). The state of the notion: knowledge management in practice. *Californian Management Review*, **40(3),** 80–89.

Scarborough, H. and Swan, J. (2001). Explaining the diffusion of knowledge management: the role of fashion. *British Journal of Management*, **12(1–3),** 3–12.

Scarborough, H., Swan, J. and Preston, J. (1999). *Knowledge Management: A Literature Review.* Institute of Personnel and Development.

Seely-Brown, J. and Duguid, P. (1991). Organizational learning and communities-of-practice: toward a unified view of working, learning and innovation. *Organization Science*, **2(1),** 40–57.

Senge, P. (1990). The leader's new work: building learning organizations. *Sloan Management Review*, **32(1),** 7–23.

Shrivastava, P.A. (1983). A typology of learning systems. *Journal of Management Studies*, **20(1),** 7–28.

Spender, J.-C. (1996). Organizational knowledge, learning and memory: three concepts in search of a theory. *Journal of Organizational Change Management*, **9(1),** 63–78.

Stata, R. (1989). Organizational learning: the key to management innovation. *Sloan Management Review*, **Spring,** 63–74.

Swart, J. and Kinnie, N. (2003). Sharing knowledge in knowledge-intensive firms. *Human Resource Management Journal*, **13(2)**, 60–75.

Swart, J. and Pye, A. (2002). Conceptualizing organizational knowledge as collective tacit knowledge (CTK): a model of redescription. The Third European Conference on Organizational Knowledge, Learning and Capabilities, held in Athens, 5–6 April.

Swart, J., Kinnie, N. and Purcell, J. (2003). *People and Performance in Knowledge Intensive Companies*. Chartered Institute of Personnel and Development.

Tsang, E.W.K. (1997). Organizational learning and the learning organization: a dichotomy between descriptive and prescriptive research. *Human Relations*, **50(1)**, 73–89.

Tsoukas, H. (1996). The firm as a distributed knowledge system: a constructionist approach. *Strategic Management Journal*, **17**, 11–25.

Venzin, M., von Krogh, G. and Roos, J. (1998). Future research into knowledge management. In G. von Krogh, J. Roos and D. Kleine (eds), *Knowing in Firms*. Sage, pp. 26–66.

Vickers, G. (1968). *Value Systems and Social Processes*. Tavistock.

Weick, K. (1979). *Social Psychology of Organizing* (2nd edn). Addison-Wesley.

Weick, K.E. (1991). The non-traditional quality of organizational learning. *Organization Science*, **2(1)**, 116–24.

Wenger, E. (2000). Communities of practice and social learning systems. *Organization*, **7(2)**, 225–46.

Winter, S.G. (1987). Knowledge and competence as strategic assets. In D.J. Teece (ed.), *The Competitive Challenge: Strategies for Industrial Innovation and Renewal*. Ballinger, pp. 159–84.

Chapter 3

Strategic human resource development

Introduction

The organization and focus of the traditional training and development function has been challenged by the emergence of the knowledge economy and the desire of many organizations to become a learning organization (see Chapter 2). This challenge has mainly been expressed through the need for training and development to become more strategic. But what does this mean? This chapter addresses the debate on strategic HRD, asking first what an organizational strategy is. Both process and product paradigms of strategy (Harrison and Kessels, 2004) will be discussed here. We will then look in particular at the links between human resource strategy and organizational strategy, and explore in more detail whether a best-fit or best-practice approach is more suitable (Purcell, 1999; Marchington and Wilkinson, 2002; Boxall and Purcell, 2003). These building blocks will then enable us to discuss the nature of the HRD strategy.

The focus of the chapter is on the criteria for strategic HRD. In other words, when is training and development considered to be strategic? The particular aspects that are highlighted here include:

1 The vertical alignment between HRD, HRM and organizational strategy
2 The horizontal alignment between various HRM practices
3 The focus of HRD on various levels in the organization
4 The role the HRD plays in creating organizational renewal processes – that is, the impact on the sustainable competitive advantage
5 The role of HRD in creating knowledge.

Objectives

By the end of this chapter you will be able to:

- Define what a strategy is
- Describe how an HR strategy is developed
- Assess whether it is possible to establish best-fit or best-practice HR strategies
- Describe and critique the development of HRD strategy
- Define the concept of strategic human resource development
- Discuss the criteria that can be used to assess whether a training and development process is strategic.

Defining strategy

Boxall and Purcell (2003) draw our attention to the differences between a firm's strategic plan and a strategy. They ask the pertinent question as to whether an organization (especially a small organization) that does not have a strategic plan and strategic objectives can be said to have a strategy. This illustrates the importance of differentiating between strategy as *plan* and strategy as *process* (Harrison and Kessels, 2004: 33). It is often observed that strategy is a field fragmented by the number of schools of thought it contains, and by its diverse theoretical foundations and research methodologies (Elfring and Volberda, 2001; Whittington, 2001). Although this diversity is often represented as the root cause of fragmentation, it could also be that the various paradigms add richness to our understanding of strategy and that various paradigms may be useful within a single organization. There is, of course, also the notion that strategy and the ability to strategize will differ from industry to industry. In some industries the market conditions change at a higher rate than others; some are characterized by novel and complex problems, whilst circumstances may be more predictable in others.

What is necessary to define and understand 'strategy' in the first instance is, therefore, not merely a summary of the various schools of thought but a representation of how various paradigms of strategy can be enacted (see Figure 3.1). The key dimension of analysis of strategy in this figure is the *degree of knowledge about the environment.*

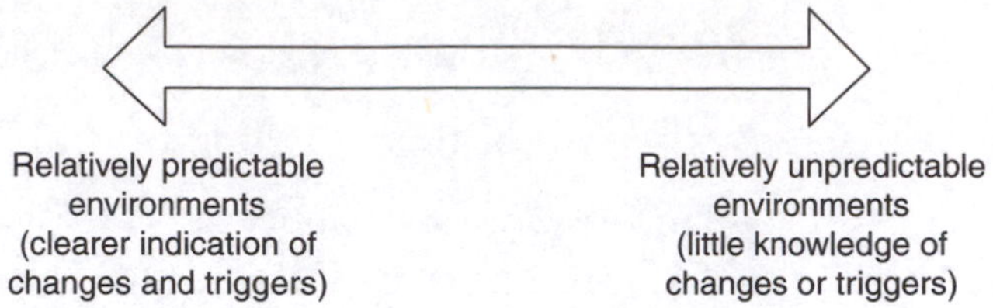

Figure 3.1
The strategy
continuum: a
knowledge-based
perspective.

Relatively predictable
environments
(clearer indication of
changes and triggers)

Relatively unpredictable
environments
(little knowledge of
changes or triggers)

At the extreme left-hand side of the knowledge continuum, organizations will have a clearer sense of how the environment may present itself in the future. In other words, the environment tends to be more stable or at least more predictable. Examples of such industries include the public sector and industries with large capital costs of configuration change – like the energy industry. It is important to note that this continuum presents the dominant market environment but does acknowledge the occurrence of surprise or catastrophic events. Moving towards the centre of the continuum, there is a notion that the market environment is slightly more unpredictable; fast-changing developments in other industries may have a significant impact on firms that can be grouped around the centre of the continuum. For example, the retail banking environment might be viewed as reasonably stable and predictable if the fast-changing nature of technology and its application to the retail banking industry is not taken into account. The centre of the continuum therefore characterizes a firm faced by some aspects of rapid change, and where the impact of the change is not certain. The knowledge about the environment and its impact on the firm is then more limited.

The right-hand extreme of the continuum represents a context wherein a firm has no clear indication as to whether its environment will change rapidly, or what may trigger a change in its environment. For example, software technology firms may not be able to predict which client influences will be the catalyst for new software applications and therefore may try to address this uncertainty by developing and creating several new applications in anticipation of a fast response to a client-driven demand. The firm responds to uncertainty in demand by creating a spread of responses at as low a cost as is practicable in order to capture the demand that eventually emerges (Powell and Wakeley, 2003).

Activity 3.1

Imagine your organization operates in a fast-changing environment.

- To what extent would you be able to write a strategic plan for a 3–5-year period?
- What difficulties would you be presented with if you try to plan ahead?

Each knowledge point in the continuum presents a different strategic paradigm and requirement (see Figure 3.2). First, the left-hand position lends itself to a view of strategy as a plan or a set of strategic objectives. This is representative of the classic perspectives on strategy (Ansoff, 1965; Porter, 1985). According to this school of thought, success or failure is determined internally through the quality of managerial planning, analysis and calculation (Whittington, 2001). The more stable and predictable environment allows for scenario planning, gap analysis and 3–5-year forecasts with their relevant action plans. This approach to strategy has been criticized severely in recent years, mainly because continuous environmental changes require flexibility in any possible plan. This raises the further question as to whether it is possible first to write a strategic plan, and secondly to implement this as planned (Boxall and Purcell, 2003).

The central point along the continuum represents the notion of strategy as process. According to this viewpoint the strategy process changes continually as a result of ongoing learning across the organization, and is therefore more adaptable throughout its enactment.

According to Pettigrew (1973), strategy as a process is influenced by individual and collective cognitions and the interplay

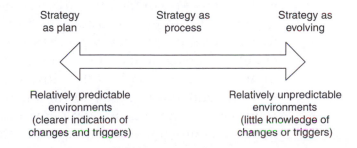

Figure 3.2
The strategy continuum: plan, process or evolving.

| Strategy as plan | Strategy as process | Strategy as evolving |

Relatively predictable environments (clearer indication of changes and triggers)　　　　Relatively unpredictable environments (little knowledge of changes or triggers)

of power and politics at every organizational level. This approach is essentially more fluid, with an emphasis on the enactment of strategy, as expressed through behaviours and cognitions. It is therefore more about seeing strategy than planning strategy.

Let us return to the example of the retail bank, whose customer accounting processes may need to change considerably due to the development of e-commerce. The retail bank may not know exactly how this technological development might impact upon its processes, but through the enactment of customer decisions and through developing relationships with the originators of advanced technologies a strategy (in response to technological change and in preparation for customer demands) is enacted.

Finally, the far right-hand side of the continuum represents an evolutionary approach to strategy (Loasby, 1991; Foss, 1994; Powell and Wakeley, 2003). Within this approach the environmental change is typically too fast, too unpredictable and too implacable to anticipate and pre-empt, and the advice is to concentrate on day-to-day viability while trying to keep options open (Whittington, 2001: 37). Responses are characterized by random generation of a spread of responses (since prediction is futile), together with a cost-sensitive trialling of these responses and a planned retention of knowledge gained by that trialling. If we return to the example of the software technology firm that develops several technology applications to an unexpected customer demand, we can see that the firm can 'keep its options open' through the design and initial development of several offerings. It then exposes these developments to the market, both through professional networks and through pilot testing. Through the process of gauging responses to possible designs the firm learns more about its environment and develops an ability to enact future strategies, and reinvests the knowledge gained in the development process.

Another critical dimension which is implied by the continuum in Figure 3.2 and by its subsequent different strategic paradigms is the focus on competence development. Given the first position, which represents strategy as a product or a plan, the key focus here is on the development of core competence that will enable the enactment of the plan. That is, the competence development focus is specific and relatively narrow.

At the mid-point in the continuum, where several options in a relatively familiar but changing environment are developed, the focus on competence development is more broadly defined. For example, the focus could be on customer service or technology development, but, given that here there is no clear end state in mind, it is impossible to define exactly which core competence will be needed to compete successfully in the marketplace.

Finally, the right-hand position calls for a development of a meta-competence that is related to multiple-offering development, trial analysis and fast response once the source of change is known. The level of the competence development is therefore higher than in the previous two cases, and the focus is even wider.

It is important to note that the continuum takes a knowledge-based view to strategy and represents strategic paradigms accordingly. It is acknowledged that several other methods of representation are possible, and one of these that deserves specific attention is the strategic option perspective. Firms at each point along the continuum may experience various degrees of freedom regarding their strategic choice. For example, a larger firm such as Toyota may not be in a position to plan for every eventuality but, given its dominant position within its local network, it has a greater degree of freedom of strategic choice (Kinnie *et al.*, 2003). Boxall and Purcell (2003: 35) believe that it is important to steer between 'hyper-determinism' on the one hand and 'hyper-voluntarism' on the other. Firms therefore neither completely control their environment, nor are they completely controlled by it. This is a general statement; we need to be cognizant of the varying degrees of freedom within and between industries that operate within each of the strategic paradigms. This holds a particular implication for human resource management and human resource development in particular because it shapes the manner in which human resources are deployed and developed to achieve sustainable competitive advantage.

Strategic human resource management

Activity 3.2

- Take a few minutes and write down your own definition of strategic human resource management.
- Compare your definition with what you think human resource strategy is. How do they differ?

There is increasing pressure for HR managers to identify the competitive issues that their companies are faced with regard to human resources, and to think strategically about how to respond (Noe *et al.*, 2003). This strategic response, as well as planning future possible responses, can be thought of as strategic human resource management (SHRM). Wright and McMahan (1992) define SHRM as a pattern of planned human resource deployments and activities intended to enable an organization to achieve its goals. For example, a life science research firm that operates within an environment where the rate of innovation is critical to survival will have an innovation strategy, whether this strategy is a plan (formal document with explicit objectives) or a process that evolves over time and has an emergent quality. Within the context of the innovation strategy, human resources will need to be deployed in order to enact the strategy. That is, employees will need to enact particular behaviours in order to achieve their personal, departmental and organizational goals and objectives.

The process wherein human resources are deployed to achieve the strategic objectives of the organization implies that the HR strategy needs to be aligned with the business strategy. That is, HR strategy needs to make the achievement of the business strategy possible. Golden and Ramanujam (1985) argue that there are various degrees of strategic integration:

1   Administrative linkage, which is the weakest form of integration between the business strategy and the HR strategy. Here, the HR focus is on day-to-day activities with little HR input into strategic planning and strategic implementation.
2   One-way linkage, which is when the focus of the HR strategy is to implement the business strategy and HR practices, and policies are shaped around the business plan.
3   Two-way linkage, where the integration point allows for input from the HRM function during the strategic planning process.
4   Integrative linkage, which is a dynamic and multi-faceted link, and calls for continuous input from the HRM function into the unfolding of the strategic process.

The varying degrees of strategic integration between the HRM function and roles and the strategy of the organization indicate that HRM strategy can be shaped during the strategy formulation or the strategy implementation phases of business strategy. The former approach results in a proactive role of HRM in the shaping of business strategy whereas the latter is more reactive, with less opportunity to voice people management issues at senior levels in the organization.

Strategic HRM and HR strategy – what is the difference?

Another important implication of these varying degrees of integration is the difference between SHRM and HR strategy. That is, to have an HR strategy does not necessarily mean that the HR practices will have strategic relevance. For example, where the HR strategy is focused mainly on day-to-day activities (administrative linkage), it may not be of strategic relevance to the organization's success. An HR department that administers a payroll effectively may have little impact on winning new business or securing a higher proportion of market share.

On the other hand, in a knowledge-intensive firm such as a professional services firm, the recruitment of specific human capital may make or break the firm. In this situation the HR strategy has a direct impact on the firm's success, and its role and impact can therefore be considered to be strategic.

The definition of SHRM usefully conceptualized by Wright and McMahan (1992) indicates that HRM can only be considered to be strategic if 'it enables an organization to achieve its goals'. In this chapter, this part of the definition will be considered as what defines strategic action, whereas the former part of their definition – 'a pattern of planned human resource deployments and activities' – will be regarded, in agreement with Boxall and Purcell (2003), as the strategy.

In summary, activities and deployments that are critical to the firm's survival are regarded as strategic (whether that refers to HR or HRD), and a pattern of planned activities are considered to be the strategy (bearing in mind that they may not be strategic). In the remainder of this section we focus on HR strategy and the various implications that this may hold for strategic action.

Best-fit approaches to HR strategy

It is important to understand that the notion of alignment between the business strategy and the HR strategy as captured by the continuum of strategic integration (Golden and Ramanujam, 1985) sits within the school of thought known as the 'best-fit' approach. This school argues that HR strategy will be more effective when it is appropriately integrated within its specific organizational and broader environmental context (Boxall and Purcell, 2003: 47).

However powerful this model may seem, it often overlooks employee interests. In other words, employees need to align their interest with the business strategy for the best-fit model to work well. It is well known that this presents challenges of its own. The mediating variable in this relationship would be the motivation of the employees.

One powerful explanatory model that can shed light on the matching of employee needs with firm needs is that of 'psychological contracting' (Schein, 1978; Rosseau, 1995; Guest, 1998; Grant, 1999; Shapiro and Kessler, 2000; Deery *et al.*, 2003). This takes into account that HR practices cannot merely manipulate employee behaviour to deliver strategic objectives and emphasizes the importance of shared expectations between the employee and the employer (Rosseau, 1995).

This approach places the individual at the heart of the employment relationship, and draws our attention to the fact that strategy alone will not achieve success, but human action is the main vehicle for strategy delivery. Within the context of the psychological contract, an employee whose expectations have not been met is not likely to engage in behaviours that contribute to the long-term success of the organization, regardless of the HR practices and the fit between the HR strategy and the business strategy. This mediating relationship is represented in Figure 3.3, and acts as a reminder of the importance of individual motivation to direct behaviours in favour of the achievement of strategic objectives.

Figure 3.3 indicates that if the psychological contract is violated, the employee might leave the organization or, more destructively, remain with the organization but reduce his or her commitment to it – i.e. be less likely to 'go the extra mile'. The reduction of organization citizenship behaviours (Boxall and Purcell, 2003) will have a severe impact on both the short-term and longer-term competitive advantage of the firm.

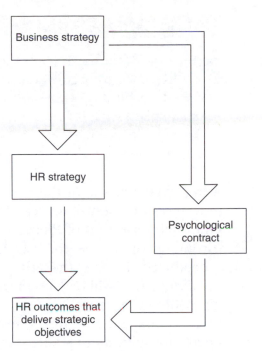

Figure 3.3
The mediating influence of the psychological contract on the delivery of strategic objectives.

Activity 3.3

Research indicates that it makes sense to align your HR strategy with your business strategy.

- What are the main difficulties within this approach?
- Identify the challenges that you may be faced with when trying to align HR and business strategy.

Best-practice approaches to HR strategy

Sceptics of the contingency approach of the best-fit models prefer a more universal prescription, and follow a best-practice approach to HRM strategy. According to the followers of this approach, particular sets of best practices will lead to performance improvements. The theoretical discipline upon which these approaches are founded is that of industrial psychology. Within this discipline decades of research have been dedicated to the prediction and development of human performance. It is the application of these findings that form the foundation of the 'best practices'.

Activity 3.4

- In your opinion, what are the HR practices that would make a difference to organizational performance?
- Would it be important to implement all these practices? If so, explain why; if not, what are the key practices that would make a difference?

A key characteristic of the best-practice model is the identification of 'lists of best practices' that would drive performance up. One such list is that of Pfeffer's (1998) practices for 'competing through people' (see Box 2.1). Often these lists are reduced and reproduced, leaving the HR practitioner wondering what the next 'big thing' will be, and in which direction they need to steer his or her HR strategy.

A dominant theme in the best-practice approaches is that of horizontal alignment – i.e. establishing a fit between the various practices within the HR strategy, otherwise known as HR bundles. Several of the bundles of practices have been divided into types with high-performance work systems (HPWS), the most well known amongst the typologies (Applebaum *et al.*, 2000).

Arguably the best-practice models are not appreciative of context, and several practitioners may find that what works best in one environment may not work as well in another (see also Figure 3.2). Another key criticism of this model is that it is highly deterministic and individualistic in its approach – it assumes that managers have control over which practices will be implemented,

Box 2.1: Pfeffer's 1998 components of best practice (adapted from Marchington and Wilkinson, 2002)

- Employment security
- Selective hiring and sophisticated selection
- Extensive training, learning and development
- Employee involvement
- Self-managed teams
- High compensation contingent upon organizational performance
- Reduction of stratus differential.

and it ignores the influence of collective employment pressures. The best-practice model also aims to unlock the secrets of human behaviour as linked to performance, and forgets the valuable context of organizational goals and an ever-changing environment.

Best-process approaches to HR strategy

The combined critique of the best-practice and best-fit models has put us in a position to shed light on an alternative approach: the best-process model. According to this approach, it is the process of implementation of HR practices that has strategic value. In the literature, this is referred to an organizational process advantage (Mueller, 1996; Boxall and Steeneveld, 1999).

The focus of this approach is therefore not continually to change current HR practices to fit in with the latest list of best practices; nor does it advocate an alignment with business strategy. It sits within the evolving model of strategy (see Figure 3.2) and believes that strategically valuable HR practices evolve through participation (Swart, *et al.*, 2003) thereby taking the collective issues into account. The commitment of line managers to people management and the unique way in which they implement HR practices will remain a source of competitive advantage. The emphasis in this model is more on people management as a process (owned by everyone on the organization) as opposed to an HR department which generates and implements HR policies and practices.

According to this model, each organization will have its unique sets of practices and process that provide sustained competitive advantage. Furthermore, this approach advocates that it is the embedded and routinized processes that sit at the heart of the strategic nature of HRM. This model supports the notion that strategic practices evolve over time, and is sceptical of the strategic process as expressed in a plan with sets of objectives. It does, however, argue that if such a plan were to exist, then the desired outcomes (behaviours) could only be achieved through HR processes that fit the organizational culture and are owned by managers and employees in the organization.

In summary, we defined HR strategy as a pattern of planned human resource deployments and activities intended to enable an organization to achieve its goals (Wright and McMahan, 1992). Several ways in which these deployments and activities take place were identified. These related to the degree of integration (Golden and Ramanujam, 1985) between the HR strategy and the business strategy: at the one extreme the business strategy merely dictated day-to-day HR activities (administrative linkage), and at the other extreme the HR function had continuous input into the unfolding of the strategic process (integrative linkage). The very notion of integration between the HR strategy and the business strategy sits within the best-fit school of thought, which believes that this strategic alignment is critical for the achievement of strategic objectives. Here we highlighted that the best-fit school does not take into account the individual motivation to act in a certain way – that is, the needs of the individual and the business needs should be matched in order to bring about the desired behaviours that will achieve strategic objectives.

Another approach to HR strategy is that of best practice. This approach adheres to a universal model of superior practices, which is believed to be linked to business performance. In a way, this model can be described as an external best-fit model. Here the HR practices in the firm fit with what is believed to be 'good practice' in the environment outside the organization. This answers the 'What are other successful businesses doing?' question. Once again, this model has a weakness in so far as it does not take into account the collective issues of the employment relationship and assumes that managers have the freedom of choice, both inside the organization and in the network that they operate in (Kinnie *et al.*, 2003) to select and implement sets of HR practices.

A final alternative was offered in the form of the best-process models. Here, the emphasis is on the unique way in which HR practices are implemented – i.e. the processes that make the achievement of competitive advantage possible. Some of the key characteristics of this model include line manager commitment to the implementation of people management practices, employee ownership of practices, and processes that are embedded in the fabric of the organization.

We previously sketched the landscape of HR strategy in its various forms and approaches. It is important for us to use this insight and ask how the HR strategy can inform the HRD strategy. Another important issue that we need to address is how we identify the difference between HRD strategy and strategic HRD. In the following section we discuss best-fit, best-practice and best-process models of HRD strategy. Our attention is then drawn to the criteria for strategic HRD. Here we answer the question: 'When would the patterns of HRD activities be critical to the success of an organization?'

Human resource development strategy

Within a knowledge economy (Drucker, 1993), the development of individuals, teams and organizations will be at the heart of survival of organizations. In this type of economy 'knowledge' is the key resource that needs to be developed and managed. In Chapter 2 we discussed how knowledge management influences the HRD practices in an organization, and here we ask what this means for the HRD strategy.

The HRD strategy can broadly be defined as the pattern of planned and unfolding activities that focuses on developing capabilities to achieve current and future strategic objectives. A few issues in this definition deserve further attention. First, HRD strategy is presented as both planned and unfolding. This links to both the strategy as plan and the strategy as process views (see above). Second, the definition captures the notion that HRD makes the achievement of business strategy possible. Here we would need to revisit the concepts of vertical integration (with the business strategy) and horizontal integration (with the HR strategy). Finally, our definition captures the notion that HRD strategy develops capabilities that are needed to deliver a current business strategy, but it also enables a firm to compete in the future. This time-horizon characteristic is what makes HRD strategic, and we discuss it further below.

Vertical integration of the HRD strategy

Activity 3.5

- HR strategy can be integrated with business strategy to varying degrees (Golden and Ramanujam, 1985). These have been presented as administrative, one-way, two-way and integrative. How would each of these linkages influence the development of the HRD strategy?

According to the best-fit models, HRD strategy should be aligned with the business strategy. In other words, the role of HRD is to develop capabilities that can deliver the business strategy. To use the previous example of the innovation strategy of the life science research firm, the HRD strategy will be focused on developing skills that are linked to innovation. These may include scientific research skills as well as business development skills. Even more challenging would be the development of capabilities that are linked to 'spotting business opportunities'. It so happens that in this case example the firm used a variety of on-the-job training strategies to develop this capability. This is because this range of skills is tacit (see Chapter 2) and can only be developed through shared practice.

As with the HR strategy, there could be various degrees of integration (see Figure 3.4) between the business and the HRD strategies. At one extreme, the HRD strategy can be focused on 'correcting previous behaviours' and be mainly reactive. At this point the HRD strategy is more focused on the previous year's strategic objectives and understanding 'what went wrong' than it is on the current strategic objectives.

The second possible variation of vertical alignment is the one-way level of integration. Here the HRD strategy is focused on implementing the current strategic objectives, as illustrated in the example of the life science firm. The key questions in this position are: 'What do we need to achieve now?' 'How can we best develop skills that will take us to the competitive position

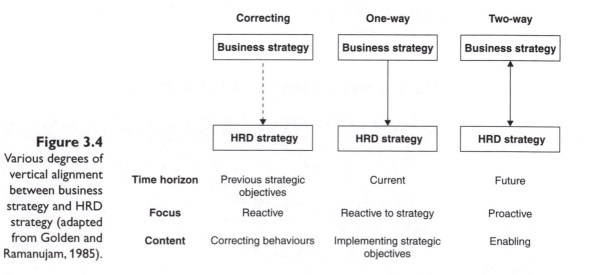

Figure 3.4
Various degrees of vertical alignment between business strategy and HRD strategy (adapted from Golden and Ramanujam, 1985).

that we have set out to achieve?' 'How can we align our human resource development with our strategic objectives?'

The final degree of integration is depicted here as two-way integration. In this context, the HRD strategy plays a much more proactive role and functions more at a meta-level. The strategy is less concerned with delivering the current strategic objectives and is more focused on continuous change. It asks: 'How can we ensure that the organization will be competitive in the future?' 'What are the key capabilities that we will need to survive long-term?' 'How could we ensure that the employees at all levels in the organization can respond to change and even create change?'

For example, a multinational consulting organization may see the value of following a t-model consultancy framework in the future. This means that all consultants need to be able to cross-sell their expertise to clients. Although the organization's current strategy could be focused on the delivery of expert advice in particular areas the HRD strategy could address future challenges not only by developing expert skills but also by introducing systems thinking and exposure to complementary areas of consulting.

A key area wherein the HRD strategy can develop future capabilities is that of change management. Here, the content of the strategy could be focused on creating readiness for change, addressing resistance to change and creating capabilities for change. It is important to note that within this framework the HRD strategy is focused on the development of organizational capabilities as well as individual capabilities. This wider focus means that the HRD strategy will encompass the organizational development (OD) activities. The ability to influence and create capacity is regarded as a key criterion for strategic HRD, and will be discussed later in this chapter.

We mentioned earlier that the HRD strategy is influenced by the HR strategy of the organization. This is referred to as horizontal integration. We will now discuss why this fit is important and how it is created.

Horizontal integration of the HRD strategy

Essentially, the fit between the HRD strategy and the HR strategy falls within the ambit of best-fit models, but here the emphasis of integration is horizontal rather than a vertical fit with the

Figure 3.5
The horizontal integration of HRD strategy.

business strategy. It also ascribes to bundles of high performance practices in so far as it calls for an alignment between the various HR practices (see Figure 3.5). The aim of horizontal integration is strategic fit and synergy. In other words, if all the HR practices complement one another the impact of the outcome is likely to be higher than the sum of the outcomes of the individual practices.

Activity 3.6

- Think of your own organization or an organization that you are familiar with. Do the various HR practices complement one another?
- If you have identified complementary practices, would you say that their combined effect is greater than the sum of the parts?
- If you have not identified complementary practices, which changes would you put in place to increase the complementary impact of the various HR practices?

For example, a software development firm that recruits graduates with cutting-edge skills would not aim to set out an HRD strategy that involves formal training programmes that focus on technical skills. The firm may, however, decide to focus on informal, employee-driven development practices through its professional networks. In this example the firm would use its available networks to enhance its capabilities whilst also building critical relationships within these networks. It is well known that these networks are often used as a further source of innovation and combined capability.

The horizontal integration will be greatly influenced by the organization of the HR and training and development functions in the organization. In smaller organizations these functions are often combined and managed within a single organizational function. However, larger (and particularly multinational) organizations often divide the HR and developmental functions, making it more difficult to integrate the various sets of practices, or patterns of planned responses (Wright and McMahan, 1992).

Within the separate organizational function design, the HR and HRD practices may start to address matters that are significantly different in nature. In one such case in a large retail bank, the HRD function focused largely on OD efforts and became far removed from what the HR strategy set out to achieve. This separate form of work organization requires a greater emphasis on co-ordination and communication, and leaves plenty of opportunities for misinterpretation and power differences between the HR and HRD functions to impact upon the possible synergies that can be established.

Best-practice models for HRD strategy

Best-practice models of HRD would aim first to identify what the leading edge practice in the area of training and development is, and then ensure that the best practice is implemented within the organization. This is the external view of the best-practice model. One such example in the United Kingdom is the practice of spending 5 per cent of the payroll cost on training and development activities. Another is to invite an external training provider to deliver management development processes. Both the US and European models rely on leading Business Schools to provide management development, in the form of either a Master of Business Administration (MBA) degree or tailor-made executive development.

Activity 3.7

Think of a new practice which your organization has embarked on recently. Examples of these include knowledge management, 360-degree performance appraisal or pay for performance.

- How did your organization decide to implement it?
- What were the key arguments for and against its implementation?
- How were these arguments arrived at?

Most of the best-practice models rely on the power of the diffusion of managerial practice. In other words, a dominant organizational practice that leads to success in a certain sector and in a certain part of the world needs to go through the following process:

1   The practice needs to become formally accepted and practised throughout the focal organization
2   The practice needs to be believed to have a significant impact on performance
3   The linkage between the practice and the organizational performance needs to be widely accepted in the organization
4   Both the practice and its linkage with performance need to become known in the network within which the organization participates
5   The linkages need to be convincing enough to justify investment from another firm in the network
6   The implemented practice needs to display the same or similar performance linkages
7   The impact of the practice needs to become known and accepted in dominant firms in other networks that lie outside the direct interconnection of the focal firm's network
8   The practice, its links with performance and its network-wide practice need to continue over a significant period of time.

It is interesting to note that the desire to follow a best-practice approach to HRD strategy often leads to a lack of horizontal integration. That is to say, if particular HRD practices are diffused across sectors and regions and are accepted and implemented, then it is likely that this 'new practice' may not fit within the wider HR strategy. Here, the best practice itself may be a cause for misalignment, and this singular and fragmented change may drive down performance (Massini and Pettigrew, 2003: 167) rather than having a positive impact on the achievement of the strategic objectives.

It is therefore important to review how the best-practice model will impact on the business success as well as how well it will fit with the current HRD and HRM models. An analysis of its strategic value is therefore necessary. Before we can embark on such an analysis, we have first to establish when the HRD practices hold strategic value.

Strategic human resource development

The aim of this section is to establish criteria for evaluation of the strategic value of HRD. Here we answer the question: 'When can HRD be considered to be strategic?' Our yardstick of strategic value will be that of Boxall and Purcell (2003) – although the original quotation refers to HRM rather than HRD, we use HRD in this context to illustrate the impact of HRD, as a sub-set of HR, on the success of the firm. They define strategic value as the ways in which HRD is critical for the firm's survival and its relative success (Boxall and Purcell, 2003: 48). That is, the particular HRD practices will have a direct impact on the competitive advantage of the firm.

The strategic value of the HRD practices has been central to many of the knowledge management debates (see Chapter 2). Furthermore, the realization that the creation and management of knowledge are central to the future success of firms has put many HRD practices into strategic focus. Many CEOs and CKOs now look to the HRD strategy to deliver strategic objectives. The implication of this heightened interest in HRD strategy is that it can easily be expected to work miracles. The dominant thinking in many organizations is, 'If we need to compete on a knowledge base, all we need to do is to enhance this knowledge base'. Unfortunately this often leads to disappointment and disillusionment with HRD practices, and a spiral of creating and managing knowledge as an end in itself (see Figure 3.6). This in turn may lead to a reduction in HRD investment and ultimately drive down business performance. What is therefore important is not blindly to believe in the strategic value of HRD but to be able to assess exactly when it will have strategic value and invest accordingly.

Activity 3.8

Think of an example where an HRD practice, such as a management development programme, has made a significant impact upon the success of your organization or an organization that you are familiar with. Compare your idea with that of a colleague or fellow student.

- How were these practices different?
- How did their impact differ?
- What did you learn from this?

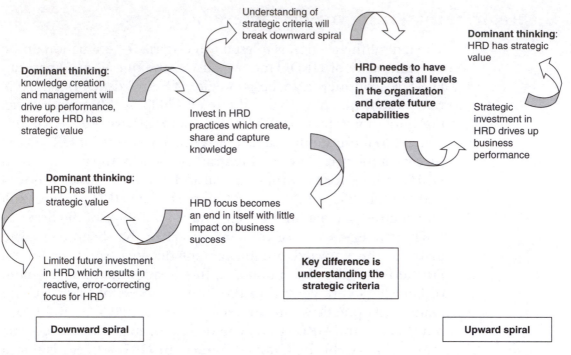

Understanding of strategic criteria will break downward spiral

Dominant thinking: HRD has strategic value

Dominant thinking: knowledge creation and management will drive up performance, therefore HRD has strategic value

HRD needs to have an impact at all levels in the organization and create future capabilities

Invest in HRD practices which create, share and capture knowledge

Strategic investment in HRD drives up business performance

Dominant thinking: HRD has little strategic value

HRD focus becomes an end in itself with little impact on business success

Limited future investment in HRD which results in reactive, error-correcting focus for HRD

Key difference is understanding the strategic criteria

Downward spiral

Upward spiral

Figure 3.6
The strategic value of HRD in a knowledge economy.

The first criterion for judging whether HRD has strategic impact is its *scope* – in other words, how far do the HRD practices reach? Is the main focus individual skill development, or do the practices address organizational level issues as well? For HRD to be of strategic value it needs to address issues at individual, team or departmental, and organizational levels. This means that the HRD focus needs to move beyond skill development (or what is widely referred to as training programmes) and extend to organizational development issues that include change processes and core competence development. In essence, the HRD practices need to enhance organizational learning in such a way as to encourage new organization-wide solutions to challenging problems that are critical to the future survival of the firm to be generated.

Second, the new practices need to be embedded in the organizational routines and become the 'way things are done around here'. Finally, these new solutions and practices need to inform new problems that are encountered. In other words, there needs to be a fine balance between renewal and preservation (March, 1991).

It is also important that the HRD initiatives at each level are linked. For example, an organization level innovation programme can be supported by team-based development that is focused on innovation, and by individual skill development programmes that have a business development focus. This refers to the need for internal best fit between the various HRD practices. As in the instance of alignment between HRM practices, this should lead to synergistic outcomes.

The second criterion for judging whether HRD is strategic is its *time horizon*. The emphasis of the strategic value of HRD will be on its impact on future business success. That is to say that HRD practices that merely correct past errors will not be valued as strategic. For example, a software development organization is solely reliant on its human capital, the knowledge and skills of its employees, to generate profits. An HRD strategy that focuses on how this knowledge base can be enriched to meet client demands will have an impact on the future success of the business, whereas practices that try to understand why last year's targets weren't met and consequently seek to develop client relationship management skills may or may not influence the business success. The key differentiator in this example is the time horizon of the practices; are they looking backwards, or are they addressing future capabilities?

The time dimension does need to include the various levels in the organization as identified in the first criterion. In other words, where the individual level is concerned, aspects such as career development and succession-planning practices would be important to the future success of the organization. At the team level, the ability to transfer knowledge to other project teams, thereby creating future solutions, would be regarded as an HRD practice that has strategic value. Finally, at the organizational level it would be important to focus on organization-wide learning practices that lead to future renewal. Argyris and Schön (1996) refer to these future-focused, high-level practices as Mode II learning. This means that the organization needs to be able to question why it engages in certain behaviours or why it responds in a certain way. Once these underlying philosophies have surfaced, the HRD practices can add strategic value either by embedding these practices or by challenging and changing these deep-rooted beliefs in a way that will impact on future organizational success.

It is often the case that the two key criteria for the strategic value of HRD practices can work against one another. For example, practices that aim to focus on all the organizational levels and that have a future perspective can bring about specific managerial tensions. Let's take the example of the software firm that relies on its human capital to compete. If this firm embarks on an organizational learning strategy and seeks to develop its key employees, it may find that these very employees become attractive to its competitors. This presents the firm with a retention-development dilemma (Swart and Kinnie, 2004) that needs to be resolved in order for the firm to be successful. In this example, the resolution of the tension itself will have strategic value.

In summary, HRD practices can be considered to have strategic value if:

■ The practices focus on all the layers in the organization (individual, team or departmental, and organizational)
■ The practices develop future capabilities
■ There is interplay between the first two criteria – that is, the HRD practice at each level has a capability-creating focus.

Summary

This chapter set out to explain what strategic HRD is and how an HRD strategy may be developed. The following issues were addressed to develop this understanding:

■ Strategy was defined both as a product (a strategic plan with strategic objectives) and as a process (that unfolds through action).
■ The degree of knowledge about the environment determines the nature of the strategic formulation process. In more predictable environments, it is easier to have a strategic plan.
■ HR strategy was contrasted with strategic HR. The main differentiator was the impact of the HR practices on the success and survival of the firm.
■ Various models of HR strategy were compared through the best-fit, best-practice and best-process models.
■ We discussed how HRD strategy is developed through vertical and horizontal integration.
■ Criteria for strategic HRD were established, and it was shown that a positive investment cycle in HRD practices depend on being aware of the criteria for judging the strategic value of HRD practices.

References

Ansoff, H.I. (1965). *Corporate Strategy*. Penguin.

Applebaum, E., Bailey, T., Berg, P. and Kalleberg, A. (2000). Manufacturing Competitive Advantage: *The Effects of High-performance Work-systems on Plant Performance and Company Outcomes*. Cornell University Press.

Argyris, C. and Schön, D.A. (1996). *Organizational Learning II: Theory, Method and Practice*. Addison-Wesley.

Boxall, P. and Purcell, J. (2003). *Strategy and Human Resource Management*. Palgrave Macmillan.

Boxall, P. and Steeneveld, M. (1999). Human resource strategy and competitive advantage: a longitudinal study of engineering consultancies. *Journal of Management Studies*, **36(4),** 443–63.

Deery, S., Iverson, R.D. and Walsh, J. (2003). Towards a better understanding of psychological contract breach: a study of non-professional employees. Paper presented at the American Academy. Seattle, August 1–6.

Drucker, P. (1993). *Post-capitalist Society*. Butterworth-Heinemann.

Elfring, T. and Volberda, H.W. (2001). Schools of thought in strategic management: fragmentation, integration or synthesis. In H.W. Volberda and T. Elfring (eds), *Rethinking Strategy*. Sage, pp. 1–25.

Foss, N.J. (1994). Realism and evolutionary economics. *Journal of Social Evolutionary Systems*, **17,** 21–40.

Golden, K. and Ramanujam, V. (1985). Between a dream and a nightmare: on the integration of the human resource function and the strategic business planning process. *Human Resource Management*, **24,** 429–51.

Grant, D. (1999). HRM, rhetoric and the psychological contract: a case of 'easier said than done'. *International Journal of Human Resource Management*, **10(2),** 327–50.

Guest, D. (1998). Is the psychological contract worth taking seriously? *Journal of Organizational Behaviour*, **19,** 649–64.

Harrison, R. and Kessels, J. (2004). *Human Resource Development in a Knowledge Economy*. Palgrave MacMillan.

Kinnie, N.J., Swart, J. and Purcell, J. (2003). Influences on the choice of HR systems: the network organization perspective. Paper presented at the International Strategic HRM Conference, Cornell University, Ithaca, USA, May 9–10.

Loasby, B.J. (1991). *Equilibrium and Evolution*. University of Manchester Press.

March, J.G. (1991). Exploration and exploitation in organization learning. *Organization Science*, **2,** 71–87.

Marchington, M. and Wilkinson, A. (2002). *People Management and Development: Human Resource Management at Work* (2nd edn). Chartered Institute of Personnel and Development.

Massini, S. and Pettigrew, A.M. (2003). Complementarities in organizational innovation and performance: empirical evidence from the INNFORM Survey. In Pettigrew, A.M., Whittington, R., Melin, L., Sanchez-Runde, C., van den Bosch, F.A.J., Ruigrok, W. and Numagami, T. (2003). *Innovative Forms of Organizing: International Perspectives*. Sage, pp. 133–171.

Mueller, F. (1996). Human resources as strategic assets: an evolutionary resource-based theory. *Journal of Management Studies*, **33(6),** 757–85.

Noe, R.A., Hollenbeck, J.R., Gerhart, B. and Wright, P.M. (2003). *Human Resource Management: Gaining a Competitive Advantage* (4th edn). McGraw-Hill Irwin.

Pettigrew, A.M. (1973). *The Politics of Organizational Decision Making.* Tavistock.

Pettigrew, A.M., Whittington, R., Melin, L., Sanchez-Runde, C., van den Bosch, F.A.J., Ruigrok, W. and Numagami, T. (2003). *Innovative Forms of Organizing: International Perspectives.* Sage.

Porter, M.E. (1985). *Competitive Advantage: Creating and Sustaining Superior Performance.* Free Press.

Powell, J.H. and Wakeley, T. (2003). Evolutionary concepts and business economics: towards a normative approach. *Journal of Business Research*, **56,** 153–61.

Purcell, J. (1999). The search for 'best practice' and 'best fit': chimera or cul-de-sac? *Human Resource Management Journal*, **9(3),** 26–41.

Rosseau, D. (1995). *Psychological Contracting in Organizations.* Sage.

Schein, E. (1978). *Career Dynamics: Matching Individual and Organizational Needs.* Addison-Wesley.

Shapiro, J. and Kessler, I. (2000). Consequences of the psychological contract for the employment relationship: a large scale survey. *Journal of Management*, **37(7),** 903–30.

Swart, J. and Kinnie, N. (2004). *Managing the Careers of Knowledge Workers.* Chartered Institute of Personnel and Development.

Swart, J., Kinnie, N. and Purcell, J. (2003). *People and Performance in Knowledge Intensive Companies.* Chartered Institute of Personnel and Development.

Swart, J., Kinnie, N. and Purcell, J. (2003). Managing competing identities and the careers of IT professionals. Paper presented at the American Academy, Seattle, 1–6 August.

Whittington, R. (2001). *What is Strategy – And Does It Matter?* (2nd edn). Thompson Learning.

Wright, P. and McMahan, G. (1992). Theoretical perspectives for strategic human resource management. *Journal of Management*, **18,** 295–320.

Chapter 4

Managing the human resource development function

Introduction

In this chapter our discussion focuses on the ways in which human resource development can be organized and managed within organizations of different sizes. HRD in small businesses is not generally organized as a specialist function, and is often dealt with in an unsystematic manner. We will see that learning and development are perceived as a financial burden and tend to be limited to short-term operational needs. The connection with overall business strategy is usually missing in smaller organizations, with the exception of development for family members engaged in the business. In larger organizations, HRD is a function with dedicated staff, budgets and objectives related to overall business strategy. The way in which HRD is managed in large organizations is dependent on the underlying philosophy of learning that they employ.

Objectives

By the end of this chapter you will be able to:

- Explain the main purposes of the HRD function
- Evaluate the degree of commitment to HRD
- Describe and critique the nature of HRD within small and medium-sized organizations
- Outline the relationship between different learning philosophies and HRD programmes
- Discuss the relationship between the HRD function and high performance working
- Describe the role of the HRD function in continuous learning.

The human resource development function

What is a HRD function for? Employees are continuously learning, but this can happen in an *ad hoc* fashion and may not be focused on skills or knowledge that have relevance to their careers in a specific organization. The purpose of a formal HRD programme is to provide a more systematic, thorough and monitored approach to learning and individual development. It seems reasonable to argue that any HRD function must be able to demonstrate that it is capable of directing learning in an organized manner, and that such learning should be compatible with the organization's HRD strategy and values (Williams, 2002).

Activity 4.1

- What do you consider to be the main purposes of a HRD function?

Nadler and Wiggs (1986: 5) highlight three main objectives:

1 To maximize the learner's (employee's) effectiveness on the job
2 To facilitate the individual's mobility to the next probable assignment
3 To increase the employee's (learner's) commitment to the organization by providing stimulating learning opportunities for personal growth and change.

A traditional 'textbook' approach to managing the HRD function typically involves a prescriptive set of activities, such as assessing training/learning needs, preparing a HRD plan, setting a budget, producing a HRD programme, allocating tasks, conducting the programme, evaluating training effectiveness and producing feedback to improve future training. In practice, a number of important variables force changes to this conventional pattern. For example, the HRD function in small and medium-sized enterprises (SMEs) is likely to be very different to that in large organizations. In the smallest companies it may be no more than one aspect of a single manager's work schedule. In the largest it may take the form of an integrated workplace learning and performance (WLP) process, defined by the American Society for Training and Development as:

> … the integrated use of learning and other interventions for the purpose of improving human performance, and addressing individual and organizational needs. It uses a systematic process of analyzing and responding to individual, group and organizational performance issues. WLP creates positive, progressive change within organizations by balancing human, ethical, technological and operational considerations.
>
> (cited in Rothwell *et al.*, 2003: 4)

Nadler and Wiggs (1986) distinguish between training, educational and developmental initiatives:

- *Training* – this produces measurable improvements in skills, knowledge or attitudes that can be used in the individual's current job, such as a course on computer spreadsheets.
- *Education* – this is learning that leads to improved skills, knowledge or attitudes applicable to a future job or assignment likely to be required within the next two years. Perceived as 'short-term investments in the future', education sponsored by the HRD function could include distance learning leading to a diploma or degree. This kind of initiative holds a greater risk for an organization, as the learner may not take up the offered opportunity and may well use the new skill or qualification to seek employment elsewhere.
- *Development* – this is broader, long-term learning that is not job-related. Developmental learning is aimed at preparing employees for the unforeseen future. It also links to an organization's retention strategy by involving workers in their own career planning, and matching learning opportunities to their career preferences. This is a high-risk investment for employers.

Garavan *et al.* (2000) identify a major gulf between those who believe that HRD as an organizational activity should promote 'performance', and those who prioritize 'learning': They argue that HRD practitioners tend to focus on performance whereas academics concentrating on research in the area of HRD are more likely to adopt a learning focus. There is also a geographical distinction, with a strong bias towards performance in the US literature while European academics focus on learning as the main objective of HRD. Interestingly, some UK authors also focus on performance.

Activity 4.2

- What is the relationship between learning and performance?

Commitment to HRD

Commitment to development and training varies from organization to organization for a variety of reasons. Well-funded and respected HRD is dependent on the way human resource development is viewed by senior managers. The HRD function plays a political as well as an operational role in the funding, management and delivery of training. For example, the HRD function may be perceived unfavourably because (Gilley and Gilley, 2002: 5):

- HRD programmes are considered to be 'outside' the mainstream of the business and viewed as internal training houses
- Training and trainers are not seen to be critical to the success of the organization
- The outcomes and impact of training are not valued
- HRD practitioners are not seen to be living in the real world.

Gilley and Gilley (2002: 5) feel that HRD practitioners may compound the situation by spending their time designing class-based training courses while others 'behave as if their mission were to conduct workshops, seminars, meetings and conferences. Consequently they view training as an end unto itself.'

A more positive view of the HRD function is likely if senior managers perceive their objectives and activities to be linked to business strategy. Nevertheless, despite the frequently voiced statement that 'employees are our greatest asset', most managers consider employees to be costs, and treat them accordingly (Bassi and McMurray, 2004). However, treating employees as assets and investing in HRD can produce positive returns in the long term. Bassi and McMurray cite investor returns on a portfolio of businesses in the US that invest heavily in employee development. The portfolio outperformed the S&P 500 index by 4.6 per cent in its first 25 months.

Thomson and Mabey (1994: 23) argue that organizations are most likely to invest in training activities when there is external support and leverage. This includes linkages with external providers and agencies, as well as grants, awards and other incentives. Thomson and Mabey contend that business structures may inhibit such investment, particularly where 'investment decisions are dominated by the finance function (fairly typical in British boardrooms) and where short-term return on capital employed by institutional investors overrides longer term considerations of people development'. They feel that the role of government is critical to strategic HRD. The article in Example 4.1, '21st Century Skills', provides an example of government policy towards HRD in England.

Example 4.1: 21st Century Skills

A Skills Strategy White Paper for England released today proposes free learning for adults who need it most, a new adult learning grant to help them meet the costs of learning, and a strengthening of Modern Apprenticeships. A new 'Skills Alliance' is also proposed – made up of the Government, the CBI, the TUC, the Small Business Council, and key delivery partners – to drive forward the strategy to ensure that skills needs are identified, mapped and met to increase national productivity and individual employability.

The strategy was launched by Education Secretary Charles Clarke, who said:

Skills matter. They help business to compete, and they help individuals raise their employability and provide a route to a better life. The success of the country depends on our skill base.

For the first time, we have produced a skills strategy based on a true partnership to enable more businesses to win in the global economy, by developing a multi-skilled flexible labour force.

Increasing the nation's skills levels is not about endless piecemeal initiatives. It's about a partnership between the Government, Business and the Unions, working together to forge a Skills Alliance.

Key reforms include:

Delivering Skills for Individuals

- introducing free learning for any adult who does not already have a good foundation of skills for employability, to help them achieve a full Level 2 qualification (5 GCSEs or equivalent);
- new opportunities for adults to gain qualifications in technician and higher craft and trade skills, through a Level 3 qualification (2 A-levels or equivalent) in regional or sectoral skills shortage areas;
- funding a new £30 weekly grant for adult learners in the priority groups to support them in studying full time courses in further education;
- expanding the successful Adult Basic Skills campaign to make Information and Communications Technology the third essential 'skill for life' alongside literacy and numeracy;
- lifting the age cap for Modern Apprenticeships so that people over the age of 25 can learn skilled trades;
- safeguarding leisure, culture and community learning, particularly focusing on pensioners, those on low incomes and benefit recipients;

contd

Example 4.1: *contd*

— reforming adult information, advice and guidance services to help adults into learning, and ensure that individuals can find out what to learn, where to learn and what they are entitled to.

Delivering Skills for Employers

— rapidly expanding the Sector Skills Council network to identify, map and meet key skills needs in employment sectors. As a major new voice for employers and employees in each sector, the Councils will develop agreements on the action that needs to be taken to tackle skills gaps;
— learning the lessons from the Employer Training Pilots, as a basis for developing a national programme for employers, to deliver training in the way that they want it, particularly for low skilled employees;
— reforming qualifications to make them more employer-friendly and responsive to business needs, by helping employers package units of training in different areas to form the training programme that best meets their needs;
— ensuring greater employer involvement in the design and delivery of Modern Apprenticeships;
— developing business support services on a 'no wrong door' approach, so that employers know who to turn to for help on skills, bringing in a wider range of intermediaries and sources of help, and joining up the work of Business Link, local Learning and Skills Councils and JobCentrePlus;
— publishing an 'Employers Guide to Good Training', bringing together clear information on everything employers need to know to improve the skills of their workforce;
— introducing a new management and leadership drive, working with Investors In People.

Trade and Industry Secretary Patricia Hewitt said:

The skills gap hits business hardest — and this strategy puts their needs first. It's a good result for business — and our economy. It recognizes that our education system must meet the needs of the workplace. This is a strategy that responds to what business needs, enabling us to meet the demands of the economy.

Although the UK is one of the most competitive places in the world to do business, we still lag behind many of our international competitors in terms of productivity, and part of that is due to the skills gap we have identified. Involving employers in vocational education, opening up education to people of all ages and focusing on adults' basic skills are all part of a far-reaching strategy that puts the UK firmly on track to the high value, high skills economy we need.

We all have a stake in higher skills — we must all work together to achieve the outcomes we want. The DfES and DTI are already working much more closely together and I will be publishing our Innovation Review in the Autumn to support this strategy.

Secretary of State for Work and Pensions Andrew Smith said the Skills Strategy and Alliance would prove invaluable in helping to build on the impressive employment record to date:

Our active labour market policies, including the New Deal and our investment in Jobcentre Plus, have ensured record levels of employment in the UK. Improving skills is central to our goal of full employment as it is often the key that can unlock the door to a job. The Skills Strategy outlines how we can go further to ensure that people have the right training and skills to fulfil their potential and continue our successful employment record.

CBI Director-General, Digby Jones, said:

Charles Clarke is right to recognize the role of employers and is giving them a greater say in the content and delivery of training programmes. For too long there has been a mismatch between the needs of employers and the services of training providers. But, the challenge now is to turn paper promises into practical realities as soon as possible.

TUC General Secretary Brendan Barber said:

> Tackling the UK's skills deficit poses a huge challenge to us all. Today's announcement that government, employers and unions are to work side by side in the Skills Alliance is a great boost to the unions and employers who are already working together to improve training in workplaces across the UK. A highly skilled workforce is ultimately in everyone's interest – the individual workers, their employers and the UK economy.

William Sargent, Chairman of the Small Business Council, said:

> I am really pleased that the need for small firms to be involved in formulating training options is being addressed. I look forward to helping the Department for Education and Skills close the skills gap, which is a critical issue in the small business community.

(Source: www.hrmguide.co.uk, 9 July 2003)

Establishing the scale and success of HRD activities is not easy. Taking the UK as an example, Matlay (2002) states that '... much of the literature that informs training and HRD policy in Britain is confused, dogmatic or biased'. According to Matlay, most of the relevant data have been collected and analysed by 'quasiofficial organizations' in the form of commercial surveys. These organizations were responsible both for the allocation of training funds and the evaluation of training activity. Not surprisingly, Matlay goes on to observe that:

> Invariably, such surveys endorsed the training policy of the day and purported to provide, on the basis of biased and/or unrepresentative samples, 'statistical proof' that government inspired and controlled initiatives were 'successful'. On some notable occasions 'resounding success' was claimed even before survey data was analysed. Furthermore, none of these statistical data were released for public scrutiny.

An Industrial Society report, 'Not very qualified – raising skill levels in the UK workforce' (Westwood, 2001) highlights a culture of learning 'apartheid' in British firms that favour high-fliers over unqualified workers. Most eleven-year-olds can read more confidently than one in five employees, but employers devote the bulk of their training budgets to their most-qualified employees. Managers and graduate recruits are five times more likely to receive work-based training than are unskilled or unqualified employees.

According to Westwood (2001), the UK averages just 99.5 training hours per year for every participating employee – 35 hours below the OECD average. This compares with an average 218.7 hours per person per year in Ireland, 159 hours in the Netherlands, and 143 hours in Poland. However, the UK beats one OECD country, the US, which averages 98 hours per person.

The report also damns the 'sitting by nellie' approach, which it calls a 'smokescreen for inactivity', and dismisses claims by employers' bodies that a major proportion of workplace training is not counted because it is informal and doesn't lead to recognized qualifications. According to Andy Westwood:

> Often referred to as 'sitting by nellie' learning that is verbally passed on to employees should not add up to much in our assessment. It is as patronising as it sounds. If the only way a firm provides training is by sitting a supervisor or manager next to an employee learning a new task, they are neither creative nor cost-efficient … neither 'winner takes all' economics nor helping 'nellie' will address the UK's productivity problem.

Similar findings came from the CIPD's third annual training survey (Cannell, 2001), which revealed that almost half of the training managers interviewed said that they found it difficult to obtain adequate assistance from senior line managers or directors to develop an adequate training strategy. Furthermore, 16.5 per cent believed that their senior managers and directors had a poor understanding of training and development. According to Cannell:

> The findings show an alarming gap between the 'haves' and the 'have-nots'. Only 8.4 per cent of our respondents said that managers and professionals in their organisations had received no on-the-job training in the past year, whereas 47 per cent said that their manual workers had received no on-the-job training during the same period. Similarly, although less surprisingly, manual workers are less likely to have a formal coach or mentor than managers and professionals.

A commitment to HRD is an important element in employee retention (Hay, 2002). In a survey of 330 companies in 50 countries, respondents were asked 300 questions regarding their satisfaction with 40 different aspects of their jobs. These included workload, treatment, benefits, pay, advancement opportunities, recognition, teamwork, job autonomy and job quality. Respondents were also asked to rate key perceptions of management behaviour, such as communication skills, leadership and management involvement in career development. Additionally, the surveyed employees were asked to indicate their long-term career strategies and commitment to their organizations, and how these were related to job satisfaction. The survey showed that employees were most likely to leave when their talents or skills were not properly developed, or when managers failed to show an interest in their career development. Only 49 per cent of employees planning to leave within the next two years were satisfied with the use of their skills and abilities. This compared with 83 per cent of those who intended to stay in their jobs.

Example 4.2 summarizes the results of the Training and Development Survey conducted by the Chartered Institute of Personnel and Development in 2004.

Ulrich (1998) identifies a number of key organizational strategies for acquiring and keeping knowledge workers:

- External talent acquisition
- Internal talent development by special assignments
- Job rotation and action learning
- Hiring talent from external agents such as consultants and freelance contract workers
- Contractually binding the most desired and talented employees to the organization.

Activity 4.3

Imagine that you are the HRD manager responsible for training and development in a medium-sized company.

- How would you justify commitment and expenditure on a learning and development programme to senior managers in that company?

Example 4.2: Skills shortage to drive training budget increases

Greater confidence in the economy, along with fears of skills shortages, is leading to more concerted investment in training and development. This is one of the main findings of the Training and Development Survey 2004 conducted by the Chartered Institute of Personnel and Development (CIPD).

The survey, launched last week at HRD 2004, showed that:

- There was little change in the size of training budgets between 2002 and 2003 but one in three private sector training managers expected to see an increase in their training budgets during 2004;

contd

Example 4.2: *contd*

- 81% of organizations have a training budget – indicating an acceptance of the 'training means business' case;
- Almost a third (32%) of respondents said that people in their organization received, on average, more than five days training per year. But almost one in five (18%) received less than three days training per year.

Warning that extra investment in training is essential in order to meet future staffing needs, Jessica Rolph, CIPD Learning, Training and Development Adviser [said]:

> If anticipated increases in training budgets do not materialize , current skills shortages could translate into wage inflation, leading to adverse implications for interest rates, growth and the economy as a whole.
>
> Economic uncertainty has led to a 'wait and see' approach to investment in training, but there is a danger that employers have not invested nearly enough in anticipation of impending skills deficiencies. A failure to invest now could leave employers in many sectors short of skilled labour, or needing to offer unsustainable salaries in order to fill vacancies for skilled workers.

Survey responses from the public sector showed a surprising disparity with the private sector with 30% of public sector training managers reporting a decrease in their training budgets last year (compared to 27% in the private sector). Just over a quarter (26%) also expected their budgets to decrease next year (compared to only 17% in the private sector).

Jessica Rolph continued:

> The Government has invested heavily in public services over the last year, and yet training budgets appear to have fallen. If, as it seems, the public sector is diverting money away from training and into pay awards in order to tackle recruitment and retention difficulties, they are taking a short-term approach which could store up problems for the future.
>
> As the private sector recovers, competition in the labour market can only increase, so reductions in public sector training budgets are ill advised. It would be ironic if the Government's investment in public services were to be undermined by a focus on pay rather than training, leading to services suffering because the public sector is failing to equip staff with the skills to do the job.

Other main findings [include the following].

Training spend

Average training spend per employee is higher in smaller firms (possibly due to economies of scale for larger employers):

Size of firm = 25–49
Average training budget = £33 833
Spend per employee = £884.06;

Size of firm = 50–99
Average training budget = £58 504
Spend per employee = £878.82;

Size of firm = 100–249
Average training budget = £111 658
Spend per employee = £660.62;

Size of firm = 250–499
Average training budget = £212 132
Spend per employee = £602.45;

Size of firm = 500+
Average training budget = £970 429
Spend per employee = Not available.

Benefits of learning

Survey respondents rated immediate job demands most highly when asked to rate the benefits of training to their organization, including:

– improvements in competence (62% said this was 'a great benefit')
– behavioural skills (61%)
– technical skills (61%)
– quality of service (61%).

These responses contrasted with the lower ratings given for general organizational benefits, such as:

– job satisfaction (33%)
– staff retention (29%)
– raised commitment (27%).

Training and time constraints

Time pressures meant that 77 per cent of respondents had to provide training in short, 'bite size' chunks. The same proportion also provided more learning materials that employees could use at times convenient for them.

Impact of Government skills initiatives

86 per cent of respondents had contact with further or higher education institutions and 81 per cent had dealings with Investors in People, but only 33 per cent had contact with Sector Skills Councils and just 28 per cent had dealt with their Regional Development Agency.
   Asked to assess the effectiveness of bodies they had contact with in meeting their needs:

– 30 per cent rated their Learning and Skills Council (or Education and Learning in Wales) as poor
– 38 per cent rated their Sector Skills Council as poor
– 43 per cent rated their Regional Development Agency as poor.

(Source: www.hrmguide.co.uk, 26 April 2004)

HRD in small and medium-sized enterprises (SMEs)

Westhead and Storey (1997) consider that training provision varies considerably in small businesses, with size being a significant factor. The British small business sector has a longstanding reputation for poor training levels, but Westhead and Storey found considerable variations between the smallest (micro-enterprises) and larger SMEs. Smaller firms conducted their training internally, with a focus on informal skills learning. Larger SMEs tended to obtain more external, formal training, with a goal of obtaining recognized qualifications.

In a survey of 6000 randomly selected SMEs in Great Britain, Matlay (2002) found significant differences in owner/manager attitudes and approaches towards the training needs of family and non-family employees in their businesses. The needs of family members were seen in terms of firm-specific HRD issues such as succession planning, whereas training for non-family employees was focused on individual career needs.

Owner/managers were mostly positive towards training, but did not regard it as a critical element in overall business strategy. Matlay also found that small business owner/managers frequently claimed to be under pressure from government agencies and private trainers to invest in HRD. In most cases (100 per cent of micro-enterprises and 93 per cent of small businesses), decisions regarding training and HRD were made by the owner/manager. A mere 7 per cent of small businesses employed a human resource manager, but even in those organizations the final decisions appeared to be taken by the owner/managers. The study encountered training plans and related budgets in under 6 per cent of micro-enterprises and fewer than 9 per cent of small businesses.

Looking at medium-sized enterprises, Matlay (2002) observed that owner/managers continued to be heavily involved in HRD issues in just over two-thirds (68 per cent) of the sample, despite the increasing levels of complexity and formality found in such organizations. HR managers took charge of training and HRD decisions in only 26 per cent of cases. All respondents claimed that they used training plans and related budgets. All respondents saw a strong link between their firms' specific training needs and sustainable competitive advantage. However, despite their positive approach to training, most owner/managers did not appear to view training as being crucial to their overall business strategy. Instead, they took a tactical perspective, relating training to the perceived HRD needs of their workforces and seeing training of non-family members as an organizational expense. Conversely, HRD in family businesses was proactive for family members as part of medium- to long-term development and succession strategies.

In line with the CIPD survey discussed in Example 4.2, Matlay (2002) found considerable dissatisfaction with the range of training available from external providers. Typically, owner/managers reported that they were faced with a significant range of skills shortages because they were unable to find relevant training for both present and future business needs. Respondents claimed to have searched at local, regional and (in some cases) national levels in order to find economically priced training programmes that were relevant to their particular HRD needs. When programmes were found, owner/managers were often reluctant to proceed because of the high costs involved and the absence of support. As a consequence, they were likely to adopt 'off the shelf' training packages with a more reasonable cost and guaranteed support despite being more general than the ideal requirements. Concern for the development needs of successors led owner/managers to devote more time and effort into searching for packages that would be of relevance to family members.

Hill and Stewart (2000) use a number of case studies to clarify the nature of human resource development in SMEs and the relationship with national policy in the UK. They confirm a tendency for short-termist and spontaneous HRD in a wide variety of companies in different industries. Training is informal, reactive, and aimed at solving immediate workplace problems rather than longer-term development of employees. Hill and Stewart also found a tendency to justify the absence of training rather than the active promotion of a development strategy. However, the business philosophy of owner/managers – as shown by their attitudes and motivation – and their perception of the link between HRD and performance have a mediating influence.

Activity 4.4

The owner of a small furniture retailing company employs a total of 57 staff, including 4 branch managers, an office manager, a delivery supervisor and several assistant managers. The owner is in his mid-50s and keen to ensure that the firm will continue after his retirement. Three family members are working in the business, all at manager and assistant manager level. An impartial observer would conclude that several of the

contd

> **Activity 4.4**   *contd*
>
> non-family management staff are more capable than the family members employed in the firm. However, the owner wishes the company to be headed by one of his family after he retires and intends to groom one of the three for the post of managing director. There is no HR or training manager, and all HRD decisions are taken by the owner. You have been commissioned as a consultant to advise on the succession plan and HRD strategy for the company.
>
> - How would you proceed and what problems are you likely to encounter?

HRD in larger organizations

Most large organizations delegate operational responsibility to a human resource section or dedicated HR function. McCoy (1993) provides the following list of objectives for a HRD function:

1. Address critical business issues and avoid common pitfalls involved in creating and managing a small training department
2. Create a realistic plan that supports your company's business goals and enhances your credibility within the organization
3. Forecast, negotiate, and manage a training budget
4. Effectively marshal resources to design and deliver HRD programs
5. Market human resource development to build company involvement in the function
6. Identify the skills and qualities essential to being an effective training manager or assistant
7. Plan appropriate developmental activities for the training staff
8. Evaluate the effectiveness of your HRD function.

It is evident that the real-life activities of the HRD function go beyond the core activities of employee development into PR, marketing and financing the HRD function itself. This includes 'playing politics' at senior management level, anticipating expectations and attitudes among employees from the highest to the lowest level. Not least, the HRD function has to pay attention to a particular point of vulnerability – that training/learning is one of the first business activities to be cut when times are hard and budgets are scrutinized.

McCoy advocates the following as a basis for a successful HRD function:

- Build a partnership with the organization by assessing what its business priorities are and how a training department can contribute to meeting them, and agree on mutual expectations to gain management's sponsorship and support of human resource development
- Create a vision and a realistic plan based on sound needs analysis, to ensure that your programs will address business-focused HRD needs and help enhance your credibility
- Be creative in finding internal and external resources to design and deliver programs and services so that HRD has an impact far beyond the direct staff power of your department
- Market human resource development so that employees understand how your department supports the company and how they are expected to participate in HRD activities to ensure that the organization gets the most out of any HRD effort
- Manage time wisely so that you stick to priorities and avoid getting bogged down in insignificant activities or projects
- Manage the budget carefully by knowing what HRD costs and what the return on investment in HRD will be
- Develop your staff and network so that you and your staff with grow professionally, remain energized, and stay on top of changes in the organization, the business world, and the professional community
- Track your effectiveness and make adjustments to keep pace with changing demands of the organization and make sure that your programs are meeting its needs.

One example of apparently effective partnerships involves the use of trade union learning representatives in the UK (see Example 4.3).

Example 4.3: Unions contribute to workplace learning

Two reports show that union learning reps have encouraged 25 000 fellow workers to try some form of workplace learning in the year since learning representatives were given new legal rights to promote learning at work.

Trade union learning representatives, a report produced by the Chartered Institute of Personnel and Development (CIPD)with the Learning and Skills Council and the TUC, states that union learning reps are collaborating well with their employers to increase learning take-up in many organizations.

The report shows that employees in junior positions are gaining the greatest benefits. Many of these workers are suspicious of learning and training initiatives, often associating learning with unpleasant experiences during their schooldays. Learning reps can provide a mixture of support and encouragement to these reluctant learners, persuading them to go on courses that can help enhance their own skills and their effectiveness in the workplace.

TUC General Secretary Brendan Barber commented:

Because of their unique position in the workplace, union learning reps are perfectly placed to encourage both their bosses and their colleagues to take learning at work seriously. In the last twelve months, with their role now backed by the law, learning reps are going from strength to strength and bringing learning to those parts of the workforce who traditionally missed out.

Victoria Gill, Learning, Training and Development Adviser at the CIPD, said:

Creating a learning culture within organizations requires a partnership between employers and employees. Learning is to everyone's advantage – boosting opportunities for individuals and generating returns for employers alike. But all too often employees on the front line view learning, training and development initiatives with suspicion. The success of legislation to assist union learning representatives has been the increased involvement of employees at all grades within organizations in learning opportunities.

The second report – *New faces* – includes results from a TUC survey of learning reps conducted last year. This shows that women seem to find the new learning roles particularly attractive. Just over a quarter (28%) of learning representatives are new to union activities, with over a half of these (59%) being women who had never before been active in a trade union.

With over 7000 union learning reps already active across the UK, and a high level of interest, the TUC believes that its target of 22 000 trained learning reps is fully achievable by the end of the decade.

Union learning reps are fairly evenly split between public (52%) and private (47%) sectors. 52% of learning representatives work in large organizations, but a considerable number are also employed in firms with fewer than 250 employees. 51% of union learning reps said their organizations had formal learning agreements with the unions in their workplaces. The TUC considers these employers to be the most likely to take employee learning seriously.

Case studies

INA Bearing Company Limited, a subsidiary of a privately owned German engineering group, has 360 people employed at its UK manufacturing facility in Llanelli, South Wales. Over the last three years the company has focused on continuous improvement and enhanced employee skills in response to increased competition from low-labour-cost countries. Management and HR staff have welcomed the involvement of the trade union Amicus in learning, together with the creation of union learning representatives.

Adrian Roberts, Personnel Manager says: 'We're trying to remove every barrier and give every opportunity for learning. For INA the new reps are key allies in the promotion of learning and lifelong learning on the shop floor.' Close collaboration between INA, the learning representatives and the union have led to a learning agreement which means that INA programmes such as learndirect are no longer seen just as management initiatives. Making information on the company training plan and budget freely available also creates an environment of trust and openness, ensuring that everyone works together.

David Preece, Amicus union learning representative added: 'We know what the production targets are and we know the business, but we also understand the pressures of shift-working and what people on the shop floor want when it comes to training.'

Learning reps from construction union UCATT have been helping workers on one of the UK's largest building sites to become computer literate and keep their health and safety knowledge up-to-date. A learning centre has been established in a portakabin at the foot of Canary Wharf Tower where the representatives have been helping construction workers from all over the 86-acre site get to grips with computers and improve their health and safety knowledge. The learning centre also offers the large number of migrant workers from Eastern Europe the opportunity to improve their English. This is of vital importance in a working environment where clear communication can mean the difference between life and death.

According to lead project worker Sean Andrew:

The construction industry at Canary Wharf has all the barriers to learning – a transient workforce; a high level of ethnic minorities with English language needs; lots of support needed for learners; lack of recognition by supervisory staff of the need for their operatives to train; and difficulty in getting paid release to do it. But because we're showing that the learning centre works and such a lot of people are using it, we've got a queue a mile long for our training.

(Source: www.hrmguide.co.uk, 27 April 2004)

Within the HRD function, individuals may be allocated roles depending on the size and organizational structure. The ASTD's WLP model identifies the following (cited in Rothwell *et al.*, 2003: 5):

1   *Manager* – plans, organizes, schedules and leads the work of individuals and groups to attain desired results; facilitates the strategic plan; ensures that WLP is aligned with organizational needs and plans; and ensures accomplishment of the administrative requirements of the function.

2   *Analyst* – troubleshoots to analyse the causes of human performance gaps or identifies areas for improving human performance.

3   *Intervention selector* – chooses appropriate interventions to address root causes of human performance gaps.

4   *Intervention designer and developer* – creates learning and other interventions that help to address the specific root causes of human performance gaps. Examples of the work of the intervention designer include material development, content preparation and instructional writing.

5   *Intervention implementor* [sic] – ensures the appropriate and effective implementation of desired interventions that address the root causes of human performance gaps. Some instances of the work performed by intervention

implementers include instructing, facilitating and organizational development.

6   *Change leader* – inspires the workforce to embrace the change, creates a direction for the change effort, helps the organization's workforce to adapt to the change, and ensures that interventions are continuously monitored and guided in ways consistent with stakeholders' desired results.

7   *Evaluator* – assesses the impact of interventions and provides participants and stakeholders with information about the effectiveness of the intervention implementation.

Activity 4.5

• What are the major differences between SMEs and large organizations in their management of HRD?

Budgetary considerations

When economic conditions are tough, learning is one of the first areas to suffer budgetary cuts. Bordonaro (2003) feels that we can gain confidence by 'recognizing that learning has matured from a discretionary curiosity into a viable function of business'. While budgets have become leaner, the HRD function has been forced to acquire a new sense of discipline and hone an innovative edge. According to Bordonaro, this involves:

- Moving the action closer to the 'customer'
- Improving measurement of return on learning
- Intercepting and incorporating recent advances in technology
- Sharpening the quality of outsourcing choices
- Acquiring a keener sense of accountability.

Bordonaro makes four suggestions:

1   *Link learning to the company's future.* Declare the learning plan to be the first year of a new 3-year cycle when learning will be increasingly innovative and have a positive impact on the organization. Ignore economic debate in the media and assume that recovery has begun and that

the business will have new requirements and abilities over the next 3 years. Focus on three questions:

■ How will our company be different in the improved economy?

■ What investments will we have made in the business to make us stronger against competition?

■ What new abilities as a total organization will we have demonstrated 3 years from now?

The next priority is to gain an understanding of how senior managers think about these issues and to point out that HRD strategy is to make their lives easier through appropriate learning and development.

2 *Take the offensive.* Look at existing activities afresh, eliminating poorly attended courses or training initiatives that do not have identifiable and measurable benefits. Almost certainly, there are some activities that have taken place for years that have never been questioned. Check the costs of outsourced activities and look for more cost-effective alternatives. Consider outsourcing those functions that have not been outsourced.

3 *Reallocate spending.* Try some new ventures. '… anticipate that today's wild new experiment will quickly become tomorrow's competitive standard'.

4 *Measure for true business impact.* Replace existing management reports on learning with new measures. Bordonaro considers that methods of evaluation have improved markedly in recent years.

From a financial perspective, Gary Steinkohl, a former controller with Fortune 500 companies and founder and President of the Lumin Group, advocates five principles for getting a training budget approved (IOMA, 2003):

1 *Make budgeting a tool, not a game.* 'Too often as managers, we try to get approved what we think is approvable by taking last year's budget and adding X per cent, building in cushions in anticipation of being asked to cut our budget at a later point.' Steinkohl argues that this turns budgeting into a game that ultimately reduces the credibility of the HRD function. Better to budget accurately. If a cut of 5 per cent is made, HRD should emphasize that this means a cut of 5 per cent in their activities.

2 *Know that no budget is ever etched in stone.* HRD's budget should be the best estimate and quantification of funding needs in the budget period. The organization and its requirements will change over that period, and learning needs will change as a consequence. Budgets are estimates and spending will differ from those budgets. Finance managers should be sufficiently astute to know this.

3 *Perform variance analyses.* Compare actual expenditure with budgeted figures and find an explanation for the difference. If a greater cost is out of your control it is 'simply business'.

4 *Go for the Big Three – responsibility, authority, and accountability.* It is difficult to meet a budget and deliver results without having full responsibility, the authority to place, modify or cancel orders and be accountable for the budgeted activities.

5 *Learn the language of leaders.* HRD specialists need to be able to communicate in a language that accountants and finance people can understand. For example, when the HRD function wishes to purchase a learning system, it is necessary to know the initial cost; ongoing annual costs such as upkeep, maintenance and depreciation; benefits in terms of staff or time savings; how training results can be tracked; and financial return on improved service due to training.

Finally, in this section, it is evident that HRD is increasingly being seen as a business function that is suitable for outsourcing. Industry experts forecast that fully one-half of all trainers will be working for outsource providers within 10 years (Tyler, 2004). Few organizations outsource their entire HRD function. In most instances HRD strategy is retained while day-to-day delivery of learning content and administration are outsourced. The motives for outsourcing range from cost-cutting to a recognition that some learning activities, such as compliance or health and safety, are generic to particular industries and can be dealt with more effectively by a specialist provider.

Activity 4.6

• Select an organization that is familiar to you. How does the HRD budgeting process take place in that organization?

Models and philosophies of human resource development

In this section we investigate some of the underlying models and philosophies of HRD that guide the thinking of practitioners and academics in their understanding of the HRD function. We consider the influence of concepts such as the traditional training model and the learning organization in real-life HRD.

HRD and the training model

Martyn Sloman (2003: 4) argues that one of the most significant trends over the last decade has been 'a recognition of the limitations of what might be called the low-cost model of competition'. Simultaneously, he contends, there has been a 'growing interest in resource-based strategy'. Advanced economies cannot compete with developing countries in Eastern Europe and Asia on employee costs. Instead, organizations in developed countries must achieve competitive advantages through the identification and development of distinctive capabilities.

Sloman also believes that trainers should adopt a new paradigm in which there is a shift from training to learning. He uses the term 'paradigm' in preference to 'model' because he perceives a need for a new mindset – hence a paradigm shift from traditional thinking. He states (Sloman, 2003: xiii) that:

> Interventions and activities that are intended to improve knowledge and skills in organizations will increasingly focus on the learner. Emphasis will shift to the individual learner (or the team), and he or she will be encouraged to take more responsibility for his or her learning. Such interventions and activities will form part of an integrated approach to creating competitive advantage through people in the organization.

Sloman looks at a number of models and highlights the problematic nature of the 'systematic training model'. This model is embedded in the 'Instructional Systems Design' perspective taught in US universities. It has also been advocated as best practice by a number of training organizations in the UK and elsewhere. In its simplest form, it is viewed as a (virtuous) circle or wheel where each of the following leads on to the next:

- ■ Identifying training needs
- ■ Designing training

- Delivering training
- Evaluating training outcomes.

It is evident that this model dates from a period when training was thought of as something 'done to' an individual, rather than one where the individual is expected to take more of a personal responsibility for what and how he or she learns.

The systematic training model has, according to Sloman (2003: 26), 'gained acceptance without adequate debate on its place', arguing that, since there is insufficient evaluation of training, 'it cannot be said that the systematic training model is governing practice'. He goes on to argue that the systematic training model is viewed as normative in the literature, that 'it is something that *ought* be taking place' – a 'signal of best practice'.

What alternatives are there to this model? Sloman concludes that the concept of learning organizations has been going out of fashion since the late 1990s. He suggests that the decline in popularity of the learning organization is due to it being a 'loose, ill-defined concept' that has 'failed to become grounded in reality'. Multiple definitions have not helped (Sloman 2003: 27):

> Most seemed to begin with the assumption that learning was a good thing, and that organizations should promote individual and organizational learning. What was lacking was a clear agreement on the steps that should be taken to make this happen and the climate in which it could take root.

A further alternative is to embed the HRD function within a high performance work system. Organizations operating within a high performance model use bundles of new working practices that require higher-level skills, so learning becomes central to high performance organizations. High performance work systems usually involve three main sets of management practices that focus on employee involvement, commitment and competencies, and emphasize the importance of HRD. The Institute of Work Psychology (2001) at Sheffield University describes these as:

1 Changing the design and conduct of jobs through flexible working (especially functional flexibility – broadening the pool of 'who does what' through training), teamwork, quality circles and suggestion schemes.
2 Ensuring that employees are given the knowledge and competencies to handle high performance work through

teamwork training, team briefings, interpersonal skills, appraisal and information-sharing.

3 Resourcing and development practices designed to attract and keep the right people with the right motivation. These include some guarantee of job security, an emphasis on internal selection, sophisticated selection techniques, and employee attitude surveys with feedback to the workers involved.

Activity 4.7

- Compare and contrast the traditional training 'wheel' model and high performance work systems models of HRD. What are the main differences in approach?

HRD and organizational learning

What is the HRD function trying to achieve in terms of learning? Holmqvist (2003) identifies a number of basic assumptions in the organizational learning literature:

1 *That organizations' learning is experiential.* This is also a central notion of most individually based approaches to learning. Learning is perceived as a 'relatively permanent change in organizational knowledge' derived from experience. This experience is encapsulated in:
  - explicit and tacit routines
  - programmes
  - standard operating procedures
  - other 'organizational rules'

  These rules are thought to change over time and to adapt to environmental changes because of the organization's experiential learning.

2 *That learning is a process that alters behaviour in a relatively permanent way.* 'It is certainly assumed that organizational learning implies changes in organizational cognitive systems albeit the explicit focus is on behavioural changes only.' Belief and behaviour are assumed to change simultaneously.

3 *That organizational learning is (effectively) individual learning that takes place in a social context* – in contrast to learning theories that hold learning to be something that only

individual minds do. So organizations are groups of individuals trying to make sense of their work activities. The organization learns by storing the outcome of these processes as organizational memories.

4   *That learning takes place within an existing system of organizational rules, practices and standards.* Individual learners are socialized into the organization's culture and use its language and accepted modes of behaviour to accommodate their learning. The single learner becomes an 'organizational practitioner', and learns on behalf of the organization. Holmqvist cites Weick and Westley (1996: 446):

> ... learning is not an inherent property of an individual or of an organization, but rather resides in the quality and the nature of the relationship between levels of consciousness within the individual, between individuals, and between the organization and the environment.

Holmqvist argues that the organizational learning literature tends to be concerned that 'although much effective organizational activity results from accumulated experience, this does not imply that organizational experience reflects cleverness'. In learning from experience, Holmqvist holds that organizations create a pattern of sophisticated beliefs about the world about them that becomes increasingly biased, leading eventually to the point where they are 'skilfully incompetent' (Argyris, 1993: 54). They cease to benefit from alternative sources of experience and their experiential learning becomes a hindrance when dealing with a changed reality. Holmqvist points to a paradoxical situation where today's organizational learning – advantageous in the short term – narrows the range of knowledge and the activities that are thought to be successful. The process of exploitation creates reliability in experience by refining and routinizing organizational activities. Short-term effectiveness may lead to long-term ineffectiveness. To counteract this drawback, organizations need to develop a matching process of exploration that emphasizes experimentation, risk-taking and innovation. Holmqvist considers that maintaining a balance between exploitation and exploration is a key concern for HRD. However, most of the literature deals with the two processes as if they were totally independent. Griseri (2002) contends that while analyses and typologies of learning make theoretical sense, in practice managers are more likely to adopt a holistic conceptual framework for dealing with real-life problems.

Rossett (2001: 25) argues that – traditionally – training professionals or instructional designers set out to create 'formal, structured learning events (typically courses or lessons)'. Such events took place outside the work context and focused on learning rather than doing. Various activities might be included, but while they might help learners apply the knowledge they gained from a course, they were rarely sufficient in scope or intensity to produce skilled performance.

Activity 4.8

- In your own words, describe the differences between academics and training managers in their understanding of the learning process.

Competency-based development and continuous learning

Over the last decade or so, a number of HRD initiatives have taken a competency-based approach to career progression and employee development. Competencies include knowledge and skills required to produce results, but also involve other characteristics such as innate ability and motivation (Rothwell *et al.*, 2003: 6). This approach involves the identification of gaps between existing employee competencies and competency requirements for positions or tasks those employees may undertake in the future (Kumar, 2003).

Competency-based HRD models have their strengths and weaknesses, sometimes producing disappointing outcomes (Garavan and McGuire, 2001). There is some controversy over the identification of competencies that are relevant to specific firms. This is partly due to the rationalistic view that characterizes advocates of the competency approach, tending to describe competencies indirectly as sets of employee and work characteristics. Garavan and McGuire argue that the concept has greater potential when competencies are viewed within the specific context of the firm.

Boon and Van der Klink (2001) are similarly concerned that many organizations use fixed generic competencies that have a global currency rather than engaging in efforts to determine competencies that are more appropriate to their own circumstances. Generic competencies may have theoretical value, but at the practitioner level they have limited use. Often they may be too broadly defined or else too detailed and prescriptive to fit reality within a particular organization.

Bell and Harari (2000) argue that the HRD function's primary asset is not the number of its permanent employees. Rather, its key resource is 'the number of contacts and networks among energetic, talented, powerful roadrunners who share information, expertise, ideas, imagination, and hard work'. The function should make best use of 'minds on loan' who cross functional, hierarchical and company boundaries. The success of the HRD organization lies in replacing traditional unempowered subordinates, working as permanent employees on hierarchically imposed tasks and processes, with collaborative alliances of powerful, driven people.

HRD leaders need to become facilitators, engaging everyone fully in their work. Participants need to be able to permeate boundaries. Bell and Harari (2000) consider that 'All organizational boundaries – departments, units, and roles – are artificial, created for convenience and efficiency' and that 'Permissions, paperwork, and red tape are byproducts of a team or organization that cares more about being procedural than about being resourceful'. Permeability, on the other hand, allows easy access to people and resources when required.

Such HRD organizations also regard continuous learning as vital to company survival, viewing learning as something to be woven into every business activity:

> Every memo, meeting, and communication carries a growth-enhancement property and helps associates sharpen their skills as learners – not just adding to the storehouse of knowledge but improving competence in focused inquiry, problem solving, efficient research, warp-speed retrieval, and extensive access.

Learning is perceived as a crucial competitive advantage giving both individuals and companies levels of competence that are more valuable than credentials. But how does the rest of the business see learning? Is it viewed as 'an exciting adventure enthusiastically pursued', or a kind of drudgery to be avoided? Is the number of people trained considered to be the key measure, rather than the impact and influence of learning? Is HRD viewed as critical to the business, or as a 'frivolous staff function to be jettisoned when times get tight'?

> **Activity 4.9**
>
> - Focus on a job that is familiar to you and list the competences necessary for effective performance.
> - How many of these competences could be improved by a suitable HRD programme?

Summary

In this chapter we have examined aspects of the role and structure of the HRD function.

The nature of the HRD function is affected by a number of variables, including the size of the organization and the prevailing attitudes towards learning and employee development. Typically, a HRD function has to justify its existence and range of activities in the face of cost-cutting and outsourcing. Whereas small organizations are generally poor trainers and give priority to family members working within the business, larger organizations take a more strategic stance regarding HRD. A complication in understanding the true nature of the HRD function arises from the different perspectives of practitioners and academics researching the field. Some longstanding textbook models are not being applied in reality, whereas other concepts, such as high performance work systems and competence-based models of learning, appear to have practical value.

References

Argyris, C. (1993). *Knowledge in Action*. Jossey-Bass.

Bassi, L. and McMurray, D. (2004). How's your return on people? *Harvard Business Review*, **82(3)**, 18.

Bell, C.R. and Harari, O. (2000). The New (beep, beep) Rules of HRD. *Training & Development*, **54(8)**, 44–8.

Boon, J. and Van der Klink, M. (2001). Scanning the concept of competencies: how major vagueness can be highly functional. 2nd Conference on HRD Research and Practice across Europe, University of Twente, Enschede, January.

Bordonaro, F.P. (2003). Budgets are getting squeezed – time to invest in learning? *Human Resource Planning*, **26(4)**, 6–9.

Cannell, M. (2001). *CIPD Annual Training Survey*. Chartered Institute of Personnel and Development.

Garavan, T.N. and McGuire, D. (2001) Competencies and workplace learning: some reflections on the rhetoric and the reality. *Journal of Workplace Learning*, **13(3/4)**, 144–60.

Garavan, T.N., McGuire, D. and Morley, M. (2000). Contemporary HRD research: a triarchy of theoretical perspectives and their prescriptions for HRD. *Journal of European Industrial Training*, **24(2/3/4)**, 65.

Gilley, J.W. and Gilley, A.M. (2002). *Strategically Integrated HRD: A Six-Step Approach to Creating Results-Driven Programs*. Perseus Publishing.

Griseri, P. (2002). *Management Knowledge: A Critical View*. Palgrave.

Hay, M. (2002) Strategies for survival in the war of talent. *Career Development International*, **7(1)**, 52–6.

Hill, R. and Stewart, J. (2000). Human resource development in small organizations. *Journal of European Industrial Training*, **24(2/3/4)**, 105.

Holmqvist, M. (2003). A dynamic model of intra- and interorganizational learning. *Organization Studies*, **24(1)**, 95.

Institute of Work Psychology (2001). *What is a High-performance Work System?* University of Sheffield.

IOMA (2003). 5 Simple Rules to Get 2004 Training Budgets Approved. *IOMA's Report on Compensation & Benefits for Law Offices, Institute of Management and Administration*, **3(12)**, 2.

Kumar, P. (2003). Retaining the best people. *Human Resource Management International Digest*, **11(1)**, 2–3.

Matlay, H. (2002). Training and HRD strategies in family and non-family owned small businesses: a comparative approach. *Education & Training*, **44(8/9)**, 357–70.

McCoy, C.P. (1993). *Managing a Small HRD Department: You Can Do More Than You Think*. Jossey-Bass.

Nadler, L. and Wiggs, G.D. (1986). *Managing Human Resource Development*. Jossey-Bass.

Rossett, A. (2001). *The ASTD e-Learning Handbook: Best Practices, Strategies, and Case Studies for an Emerging Field*. American Society for Training and Development.

Rothwell, W., Lindholm, J. and Wallick, W.G. (2003). *What CEOs Expect From Corporate Training: Building Workplace Learning and Performance Initiatives That Advance*. AMACOM.

Sloman, M. (2003). *Training in the Age of the Learner*. Chartered Institute of Personnel and Development.

Thomson, R. and Mabey, C. (1994). *Developing Human Resources*. Butterworth-Heinemann.

Tyler, K. (2004). Carve out training? *HRMagazine*, **49(2)**, 52–8.

Ulrich, D. (1998). Intellectual capital = competence × commitment. *Sloan Management Review*, **39(2)**, 15–26.

Weick, K.E. and Westley, F. (1996). Organizational learning: affirming an oxymoron. In S.R. Clegg, C. Hardy and W.R. Nord (eds), *Handbook of Organization Studies*. Sage, pp. 440–58.

Westhead, P. and Storey, D. (1997). Training and development of small and medium-sized enterprises. *Research Report No. 26*. HMSO.

Westwood, A. (2001). *Not Very Qualified – Raising Skill Levels in the UK Workforce*. Industrial Society.

Williams, S.L. (2002). Strategic planning and organizational values: links to alignment. *Human Resource Development International*, **5(2)**, 217–33.

Chapter 5

The role of learning in a human resource development context

Introduction

From the moment we are born we are exposed to experiences from which we may, or may not, learn something. Some of our learning may occur spontaneously and in unstructured situations, whilst in others learning is planned and structured. Throughout our lives we continue to learn and the process of acquiring new skills or behaviours often appears to be automatic. It is as if no conscious effort is required on our part. For example, locating the correct place of items at the supermarket may appear to be automatic and is influenced by our experience at other super-markets. Other forms of learning require much greater attention, practice and reflection. For example, a doctor learns to diagnose and treat illness through study, practice and feedback. Much of our learning takes place within a social context where the behaviour of others influences our learning. For example, we learn to display appropriate behaviour in different situations. Our behaviour at an informal party with friends is very different to that at a job interview. Such appropriate behaviour may result from direct feedback, or from observation and reflection.

The ability to learn is influenced by our own innate potential and our social experiences. Instead of being 'empty vessels' ready to be filled with knowledge, we are active participants interacting with and relating to the environment around us. Learning provides a framework for further learning, otherwise experience would be of little value. Experience is, of course, an invaluable tool, especially when there is no opportunity for structured feed-back. As individuals, we learn to become members of society who must acquire appropriate responses if we are to function effectively. Such responses are largely shaped by cultural expectations. Much of this early learning takes place within the family. This shapes much of our later learning in a wide variety of social contexts, such as school, university or employing organizations.

Within organizations it has been the responsibility of management to identify and organize training activities, usually in conjunction with a HRD specialist. As the emphasis has shifted from training to development and learning it has become the responsibility of management to create an effective learning environment that embraces both the traditional planned and structured training/learning activities and the incidental, accidental or informal learning that occurs in the workplace. However, responsibility for learning is now being viewed as a *shared* responsibility between the employer and the employee. This shift reflects the growing importance, and relevance, of the *psychological* or *unwritten* contract between the employer and employee. Much emphasis is now placed on the importance of the learning organization (see Chapter 2).

Such change is a common feature of modern organizations, and if organizations are to survive and be competitive they must ensure the continual development of their human resources. As organizations 'flatten' their structures and retain fewer layers of management, individuals are becoming more 'empowered' to make decisions at every level in the organization. The increasing use of teamwork means that people learn in groups and within complex social and psychological environments. Indeed, it is through the sharing of ideas, experiences and problems in groups, in the exchange of stories about these issues, that knowledge is transferred not only between individual employees but also between different parts of the organization.

As discussed in Chapter 1 the nature of work has changed dramatically, not least due to rapid changes in technology and the speed of communication. These changes require that people continuously adapt and develop in their jobs. An increasing number of workers are now known as 'knowledge workers', whose importance to an organization lies as much in their ability to adapt to new technology as in their skills and ability to learn. New patterns of work have emerged, such as teleworking and 'portfolio' careers, which have implications for the context in which learning occurs. It is within this context that learning has acquired a strategic significance to organizations.

Traditionally, organizations have relied on stable structures and formal channels of communication to transmit knowledge and socialize their workforces. However, as organizations respond to changing external circumstances, there is inevitable internal change to company structures, management, communication, and decision-making processes. SHRD has a major role to play in assisting in the preparation and response to ongoing change. However, greater focus must be placed on creating cultures and environments in which people continuously learn and adapt to change. It is now a government strategy to improve attitudes and resources towards learning to cope with change. Organizations are now beginning to appreciate the importance of developing a culture of learning and self-development if they are to resource their businesses effectively, and if they are going to maximize the levels of creativity, innovation and improvement necessary to remain competitive.

These increasing demands for continuous development pose enormous challenges for organizations and educational providers. Understanding how individuals learn and how this can be used to underpin SHRD provision is the precursor of effective learning strategies.

In this chapter, we will examine in detail the nature of the learning process and how people can be encouraged to learn. As you would expect, we outline the main theories of learning, which seek to explain how and why people learn. A knowledge and application of these is essential if learning events are to be effective. You will also need to understand the concept of the learning cycle. This chapter is more pragmatic in nature, rather than being an academic debate of theory. This allows the reader to focus on application rather than in-depth discussion of competing theories. However, it relies on an understanding of the SHRD principles discussed in earlier chapters.

Objectives

By the end of this chapter you will be able to:

- Describe the factors influencing individual learning
- Explain how people learn
- Evaluate key motivation theories in understanding personal motivation to learn
- Distinguish between the main theories of learning.

What is learning?

This chapter seeks to define learning and to identify exactly why people learn. Understanding personal motivation to learn is important in establishing how people learn, as well as reasons for their reluctance or inability to do so. Numerous theories exist which attempt to understand human motivation, and several theories of specific relevance to learning are considered. These are of importance in numerous learning contexts, but we will concentrate specifically on educational and organizational settings. Individuals learn at different rates, and the many factors that influence the speed and effectiveness of their learning will be discussed. Finally, we will consider the concept of the experiential learning cycle and its implications for understanding learning processes; and, particularly, its role in the development of workplace learning.

We are exposed to the concept of 'learning' from an early age, and so we have some idea of what we mean by the term 'learning'.

Activity 5.1

Before we explore this topic in depth, think through what you understand by the term *learning*.

- Try to write as precise a definition of learning as possible. In answering this question, it may be useful for you to identify what happened to you whilst you were learning something or as a result of learning taking place.

Your answer probably included something to do with 'change' in your knowledge, skills, understanding or attitudes. Most definitions of learning include the concept of change. Bass and Vaughan (1966) defined learning as: 'A relatively permanent change in behaviour that occurs as a result of practice or experience'.

From this definition we can draw several important features of learning:

- ■ Learning involves a change, which must be relatively permanent. A temporary change is then *not* learning. Therefore changes in our behaviour due to psychological state or fatigue are not learning.
- ■ The learning experience can be direct or indirect. Direct learning comes from an immediate personal experience

as a result of doing something – for example, practising playing football. Indirect learning comes from observing something, or hearing about the experiences of others – for example, watching a professional play football, or watching a video about football.

■ Physical maturation, although involving change, is not learning. For example, when we are older we are able to solve more complex problems; this is the result of physical maturity and cognitive development rather than learning.

■ Learning does not *always* result in a desirable change in our behaviour, since the opposite may occur. For example, you might learn the habit of driving recklessly.

■ This permanent change may take place informally or through planned training interventions. It is useful at this stage to differentiate between learning and training.

Training and learning

Learning has been defined above as the relatively permanent change in knowledge, skills or attitudes by an individual. Training can be viewed as a planned and structured process – usually characterized by an individual acting as an instructor/trainer – which attempts to accelerate and structure such learning. However, because it is now acknowledged that the majority of learning takes place informally, it has become even more important for managers, HRD specialists and employees to understand how people learn in a variety of settings.

Learning is not just adding to what you know. It also concerns skills, emotional development, motivation, social behaviour and personality. This change means that you actually do something in a different way. It may not be evident until a situation arises in which the new behaviour can occur, and this may be much later. Thus, by understanding the factors contributing to learning, we can facilitate individual development and the success of planned HRD interventions.

However, is it reasonable to define learning purely in terms of relatively permanent changes in behaviour? As Harrison (2000) comments, this definition does not refer to any changed ways of perceiving, thinking and knowing in relation to an individual's understanding of the 'real world', and she argues that learning is as much about knowledge as it is about behavioural change. This is consistent with the growing emphasis on the idea of the 'knowledge-productive organization'. In such an organization, learning at the individual, group and organizational levels is closely associated with the generation, acquisition and utilization of knowledge. Consequently, managers need to develop a learning environment in which both behavioural changes and knowledge acquisition are achieved. As Harrison (2000: 238) observes:

> Management must foster the kind of individual and collective learning that not only produces changed behaviour, but that also adds to the store of valuable knowledge which the organization possesses and on which its long-term future depends.

It is important to note that some changes in behaviour are not learning, so relatively permanent change excludes temporary conditions such as fatigue or the influence of alcohol or drugs. By including the result of experience, we exclude changes due to physical maturation, illness or suffering physical damage.

Reid and Barrington (1999) point out that learning is an interactive process involving other people or activities. This is consistent with the view that knowledge acquisition and transfer requires a social or group context in the workplace. Often learning appears to occur automatically without conscious effort as people come together and share stories and experiences. For example, people in organizations learn:

- Other people's names and roles
- Technical terms and jargon
- How an organization is structured, and the responsibility of different departments.

After this initial acquisition of knowledge, more complex learning occurs as people learn about:

- Other people's attitudes and beliefs
- Their behaviour and styles of working.

This has an influence on the learner, whose change in behaviour in turn influences the behaviour of others. As Reid and Barrington (1999: 60) point out: 'People learn by imitating others (modelling), by perceiving and interpreting what happens in the organization and by the cumulative experience of trial and error'. Thus, it appears that individual learning within a work context occurs through observation, interpretation and reflection within a social/group context.

Why people learn

Learning is a natural feature of human behaviour. At the most basic level, people and animals learn because they have to in order to survive. At work, many people are under constant pressure to learn and develop in order to meet the challenges of new work activities and organizational changes.

Yet controversy exists amongst psychologists over the reasons for learning. People want to learn well beyond the needs of basic survival. Why? Individual differences and social and cultural pressures play a part in the desire to learn and achieve desirable outcomes. Much of the research into why people learn concerns learners' recognition of the results of learning. You can think of these results as rewards of various kinds. These rewards of learning can be classified into five groups:

1   Achievement – the success that results from the learning
2   Anxiety – the avoidance of failure
3   Approval – the approval of family, friends, teachers or colleagues
4   Curiosity – the increased opportunity to explore the environment and be exposed to new stimuli
5   Acquisitiveness – something tangible, such as money or material benefits.

In any given situation more than one reward may play a part, so the items are not mutually exclusive.

The 'nature–nurture' debate also adds to the argument regarding how people learn. Are people born with a certain capacity for learning, which they will naturally achieve but not exceed? Or is everyone capable of limitless achievement if they have the right upbringing? The two extreme viewpoints are:

1   *Nature.* Nativist psychologists insist that an individual's entire potential is present at birth, and that during life this potential is simply reached. Some people's potential is greater than that of others. A nativist would argue that one person could learn more than another because he or she was born with more potential ability.
2   *Nurture.* Behaviourist psychologists insist that an individual's potential is unlimited, and develops wholly under the influence of the environment. A behaviourist would argue that one person learns more than another because

he or she has been encouraged as a child to learn and rewarded for being successful.

Most psychologists believe that the truth lies somewhere between these two extremes, so we need to see how we can combine the views of the nativists and behaviourists to find the most effective ways of learning. The organization needs to ensure a balance between effective staff selection and the potential to learn and develop. There is also a political issue here, with the nativist believing ability is a function of one's genes. It is similar to the notion of inherited intelligence, a view that can be traced back to Sir Francis Galton in the nineteenth century, who formed the Eugenics Society. This society believed that it was desirable for individuals to be bred to be of superior intelligence, thus ignoring the belief that others had any ability at all.

Individuals are born with an immense capacity to learn and achieve. Even as children we have enormous potential to learn to walk, talk, read, write, paint and so on. That potential can be encouraged, nurtured, developed and expressed, or distorted and repressed by how we are treated and the environment we grow up in. Personal motivation is a major influence on an individual's willingness and desire to learn. This is important, because without an active desire to learn, development will be limited.

Activity 5.2

- Outline the factors that you consider important in your motivation to study successfully and understand this material on employee development – for example, completion being necessary for formally approved qualification, or developing an understanding of the topic for later application to your job.

Your answer to a large extent depends on your particular circumstances. Your initial motivation was probably influenced by a number of factors – e.g. needing to complete the module as part of a formal qualification, for knowledge improvement, or owing to organizational pressure or interest. As far as success during study is concerned, you probably mentioned issues to do with the content and presentation of materials, ease of understanding, quality of explanation and examples, relevance and application.

Perhaps motivation to learn is influenced by other people. This may be in the form of pressure from others, or their position as a role model or comparison. All these factors play a part in our motivation to learn in both everyday life and formally organized training programmes.

The motivation to learn

Most research into human motivation has been carried out in respect of work in general, not learning in particular. A number of researchers have analysed the factors contributing to (or inhibiting) motivation at work. Before we look at these, it will be useful to consider your own working experiences.

Activity 5.3

This activity requires you to consider your working experience. If you are a student and haven't held a job, you may complete the activity by asking a friend or colleague for their responses to the questions.

- Think of a situation when you did a job that you particularly enjoyed. Outline exactly what made that job enjoyable – e.g. supportive boss, feeling of making a contribution. Identify as many factors as possible that you think contributed to you enjoying that job.
- Now, complete the same task for a job that you particularly disliked or from which you derived little or no satisfaction. You may also complete this task by considering the enjoyable and dissatisfying aspects of one specific job.

You will have mentioned a variety of factors for the enjoyable and dissatisfying jobs. Each of these has implications for motivation and de-motivation respectively. The likely factors present in the enjoyable job probably related to:

- Feedback and support from others
- Involvement and sense of contribution
- Ability to see the job through to the end
- Belief in your ability to do the job well
- Sense of responsibility and accomplishment

■ Fair treatment in relation to others
■ Good benefits and rewards.

The likely factors present in the dissatisfying job probably related to:

■ Lack of interest and mundane nature of the job
■ Lack of feedback and recognition
■ Unfair rewards and treatment relative to others
■ Poor or inadequate equipment to do the job effectively
■ Effort not being regularly or fairly rewarded
■ Inadequate remuneration and rewards.

These factors underpin a number of motivation theories, which seek to explain motivation and its influence on subsequent behaviour and performance. Any rudimentary text on motivation will provide a discussion of the major theories. However, many have relevance for understanding an individual's motivation to learn at work and how they can benefit from training – or indeed, how training can arouse or respond to such needs. Four theories have been chosen to highlight the importance of personal motivation in learning:

1   Need for achievement (McClelland, 1988)
2   Two-factor theory (Herzberg, 1974)
3   Equity theory (Adams, 1965)
4   Expectancy (Vroom, 1964).

Whilst these theories might appear dated in terms of age, the principles that underpin learning are the same and they have great relevance in understanding the learning process.

Need for achievement

McClelland (1988) identified four main motives, which he believed were arousal-based and socially developed. Thus, they are a function of social expectation and culture. Those motives are:

1   Achievement
2   Power
3   Affiliative
4   Avoidance.

The Achievement motive (nAch) is the most relevant for our discussion. Research indicates that nAch varies between different occupations, with managers appearing to have higher nAch motives than need for Affiliation (nAff) (Mullins, 1999). Because McClelland saw nAch as being a major determinant of a country's growth and economic success, it has relevance for wider development strategies and individual behaviour and learning. Whilst his research has been criticized in terms of its methodology and subjective assessment of needs, he presented empirical evidence of four characteristics associated with high nAch. Thus people with high nAch display the following preferences:

1   *Moderate task difficulty.* They prefer tasks that are moderately difficult. This is because such tasks are both achievable and challenging. A task that is too easy will have no sense of accomplishment or reward, while a task that is too difficult is unlikely to result in success and resultant reward.

2   *Personal responsibility for performance.* To rely on others for success would only mean relinquishing control. Because their sense of accomplishment is derived from the goal achievement itself, recognition from others is not important.

3   *Need for feedback.* Clear and unambiguous feedback is required to enable them to monitor their performance and to provide satisfaction from the activities themselves.

4   *Innovativeness.* They appear to display greater innovation and constantly seek new challenges, variety and information about new ways of doing things.

An individual's need for achievement can be identified through questionnaire responses and validated by establishing a relationship between their responses and actual behaviour and performance. From this definition of high nAch characteristics, the relevance to learning is important. If different motivations predispose individuals to seek out and benefit from different task situations, the learning environment and opportunities must surely reflect this. Individual differences in need for achievement must be taken into account in providing learning opportunities in both education and occupational settings.

Two-factor theory

Herzberg's (1974) theory was derived from investigations into the factors that determine satisfaction or dissatisfaction at work. Through the use of critical incident technique (Flanagan, 1954), his study of work motivation culminated in a two-factor theory of motivation. The absence of one of these sets of factors causes dissatisfaction, and the factors are *extrinsic* to the job. If present, such factors might remove dissatisfaction – but they do not increase satisfaction and motivation. They are known as *hygiene factors* or *context factors*. Such factors include such things as:

- Salary
- Company policy
- Supervision
- Working conditions
- Security and status.

Factors that have motivating potential are *intrinsic* to the job, and offer the potential for growth and development. If these *motivating factors* are absent this will affect feelings of satisfaction, but will *not cause* dissatisfaction. Such factors include:

- Achievement and autonomy
- Recognition and responsibility
- Advancement and growth
- The work itself
- Meaningfulness.

Thus, dissatisfaction is *not* merely the opposite of satisfaction. Different factors influence these two very different psychological states. Herzberg's (1974) theory has been criticized in terms of ignoring situational variables, poor methodology, reliability (Robbins, 1998) and the link between satisfaction and productivity (Caston and Braito, 1985).

Activity 5.4

- Look back at your responses to Activity 5.3. How do your responses relate to the hygiene and motivating factors of Herzberg's theory?

You have probably found that many 'motivating factors' were present in the 'enjoyable' job. Likewise, a lack of these factors, together with poor hygiene factors, probably influenced the dissatisfaction felt in the job that you found demotivating. If this distinction is not clear, it is worth considering your perception of the rewards or conditions present in these two jobs. Remember, of course, that some people place greater importance on hygiene factors than motivators, and seek to gain satisfaction outside of work.

Herzberg's two-factor theory has important implications for learning. If the motivating potential of a task is derived from factors intrinsic to the job, these factors should be focused on any learning opportunity. Any learning opportunity must ensure that such motivators are linked to the learning event, or form part of the tasks back in the environment in which the learning will be used. Likewise, the potential for dissatisfaction from hygiene factors (extrinsic to the event) must be limited.

Equity theory

Adam's (1965) theory is based on social exchange, and focuses on people's perception of how they are treated in relation to the treatment received by others. An individual in any exchange inputs to a situation and receives rewards (outputs) from that exchange. Adams argues that we seek equity or fairness. Therefore, in a work situation, for example, skills, experience, ideas and time are exchanged for a range of financial, social and psychological rewards. Equity theory proposes that each individual will have a notion of what represents a fair or equitable exchange and will respond to any imbalance. Equity is sought in this situation, and any inequity serves as a motivating force to correct the balance. The theory goes further to argue that we evaluate our balance of inputs and outputs against those of others with whom we seek to compare ourselves. Again, inequities influence our motivation and behaviour.

Problems arise due to:

■ Our subjective evaluation of the inputs and outputs
■ The appropriateness of those with whom we compare ourselves.

How is this theory of relevance to an individual's motivation to learn? Certainly, individuals' willingness to learn will be influenced by their perception of the fairness and value of the exchange – i.e. their effort and the rewards involved. Individuals' responses to inequity will vary. For example, they may attempt to alter the outcomes, modify their inputs or change their comparison group. Whether in a structured learning event or in the workplace, the perception of the balance of inputs and outputs will certainly influence their willingness to continuously develop and grow. Culture and management style are also key in influencing perception, and thus play a major part in the motivation to learn.

Activity 5.5

Look back at your responses to Activity 5.3.

- Identify any mention of equity or fairness in relation to your input and rewards.
- List how Adam's equity theory might explain any satisfaction or dissatisfaction felt in the jobs you mentioned.

It is likely that any mention of inequitable or unfair treatment was listed under the job you found to be dissatisfying. When we perceive fair treatment in relation to our inputs or those of others, we often do not notice this, except where there is a specific reward or recognition given. However, if we increase our input (e.g. by working overtime) and are not praised or rewarded, we often become dissatisfied. In the same way, we become dissatisfied when we perceive that others are being treated more favourably for the same work performance. The same process can also be applied to effort given to academic work and the resultant rewards in terms of course grades. These principles may appear simplistic in view of the strategic focus on learning in organizations. However, these basic principles are often overlooked.

Expectancy theory

Vroom's (1964) theory has greater complexity and offers a formula to determine motivational force. A detailed explanation can be gained from any rudimentary text on motivation.

In brief, the theory states that people have preferences for certain outcomes over other outcomes. For individuals to be motivated, they must not only value the reward or outcome offered but also feel that it is 'their' behaviour that will result in the achievement of the reward.

Expectancy theory has real relevance to learning. If individuals are to commit to learning, they must value the rewards offered (whether financial, social or psychological) and feel that it is their actions that will result in success. Focus must thus be placed on matching expectations and designing events or environments that facilitate individual achievement. This is in line with the

Example 5.1: Expectancy theory 1

Consider an individual who has joined an organization as a graduate trainee in an accounts department. She is ambitious and works hard, and her grades at university indicate that she is an above-average student. She is keen for promotion, and is motivated to work hard to achieve it. However, after joining the organization her own observations and discussions with others in the organization lead her to believe that, as a woman, it is highly unlikely that she will be promoted. She believes this to be unfair and potentially to have legal implications, and her motivation to work for promotion is affected by this. Expectancy theory would indicate that her motivation to succeed is insufficient in influencing her behaviour. Even if she is encouraged, her experiences lead her to generally believe that her efforts will not result in the desired reward.

Example 5.2: Expectancy theory 2

Consider a student who is keen to succeed in her Business Studies degree programme. Her grades indicate that she is capable of obtaining a good degree classification. To date she has valued the possibility of obtaining her degree, and her efforts so far have been rewarded with high marks. Expectancy theory would indicate that she will be motivated to work hard because she values the final reward (the degree) and believes she will achieve it through her own efforts. However, if the student unexpectedly wins a substantial amount of money on the lottery she may no longer value the possibility of obtaining a good degree since this was needed to secure a highly paid job. In this situation, her motivation changes along with her hard work although she is capable and has been rewarded for her hard work so far.

concept of the learning organization (discussed in Chapter 2) that underpins such environments. There is considerable research on expectancy theory and good review articles are available. See Mitchell (1974) and Connolly (1976).

How people learn

People learn by adding to their current stock of knowledge, skills and attitudes. Later in the chapter we will describe several theories that explain precisely how learning happens, but let us first take some simpler models.

At work, when you are required to use new techniques or new machinery, learning needs to take place. There are a number of ways you can approach this need to learn. You can:

- Try it on a trial-and-error basis
- Be told how to do it and then get on with it
- Be shown how to do it so that you can imitate the demonstrator
- Think about how to do it
- Observe the successes and mistakes of others
- Adapt previous learning to trying out the new activity.

Each method has some advantages. Some people like to experiment and find things out for themselves. They may find it interesting; also, experienced workers can use their skills and experience in different circumstances. When people are told how to do something, they can be given good directions on how to proceed. When people are shown, they tend to have a model to follow in their minds. When people think about the problems, they can use their existing knowledge to devise effective solutions. In all these cases, the learning takes place when the workers 'think about the results of their actions and apply the results at work'.

It is important to understand that learning does not occur in a linear fashion – i.e. learning is not a matter of simply adding one piece of knowledge to another. The speed of progress varies enormously. If you put learning on a graph with time on one axis and achievement on the other, you will see that learning does not advance in a straight line. Early success can be quickly followed by apparent failure. Learners will say, 'I thought I was really beginning to understand this, but it doesn't make any sense now'.

If you have learned to drive a car or play a musical instrument, you will know that after the earliest stages the rate of increase in competency tends to fall off sharply. To achieve continued progress, greater persistence on the part of the trainee and encouragement on the part of the trainer are needed. This is the case particularly for sensory motor skills, where, for example, hand movements are combined with careful judgement.

Learners can be encouraged to plot their own progress on learning curve graphs. They will make greater progress as they come to understand the nature of learning, especially when they realize that a plateau can soon be followed by a burst of achievement. If a learner encounters one plateau after another, it may be possible to redesign the training programme to help him or her to overcome the barriers and become recommitted to learning. Encouragement from the trainer can result in extra energy and effort from the trainee or learner.

Activity 5.6

- List three things you have learned recently and describe how you learned them.
- Think of ways in which you might have learned them more effectively.

Activity 5.6 should help you see that there are different ways of learning things, and that different people have different approaches. The important point is to find a learning method that works well for you. Consider the impact of others on your learning. How does this influence your motivation and method of learning? Organizations are beginning to appreciate the importance of a supportive culture if workplace learning and change is to be successful.

Learning in the workplace

Organizations are beginning to embrace the necessity for a culture of learning and self-development if they are to survive continuous change. The concept of 'continuous development' presupposes that people must learn from real experiences at work and everyday life, rather than occasional injections of training.

The Chartered Institute of Personnel and Development's (CIPD's) first Annual Report on Training and Development in Britain 1999 highlighted the directions organizations are taking in securing an environment of continuous development. Interested readers can access the entire report, but an overview is given here to highlight training and development practices in British organizations.

A sample of 800 training managers were interviewed to:

- Investigate trends and developments in training policies in UK establishments
- Identify what budgets exist and how they are managed
- Identify the link between training and workplace practices
- Evaluate delivery mechanisms and compare traditional approaches with advances in new technology
- Consider the changing role of the training manager in the millennium.

The key findings are summarized below:

- Training appears to be more closely linked to the strategic business objectives – 81 per cent of trainers report that their activities are designed to link directly with strategic business objectives. Of the respondents, 63 per cent used an analysis of the business plan to identify training needs and 61 per cent used a training audit.

■ Training is increasingly used as a tool for change and a vehicle for increasing quality standards. It is further used to support change initiatives.

■ On-the-job training is seen as the most significant and important training method, and increasing use is being made of it.

■ Training is believed to be a major factor in employee commitment.

The most significant outcome of the research is that managers consider a culture of learning and development to be key to organizational growth. The close link with strategy and change initiatives highlights this move.

Activity 5.7

The 1999 CIPD Report identified that on-the-job training was the most significant and important training method, and increasing use is being made of it in British industry.

• List the key issues that might arise in ensuring the effectiveness of this approach in organizations and make suggestions for addressing potential problems (e.g. creating a culture in which sharing of information is valued and rewarded).

On-the-job training can be a valuable method where the skills, attitudes and knowledge learnt are directly relevant to the job being carried out. Learning on external training courses may not be easily transferred to the workplace. The success of on-the-job training depends to a large extent on the purpose of the training. Learning might take place whereby a new skill is learnt which is useful, and where the individual was previously unaware of its relevance. On the other hand, new learning might improve the effectiveness with which existing tasks are carried out. It is the latter situation that highlights the importance of management style and organizational culture in encouraging new and better ways of task performance. This is particularly the case where interpersonal skills are concerned. A culture of openness to new ideas, open communication and shared problem-solving is crucial if workplace learning is to be successful. This is at the very heart of the learning organization, which was discussed in Chapter 2.

However, you might like to consider how individuals really *feel* about training at work. Training managers may paint positive pictures of continuous growth through training, but in the long term it may not be the actual training organization that benefits from such investment. How can such development be harnessed? As individuals become increasingly viewed as commodities in a free market, to what extent do they feel that such development is for furtherance of their 'own' career (in or out of their organization) rather than for the benefit of their current employer?

Let us now consider a range of learning theories on which HRD interventions are based.

Learning theories

Any HRD intervention must be based on sound principles of learning and on assumptions of how people actually learn. There are no clear-cut rules to explain how learning takes place. This is because the range of learning activities is enormous – for example, from cooking a meal to writing a novel or managing a department. However, an understanding of the underlying principles of learning is necessary and should underpin different aspects of the complex process of learning. The main theories or approaches we will consider are:

- Reinforcement theories
- Cybernetics and information processing
- Cognitive theories and problem-solving
- Experiential learning
- Neurolinguistic programming.

Reinforcement theories

Early reinforcement theories date back to the nineteenth century, when researchers like Pavlov (1927) identified the nature of conditioning. Pavlov noticed that a hungry dog would salivate when presented with food. Over time, the dog would learn to associate the sound of a bell with the arrival of food. Then the animal would 'learn' to salivate to the sound of a bell without food being present. The association of stimulus (bell) and response (food) became known as *classical conditioning*, and has been generalized to certain, if not all, aspects of human learning.

It is Skinner's (1965) reinforcement theory that builds on this early conditioning approach. He worked with pigeons, and gradually modified their behaviour through a series of rewards. Rewards, in the form of food, were given to 'reinforce' required behaviour and increase the probability of the behaviour being repeated. This became known as *instrumental conditioning*. These principles have been linked to all human learning. Human learning is seen by behaviourists like Skinner to be a result of a series of stimulus–response reactions, where positive reinforcers increase the probability of the response being repeated and negative reinforcers decrease the probability.

It is probably fair to say that reinforcement and feedback do not accurately reflect more sophisticated and complex human behaviours. However, this does highlight some very basic principles important in many types of learning.

Activity 5.8

- Identify something that you recently learnt. What role did reinforcement play in facilitating that learning?
- How could the reinforcement have been stronger, more direct or continuous?
- What rewards would you put in place to reinforce the learning of this task by others?

Your answer probably included some comments regarding the importance of direct, continuous and immediate feedback. The *immediacy* of reinforcement is often important so that an association can be made between the desirable or undesirable behaviour and the feedback. However, reinforcement that is delayed may result in a less developed desirable response. For example, failing to give an individual positive praise for work well done may be a lost opportunity. On the other hand, positive reinforcement that is *delayed* may strengthen the behaviour, since the individual learns that the longer the wait, the greater the probability of the behaviour being rewarded. Parents who respond to an infant only after a long period of crying may unknowingly reinforce the crying behaviour.

Whilst positive reinforcement may bring about relatively permanent changes in behaviour, negative reinforcers, such as criticism and various forms of discipline, may only be effective whilst the threat appears imminent. This is because the negative reinforcer is being used to ensure that the individual 'learns' to avoid possible punishment. This is a major factor in designing effective safety training.

Reinforcement theory in the workplace

In the workplace, reinforcements ranging from bonuses to praise play a part in facilitating an individual to continue the rewarded behaviour. In terms of training, feedback and praise reinforce learning and correct responses. Conversely, negative reinforcement or even punishment may reduce or extinguish inappropriate learning.

The management literature offers many examples of attempts to incorporate reinforcers into different aspects of organizational development. For example:

- Compensation – where financial rewards are given to reward individuals' performance to encourage them to maintain their effective output
- Performance management – which links performance and development, goal setting and rewards for successful achievement
- Performance-related pay – where an individual's output is directly related to financial pay awards
- Performance appraisal – where effective performance is rewarded through praise and positive feedback, and less effective performance is discouraged by discipline or unfavourable feedback.

Traditional performance appraisal systems are criticized as poor development techniques because the period between the behaviours and reinforcement is so long. Other influential factors in learning through reinforcement include, for example:

- Organizational culture – which defines and reinforces the acceptable collective behaviour of organizational members
- Management style – which plays a large part in encouraging or discouraging individual effort and effective output
- Organizational structure – which facilitates effective communication and feedback between different parts of the organization

■ Power and politics – which influence the behaviours that will result in positive outcome for individuals and small groups. Such influences may be outside of the blueprint of the organization.

These will be considered in more detail in Chapter 7, when we consider factors contributing to a shortfall in desired performance. Thus, if desirable learning is to be encouraged it must take place within a system of performance management, which creates a culture and environment in which learning is part of everyday experience and reinforced and rewarded accordingly.

Cybernetic and information theories

This category of theories concentrates on how information is received and monitored. Feedback of performance may control human performance by operating like a thermostat that controls a heating system (Stammers and Patrick, 1975; Duncan and Kelly, 1983). The temperature is monitored and regulated because information fed back from the thermostat determines the level of power input to the system.

For example, experienced drivers monitor their speed and reactions through experience as a result of receiving stimuli from the environment via the senses (i.e. sight, touch, kinaesthesis, hearing and balance). The same occurs for the machine operator, who must learn to co-ordinate hand and eye movements, or an individual competing in a sport. In a training situation the most usual form of feedback is provided by comments from an instructor, but sometimes it can be given by simulators, which act as artificial 'thermostats' and help trainees monitor their own performance.

It is important to ascertain which cues or stimuli are guiding the learner – for example, a typist who looks at the keys will never learn to touch-type because skilled performance depends on kinaesthesis and position and feel of the keyboard.

In a formal training programme, it is important to ascertain which actual cues or stimuli trigger responses and monitor performance. Thus learners need to be shown and to practise recognizing and reacting to stimuli used by the skilled performer. Both recognition of stimuli and perception are important in acquiring new skills.

Thus, during the effective learning process, the 'selectivity' of stimuli becomes increasingly automatic, and the experienced worker ceases to think consciously about it. For example, a learner-driver initially concentrates hard on braking, accelerating and changing gear. However, after sufficient practice these operations become virtually automatic and are carried out almost without conscious thought or effort. Training programmes could have tasks subdivided into smaller units so that the learner can concentrate on one part at a time. Therefore, each part becomes programmed more quickly and the training period is shortened, with fewer resultant errors.

Cybernetic and information theories are largely applicable where effective co-ordination between the different senses needs to become automatic.

Experiential learning

A considerable amount of learning occurs through observation and reflection. For example, a manager who conducts a poor selection interview may, after the event, feel that his or her lack of preparation and structure did not allow sufficient information to be obtained from a candidate. This experience may lead to the decision to plan, structure, set objectives, decide key questions areas etc. in the future. When this is tried out and results in a better outcome, the revised method is used in future.

Kolb *et al.* (1974) highlight four stages in experiential learning (see Figure 5.1):

1 The experience
2 Observation and reflection

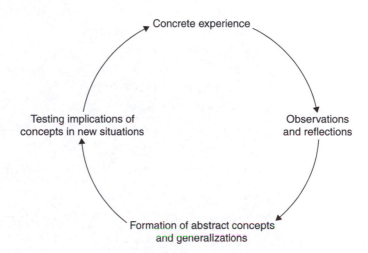

Figure 5.1
Kolb's experiential learning cycle (Kolb *et al.*, 1974: 28).

3   Theorizing and conceptualizing
4   Testing and experimentation.

All stages are necessary if learning is to take place. However, the different stages of this model require very different abilities, and people may have a preferred learning style that means they are better at some stages than others. Thus a model of continuous improvement and learning can be developed, with the learner growing in confidence and becoming more willing to embrace new learning. This method is popular in higher education, and explains why, in student texts, it is important to get the individual to do something to get the cycle started.

Activity 5.9

- Think of an example of something you have learnt recently. It may be a relatively simple task (like baking a cake) or a more sophisticated one (e.g. driving a car or giving a presentation). Using the four stages of Kolb *et al.*'s (1974) experiential learning cycle, consider how the stages might be of relevance in explaining how you learnt (see table for an example).

Learning – e.g. improving one's assertiveness skills	*Stages in Kolb's cycle*
Observation of manager using appropriate skills in practical setting	Concrete experience
Reflecting on how effective the action had been and its success in terms of the reaction of respondent and the subsequent improved working relationship	Observation and reflection
Considering how the effective skills could be used in one's one job (*theorizing*)	Formation of abstract concepts and generalizations
Practice of assertiveness skills in new setting (*pragmatism*)	Testing of concepts in new situation

Whilst you may have broadly identified your learning according to Kolb's four stages, it is sometimes difficult to identify the actual stages because much of our learning progresses through one stage to another without any real conscious effort. Learning is only complete when the learner progresses through the four stages and extrapolates their learning to different situations.

In organizations, a social environment can be created to facilitate the learning process. Structured experiences include coaching, mentoring and peer relationships. These structured experiences are important in encouraging individuals to be responsible for their own learning. According to Hicks (1999, in Mullins, 1999), it may be the only way to create and establish a learning culture. However, experiential learning is just as important to the vast array of informal, incidental or accidental learning that takes place in the workplace. Improving individuals' understanding of how they learn can improve the quality of such informal learning as individuals learn how to maximize their learning (e.g. through improving the level of reflection). Unfortunately, the frenetic nature of many work environments may be such that individuals may not have time to consciously think about learning; and many of the suggested learning aids, such as keeping a learning diary, can be seen as being too time-consuming or mechanistic by many people.

Honey and Mumford's (1989) Learning Styles Questionnaire has been derived from Kolb's cycle to ascertain preferred styles. We will return to this when we look at factors affecting individual learning. However, it is evident that different people prefer different learning opportunities, since their learning is more suited to one of the four stages. For instance, a manager may be more concerned with the practical application of a solution than is an academic who is looking for underpinning concepts.

In human resource development now there is a move away from static objectives and conditions that surround learning to a focus on creating an environment to facilitate the learners taking responsibility for their own learning. We have seen that learning does not exist in a static environment, but is influenced by wider organizational factors as well as those peculiar to the individual. This does mean, though, that HRD specialists are often attempting to create a rational understanding of learning in a work environment that is characterized by confusion, ambiguity, and apparent chaos – this is the reality of life in most organizations. This is why it can be so difficult to transfer the knowledge gained from formal programmes of study to the workplace. We will consider these issues in Chapter 6.

It is not sufficient simply to learn new skills and knowledge. The process must be dynamic and ongoing, and occur within a culture that is supportive and develops employee confidence to learn on a daily basis. The notion of a 'learning organization' may be aspirational, but this should not prevent individuals (directors, managers, HRD specialists or employees) from incorporating best practice from the concept into the daily workings of their own organization.

Cognitive theories and problem-solving

Cognitive learning theory asserts that 'learning occurs through individuals accessing, processing and transforming information from their physical and social environment' (Stewart, 1999: 107). The terms *cybernetics* (Marchington and Wilkinson, 1996) and *information processing* (Huczynski and Buchanan, 1991) have been used to describe this theory; which is not very surprising given that it is modelled upon computer science. However, cognitive learning theory was built upon to arrive at learning by and through insight (Hilgard *et al.*, 1971), which 'focuses on the individual's free capacity to make sense of problems and reach their own solutions ... Insight occurs when new and different relationships between elements in a situation or problem are formulated' (Stewart, 1999: 111). Thus a learner sees a situation as a whole and begins to organize it. The method of solving the problem is conceptualized and internalized, and then used in other similar situations. This is often recognized as 'insight', where a person suddenly realizes that a solution has been found – often referred to as the 'aha' factor (Marchington and Wilkinson, 1996).

A particular training approach arises from cognitive theory called 'Action Learning' (see Table 5.1). Case studies and project work are used to assist learners in analysing problems and developing insight, which can then be transferred to a similar real-life situation. Because the solution is actually found by the learner, it is internalized and the possibility of transfer is greater. Action learning is a concept that can be traced back to Revans (1972), who believed that in order to learn, individuals do not merely need education but also the ability to solve problems. He brought together managers from different organizations for several

Table 5.1
Comparison of training and action learning

Traditional training	Action learning
Individual-based	Group based
Knowledge emphasis	Skills emphasis
Input-orientated	Output-orientated
Classroom-based	Work-based
Passive	Active
Memory tested	Competence tested
Focus on past	Focus on the present and future
Standard cases	Real cases
One-way	Interactive
Teacher-led	Student-led
Source: based on Margerison (1991).	

months for discussion and debate. He concluded that learning stemmed from achieving a solution by working through:

■ The immediate problem presented
■ The new ones that emerge
■ Dealing with the problems one by one.

Such an approach means that learning is seen in terms of what individuals discover they 'need to learn' rather than what someone else feels is necessary.

This method is very simple and explains why delegates on courses with individuals from many different organizations learn so much more from each other. Many organizations have been unwilling to embrace such an approach and link it to their development programmes in order to avoid the risk of upheaval or constant change. However, the move towards an environment of continuous development means they must. Indeed, approaches such as action learning may be important in helping to improve our understanding of the link between individual learning and knowledge, and organizational learning and knowledge. Empirical research on this important topic continues. For example, Ellis and Phelps (2000). As has already been illustrated, the subject of individual learning has received much attention in psychology. However, the concept of organizational learning is far less well understood (Starkey, 1996; Probst and Büchel, 1997). Indeed, the 'connection between the individual level and organizational levels is perhaps the weakest link in the chain of arguments forwarded by organizational learning theorists' (Probst *et al.*, 1998: 244). Often, 'there is a leap from individual learning processes of action and reflection ... to applying these concepts somewhat cavalierly to an organization' (Fenwick, 2001: 78).

However, careful choice of tasks in terms of ability of the learner and the appropriateness is essential. If learners cannot find a solution because the task is beyond their capability, it can be frustrating and demotivating. Finding the solution thus acts as a reinforcer but, discovery learning naturally takes longer than many traditional approaches.

Neurolinguistic programming

Neurolinguistic programming (NLP) is increasingly being used in learning programmes to assist individuals to learn and process information more effectively. It is a fairly difficult concept to define and one which 'explores the subjective experience of the processes by which people learn things' (Bandler, 1985: 118). The term NLP can be broken down into:

- *Neuro*: the neurological processes of hearing, smell, touch, taste, sight and feeling. The world is experienced through these senses, and our neurology covers our thought processes and our physiological reactions to ideas and experiences
- *Linguistic*: the use of language or our thoughts and behaviour and how we communicate with others
- *Programming*: how we chose to organize our ideas and actions to produce results.

O'Connor and Seymour (1994: 3–4) highlight the subjective and perceptual experience of the individual:

> NLP deals with the structure of human subjective experience, how we organize what we see, hear and feel, and how we edit and filter the outside world through our senses. It also explores how we describe it in language and how we act both intentionally and unintentionally, to produce results.

Let us now undertake an activity to explain an application of NLP.

Activity 5.10

- Think of a time when you had to learn to drive a car. Try to identify the actual stages you went through before the skill became automatic. If you do not drive a car, ask a driver to identify the various stages for you.

This was probably quite a difficult exercise for you. It is often difficult to remember the stages we went through in developing this complex skill. However, you will, as will any person learning to drive a car, have gone through a number of key stages:

- *Unconscious incompetence*, where you are unaware of what you don't know
- *Conscious incompetence*, where you are aware of your lack of skill
- *Conscious competence*, where the skill is learnt but you are conscious of the actions needed for success
- *Unconscious competence*, where the skill is performed without conscious effort.

Practice is needed to achieve the final stage. However, bad habits are learnt and often these have to be 'unlearnt' before a more efficient pattern is developed. NLP can assist in this process.

NLP constantly refers to conscious and unconscious learning. Something is conscious when it commands our attention. However, many of our skills have become habitual and no longer require conscious thought. An individual is often unable to tell you how he or she learnt something because it is so difficult to remember the learning stages. NLP uses modelling skills (replication of successful skills observed in others) to identify the invisible successful learning strategies from words and body language to assist people in learning better and more flexibly. If it is possible to improve the processes of skill acquisition, this will have important implications for developing competence. Effective techniques have reputably been developed to engender more effective responses in education, counselling and therapy.

Research into NLP by neuroscientists and educational psychologists has culminated in a programme called *accelerated learning*. This mode of learning facilitates people learning faster, remembering more and thinking creatively. It is based on reprogramming how a person filters information through their senses, and learning how to learn and thinking creatively. Accelerated learning is based on the belief that each of us has an individual preferred way of learning quickly and easily. (Readers who wish to explore this approach further can access a wide range of texts on NLP. See Rose and Nicholl (1997) and Knight (2002).

As a theory of learning, it has been criticized in terms of the paucity of empirical evidence of its application. However, an increasing amount of research is becoming available to support NLP as a valid and reliable technique in facilitating effective individual learning.

Learning cycles

From the various theories of learning we have examined so far, you can see that the learning process is complicated. In recent years, there have been several attempts by academic researchers and training practitioners to rationalize this process and make it more clearly recognizable.

Honey and Mumford (1989) have developed a simpler definition of learning. Dispensing with a complicated definition, they state: 'People have learned when they know something they did not know earlier and can show it, and/or they are able to do something they were not able to do before'.

Their theory contains four stages related to the way in which individuals carry out tasks:

1   Taking action
2   Seeing results
3   Thinking about the results
4   Planning next time.

After extensive research in business and industry, they suggest that the learning cycle for an individual follows a similar path, in that a learner will:

- Have an experience
- Reflect on what happened
- Draw conclusions from it
- Relate the experience to their own situation.

Honey and Mumford related their version of the learning cycle to the basic task cycle, which they see as: taking action, seeing results, thinking about results, and planning next time. In Figure 5.2

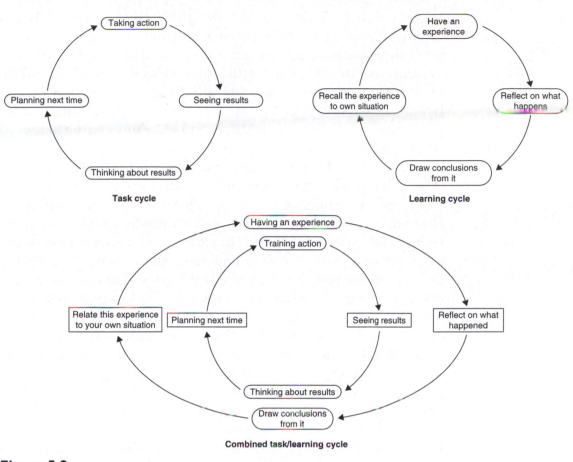

Figure 5.2
Combined task/learning cycle.

you can see the task cycle, the learning cycle and a combined version of both of these.

One of the most important aspects of a learning cycle is that there is a basic framework for both 'design' and 'evaluation' of learning. If effective learning has to comprise all four stages of the cycle, then close examination of any learning activity, planned or accidental, can be carried out by checking how, when, where and what were the activities involved in each stage. We examine the application of this concept in greater depth later in this book.

Summary

Learning processes are critical in organizations. The everyday behaviour of individuals and groups will either help to achieve organizational goals or impede their achievement. When organizational goals change, or when people are required to meet these goals in new ways, it is essential that people learn new behaviours effectively and efficiently. Hence an understanding of learning processes is important both in ensuring that people behave in ways that are desirable from an organizational stand-point, and to ensure that changes in behaviour can be achieved when they are needed.

A number of factors influence an individual's learning. Motivation plays a big part in influencing the desire to learn and its success. A number of key theories have been considered in this chapter, namely need for achievement, two-factor theory, equity theory and expectancy theory. In addition, you have seen that the contending theories of learning have their own place in the process of learning. For example, we can see that cybernetic theories of learning may be useful for safety training purposes and for training young people just starting work. As we outlined, cybernetics breaks down tasks and makes the learning process easier. Reinforcement theory, although simplistic in its approach, forces the trainer and facilitator to look at the organization's culture, policy, procedures, management style and employee practices. Therefore, in 'learning organizations' there is a supportive climate that develops employees' confidence in their abilities to tackle and overcome barriers to learning. There is also a strategic perspective taken with employee development programmes directly linked to business plans. Neurolinguistic programming, although highly controversial, is also an increasingly valuable tool in training.

References

Adams, J.S. (1965). Injustice in social exchange. In L. Berkowitz (ed.), *Advances in Experimental Social Psychology*. Academic Press.

Bandler, R. (1985). *Using your Brain for a Change*. Real People Press.

Bass, B.M. and Vaughan, J.A. (1966). *Training in Industry – The Management of Learning*. Tavistock Publications.

Caston, R.J. and Braito, R. (1985). A specification issue in job satisfaction research. *Sociological Perspectives*, **April,** 175–7.

Connolly, T. (1976). Some conceptual and methodological issues in expectancy models of work performance motivation. *Academy of Management Review*, **1,** 37–47.

Duncan, R.D. and Kelly, C.J. (1983). *Task Analysis, Learning and the Nature of Transfer*. The Manpower Services Commission.

Fenwick, T. (2001). Questioning the concept of the learning organization. In C. Paechter, M. Preedy, D. Scott and J. Soler (eds), *Knowledge, Power and Learning.* Paul Chapman Publishing/The Open University.

Flanagan, J.C. (1954). The critical incident technique. *Psychological Bulletin,* **51,** 327–58.

Harrison, R. (2000). *Employee Development.* Beekman.

Herzberg, F. (1974). *Work and the Nature of Man.* Granada Publishing.

Hilgard, E.R., Atkinson, R.C. and Atkinson, R.L. (1971). *Hilgard's Introduction to Psychology,* 5th edn. Harcourt Brace Jovanovich.

Honey, P. and Mumford, A. (1989). *A Manual of Learning Styles.* Honey.

Huczynski, A. and Buchanan, D. (1991). *Organizational Behaviour: An Introductory Text,* 2nd edn. Prentice Hall.

IPD Survey Report (1999). Training and Development in Britain 1999. The First IPD Annual Report. Institute of Personnel and Development.

Knight, S. (2002). *NLP at Work: The difference that makes the difference in business,* 2nd edn. Nicholas Brealey Publishing.

Kolb, D.A., Rubin, I.M. and McIntyre, J.M. (1974). *Organizational Pyschology: An Experiential Approach.* Prentice Hall.

Marchington, M. and Wilkinson, A. (1996). *Core Personnel and Development.* Institute of Personnel and Development.

Margerison, C. (1991). *Making Management Development Work.* McGraw-Hill.

McClelland, D.C. (1988). *Human Motivation.* Cambridge University Press.

Mitchell, T.R. (1974). Expectancy models of job satisfaction, occupational preference and effort; a theoretical, methodological, and empirical appraisal. *Psychological Bulletin,* **81,** 1053–1077.

Mullins, L.J. (1999). *Management and Organizational Behaviour,* 5th edn. Pitman.

O'Connor, J. and Seymour, J. (1994). *Training with Neurolinguistic Programming: Skills for Managers, Trainers and Communicators.* Harper Collins.

Pavlov, I.P. (1927). *Conditioned Reflexes* (transl. C.V. Anxel). Oxford University Press.

Probst, G. and Büchel, B. (1997). *Organizational Learning: The Competitive Advantage of the Future.* Prentice Hall.

Probst, G., Büchel, B. and Raub, S. (1998). Knowledge as a strategic resource. In G. von Krogh, J. Roos and D. Kleine (eds), *Knowing in Firms: Understanding, Managing and Measuring Knowledge.* Sage.

Reid, M.A. and Barrington, H. (1999). *Training Interventions: Promoting Learning Opportunities,* 6th edn. Chartered Institute of Personnel and Development.

Revans, R.W. (1972). Action learning – a management development programme. *Personnel Review,* **Autumn.**

Robbins, S.P. (1998). *Organizational Behaviour: Concepts, Controversies & Applications,* 8th edn. Simon & Schuster.

Rose, C. and Nicholl, M.J. (1997). *Accelerated Learning for the 21st Century.* Judy Piatkus (Publications) Limited.

Skinner, B.F. (1965). *The Behavior of Organizations.* Appleton Century.

Stammers, R. and Patrick, J. (1975). *Psychology of Training.* Methuen.

Starkey, K. (1996). Introduction. In K. Starkey (ed.), *How Organizations Learn.* International Thomson Business Press.

Stewart, J. (1999). *Employee Development Practice.* FT Pitman.

Vroom, V.H. (1964). *Work and Motivation.* John Wiley & Sons.

Chapter 6

Factors affecting learning

Introduction

In this chapter we will examine numerous factors that might influence learning. We have already examined a number of learning theories in Chapter 5, which are useful in underpinning the design of structured learning events and are also important in helping individuals understand better how they learn and how they might improve their ability to learn. Individual differences in the way people prefer to learn indicate the type of learning environment or process they will benefit from most.

As argued earlier, directors, managers, HRD specialists and employees have a joint responsibility for developing an effective learning environment, or collection of learning activities, which will lead to effective learning by individuals or groups. In this chapter, we will explore a number of factors that impact upon this process. These include:

- Organizational culture
- Group and social processes
- Individual learning styles
- Learning opportunities that may be intentional or not
- Personality differences and their influence on different aspects of performance including learning
- Emotional intelligence (this approach to understanding individual behaviour and style is currently under strong debate in academic circles and warrants discussion in terms of its alleged influence on learning behaviour).

> **Objectives**
>
> By the end of this chapter you will be able to:
>
> - Describe the factors influencing the effectiveness of an individual's learning
> - Outline the conditions for effective adult learning
> - Describe how personality and other factors affect learning.

Organizational culture

The role and importance of organizational culture has increased over the years. In the post-Fordist era, it has been described 'as the new technology for managing work and managing people' (Solomon, 1999: 121), and is seen as an integral part of the organization for influencing behaviour. Organizational culture has been defined as: 'a set of meanings to be shared by all members of the organization which will define what is good and bad, right and wrong and what are the appropriate ways for members of the organization to think and behave' (Watson, 1994: 111–12). However, Schein believes that organizational culture needs to be defined at a deeper level than merely a set of shared meanings. He defines organizational culture as: 'A pattern of shared basic assumptions that the group learned as it solved its problems of external adaptation and internal integration, that has worked well enough to be considered valid, and, therefore, to be taught to new members as the correct way to perceive, think and feel in relation to those problems' (Schein, 1992: 12).

These basic assumptions may operate unconsciously, defining in a 'taken-for-granted' fashion an organization's view of itself and its environment. This perspective highlights not only the role of learning in the development of organizational culture, but also the importance of groups and social processes (see below). Consequently, organizational culture influences how individuals learn to behave and think. At the same time, the interaction between individuals within a group or social context helps to consolidate further, or even change, the organizational culture itself.

A traditional perspective has been one in which the role of management is seen as ensuring that employee actions conform to the prevailing rules and procedures that exist in an organization to guide, constrain and control behaviour (Starkey, 1996). However, this is very much a one-way process, and denies the two-way interaction between individuals at the same and different levels in the organization, as well as ignoring the implications of the psychological contract which, by definition, must be two-way.

Group and social processes

The *social* perspective on organizational learning focuses on the way people make sense of their experiences at work. Consequently, 'learning is something that emerges from social interactions, normally in the natural work setting' (Easterby-Smith and Araujo, 1999: 4). This perspective emphasizes the role of groups or, as they are often termed, 'communities-of-practice'. It also highlights the importance of organizational culture. Yet, as Huysman (1999) comments, the tendency in much of the literature is to emphasize the role of individuals (usually as organizational 'agents' of learning). This means that the role played by culture, along with other structural conditions (such as organizational histories, group structures, power structures), tends to be overlooked.

To focus on the social perspective means that the analysis of learning in the workplace will be more messy, confused and ambiguous than the more 'clinical' perspective of those ascribing to the technical/rational perspective (i.e. organizations as information-processing entities). However, given the amount of time individuals spend working in groups it is important to understand how group/social bonds or attachments may influence, for example, how individuals learn or whether they wish to learn something. That said, individuals still retain a large degree of independence. For instance, their learning styles or preferences will differ. Also, as learning can be a deeply emotional and personal process, individuals within a group will not learn in exactly the same way when confronted by a common/shared problem (Elkjaer, 1999). Jarvis (2001) argues that any learning will affect what he terms the 'learner's biography' (i.e. the individual's knowledge, skills, attitudes, values, beliefs, emotions and senses).

Learning styles and learning to learn

Kolb's experiential learning cycle was introduced in Chapter 5, and is reproduced in Figure 6.1 for ease of reference.

According to Kolb *et al.* (1974), learning can be viewed as a circular process. The circle has no beginning or end, and people often work through the stages almost instinctively. Sometimes they appear to do this so skilfully that they often seem to produce more effective behaviour in situations that initially caused them problems. However, behaviour change may be slow, or fail to occur, because they make mistakes or become stuck at one or more points. For learning to be most effective, individuals must pass through all the stages.

The cycle or learning process, although not always easy to understand, may provide useful insights into where learning is inhibited, since an individual may find it difficult to progress from one stage to another. For example:

■ An experience may be so novel or different that an individual does not have the means of analysing it
■ Simulated training experiences may be seen as artificial or irrelevant
■ There may be insufficient time, willingness or encouragement to reflect and learn from experience (whether a work project, unexpected event or exercise in a training programme)
■ An individual may lack the skills to diagnose the situation or generalize and test out new responses.

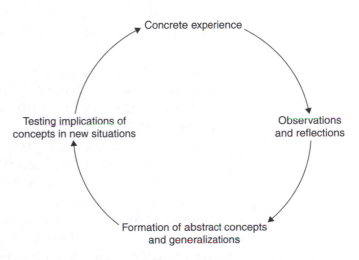

Figure 6.1
Kolb's experiential learning cycle (Kolb *et al.*, 1974: 28).

Therefore, learning and training must ensure the correct kind of stimulation, practice and feedback (continuous stages of learning). The model sees learning as an active process that involves problem-solving. Whilst each of the four stages is critical in effective learning, few people are strong at each stage. People appear to develop a preference for one or more of the skills required at the four different stages. A questionnaire to identify where people's strengths and weaknesses lie (Honey and Mumford, 1992) categorizes an individual's learning styles as:

- Activist
- Reflector
- Theorist
- Pragmatist.

By understanding our strengths and weaknesses, it is possible to choose or be subjected to learning activities that suit our style, and to attempt further to develop a weak learning stage in our learning cycle. The following characteristics tend to be associated with each of the learning styles:

1   *Activists.* Activists involve themselves fully and without bias in new experiences. They enjoy the here-and-now, and are happy to be dominated by immediate experiences. They are open-minded and not sceptical, which tends to make them enthusiastic about anything new. Their philosophy is 'I'll try anything once'. They tend to act first and consider the consequences later. They tackle problems by brainstorming. As soon as the excitement from one activity has died down, they are busy looking for the next. They tend to thrive on the challenge of new experiences, but are bored with implementation and longer-term consolidation. They are often gregarious people, constantly involving themselves with others, but in doing so they try to centre all activities on themselves.

2   *Reflectors.* Reflectors like to stand back to ponder experiences and observe them from many different perspectives. They collect data, both firsthand and from others, and prefer to think about them thoroughly before coming to any conclusion. The thorough collection and analysis of data regarding experiences and events is what counts to them, so they tend to postpone reaching definitive conclusions for as long as possible. Their philosophy

is to be cautious. They are thoughtful people, who tend to take a back seat in discussions and enjoy observing other people in action. They listen to others and get general focus of discussions before making their own points. When they act, it is as part of a wider picture that includes the past as well as the present, and others' observations as well as their own.

3   *Theorists.* Theorists adapt and integrate observations into complex but logically sound theories. They think problems through in a vertical, step-by-step, logical way. They assimilate disparate facts into coherent theories. As perfectionists, they like to analyse and fit facts into a rational scheme. Their philosophy prizes rationality and logic: 'If it's logical, it's good'. Questions they frequently ask include: 'Does it make sense?', 'How does this fit with that?', 'What are the basic assumptions?'. This is their 'mental set', and they rigidly reject anything that doesn't fit with it. They prefer to maximize certainty, and feel uncomfortable with subjective judgements, lateral thinking and anything flippant.

4   *Pragmatists.* Pragmatists are keen to try out ideas, theories and techniques to see if they work in practice. They search out new ideas, and take the first opportunity to experiment with applications. They are the type of individual who returns from management courses brimming with new ideas that they want to try out in practice. They like to get on with things, and act quickly and confidently. They tend to be impatient with ruminating and open-ended discussions. They are essentially practical, down-to-earth people who like making practical decisions and solving problems. They respond to problems and opportunities as a challenge. Their philosophy is: 'There is always a better way' and 'If it works, it's good'.

Whilst learning design is considered in detail in Chapter 8, you can already see that, based on this concept of learning styles, good learning design should ensure that any learning activity has:

- An experience of some kind
- A period of facilitated reflection
- A period of facilitated conclusion
- An opportunity to plan the use of the experience in practice.

Whilst Honey and Mumford (1992) suggest that design should be tailored to individuals and each group of people, depending upon their learning style preferences, in practice this is impossible. Computer-aided learning packages may be able to provide learners with four different options, which they can select to suit their learning styles. This is imaginative learning design, and important where the trainer understands more about the process of learning than the trainees.

Thus, learning is likely to be more effective if all stages of the cycle are completed. Trainers should use this knowledge not only in their learning design but also in the way they actively help learners to understand their own learning styles in relation to the choice of learning opportunities available. Better still, they should encourage learners to develop their less-preferred learning styles. For example:

- Activists can be encouraged to reflect a little rather than rush off to try something else
- Reflectors can be encouraged to try new things rather than just think about issues
- Theorists can be helped to look for practical applications
- Pragmatists can learn to value theoretical models and concepts developed by others.

Experienced and skilled learners will make the best use of learning opportunities and use their learning skills effectively. They will manage their own learning. Such an understanding of the different responses to learning events has culminated in management development moving away from formal training and classroom tuition to practical experiential events such as action learning.

Activity 6.1

- Complete the Learning Styles Questionnaire (LSQ) below. This is designed to find out your preferred learning style(s).

Learning Styles Questionnaire

This questionnaire is designed to find out your preferred learning style(s). Over the years you have probably developed learning 'habits' that help you benefit more from some experiences than from others. Since you are probably unaware of this, this questionnaire will help you identify your learning preferences so that you are in a better position to select learning experiences that suit your style.

There is no time limit to this questionnaire, although it will probably take you up to 15 minutes. The accuracy of the results depends on how honest you can be. There are no right or wrong answers. If you agree more than you disagree with a statement, put a tick by it. If you disagree more than you agree, put a cross by it. Be sure to mark each item with a tick or cross.

1 I have strong beliefs about what is right and wrong, good and bad
2 I often 'throw caution to the winds'
3 I tend to solve problems using a step-by-step approach, avoiding any 'flights of fancy'
4 I believe that formal procedures and policies cramp people's style
5 I have a reputation for having a no-nonsense, 'call a spade a spade' style
6 I often find that actions based on 'gut feeling' are as sound as those based on careful thought and analysis
7 I like to do the sort of work where I have time to 'leave no stone unturned'
8 I regularly question people about their basic assumptions
9 What matters most is whether something works in practice
10 I actively seek out new experiences
11 When I hear about a new idea or approach, I immediately start working out how to apply it in practice
12 I am keen on self-discipline, such as watching my diet, taking regular exercise, sticking to a fixed routine etc.
13 I take pride in doing a thorough job
14 I get on best with logical, analytical people and less well with spontaneous, 'irrational' people
15 I take care over the interpretation of data available to me and avoid jumping to conclusions
16 I like to reach a decision carefully after weighing up many alternatives

contd

Activity 6.1   *contd*

17 I'm attracted more to novel, unusual ideas than to practical ones

18 I don't like 'loose ends' and prefer to fit things into a coherent pattern

19 I accept and stick to laid down procedures and policies so long as I regard them as an efficient way of getting the job done

20 I like to relate my actions to a general principle

21 In discussions I like to get straight to the point

22 I tend to have distant, rather formal relationships with people at work

23 I thrive on the challenge of tackling something new and different

24 I enjoy fun-loving, spontaneous people

25 I pay meticulous attention to detail before coming to a conclusion

26 I find it difficult to come up with wild, off-the-top-of-the-head ideas

27 I don't believe in wasting time by 'beating around the bush'

28 I am careful not to jump to conclusions too quickly

29 I prefer to have as many sources of information as possible – the more data to mull over, the better

30 Flippant people who don't take things seriously enough usually irritate me

31 I listen to other people's point of view before putting my own forward

32 I tend to be open about how I'm feeling

33 In discussions, I enjoy watching the manoeuvrings of other participants

34 I prefer to respond to events on a spontaneous, flexible basis rather than plan things out in advance

35 I tend to be attracted to techniques such as network analysis, flow charts, branching programmes, contingency/planning, etc.

36 It worries me if I have to rush out a piece of work to meet a tight deadline

37 I tend to judge people's ideas on their practical merits

38 Quiet, thoughtful people tend to make me uneasy

39 I often get irritated by people who want to rush headlong into things

40 It's more important to enjoy the present moment than to think about the past or future

41 I think that decisions based on a thorough analysis of all the information are sounder than those based on intuition

42 I tend to be a perfectionist

43 In discussion, I usually pitch in with lots of off-the-top-of-the-head ideas

44 In meetings, I put forward practical, realistic ideas

45 More often than not, rules are there to be broken

46 I prefer to stand back from a situation and consider all the perspectives

47 I can often see inconsistencies and weaknesses in other people's arguments

48 On balance, I talk more than I listen

49 I can often see better, more practical ways to get things done

50 I think written reports should be short, punchy and to the point

51 I believe that rational, logical thinking should win the day

52 I tend to discuss specific things with people rather than engaging in 'small talk'

53 I like people who have both feet firmly on the ground

54 In discussion, I get impatient with irrelevancies and 'red herrings'

55 If I have a report to write, I tend to produce lots of drafts before settling on the final version

56 I am keen to try things out to see if they work in practice

57 I am keen to reach answers via a logical approach

58 I enjoy being the one that talks a lot

59 In discussions I often find I am the realist, keeping people to the point and avoiding 'cloud nine' speculations

60 I like to ponder many alternatives before making up my mind

61 In discussions with people, I often find I am the most dispassionate and objective

62 In discussions, I'm more likely to adopt a 'low profile' than to take the lead and do most of the talking

63 I like to be able to relate current actions to a longer-term bigger picture

64 When things go wrong, I am happy to shrug it off and 'put it down to experience'

contd

Activity 6.1   *contd*

65 I tend to reject wild, off-the-top-of-my-head ideas as being impractical

66 I feel it's best to 'look before you leap'

67 On balance, I do the listening rather than the talking

68 I tend to be tough on people who find it difficult to adopt a logical approach

69 Most times I believe the end justifies the means

70 I don't mind hurting people's feelings so long as the job gets done

71 I find the formality of having specific objectives and plans stifling

72 I'm usually the 'life and soul' of the party

73 I do whatever is expedient to get the job done

74 I quickly get bored with methodical, detailed work

75 I am keen on exploring the basic assumptions, principles and theories underpinning things and events

76 I'm always interested to find out what other people think

77 I like meetings to be run on methodical lines, sticking to laid down agenda, etc.

78 I steer clear of subjective or ambiguous topics

79 I enjoy the drama and excitement of a crisis situation

80 People often find me insensitive to their feelings

Scoring

You score one point for each item you ticked. There are no points for items that you crossed. Simply indicate on the lists below which items were ticked.

2	7	1	5
4	13	3	9
6	15	8	11
10	16	12	19
17	25	14	21
23	28	18	27
24	29	20	35
32	31	22	37
34	33	26	44
38	36	30	49

40	39	42	50
43	41	47	53
45	46	51	54
48	52	57	56
58	55	61	59
64	60	63	65
71	62	68	69
72	66	75	70
74	67	77	73
79	76	78	80

Totals

Activist　　　Reflector　　　Theorist　　　Pragmatist

(Source: Honey and Mumford, 1992).

We assume that you have completed the questionnaire and scored it. You therefore have four scores, ranging from 0 to 20 for Activist, Reflector, Theorist and Pragmatist. The question is, what do these four scores tell you?

Since the maximum score for each style is 20, at first sight you might conclude that the highest of your four scores indicates your predominant learning style. This, however, is not necessarily so. Before drawing a conclusion, you need to view your scores in relation to those obtained by other people who have completed the questionnaire. Norms have been calculated for various groups of people, and you need to decide with which group to compare your scores. If in doubt, use the general norms in Table 6.1, which are based on the scores obtained by well over 1000 people. The norms are calculated on the scores obtained by:

A	The highest scoring 10 per cent of people
B	The next 20 per cent of people
C	The middle 40 per cent of people
D	The next 20 per cent of people
E	The lowest scoring 10 per cent of people

To illustrate how to use norms to interpret your LSQ result, let us suppose your scores are: Activist 11, Reflector 11, Theorist 11 and Pragmatist 11. (We have chosen these scores deliberately because they admirably demonstrate the importance of using

Table 6.1

Learning Styles Questionnaire norms

	Very strong preference	Strong preference	Moderate preference	Low preference	Very low preference
Activist	13–20	11–12	7–10 (Mean 9.3)	4–6	0–3
Reflector	18–20	15–17	12–14 (Mean 13.6)	9–11	0–8
Theorist	16–20	14–15	1–13 (Mean 12.5)	8–10	0–7
Pragmatist	17–20	15–16	12–14 (Mean 13.7)	9–11	0–8

Source: Honey and Mumford (1992).

norms to reach an interpretation.) The norms give the identical raw scores of 11 with different weightings as follows:

- A score of 11 for *Activist* falls in the B range, indicating a strong preference for this style
- A score of 11 for *Reflector* falls in the D range, indicating a low preference for this style
- A score of 11 for *Theorist* falls in the C range, indicating a moderate preference for this style
- A score of 11 for *Pragmatist* falls in the D range indicating a low preference for this style.

The LSQ may be a useful tool. However, it is worth considering the acceptability of the instrument to the user in terms of its relevance, ease of completion and likely application (i.e. its face validity). You might feel that some questions include phrases that may be culturally specific to certain Western populations. Individuals whose first language is not English may find the questions ambiguous. Thus, any norms and assumptions drawn from data collected may lack validity in that we cannot be sure that individuals have fully understood the questions. Issues regarding psychological questionnaires of this nature will be discussed in greater depth in Chapter 7.

Learning opportunities

Any learning activity requires a recognizable beginning and an experience, which is practical, psychological, emotional or spiritual. In a sense, any experience is a learning opportunity. It may be positive or negative, planned or unplanned, conscious or

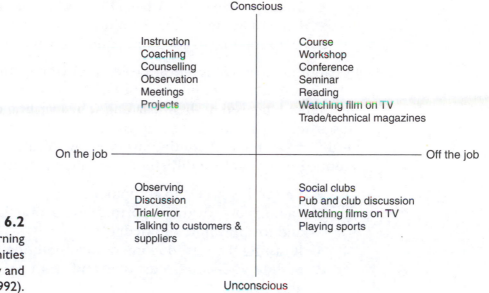

Conscious

Instruction	Course
Coaching	Workshop
Counselling	Conference
Observation	Seminar
Meetings	Reading
Projects	Watching film on TV
	Trade/technical magazines

On the job ——————————————————————— Off the job

Observing	Social clubs
Discussion	Pub and club discussion
Trial/error	Watching films on TV
Talking to customers &	Playing sports
suppliers	

Unconscious

Figure 6.2
Learning
opportunities
(*Source*: Honey and
Mumford, 1992).

unconscious. As they do not come neatly packaged and labelled, many experiences are easily overlooked. This is especially true for learners who do not have the skills to manage their own learning. They may wait for a trainer to 'give' them learning rather than taking charge of their own learning. Honey and Mumford (1992) have categorized the learning opportunities, on and off the job, both conscious and unconscious, as illustrated in Figure 6.2.

Employees can be helped to identify learning opportunities and to couple job activities with learning. So, instead of work and learning being 'either/or' activities, they can be integrated as complementary pursuits. The ability to identify, plan for and capitalize upon experiences can be developed and expanded. Creating an environment where learning is part of the daily experience has many potential benefits in that it:

- Adds a 'learning' dimension to normal activities
- Enables learning from any experience to be a more conscious and deliberate process
- Enables people to derive learning even from unremarkable routine events
- Improves an individual's ability to learn from successes, not just from mistakes
- Improves an individual's ability to transfer learning from one specific situation to other situations

■ Helps people to describe in detail what they have learned
■ Offers a framework for continuous personal improvement
■ Helps people to cope with, and keep ahead of, change.

Organizations play a significant role in providing employees with the range of learning opportunities outlined above, and in helping them to succeed in their learning. The learning organization (discussed in Chapter 2) reflects this approach by seeking to create an environment of continuous learning. A culture that is non-supportive may make it difficult for learners to learn, by:

■ Preventing access to equipment
■ Failing to provide opportunities to practise new skills and to apply new knowledge
■ Resisting the introduction of new methods
■ Stifling individual curiosity and enthusiasm to learn and grow.

Learning opportunities exist beyond those that are intentional and planned (e.g. training). Activity 6.2 illustrates this.

Activity 6.2

- Identify five situations that offered you or your colleagues a learning opportunity. These might exist in your social life or at work, but they should not be conscious, on-the-job opportunities.
- Describe each of the opportunities. Write an objective for one learning opportunity for yourself that you would have set if it had been a formal learning event.

The result of this activity might surprise you in that it should reveal opportunities for learning that you had not been aware of. For example, learning may arise out of job sharing, job-swapping, reading, researching, visiting suppliers and customers, spending a day in a different department, meeting fellow students on your course, etc. Individuals need to be aware of these opportunities in order to gain maximum benefit from them and generalize the learning into the workplace. In addition, managers should create opportunities to facilitate the transfer of learning to work.

You could, of course, argue that learning styles and preferred learning opportunities are two aspects of personality. We now turn our attention to the importance of personality in the learning process.

Personality and learning

Before we consider how personality might influence learning, it will be useful for you to reflect on what you consider personality to be. Personality is a term in common use, and it is important to define it appropriately.

Activity 6.3

- Write down your own definition of the term *personality*. You might find it useful to use some adjectives to explain your answer more fully (e.g. personality aspects: outgoing, lively, tough-minded).

The term *personality* is used in everyday life in a highly subjective way. People refer to someone as 'Having no personality at all' or 'Having lots of personality'. You may have found it hard to define the term, but your answer probably included something to do with recognizable aspects of someone's behaviour.

In identifying someone's personality, we are really referring to those enduring characteristics of an individual that are consistent over time and situations, despite their observable behaviour changing due to life events or circumstances.

There are many explanations of how personality develops, and it will not surprise you that the 'nature vs nurture' perspectives are very different. Clearly, the development of personality is a function of both innate characteristics and early socialization. Any rudimentary text on personality will assist you in understanding the different theoretical approaches and their philosophical basis. However, some key perspectives are mentioned here in terms of their implications for learning and development.

The scientific approach to personality study has culminated in the development and widespread use of psychometric tests. These are instruments that attempt validly and reliably to measure and predict performance in both educational and occupational settings. In terms of HRD, we are interested in how personality might influence an individual's ability to learn from different opportunities. We will briefly discuss three scientific approaches to personality measurement in terms of their relevance in learning:

1 Cattell's 16PF
2 Holland's theory of personality and job fit
3 The Myers–Briggs type indicator.

In contrast, Carl Rogers' (1947) ideographic approach to personality will be discussed – i.e. focusing on individual development instead of comparable norms of behaviour.

Cattell's 16PF

Using factor analysis, Cattell and Kline (1977) identified clusters of behaviour that relate to commonsense descriptions of personality. He explained these as products or underlying sources called *source traits*, identified 16 of them, and produced the 16PF (personality factors) test to measure them. The 16PF therefore identifies 16 personality factors called source of primary traits, as set out in Table 6.2.

Table 6.2
Cattell's 16 personality factors

#			
1	Reserved	vs	Outgoing
2	Less intelligent	vs	More intelligent
3	Affected by feelings	vs	Emotionally unstable
4	Submissive	vs	Dominant
5	Serious	vs	Happy-go-lucky
6	Expedient	vs	Conscientious
7	Timid	vs	Venturesome
8	Tough-minded	vs	Sensitive
9	Trusting	vs	Suspicious
10	Practical	vs	Imaginative
11	Forthright	vs	Shrewd
12	Self-assured	vs	Apprehensive
13	Conservative	vs	Experimenting
14	Group-dependent	vs	Self-sufficient
15	Uncontrolled	vs	Controlled
16	Relaxed	vs	Tense

Source: adapted from Cattell and Kline (1977: 44–5).

These 16 traits have been found to be generally sound and constant sources of behaviour. They do offer some prediction of an individual's behaviour by weighting the characteristics for their situational relevance. In recent years, there has been enormous research (Mount *et al.*, 1994) that supports the notion that, regardless of the variability of dimensions offered by different theories, five basic personality dimensions underlie all others. These dimensions are:

1 Extraversion
2 Agreeableness
3 Conscientiousness
4 Emotional stability
5 Openness to experience.

Research also indicates a relationship between these dimensions and important aspects of job performance. A broad spectrum of occupations has been considered, such as professionals (including lawyers and accountants), police, managers, salespeople, semi-skilled and skilled employees. Job performance was defined in terms of performance ratings, training proficiency and personal data – for example, salary progression. The results indicated that *conscientiousness* predicted job performance for all occupational groups (Mount *et al.*, 1994). *Extraversion* predicted performance in managerial and sales jobs.

Commonsense tells us that there is a relationship between personality and different aspects of performance. As training proficiency – the ease and skill with which an individual is able to benefit from training – was one of the measures of job performance, it is evident that personality influences learning. Clearly, personality will influence a wide array of an individual's work behaviour, including their learning behaviour. A valid and reliable measure of personality is thus a valuable source of information in understanding how best an individual learns and benefits from different learning opportunities.

Holland's theory of personality and job fit

Holland's (1997) theory is based on the notion of fit between an individual's occupational environment and their personality characteristics. Holland presented six personality types, and

Table 6.3
Holland's personality types

Personality type	Typical personality characteristics include:
Realistic: preferring physical activities requiring strength and co-ordination	Practical, conforming, shy, persistent, genuine
Investigative: preferring activities involving thinking, understanding and organizing	Independent, analytical, original, curious
Social: preferring activities involving developing and helping others	Social, practical, imaginative, inflexible, efficient
Conventional: preferring unambiguous orderly and rule-regulated activities	Efficient, practical, conforming, unimaginative
Enterprising: preferring verbal activities with opportunities to attain power and influence others	Ambitious, energetic, self-confident, domineering
Artistic: preferring unsystematic activities allowing creative expression	Disorderly, idealistic, impractical, imaginative
Source: adapted from Holland (1997).	

suggested that satisfaction and tendency to leave a job depend on the extent to which an individual's personality is matched to the occupational environment. The six personality types are briefly outlined in Table 6.3, together with associated typical personality characteristics.

For each of these personality types, Holland's research indicates congruent occupations. For example, the *social* type is more suited to work as a teacher, counsellor or social worker – occupations involving social interaction and helping others. *Artistic* types are more suited to work as writers, actors or interior designers. Likewise, congruent occupations are offered for each of the six personality types. A fuller explanation of the types and best-fit occupations can be found in Holland (1997).

If, according to Holland, personality predisposes an individual to be more satisfied with certain occupations, this must surely influence both the willingness to learn and the manifestation of newly acquired skills. It also highlights the importance of providing tasks and job content that is compatible with an individual's personality preferences.

The Myers–Briggs type indicator

The Myers–Briggs type indicator (MBTI) measure of personality is derived from Jungian psychology, which asserts that seemingly random behaviour is consistent and orderly due to basic differences in how individuals prefer to use their perception and judgement. It provides a useful measure of personality preferences that all people use at different times. These eight preferences are organized into four scales with two opposite preferences for each scale. Any combination of these preferences is possible, resulting in 16 possible types (see Table 6.4).

The MBTI has been used in a variety of settings, including counselling, career guidance, teamworking and communications. It has also been readily applied in education and training for a number of purposes:

- To meet the needs of different personality types by developing different methods

Table 6.4
Myers–Briggs type indicator characteristics of each of the four scales

Characteristics of each of the four scales	
Where do you prefer to focus your attention? The EI Scale	
Extraversion	*Introversion*
Preference for drawing energy from the outside world of people, activities and things	Preference for drawing energy from one's internal world of ideas, emotions, and impressions
How do you take in information, find out about things? The SN Scale	
Sensing	*Intuition*
Preference for taking in information through the five senses and noticing what is actual	Preference for taking in information through a 'sixth sense' and noticing 'what might be'
How do you make decisions? The TF Scale	
Thinking	*Feeling*
Preference for organizing and structuring information to decide in a logical, objective way	Preference for organizing and structuring information to decide in a personal, value-oriented way
How do you orient toward the outer world? The JP Scale	
Judging	*Perceiving*
Preference for living a planned and organized life	Preference for living a spontaneous and flexible life
Source: adapted from *The Myers–Briggs Type Indicator*. Consulting Psychologists Press Inc. (1998).	

- To understand what motivates different personality types to learn
- To provide extracurricular activities to meet the needs of all types
- To consider the value of different teaching and learning methods.

Thus, personality as measured by the MBTI has major implications for teaching and learning in educational and occupational settings. It can offer insight into how an individual's preferred approach influences his or her response to different learning environments and learning groups. It is useful to consider the effects of preferences in work situations, because they have direct implications for learning styles and opportunities from which different types can benefit. The interested reader can find a fuller explanation of how types influence behaviour in a variety of situations by reading Briggs–Myers and Myers (1985).

Rogers' humanistic theory

Humanistic theories of personality focus on subjective experience and human potential for growth and development. Carl Rogers (1947) was interested in the fact that people strive to grow throughout their lives. He believed that personality problems arise when people are consistently prevented from developing their potential.

Rogers believes that there are two sharply different approaches to the learning process: the traditional approach and the person-centred approach. He advocates the person-centred approach and, if preferred, this has implications for learning in education and the workplace.

1 *The traditional approach.* Some of the features of traditional education include the following:
    - The teacher is the possessor of knowledge, the student the expected recipient
    - The lecture, the textbook or some other means of verbal intellectual instruction are the main methods of getting knowledge into the recipient; the examination measures the extent to which the student has received it
    - The teacher is the possessor of power, the student the one who obeys

- Trust is at a minimum
- The students are best controlled by being kept in a constant state of fear.

It is the idea of an 'empty vessel' theory of education, whereby the teacher fills the willing student with knowledge and information. The student is passive and the process is one way, with the teacher leading the process rather than the student interacting with the information. Such an approach takes no account of individual differences in learning style or personality, and as such limits the extent to which the student can learn effectively.

2 *The person-centred approach.* The person-centred approach is in contrast to the traditional approach, and Rogers concludes that 'we cannot teach another person directly, we can only facilitate his or her learning'. The features of this approach are:

- The facilitative teacher shares with others the responsibility for the learning process
- The facilitator provides learning resources, from within him- or herself and personal experiences, from books or materials or community experiences
- The student develops a personal programme of learning, alone or in co-operation with others
- A facilitative learning climate is provided
- The focus is on fostering the continuing process of learning
- The discipline necessary to reach the student's goals is self-discipline
- The evaluation of the extent and significance of the student's learning is made primarily by the student.

In this growth-promoting climate, the learning tends to be deeper, proceeds at a more rapid rate, and is more pervasive in the life and behaviour of the student than the learning acquired in the traditional classroom.

Rogers therefore sees the role of the manager or trainer as one of creating a supportive and stimulating learning environment. Such an approach is similar to the culture of the learning organization, whereby continuous development is actively encouraged.

Personality factors can affect how we learn and how effective we are at learning. We have already seen how different preferences for thinking and dealing with the world predispose us to behave in certain ways. Individuals will not be effective learners if they have not been encouraged to develop their preferred ways of operating in the world. In such cases, their curiosity or enthusiasm may become stifled, as is often the case in early formal educational experiences.

The use of psychometric instruments to measure ability and aptitude as well as personality now forms an integral part of many organizational recruitment processes. Such instruments are also used in determining training and development needs, and will be discussed further in Chapter 7. Before we do this, let us consider a controversial issue in learning in terms of its definition and influence on behaviour – namely, emotional intelligence.

Emotional intelligence

Since Goleman (1997) published his text on emotional intelligence (EQ), there has been an increasing interest in the role that emotions play in decision-making, personal success and workplace behaviour.

The theory of EQ can be traced back to Jack Mayer, of the University of New Hampshire, who defined EQ as 'The ability to perceive, to integrate, to understand and reflectively manage one's own and other people's feelings' (Salovey *et al.*, 2004). Mayer and his colleagues have been studying the interaction between emotion and cognition since the 1980s to try to identify how emotions interact to improve thinking.

Attempts to use traditional methods of intelligence testing to predict individual and occupational success have been criticized as having limited value. Goleman believes that this is because the component of recognizing and managing the emotional elements of life has been omitted. He identified the main components of emotional intelligence as being:

- Self-awareness
- Emotional management
- Self-motivation
- Empathy
- Managing relationships
- Communication skills
- Personal style.

Goleman's work *Working with Emotional Intelligence* (1998) has incorporated the main domains of EQ and translated them into a five-point competency framework.

Whilst the concept of EQ appeals at the intuitive level, there is a need for more rigorous research to prove its validity. Research continues, with people like Dulewicz and Higgs (1998) offering evidence of EQ's predictive validity of managerial performance. One of the biggest criticisms is that, as a test instrument, it identifies nothing more than the 'big five' personality factors discussed earlier (see Mount *et al.*, 1994). However, with Goleman believing that EQ is twice as important as technical skill or cognitive development, more rigorous scientific research is needed to substantiate its claims.

EQ as a predictor of leadership potential has major implications for organizations (Higgs and Dulewicz, 2004). Therefore EQ as a predictive factor in individual and occupational success certainly has implications for learning and development. It may be that individuals with different amounts of emotional intelligence benefit differently from learning opportunities. It may also be a useful measure to identify the preferred learning environments that individuals benefit most from. The practitioner and trainer need to know if EQ differentiates competencies that have an emotional basis from those that have their roots in technical or academic achievement. Any instrument that differentiates competencies on this basis can assist trainers in developing methods more closely matched to an individual's needs.

According to Pickard (1999: 56), '[Goleman] has provided a scientific basis for what many trainers knew instinctively, but had difficulty explaining: that a change in behaviour cannot be achieved by simply going on a course'.

The debate continues as to its real contribution and application, and more research is needed to establish its real links with performance and learning.

Summary

Learning is a continuous, never-ending process occurring in all spheres of our lives. Many factors contribute to the ease or difficulty with which we learn from opportunities that are presented to us. Many factors facilitate or inhibit the effectiveness of our learning.

In order to understand how learning can be maximized, we have considered a number of important factors – namely organizational culture, group and social processes, learning theories, learning styles, personality characteristics and how learning can be facilitated. The implications of these factors can be considered in the design of planned training and developments pursuits, or indeed everyday learning opportunities. An understanding of learning theory is essential, and must be taken into account throughout the whole process of identifying needs, establishing objectives, and planning learning and training. In addition to these factors, it is important for us to consider in more detail what trainers need to know about learning in order to design effective learning strategies. This has direct implications for creating a culture of continuous learning in organizations.

References

Briggs-Myers, I. and Myers, P.B. (1985). *Gifts Differing: Understanding Personality Type.* Davies-Black Publishing, Division of Consulting Psychologists Press Inc.

Cattell, R.B. and Kline, P. (1977). *The Scientific Analysis of Personality and Motivation.* Academic Press.

Dulewicz, V. and Higgs, M.J. (1998). Emotional Intelligence: Can it be measured realiably and validly using competency data? *Journal of Competency,* **Autumn**.

Easterby-Smith, M. and Araujo, L. (1999). Organizational learning: current debates and opportunities. In M. Easterby-Smith, J. Burgoyne and L. Araujo (eds), *Organizational Learning and the Learning Organization: Developments in Theory and Practice.* Sage.

Elkjaer, B. (1999). In search of a social learning theory. In M. Easterby-Smith, J. Burgoyne and L. Araujo (eds), *Organizational Learning and the Learning Organization: Developments in Theory and Practice.* Sage.

Goleman, D. (1996). *Emotional Intelligence: Why It Can Matter More Than IQ.* Bloomsbury.

Goleman, D. (1998). *Working with Emotional Intelligence.* Bloomsbury.

Higgs, M.J. and Dulewicz, V. (2004). The emotionally intelligent leader. In R. McBain and D. Rees (eds), *Future People Management.* Macmillan.

Holland, J.L. (1997). *Making Vocational Choices: A Theory of Vocational Personalities and Work Environments* (3rd edn). PAR Inc.

Honey, P. and Mumford, A. (1992). *The Learning Styles Questionnaire: 80 Item Version.* Peter Honey.

Huysman, M. (1999). Balancing biases: a critical review of the literature on organizational learning. In M. Easterby-Smith, J. Burgoyne and L. Araujo (eds), *Organizational Learning and the Learning Organization: Developments in Theory and Practice.* Sage.

Jarvis, P. (2001). *Universities and Corporate Universities.* Kogan Page.

Kolb, D.A., Rubin, I.M. and McIntyre, J.M. (1974). *Organizational Psychology: An Experiential Approach.* Prentice Hall.

Mount, M.K., Barrick, M.R. and Strauss, J.P. (1994). Validity of observer ratings of the big five personality factors. *Journal of Applied Psychology,* **79(2),** 272–80,

Pickard, J. (1999). Sense and sensitivity. *People Management*, **28 October**.

Rogers, C. (1947). Some observations on the organization of personality. *American Psychologist*, **2**, 358–68.

Schein, E.H. (1992). *Organizational Culture and Leadership*, 2nd edn. Jossey-Bass.

Salovey, P., Brackett, M.A. and Mayer, J. (2004) *Emotional Intelligence: Key Readings on the Mayer and Salovey Model*. National Professional Resources Inc.

Solomon, N. (1999) Culture and differences in workplace learning. In D. Boud and J. Garrick (eds), *Understanding Learning at Work*. Routledge.

Starkey, K. (1996). Introduction. In K. Starkey (ed.), *How Organizations Learn*. International Thomson Business Press.

Watson, T.J. (1994). *In Search of Management: Culture, Chaos and Control in Managerial Work*. Routledge.

Chapter 7

Training and learning needs assessment

Introduction

This chapter considers the assessment of training and development needs at different levels within the organization. In Chapter 3, we examined HRD from a strategic perspective and examined the link between the development of employees and performance management. Armstrong and Baron (1998: 7) define performance management as 'a strategic and integrated approach to delivering sustained success to organizations by improving the performance of the people who work in them and by developing the capabilities of teams and individual contributions'. Thus, performance management is a strategic approach integrated with the wider business functions and concerned with improvement and continuous development. In order to design effective training and learning events within this context, it is essential to assess the needs of the organization, the department or group, and the individual effectively.

A number of needs arise at the organizational level due to changes such as legislation or new technology and the need to remain competitive. At the job level, new demands are placed on jobholders, which have training, learning or development implications. As virtual teams and more flexible forms of working increasingly become the means of achieving work objectives, new training, learning and development needs become apparent. The individual also has to adapt in response to those changes arising in the job, group and organization. However, it is important to ascertain from the outset whether identified problems or shortfalls in performance will benefit from a training or learning intervention.

Many factors influence performance, and it is important to identify whether training is likely to facilitate more effective performance or whether attention should be given to other management issues. Considerable time is devoted to considering this argument. Two broad models are considered, which take quite different philosophical approaches to training and learning. First, the *individual model of training* (Bramley, 1991) will be examined. This model assumes that a change within the individual will result in improved job performance and subsequent increased organizational effectiveness. *The increased effectiveness model* (Bramley, 1991), on the other hand, provides an alternative perspective which ensures more systematically that the correct steps are taken to ensure the success of any training intervention.

In order to carry out a training or learning needs analysis at the various levels, the HRD specialist needs to understand the methods available for data collection and interpretation (e.g. of company policies and strategies at an organizational level; appraisals; job analysis; questionnaires; interviews at an individual or departmental level). The reason for this is quite simple – it is important to carry out any analysis in as organized and systematic manner as possible in order to maximize the potential benefits of any training or learning intervention.

Conducting an organization-level analysis enables the HRD specialist to ask some important questions, such as: How well matched is our workforce to the needs of the business? What expertise do we have now; and what will we require in the future in order to achieve our business objectives? The HRD function can assist line managers in identifying the training and learning needs of their subordinates. These needs will differ greatly depending on the job a person is doing and the level of skill they possess. Even in a team where everyone does the same job, the training/learning needs may vary significantly – some team members may already carry out tasks competently; others may have little experience and be less competent; others may be interested in developing themselves for future roles.

Objectives

By the end of this chapter you will be able to:

- Consider the significance of aligning departmental, group and individual HRD objectives with business goals
- List possible reasons for a shortfall in effective individual work performance
- Identify key factors that might influence work performance
- Discuss how an understanding of these factors might ascertain the likely causes of poor performance
- Compare and contrast the individual model of training and the increased effectiveness model of training and development
- Identify a range of methods for assessing individual, group and organizational training and development needs
- Understand the role of performance appraisal and development centres as means of assessing needs as well as developing individuals.

Identifying performance shortfalls

Organizational objectives and human resource developmental needs

For effective development to occur within an organization, the department, group and individual human resource development objectives must be aligned with the business goals. Linking longer-term development with performance management systems (PMS) is essential to an organization's continued success (Armstrong and Baron, 1998). Much of the current literature on employee development echoes this (see Reid and Barrington, 1999; Stewart, 1999; Harrison, 2000).

A good performance management system should be able to identify and link the development needs of the organization, the group and the individual. This has already been discussed in Chapter 3 and highlighted in subsequent chapters. If HRD is effectively integrated with business objectives, the organizational and departmental objectives should be established at senior management level. It should never be forgotten that the primary purpose of most (if not all) organizations is to maximize performance – however performance may be measured. A number of variables are recognized as having a positive impact on performance, and are thus important in development and change. The following list is adapted from the work of Harrison (2000), and also reflects some of the experiences of the authors:

- *Commitment.* The commitment of individuals to their job and organization in terms of their values and behaviour is crucial in realizing organizational objectives, and must involve both their values and their behaviour.
- *Empowerment and involvement.* The organization will benefit by releasing the untapped reserves of labour resourcefulness, by facilitating responsibility, commitment and involvement. Empowerment is seen as a means of enhancing organizational performance and employee satisfaction simultaneously. However, as Sisson (1995: 72) observes, 'It is a moot point, however, whether it is appropriate to dignify what is going on with the label of "empowerment". "Managed autonomy" is a much better description of what is actually happening'.
- *Leadership.* This has been identified as a key to the high performance organization. Leadership is seen as power to inspire, motivate and fill employees with the desire to change the organization and to be the best. Leaders can act as change role models within the organization.
- *Teamwork.* There has been much emphasis placed upon the notion of 'high performance teams' in recent years. Individuals draw support from colleagues, and in turn give this back. This is a powerful and important motivator, as is evidenced by the earlier references to the importance of teams to the organizational learning and knowledge processes.
- *Culture.* Because culture is a major determinant of organizational behaviour, it is assumed to be instrumental in uniting all employees behind the stated organizational gaols. Whilst it is a powerful force in influencing behaviour, it is notoriously difficult to change; however, it should be the vehicle to facilitate strategic change.
- *Communications.* Good, effective, two-way communications are important in helping to change organizational culture and help people understand how important they are to the future of the organization. Indeed, 'they are

critical in informing, educating and encouraging people to adopt new behaviours' (Holbeche, 1998: 38).

■ *Flexibility.* Flexibility, together with choice of job tasks and use of a wide range of skills, can have a motivating influence on employees whose increased feeling of responsibility can lead to improved performance. However, flexibility needs to be nurtured at all levels of aggregation within the organization, from individual through team to organizational levels.

■ *Learning.* Organizational and individual learning is associated with organizational performance. The emphasis now is on enabling the whole organization to learn on a continuous basis rather than focusing on individual learning. This can only be done in a strategic HRD context.

Unfortunately, organizations have tended to underestimate the importance of employee motivation:

> Many organizations are waking up to the need to address issues of employee motivation, but managers often express a sense of impotence about how to deal with them.
>
> (Holbeche, 1998: 10)

This is one of the key areas where HRD can make a valid and significant contribution to the development of a successful organizational culture; and one of the reasons why the psychological contract is so critical to the effective role of HRD within organizations (Mankin, 2001).

In order to improve performance, supporting initiatives must be implemented in a cohesive and integrated manner. Harrison (2000) says that an organization's employee development programme and performance management system identifies learning needs, since they are derived from:

■ The overall vision of the business, the long- and short-term objectives and strategies and plans to achieve it
■ Characteristics of specific jobs
■ Individuals' job performance and their desired developmental path in the organization in the longer term.

However, it is important to clarify what Harrison means by 'employee development programme'. This has already been outlined in Chapter 3, but is repeated here for clarification. It is not merely a detailed plan of development, which would need constant amendment to ensure it kept pace with change. Instead, an employee development programme refers to the overall activities used by an organization continuously to develop its staff and link with its performance management system. Thus, it is *not* always necessary to have planned learning events, since an organization can promote workplace learning. However, planned events are a core component of an organization's employee development plan. Linking individual needs with an organization's performance management system and its long-term direction is crucial if change is to take place. As Harrison (2000) points out, the PMS must:

■ Be driven by vision, corporate goals and business strategy
■ Ensure that top management communicates the vision, goals and strategies to achieve it.

This communication of business strategy must be linked directly to plans to develop the workforce. Business leaders need to be seen to be acting out, as well as espousing, the values of the organization. Indeed, leaders can also use stories to teach employees what is valued within the organization (Holbeche, 1998). Harrison (2000) indicates however, that this is rarely satisfied because:

■ There is often a direct focus on business performance and output rather than taking the time to develop a learning culture and blame-free discussion of needs
■ The culture required to foster continuous learning does not exist.

Thus, before any real discussion of training needs assessment can take place, it is important to ensure the appropriate underlying culture and link with business objectives exists. However, if these links are not directly apparent, it does *not* mean that training has no value. Under these circumstances, training or other forms of learning activities will not be as beneficial to an organization as it could be.

Activity 7.1

• Outline the key phrases that would describe an organizational culture that would facilitate continuous development. You might find it useful to include some key adjectives in your answer (e.g. two-way communication between senior management and all employees).

The phrases and adjectives you used to describe a culture necessary to facilitate continuous learning might have included openness to new ideas; participative, consultative, encouraging; one that listens, encouraging involvement of all members; one with vision and integrity. Many of these words underpin the concept of the learning organization and mirror the soft HRM approach. The concept of the learning organization was discussed in Chapter 2 as being an organization that facilitates continuous learning and creates an environment in which all its members grow and develop. Example 7.1 highlights one company's innovative attempt to create a learning culture and the associated activities.

Example 7.1: Learning culture and associated activities

A large blue chip organization in the UK has undertaken a large variety of innovative programmes, both formal and informal, in order to break down functional barriers and get people learning. It has called these Anarchic Circles, and they include:

- Business improvement groups – cross-functional groups working on deep-seated organizational problems
- Organizational improvement groups – similar to the above, but focusing on smaller issues and reporting over a shorter time
- A virtual learning centre – an Internet-based learning resource that allows employees to access data on company business initiatives, engage in discussions, contact other staff members and look up other useful websites
- Process mapping – training people to make visual representations on how they do their jobs
- The learning table – a free lunch is given as long as attendees focus their conversation on learning
- Mentoring and shadowing
- Reviewing – by teams at the end of each day
- A regular newsletter with alternating editors, celebrating learning achievements and giving information about future events
- A learning notice board – teams rotate responsibility for this board, which has a different theme every month
- Partnering – pairs of employees who do not normally meet at work have to find each other, introduce themselves and explain what they do.

Training, learning and development should thus be planned and managed within a wider business context. Whatever approach is taken, it is essential to assess human resource development needs at different levels within the organization. This will be considered in detail later in this chapter. At this stage, we will examine more closely the factors that contribute to a shortfall in performance. The following sub-sections deal with HRD needs assessment at different levels of analysis.

Why a shortfall in performance?

Before adopting a training solution, it is important to be satisfied that the actual shortfall in performance is a function of lack of training. If it is not, then the time and effort spent in designing and conducting training or encouraging individuals to learn will be wasted. This part of the chapter examines the factors contributing to effective performance, and explains the importance of identifying those problems that will benefit from a training or learning and development solution.

Stewart (1999) offers an interesting link between organizational objectives and training needs, indicated by two factors:

- Organizational objectives are achieved through the combined activities of individuals, departments and functions. However, people need training to meet their own personally defined objectives.
- If the organization does not meet its stated objectives, it is likely that the department and individual objectives will not be met either.

Therefore, as Harrison (2000) highlights, training, learning and development must take place within an effective performance management system if it is to be most effective – i.e. integrated with the wider business functions and managed strategically. Within a more learning-oriented organizational culture, it is likely that individuals will be better prepared to identify gaps in their own knowledge and performance as well as in others (colleagues and/or subordinates). In such organizations there are likely to be HRD processes and activities in place that attempt to ensure that the performance management system itself is a vehicle for learning and development as much as it is one for measuring and evaluating performance. Again, this reflects the emphasis placed upon process learning in Chapter 2.

The failure to meet organizational objectives could stem from a variety of causes, such as inappropriate strategy, unreliable technology, poor control systems or indeed lack of training and development. Performance management seeks to address such issues in a strategic and integrated manner, rather than assuming that training or self-managed learning will bridge the performance gap. The failure of individuals to meet their personal objectives may indicate a training or learning need. However, the non-attainment of personal goals may not be due to lack of training or self-development. Other reasons may be identified. Thus, training and learning needs are associated with current individual and organizational performance compared to the stated and desired objectives of the business.

Activity 7.2

List the possible reasons, other than lack of training, why an individual may not be performing his job as effectively as he could. Do this from the following perspectives:

- Individual reasons
- Interpersonal reasons
- Organizational reasons.

There is a vast number of reasons why individuals may not perform their job effectively. Some of the reasons may be within an individual in terms of lack of motivation or interest in the job. Others may be due to the individual's relationship with others. Wider reasons also exist in terms of the structure and culture of the organization. We will examine the possible causes at individual, group and organizational levels in much greater detail as we work through this chapter. At this stage, it is important that you understand that training or self-managed learning are only some of the ways of improving individual job performance.

The two factors mentioned above – i.e. achieving organizational objectives and individual objectives (Stewart, 1999) – denote training or learning needs as a 'gap' (Truelove, 1997) between existing capability and that required to achieve performance objectives. This gap is *not* the same as the gap between current and desired performance. This occurs for a variety of reasons (Truelove, 1997).

A performance gap is a training or learning gap *only* if performance will be improved by the development of knowledge, skills and attitudes to close the gap. In this case, the 'gap' would be as in Figure 7.1.

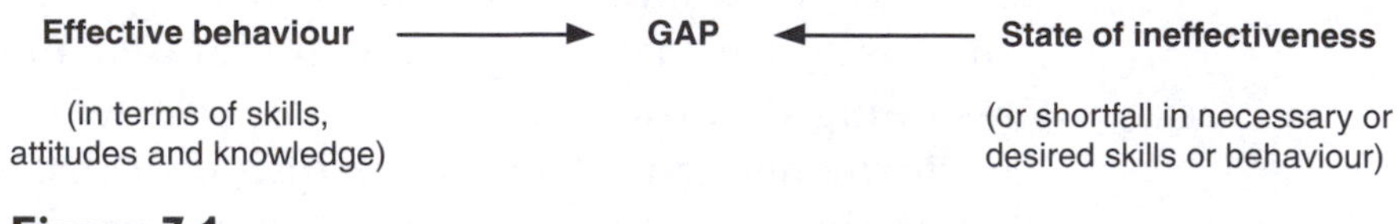

Effective behaviour ⟶ **GAP** ⟵ **State of ineffectiveness**

(in terms of skills, attitudes and knowledge)   (or shortfall in necessary or desired skills or behaviour)

Figure 7.1
The gap between effective behaviour and ineffectiveness.

It is the gap that needs to be bridged, and training is often used to bridge it – or, alternatively, improved self-managed learning and development. However, as we have stated, if the shortfall or gap is *not* due to the deficiency of training or workplace learning *but* due to some other organizational, group or individual factor, then no matter how good a training programme, it will not be effective in terms of improving the performance of the individual. For example, a person may be sent on an assertiveness training course in an attempt to improve his or her ability to gain co-operation from other people. If the difficulty in gaining co-operation is found to be because of a particularly autocratic style on the part of those unco-operative people, then no matter how assertive an individual becomes after training, co-operation is unlikely to be forthcoming.

This example does illustrate the difference between a training-only approach and a broader training, learning and development one in which self-managed or workplace learning may be seen to be a potential alternative to a formal training programme. This is particularly the case where effective group-learning processes are in place and individuals are willing to share their knowledge and experience with each other. In this situation, it might be that there is a learning solution rather than a training one. However, it would be too idealistic to argue that all organizations would be effective in developing learning solutions to all organizational issues.

The manager must ascertain which factors constitute ineffectiveness and then make changes, *maybe* through training or learning and development, but *maybe* by changing other factors in the organization – e.g. the reporting lines, the structure, the way people are rewarded, or how groups work together.

However, many organizations rarely stop to consider the causes of ineffectiveness, and just take yet another training package off the shelf in an attempt to improve the performance of the workforce. Other organizations will seek to identify what can be learnt as a result of the ineffectiveness, and attempt to embed solutions that also prevent a future reoccurrence of the problem.

Traditional assumptions about learning

Various assumptions about learning underpin all training models. It is still a training rationale, rather than a learning one, that underpins much what is happening in organizations – as stated in Chapter 2, the learning organization is still very much an aspirational model rather than a description of organizational reality. Many of these assume that individual effectiveness will improve following training and that improved group and organizational performance follows as a result. However, this may not be the case, particularly if training does not bridge the gap between current and desirable performance. It is useful to examine a commonly used model of training to examine the correct choice of management intervention further. This model makes certain assumptions regarding how individual behaviour will change as a result of some training intervention (see Figure 7.2).

This model assumes that individuals' job performance will improve in line with their enhanced skills, knowledge or behaviour. This, in turn will impact on wider organizational performance. How correct are these assumptions? To what extent can trained individuals influence the wider organization? Often, trained individuals have little power to change systems or performance beyond their own job role. The model might be very effective when minor changes are being made to the ways in which people work (such as using a new software package). However, problems occur when the skills to be changed are more sophisticated (such as leadership skills) and their successful use is influenced by a variety of factors (e.g. organizational culture or structure). Let us examine each stage of this model.

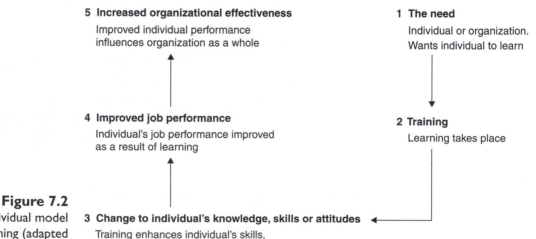

Figure 7.2
The individual model of training (adapted from Bramley, 1991).

5 Increased organizational effectiveness
Improved individual performance influences organization as a whole

1 The need
Individual or organization. Wants individual to learn

4 Improved job performance
Individual's job performance improved as a result of learning

2 Training
Learning takes place

3 Change to individual's knowledge, skills or attitudes
Training enhances individual's skills, knowledge or behaviour

The need

Often training is required because the organization (i.e. the manager) perceives that specific individuals are not doing their job as effectively as they could and that an improvement in their knowledge, skills or behaviour is necessary. Alternatively, a change might occur in the organization that requires a number of individuals attending training (e.g. introducing a new computer system into a department).

Activity 7.3

- List five reasons why an individual's job performance may not improve following a training course.

Numerous reasons might explain why an individual may not benefit from attending a training course, and possible problems existing at this stage in the training process are outlined here (amended from Bramley, 1991).

The individual

The individual may:

- Not be motivated to learn
- Lack the ability to acquire the skills
- Know that necessary equipment will not be available on their return to the workplace
- Feel resistant that the boss considers that he or she is unable to work effectively
- Lack the time to attend training
- Feel that there will not be the opportunity to practise the skills back in the workplace
- Face jealousy back in the workplace
- Find it easier to conform to their previous performance
- Consider that his or her needs and expectations were not taken into account in planning the training
- Find that his or her job is designed in such a way that the new skills are incompatible with the old ones.

As we can see, a number of factors within the individual or their job environment may inhibit the effectiveness with which new skills are acquired during training or used thereafter.

The training

When training is considered, it is often in the form of a training programme. However, closer examination of the particular needs might reveal that a course or workshop is not the most effective way of learning. Giving someone a book to read or sitting that person next to an experienced worker might be more effective than sending him or her on a training course.

Activity 7.4

- List five reasons why a training course may not meet its objective of improving an individual's job performance (e.g. the content of the training is not related to the individual's needs).

There are many reasons why a training course may fail to achieve its objectives. Courses often occur away from the workplace, and may be seen as artificial and lacking the reality of work pressures. Exercises on a training course tend to reflect a rational–logical perspective of organizational life, and encourage participants to 'learn' rational models. The reality of day-to-day life in an organization is very different; it is, messy, ambiguous, full of conflict and riddled with rumour and differences of perspectives. Little wonder that so many participants struggle to transfer logical frameworks and models to such an environment.

A number of problems may occur at this stage in the training process:

- The content and design of training may be inappropriate for the particular need
- Trainees may have little opportunity to practise newly acquired skills
- The trainer may be inexperienced and unable to facilitate effective learning
- The examples given during training may not be relevant to the work in question
- The setting may be artificial, and transfer of newly acquired skills to the workplace may be difficult
- The needs of trainees may differ and the course may be inappropriate for certain members.

Change to individual knowledge, skills and attitudes

The individual model assumes that training will result in some change in individuals in terms of their effectiveness. However, the extent to which there is individual improvement will depend on various factors, including:

- The quality of training
- The motivation of the individual
- The individual's needs.

Personal change within an individual is therefore not necessarily a direct outcome of attending a training course. Even if it does occur, it does not mean that the change will be expressed through behaviours that are beneficial to the organization.

Improvement in job performance

It is often assumed that an individual's job performance will change directly as a result of training.

Activity 7.5

- List five reasons why an individual's job performance may not change as a result of attending a training course (e.g. colleagues may resist the individual's new approach to work).

There are many reasons why job performance does not improve following attendance on a training course. Individuals might find it difficult to demonstrate their new skills in their work environment. They may lack the necessary equipment, or face resentment from colleagues who did not attend training. Numerous factors exist in the working environment that may inhibit the use of newly acquired skills or attitudes. It therefore does not follow that changes within an individual are expressed in desirable improvements to job performance.

Increased organizational effectiveness

It is often assumed that the cumulative effect of training impacts on the organizational performance as a whole. The belief that sufficiently well-trained individuals will collectively impact on

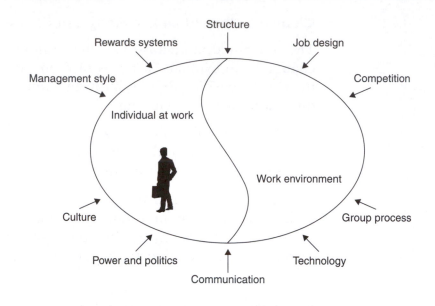

Figure 7.3
Factors affecting
individual job
performance
(*source:* Training &
Development
Module, 1999;
Unpublished
materials from the
Open Learning
Foundation).

organizational productivity is often unfounded. The same argument exists following individual change and improved job performance. However, many training programmes are chosen on the basis that they will eventually impact on enhanced organizational performance. Possible factors that inhibit this will be examined in greater detail in Figure 7.3. Indeed, as indicated in Chapter 2, this same assumption is replicated in much of the literature on organizational learning and the learning organization.

Factors influencing improved job performance

Many factors influence an individual's job performance. It will be useful at this stage for you to list possible influences to clarify your understanding of organizational dynamics.

Activity 7.6

List two possible influences on an individual's work performance under the following three headings:

- Influences within the individual; e.g. motivation
- Influences within the individual's immediate working environment – e.g. adequate equipment
- Broader organizational influences – e.g. the vision and values of the company.

There are many influences on job performance. Some of these exist within individuals and relate to their ability, style of working or attitudes. Others arise from their immediate working environment and include their relationship with others, their roles and work experiences. Broader organizational influences include the organizational structure, culture, management style and values. These may exert enormous influence on how individuals perceive their role or perform their job. Figure 7.3 illustrates the many factors that may impinge on an individual's job performance.

A number of influences within individuals and their immediate environment were identified when we evaluated the individual model of training. From the figure, let us consider some of the wider organizational influences on individual performance, all of which are powerful determinants of job performance.

Organizational structure

The pattern of relationships between the different roles and functions in a company can be seen in the organizational chart. A newly trained individual may find it difficult to demonstrate his or her new skills because of the formal authority and behaviour of those in different roles.

For example, an individual who returns from an assertiveness training course might demand a report from someone in a different department. Although the recently trained individual might be willing to demonstrate newly acquired skills, success depends on the response of someone else. If that person resists this request, believing that his or her role does not require direct co-operation with the individual, or provision of reports, the person may fall back on the structure by referring it to a direct boss, thus delaying the report. If the aim of the assertiveness training course was to facilitate a speedy collection of regular reports, it will have been unsuccessful. Changes to the structure, communication mechanisms and working systems will need to take place if co-operation is to occur.

Organizational culture

The shared norms, values, attitudes and behaviour operating within an organization or department are major determinants of people's behaviour. A highly bureaucratic culture, for instance, may resist any intervention to modify behaviour in terms of customers' treatment, pace of work, relationships between bosses and workers etc.

A manager has to consider the culture in which people work before planning training, because a mismatch in the cultural expectations of working behaviour and the course can inhibit behavioural change back in the workplace. For example, newly acquired customer care skills may be difficult to implement in an organization that is resistant to innovative ways of working. The individual who tries to use these skills to improve customer relations may find others are resistant to the changes, or systems within the organization do not support such initiatives.

Rewards systems

Many rewards and incentives are available for individuals at work. Some of these are financial, including pay, benefits and perks. Others are psychological, and include recognition, autonomy, status, job satisfaction and social support. How these systems operate has implications for the effectiveness of training. For example, an individual returning with newly acquired skills who feels unfairly rewarded in terms of more money or recognition may feel de-motivated and, as a result, fail to demonstrate the new skills.

Job design

The way a job is designed in terms of its pace, the variety of tasks and the timing of activities has implications for the effective use of newly acquired skills. For instance, imagine a person has been sent on a customer care training course and is now working on the reception of a busy leisure centre. The customer care training programme might have trained the receptionist to do the following:

- Answer the phone within three rings
- Attend to each visitor within 1 minute of their arrival
- Avoid keeping customers waiting more than 4 minutes
- Make an entry on the ISO 9000 quality form in respect of each customer.

Whilst the purpose of these activities might be to improve the quality of customer care, it may be impossible to achieve the individual tasks on some occasions. In the leisure centre, it is possible that the phone may ring, three customers arrive and an accident occurs in the reception area simultaneously, thus preventing the individual tasks from being achieved. The combination of these demands makes it impossible for the receptionist to implement his or her new skills meaningfully. There might therefore be the need for some changes in how the job is designed in order to achieve improved customer care in the leisure centre. Lack of practice and inefficient equipment that is incompatible with the new skills might also inhibit effectiveness. Often it is easier for an individual to revert to their old ways of working.

Group processes

After training, an individual returns to the workplace where he or she is part of a formal working group. Relationships are usually formed with certain members, who develop their own values and norms of behaviour. This 'informal' influence exerts enormous pressure on individuals to conform to the group norms and patterns of behaviour. An individual who returns from the course may face pressure to conform to the previous way of working because the others, especially if they have not been on the course, believe that the older ways are preferable.

Conformity often occurs, as the individual reverts to the old means of carrying out his or her role. In addition, jealousy might occur where some have been trained and not others, and their resistance to the new ways (or to the individual personally) might inhibit the display of the more effective behaviour.

Power and politics

Some sources of power may be legitimate and embodied within the structure and authority systems of an organization. Others exist outside the blueprint of the organization and can be defined as politics. In essence, people do not leave their careers to chance, or to the belief in rational organizational decision-making (Buchanan and Huczynski, 2004). Instead they engage in a range of behaviours that increase their power base. Power and politics exert an enormous influence on the way in which people carry out their work, the relationships they make and the decisions they take. It is outside the remit of this text to examine power in greater detail, but it is important to note the determining influence on organizational behaviour (see Morgan, 1998).

Activity 7.7

Think of a job you have held or currently hold. If you have not held a job before, ask a colleague or friend for an example.

- Place yourself at the centre of Figure 7.3 (Factors affecting individual performance), and list the factors that you consider currently have a negative effect on your performance.
- Which of these factors do you feel could be resolved through a training and development solution?
- Which factors could be resolved partially through a training and development solution?
- Which factors do you feel have a non-training solution?

Your answer to this activity will depend on your own job situation and experiences. However, some key issues arise. One of the unfortunate features of many organizations is the lack of awareness and attention to some of the factors that contribute to poor performance. Instead of considering a problem carefully and dispassionately, many managers are content to terminate the employment of a poor performer or assume that the answer to the problem is a training intervention. At some stage of the analysis, of course, a training need may emerge. When this happens, the organization is faced with a choice of action. It could:

- Design a custom-built training activity specifically to suit the needs of the individual
- Place the individual in an already well-established internal training activity
- Send the individual on an external training activity.

Owing to the unique nature of each individual's training and development needs, it is difficult for a single organization to provide all the necessary facilities and opportunities from within itself. Only very large organizations are able to design and run cost-effective training activities for groups with similar needs, and only these organizations are able to employ sufficiently skilled trainers to run the programmes effectively. In most circumstances learning is carried out by the individual either alone (as in distance learning) or in an external learning environment (such as a course).

The increased effectiveness model of training

From the above discussion, it is clear that training may *not* be an effective way of improving organizational, group or individual performance. This does not mean that training has no advantages. Indeed, the benefits of training can be enormous, and include, for example:

- Increased motivation of workers
- Recognition
- Enhanced responsibility
- Implications for pay and promotion
- Personal satisfaction
- Opportunities for career progression
- Improved quality and availability of staff.

However, the manager has to consider very carefully what he or she is trying to achieve through training, and decide how to bridge the gap between desirable performance and current performance. Sometimes training is the answer to improving individual performance and, ultimately, organizational effectiveness. Close examination of the problems will highlight other factors that need addressing, either solely or in conjunction with a training programme. Effective performance management systems integrate human resource development strategically in a systematic and holistic way. Training, learning and development is part of that process, as is the development of a learning culture. Once training and development has been decided upon, a more operational approach is necessary.

An alternative to the individual model is the increased effectiveness model (Bramley, 1991). This comprises a number of decision-making steps that should be made by a manager in order to ascertain the gap between desirable and current performance. The steps are shown in Figure 7.4.

In working through these stages, the manager must to ask a number of questions, including:

1 What do I (or the organization) want to achieve?
2 How will I know it has been achieved once an intervention is made?

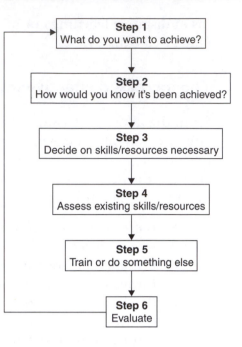

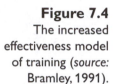

Figure 7.4
The increased effectiveness model of training (*source:* Bramley, 1991).

3   What skills/resources will be necessary to achieve my aim (i.e. the desired performance)?
4   What are the current skills/resources (i.e. human performance)?
5   What do I need to do to bridge the gap – train, or change something else in the organization?
6   How can I evaluate success? This will only be possible if I ascertain what desirable performance looks like.

The two models presented make very different theoretical assumptions regarding how people learn and the influences on their performance. The individual model of training is limited because it assumes that the changes in the trained individual translate effectively into the workplace. It takes no account of the wider influences on effective performance.

The stages of the increased effectiveness model allow the manager to pinpoint the problem areas, and to decide whether training will bridge the gap or whether some other organizational issue should be addressed. Note that evaluation of training is only possible if Step 2 has been considered. Step 2 indicates that clear criteria must be developed against which subsequent change will be measured, and is an essential stage if interventions are to be meaningfully evaluated.

The increased effectiveness model is a useful model to use in a strategic HRD context. Because it considers the many reasons for a shortfall in effective performance, it places training within a wider business context. It is thus a more valuable approach than the individual model of training, and identifies those organizational problems that may be solved by a training solution and those that may not.

Methods of assessing needs

Assessing needs at different levels of analysis

There is a variety of methods or techniques that can be used to help to assess or identify training, learning and development needs. Which ones are used will vary from organization to organization, and will often be determined by the nature of the organization's culture. Commonly used methods include:

- Interviews
- Observation
- Self-assessment.

Traditionally, trainers have favoured using the above methods as part of a job analysis approach which involves analysing the job description and specification, and arriving at a training specification following the detailed study of how an individual carries out the various tasks required to do the job. As organizations attempt to develop a learning culture, the emphasis shifts from someone else (e.g. trainer) carrying out an analysis on the individual to the individual carrying out some form of self-analysis (or assessment) with support from the line manager or HRD specialist. In this context, the process can be described as a learning needs analysis rather than a training needs analysis.

The growth in emphasis on the concepts of organizational learning and knowledge management now reinforce the need to view team needs as something more than the sum total of all the individual needs within a team. Consequently, it is important to consider team or group learning needs in more holistic fashion.

We will briefly identify these in turn before discussing how exactly needs may be analysed at the respective levels.

Organization level needs

HRD needs often exist across the organization as a whole. For example, a change in legislation to limit working hours to 48 hours per week in Europe has communication and training implications for the organization as a whole. An assessment of the organization's needs is an essential precursor to any HRD intervention. Stewart (1999) suggests that it is useful to think of needs as being of two types:

1   Those arising from collective needs identified at individual and job level
2   The knowledge, skills and attitudes which all members, irrespective of their job, are required to develop, due to:
    ■ policy change
    ■ objectives
    ■ new technology
    ■ new legislation.

Team level needs

As the motivation to learn can vary so much from individual to individual, it is important to identify and develop shared goals. Within a team context, individuals can give each other mutual support and assist with achieving team synergy, thereby enhancing the quality of learning achieved by each member. This perspective reflects the constructivist theories, in which the learner is central to the learning process and uses explicit knowledge and interaction with other people to arrive at a shared understanding (Reynolds *et al.*, 2002). This moves beyond a more traditional perspective in which team level needs have often been described in terms of 'teambuilding' or 'teamworking'; thought to be resolved by formal training interventions (e.g. the classic outdoor teambuilding course).

Job level needs

Effective job performance depends on a complex set of factors. A number of training needs arise from the job itself, and close examination of the job identifies how training needs arise as a function of changes in job requirements and working environments. We have already seen the wider interrelated factors that may inhibit or facilitate an individual's performance (see Figure 7.3).

One set of factors that indicates training needs, regardless of the jobholder, includes:

- Knowledge
- Skills
- Attitudes.

Thus, a specification of what an individual needs to know and do indicates the training needs at the job level, regardless of the jobholder. It is important here to recognize that 'skills' may be categorized in a variety of ways – for instance, cognitive, perceptual and motor (Craig, 1994).

Individual level needs

Individual needs exist to the extent to which there is a 'gap' between the knowledge, skills and attitudes currently held by the individual, and those specified by the job.

A useful model from Vinton *et al.* (1983) contains all three levels of analysis (see Figure 7.5).

This is a useful framework when focusing solely on training needs. It links training needs analyses with organizational goals. The process begins by examining the performance of the organization, or a part of it. If this suggests a possible training need, then the group of jobs in the area under review is examined. This may lead to an analysis of the individuals in post to discover whether training is likely to change the current level of performance into one that is nearer the optimal level for the job. At all three levels of analysis, alternative solutions are considered.

Whilst this is a simple model, it is one that is included, in principle, in many PMS and HRD approaches. Whilst the focus may be on training needs, the outcomes/solutions may embrace self-managed learning or team learning. We will now look more closely at identifying HRD needs at these three levels.

Organizational level needs

A number of factors within organizations indicate the need for HRD interventions. Some of these are in direct response to the business activities, and others are in response to internal and external change.

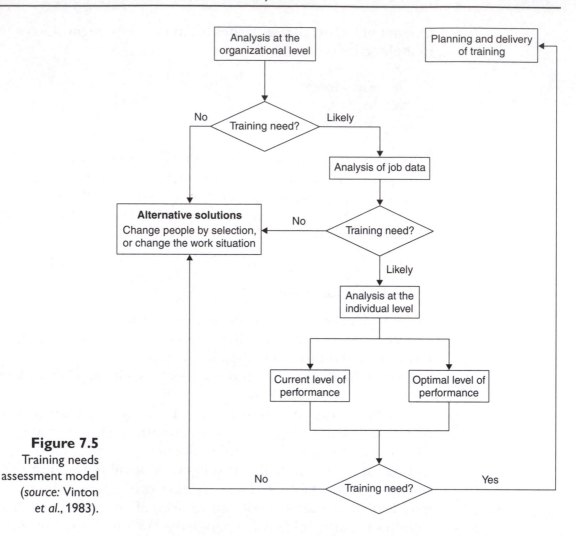

Figure 7.5
Training needs
assessment model
(*source:* Vinton
et al., 1983).

Activity 7.8

• Make a list of the organizational activities and processes that might indicate HRD needs at the organizational level (e.g. long and short business objectives).

Identifying organizational HRD needs involves a review of organizational activities – for example:

■ Long and short-term business objectives
■ Major changes in the organization's activities
■ Ensuring strategic requirements are met

- Defining competencies
- Benchmarking
- Linking HRD and PMS
- Responding to social, political and economic changes affecting the business.

Stewart (1999) outlines the extent and range of information needed to assess HRD needs under two main headings:

1   *Hard data*, which includes a range of information produced by management information systems, such as:
    - productivity reports
    - market share
    - labour turnover.
2   *Soft data*, which includes individual and collective beliefs, values, opinions and predictions. Interviews, focus groups and feedback from team meetings will provide a rich source of information about organizational HRD needs.

Activity 7.9

Think about the types of data that an organization can gather under the headings of *hard* and *soft* data.

- Do you feel that the data from these two different categories are separate or linked in some way? Make some notes to support your answer. (For example, labour turnover statistics may indicate an increase in labour turnover. This may be linked to some other organizational changes, and indicate increased levels of dissatisfaction, lack of training etc.)

Whilst data regarding organizational activities can be divided into hard and soft categories, the data gathered are closely connected. These two categories of information are not mutually exclusive. For example, an organization may try to gain objective statistical information from the workforce in the form of an attitude survey. Whilst the results can be presented in statistical form, they do, of course, have major 'soft' implications. For example, results may indicate dissatisfaction with working hours, or unhappiness regarding management style or culture in the organization.

A useful model for integrating these two sets of data to ascertain organizational HRD needs is presented by Stewart (1999; see Figure 7.6).

Thus, an organizational review is a precursor to identifying organizational and later job and individual HRD needs. This assessment of organizational needs can identify a number of organizational problems for which a job-specific, formal or informal learning solution can be identified for individuals and groups. Reid and Barrington (1999) offer a useful system process for identifying training needs at the organizational level (see Figure 7.7).

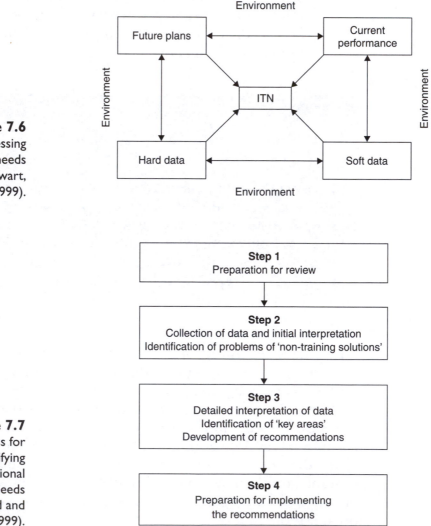

Figure 7.6
Assessing organizational needs (*source:* Stewart, 1999).

Figure 7.7
System process for identifying organizational training needs (*source:* Reid and Barrington, 1999).

For a more thorough outline of the actual details of this process, see Reid and Barrington (1999: 165).

Job level needs

There are many different approaches that can be taken to analyse actual jobs and the training, learning and development necessary to perform that job well. The traditional approach was to consider job requirements in terms of knowledge, skills and attitudes (KSAs), and to define behaviourally the objectives specifying what a 'trainee' should be able to do at the end of a training activity. Since the 1980s, the competence approach and use of NVQs has taken a slightly different perspective and employed different terms and methodology.

In order to identify job level needs, it is essential to conduct what is traditionally described as a job training analysis (JTA) in which the purpose of the job under consideration is identified and the job is then 'broken down into a number of tasks and procedures. The skills, knowledge, and perhaps attitudes and values required to carry out tasks are then identified' (Boydell and Leary, 1996: 175). The aim of the JTA is to identify what must be learnt by the jobholder in order for an improvement in his or her performance. Harrison (2000) observes that a key outcome of any JTA is usually a job training specification, which enables learning objectives to be established and appropriate HRD solutions to be designed.

There are many different approaches and techniques for conducting a JTA. Figure 7.8 demonstrates an amalgam of best practice.

Let us consider each stage in Figure 7.8 in turn, and the points that arise at each stage.

1   *Gain co-operation of all concerned*:
    - Do all individuals understand what a JTA is?
    - Has it been explained why a JTA is being conducted?
    - Have any concerns that individuals may have been identified and addressed?
2   *Initial investigation*:
    - What is the cost to the organization of not addressing the performance problem?
    - Is there enough information already to make a JTA unnecessary?

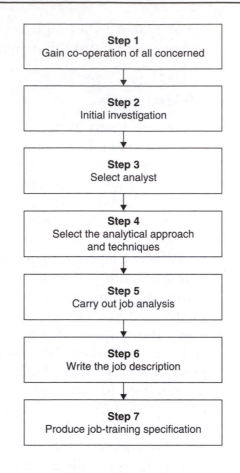

Figure 7.8
Seven-step strategy for conducting job training analysis (*source:* Harrison, 2000).

- Is training really the answer?
- Is training the most cost-beneficial answer?
- Are there specific incentives for individuals if training is given for this task?
- Is analysis really necessary?
- Is the job likely to change?
- Should the person be adapted to the job, or the job to the person?

3 *Select the analyst:*
- Should a specialist or line manager do the job?
- If done by a specialist, this may uncover other issues that inhibit effective performance.

4 *Select the analytical approach and techniques:* Stages 1–3 enable the analyst to decide the approach and techniques to choose. There are many techniques available (these will be discussed in detail later in this chapter).

5　*Carry out job analysis*: Harrison stresses the need to address both the sources of information to be gathered and the depth of analysis required:

■ *Sources of information* may be written or oral. Written sources include job descriptions and performance records of problems in performance where the norm indicates good standards of performance are achieved. Trends in turnover, sickness etc. may indicate difficulties in conducting jobs. Oral sources of information can be gathered from a wide range of people, including the jobholder and his or her line manager and colleagues, as well as internal and/or external customers, and suppliers. It is important to note that perceptions and the order of priorities may differ. The analyst will need highly developed interpersonal and political skills to gather effective information.

■ *Depth of analysis required* needs an answer to the question: How much information is needed? The social and work environment needs to be identified, together with the inhibiting factors that might affect application of later learning. It is important that any learning event or intervention prepares the individual for his or her return to work.

6　*Write the job description*: At this stage a new job description should be written, rather than simply relying on amending the old one.

7　*Produce job training specification*: Reid and Barrington's (1999: 165) definition of a JTS finalizes this seven-stage process. 'The job training specification describes in overall terms the job for which training is to be given or the key problem areas in a job which training will enable learners to tackle; it then specifies the kinds and levels of knowledge, skill and, where relevant, attitudes needed for effective performance, together with the standards that will operate in the job and the criteria for measuring achievement of standards.'

Job training analysis approaches

There is a wide number of approaches available, all of which can be used for job analysis for selection and other resourcing options. However, a JTA focuses on training requirements. Pearn and Kandola (1990) offer over 18 different job analysis approaches. (For a more comprehensive discussion of JTA, see Mills, Pace and Peterson, 1988; Boydell and Leary, 1996; Hackett, 1997; Reid and Barrington, 1999.) Probably the most popular, as discussed by Reid and Barrington (1999) and Stewart (1999), are as follows:

1 *Comprehensive analysis.* This approach is highly analytical and time-consuming, and comprises a detailed examination of all facets of a job. Each aspect of the job is identified in terms of the knowledge, skills and attitudes required for effective performance. Because it is time-consuming, it is really only necessary where a new job has been created or where a highly prescriptive job performance is required. A job description and job training specification is designed from the analysis to identify the KSAs necessary to achieve the tasks and sub-tasks. This information is then used to design appropriate training interventions.

2 *Key task analyses.* This approach identifies critical or core job tasks essential to competent performance. It is used for jobs which are more complex, and where there is greater discretion and change in terms of the pace, variety, problem-solving or decision-making – e.g. a university lecturer or marketing director. Key task analysis is useful in analysing managerial jobs or those requiring reflection, creativity, analysis and problem-solving. Instead of analysing the entire job, the essential tasks are identified to produce a job description and job training specification. These are expressed in general terms such as:
    ■ tasks crucial to competent job performance
    ■ objectives and targets
    ■ key areas to be covered.

3 *Problem-centred analysis.* This approach focuses on the difficulties encountered (or likely to be encountered) for which a training solution is required. For example, certain managers in a company may require specific help on improving their presentation skills or report writing. This method is often used with key task analysis. The analysis frequently reveals common training needs for all or a certain number of staff. The approach has the

benefit of gaining commitment because the jobholders analyse their own problems and needs.

4   *Competence-based approaches.* These approaches have grown in popularity for a range of managerial and non-managerial functions. They were originally developed to identify how young trainees could be given organizational learning experiences that could be transferred to other organizations. Such early approaches culminated in:

■ occupational training families
■ key competencies
■ transferable learning objectives.

Management competencies can be seen from either an input or output perspective:

■ the input perspective identifies the individual characteristics that individuals bring to the job and are necessary to perform effectively
■ the output perspective focuses on what high performers achieve – the NVQ approach.

(See Hayes *et al.*, 1983 for a fuller explanation.) A competence-based approach is highly useful for identifying training needs. Performance standards for one or more occupational groups can be defined. In addition, core behavioural attributes can be identified across a job sector. Such analysis is, of course, used when training needs are required to relate to NVQ training standards and qualifications, and identifies:

■ Job or role requirements
■ Competence required for different aspects of the job
■ Competence in each area
■ Behaviour definitions of the competencies necessary to perform well.

Activity 7.10

• Take each of the four job training analysis approaches (comprehensive, key task, problem-centred, competence-based). For each of them, give three examples of jobs for which they would be most suited in terms of analysing job training needs. Give reasons for your answers.

You may have found this quite a difficult task, since the depth and range of information may be a function of the organizational context of a particular job. The type of job training analysis might therefore vary for the same jobs in different organizations. The size, competition and prevailing social and economic context may dictate very different demands on the job holder.

Comprehensive analysis comprises an in-depth investment into an individual's job. An air traffic controller's job may need to be explicitly defined in order to ascertain training, since any mistakes in certain procedures or performance may have far-reaching consequences.

Key task analysis identifies critical job tasks rather than outlining specific details of actual demands. The job of university lecturer would lend itself well to key task analysis, since the role contains a high degree of discretion and autonomy. Key objectives must be achieved within broad parameters, but the lecturer has enormous discretion in the choice of the methods, content and teaching style used to facilitate student learning.

Problem-centred analysis may be used for a range of jobs – e.g. newly promoted managers whose new role entails tasks not previously encountered, such as report writing or maintaining a budget. An accountant's role may suddenly demand a larger degree of people management, or a secretary may have to learn the skills of budgetary control. Each of these new demands represents potential problems to be overcome, and problem-centred analysis is a useful tool to identify individual and collective training needs.

A number of job roles can benefit from competence-based approaches to training needs analysis. For example, bank clerks, teachers, engineers and marketing professionals have jobs that indicate levels of competence essential at different levels of seniority. By identifying the actual behaviours necessary to indicate effective performance at different levels, decisions can be made regarding those that indicate a training need.

Analysing human resource development needs of groups and teams

The importance of groups in the sharing of knowledge and development of learning processes has already been discussed. With the increasing use of teamwork in organizations, it is important to ascertain a group's effectiveness in terms of task achievement and interactions between group members. This question raises another important issue of training needs analysis. Much research has been carried out in this area, and various methods, including questionnaires, have been devised to identify individual styles and skills within a team. The correct mix of skills is essential if the benefits of group working are to outweigh those of separate individuals. An analogy can be with a team game like football. In this game, players develop special skills and become good at playing in certain positions depending on their height, weight, speed, reaction time, ball skill etc. The requirements of each position are so different that players skilled in one position would be quite ineffective in another. In the same way, a task group needs a diversity of skills and knowledge. If the diversity can be managed and built on, the group's achievements are likely to be greater than those of a group of people who are all very similar. In both cases, the ability and willingness to co-operate with the others for the good of the team are the overriding requirements. Compatibility with colleagues is therefore very important, particularly if the task is complex.

A number of different studies have been carried out on the different roles, styles and skills within teams (see Adair, 1996; Anderson and West, 1994). These can be useful as job training analysis techniques to assess and develop interpersonal relationships and teamwork. Examples include Belbin's (1981) team-type inventory and Anderson and West's (1994) team climate inventory. These are briefly discussed here.

Belbin's team-type inventory

Belbin's (1981) original research suggested that the most effective teams exist where eight team-roles (or useful types of contribution) exist. The eight key team-roles are:

1 Company worker – a practical organizer
2 Chairman – a coordinator of efforts
3 Shaper – outgoing and dominant; the task leader
4 Plant – most creative and intelligent, but introverted; ideas' person
5 Resource investigator – the most popular salesman or diplomat; Mr Fix-it
6 Monitor-evaluator – analytically rather than creatively intelligent
7 Team worker – supportive, uncompetitive; mediator

8   Completer finisher – checks details, worries about deadlines, chivvies others.

Since then a ninth role, the Specialist, has been added.

Belbin developed a self-perception inventory for individuals to assess their preferred team role/s. His theory holds that an individual's personality predisposes him or her to prefer to play certain roles. Belbin's (1993) later work renamed certain roles (i.e. Co-ordinator replaced Chairman, and Implementer replaced Company worker). This was done for reasons of acceptability. The most significant change is the addition of a ninth role, that of Specialist. This role was added because of the increasing importance of the professional expertise so important in project work.

The Belbin self-perception inventory can be a very effective job training analysis technique. It can be used as a yardstick against which individuals can analyse their particular preferences and behaviour in groups. It can also be used to understand other people's reactions and behaviour, and related team dynamics.

Example 7.2 outlines a training workshop using Belbin team-type roles to identify individual and group team dynamics and potential training gaps.

Example 7.2: Identifying group training needs using the Belbin's team-type inventory (BTTI)

In the early 1990s, a large public relations and advertising company in the UK employed an occupational psychologist to conduct a teambuilding workshop to identify issues inhibiting the optimum performance of their senior management team. The 1-day workshop used the BTTI together with a variety of problem-solving exercises. The individual styles of team members and the dynamics and interactions of this intact team were identified.

Members completed the BTTI prior to the workshop. A series of problem-solving exercises were given to members for solution requiring the agreement of all directors. This exercise was videoed and played back to the team after the task was completed. Prior to seeing their interactions on video, the individual team roles were discussed with the members. The implications of missing roles and an overemphasis on certain team role behaviours were discussed. A playback of the video was used to demonstrate different behaviours, many of which were compatible with the reported team role types. Discussion was then able to take place regarding individual contributions to the team, and sources of miscommunication and misinterpretation of others' behaviour.

By using the team role model as a basis for discussion and interpretation of behaviour, members were better able to appreciate the contributions of their colleagues. They could establish ways in which they could change their own behaviour and reactions for the overall benefit of team. Thus, the team-type inventory, together with facilitated problem-solving exercises, provided an excellent means of identifying individual and group training needs. Because the members comprised the senior management team, the culture, structure and political environment in which decisions were made could also be addressed.

Anderson and West's team climate inventory

The team climate inventory (TCI) is a multidimensional measure of work group climate. In trying to define climate, Anderson and West (1994) refer to Reichers and Schneider's (1990) definition: 'Climate is widely defined as the shared perception of "the way things are around here". More precisely, climate is shared perceptions of organizational policies, practices and procedures, both formal and informal'. This definition may appear very similar to that of organizational culture. Whilst the two concepts are interrelated, climate, with its shared perceptions by members, is more open to change over shorter periods and quickly indicates levels of morale, commitment and motivation in an organization. The TCI measures climate in terms of the different aspects of working together that the team has evolved, which include:

- Communication patterns – how team members interact with one another, and the structure and style of team meetings
- Participation – the level of participation team members have in decision-making and other group activities
- Safety – how much interpersonal trust there is in the team, and how safe individuals feel as a team
- Cohesiveness – how cohesive the team perceives itself to be, and how cohesive it is perceived to be by others outside the team
- Task style – how the team typically goes about tasks in hand, and how it pursues the accomplishment of team objectives
- Vision – the team's overriding objectives and targets as specified in the 'vision' or 'mission' statement
- Innovativeness – how creative the team is in developing new and improved ways of doing things.

The TCI can be used as a useful job training analysis technique to identify team climate and dynamics. Belbin's (1981) work has been criticized in terms of role holders becoming typecast. The TCI, on the other hand, may be a more useful tool than Belbin's because it provides a more thorough analysis of team atmosphere or climate within the group, essential for effective team functioning. It would be an excellent JTA technique to use within a culture of continuous development. Identifying training needs with the TCI is possible with a similar workshop scenario mentioned in the previous example using Belbin team-type roles.

Individual human resource development needs analysis

A wide number of methods exist to assess an individual's ability to perform a job effectively, and to identify the gap between effective and current performance for which a training solution will contribute to closing the gap. A manager or HRD specialist can question individuals about their job, their problems or perceived learning needs. Observation can also be used to investigate work methods or work flows. Where simple observation fails to yield clear results, HRD specialists may need to devise special tests. Another source of information is internal records of performance or production output. Such data must be analysed to identify patterns and trends. Here, we consider four approaches:

1   Performance appraisal
2   Development centres
3   Self-assessment
4   Psychometric testing.

Performance appraisal

Performance appraisal is a means of rating individual performance, highlighting performance shortfalls and development needs. In many companies it is something that happens to employees, rather than being a process in which the individual plays a valued and important part. However, if it is to be a valuable performance management tool, it should be seen also as a means of motivating the individual and gaining commitment and identification with the organization and departmental goals. Often appraisals fail because they seek to meet too many objectives. Where appraisals attempt to identify training needs together with pay increases, they fail to have any developmental value at all (Fletcher, 2004). In order to overcome this, separate appraisals are often held to address these very different objectives. Appraisals may take a number of forms:

- *Self-assessment,* where individuals assess themselves against rating criteria or targeted objectives
- *Peer assessment,* where fellow team members, colleagues selected or others with whom the individual works provide assessments of the individual's performance

■ *Line management,* where the employee's immediate supervisor provides the assessment

■ *Upward appraisal,* which is a rare form of appraisal (but one that is growing increasingly popular) whereby managers are appraised by their staff

■ *360-degree feedback,* where different groups within the work situation appraise an individual. These different groups may include peers, subordinates as well as bosses and, possibly, internal and external customers.

Activity 7.11

- Consider each of the forms of appraisal set out below:
  - self-assessment
  - peer assessment
  - line management
  - upward-appraisal
  - 360-degree feedback
- List the advantages of using each method, and the potential limitations in terms of assessing individual training needs.

There are a number of advantages and disadvantages of using different methods of performance appraisal for assessing training and development needs:

■ Self-assessment allows individuals to reflect on their own needs and HRD requirements, and may identify needs of which only they are aware. Individuals are also likely to be more motivated to undertake any training or self-managed learning that occurs as a result of the appraisal. However, they may identify needs that directly relate to training or learning they would *prefer to* undertake, rather than training or learning that is essential in terms of their effective job performance.

■ Peer assessment may be a valuable means by which colleagues and fellow workers can highlight individuals' HRD needs. Individuals may feel more comfortable discussing their needs with colleagues rather than with managers, who might use the information for wider assessment purposes. Individuals who feel that a manager's assessment might influence other decisions (e.g. promotion or pay awards) might not be as willing to admit to limitations in their current job performance.

■ Appraisal by an immediate line manager may be a useful means of identifying HRD needs. To a large extent, this depends on the quality of the manager–subordinate relationship. If the relationship is a good one, HRD needs may be discussed within the wider context of the job and future development. The joint decision-making will also ensure commitment and support for training or learning solutions from both sides. However, if the relationship between the manager and subordinate is not a good one, there may be distrust, lack of support and apathy towards future individual HRD plans.

■ Upward appraisal is a rare form of appraisal that often reflects a culture of openness and participation. It encourages subordinates to offer feedback to their manager in terms of that manager's style and the support and direction needed for future development. It is probably very valuable if the culture supports such openness, but can lead to distrust and cynicism if such openness is not reflected in other aspects of organizational performance. As a means of analysing HRD needs, it may be a useful way for individuals to identify joint training or learning needs but, because of its nature, is highly politically sensitive.

■ 360-degree appraisal is designed to enable all the stakeholders in an employee's performance to comment and give feedback (Ward, 1997). These stakeholders include colleagues, subordinates, managers, peers and internal or external customers. 360-degree appraisal is considered to be the only means of comprehensively revealing how successful individuals are in their work relationships. It shows what individuals think about their own strengths and weaknesses, compared with what others think, as well as identifying areas for development. Therefore it is a balanced process that can be used at any level of the organization.

Most 360-degree instruments examine a number of specific competencies or skill areas with detailed questions or items stemming from each one. Some companies have developed their own competencies and are finding that their own 360-degree instruments are an excellent way of measuring the extent to which people perform against them.

The resulting feedback can be presented in a number of ways. One way is to examine what the individual does now and compare it to what the respondents actually would like to see. There are a number of sources of feedback, which include the boss, direct reports, peers, customers and the individual's own self-assessment. Most participants, from companies, who are successfully using the 360-degree feedback methods, have suggested that they have never experienced such powerful and apparently insightful feedback about their performance.

One of the key principles of 360-degree feedback is that people see you differently. Some people receive uncomfortable surprises on receiving feedback and may need help to benefit from the information. A trained internal or external facilitator should handle feedback and this also may involve training line managers in facilitation skills. Consequently the 360-degree approach can be used in a number of areas to improve training and development. For example, self-development can be encouraged where the employee takes responsibility for their own learning at all times in the workplace. In addition, HRD specialists can analyse the feedback to target training efforts where they are most needed (Ward, 1997).

The use of the 360-degree is increasing in the UK, and it is set to become a very popular and important measurement tool whenever companies need accurately and comprehensively to assess competency in given areas of performance. Organizations are becoming increasingly innovative in the use of performance appraisal to develop staff. Squires and Adler (1998) highlight that large organizations are currently conducting developmentally oriented appraisals outside the normal performance appraisal process. Example 7.3 identifies how innovative organizations can be.

Example 7.3: The use of performance appraisal for development purposes

A large American computer company developed an innovative means of preparing managers for the changes facing them in the twenty-first century. A 4-hour simulation of a 'Year in the Life of the Senior Executive' appraised effective change leadership skills. Restructuring, downsizing, emerging marketplace opportunities and staff movement typified the executives' experience.

contd

Example 7.3   *contd*

A team of external assessors appraised the executives' change leadership skills during the simulation. The diagnosis included an analysis of competency strength and weakness of each type of change situation encountered, and as such was far more detailed than the typical skill appraisal.

Following a feedback session, a 6-month skill development plan was developed for the executives, who then worked closely with a coach to improve their change leadership skills. Developmental activities include formal training, standard resources (books, videotapes) and on-the-job action learning (experimentation and reflection).

(Source: Squires and Adler, 1998)

In a very large number of appraisals, the immediate supervisor provides the assessment with the comments added by the supervisor's own manager. Appraisal forms are used to rate the individual's performance in line with required goals. Management assessments tend to feature results-oriented criteria, typically against objectives agreed at the beginning of the year.

Of course, to be truly effective it is crucial for performance appraisal to form part of a wider performance management system (Armstrong and Baron, 1998). Objective setting and general appraisal is at the heart of PMS, where individual goals and responsibilities are linked to departmental objectives and the business as a whole.

More junior staff are often rated on traits that are really no more than crude personality measurements. As most assessors are totally unqualified to assess personality, the traditional form offers fixed-choice ratings. Because such an assessment is highly subjective, it is prone to numerous errors of judgement in terms of the individual's performance. This has implications for the poor diagnosis of training needs, and negative effects on motivation and trust by the individual.

Performance management systems attempt to reduce the extent to which subjective assessments are made. They tend to focus on one or more of the following criteria:

- *Results*: employees are rated on their achievements expressed in well-defined personal or organizational targets.
- *Processes*: the emphasis is on how the outcomes are achieved rather than measurable results. It is argued that compliance with a system or provision of a service is an example of process assessment. Such processes are measurable in some way because they can be related to mistakes or customer complaints.

■ *Behaviour:* less objective assessments focus on employee performance that is only tangibly connected with either achieved results processes. Managers often dwell unnecessarily on personal prejudices or appearance, dress and manners, which perpetuate a certain type of preferred culture.

To overcome such subjective assessments further, many large organizations have adopted the use of a number of techniques. Behaviourally anchored rating scales (BARS) are used to develop rating scales anchored to real-life behaviour through critical incidents. These more clearly define observable behaviours that are necessary to achieve a certain rating. They are time-consuming to develop, but provide a more valid measure of behaviour than impressionistic scales of traits or attributes. Behavioural observation scales are used where assessors list the frequency of occurrence of particular behaviours within a particular period, rather than making comparative judgements of better or worse performance – like BARS. (For further discussion, see Harrison, 2000.)

Development centres

A development centre, rather than being a place, is a process of assessing managerial potential within an organization. Performance appraisal systems are a means through which career potential can be assessed, and are a useful vehicle through which employer and employee agree appropriate action. However, performance appraisal alone is insufficient in gaining a comprehensive analysis of potential. Development centres are an ideal way of conducting an in-depth study of potential.

A development centre comprises a series of exercises to assess managerial potential. It is similar to the assessment centre used for recruitment and selection purposes. Development centres focus on development rather than job selection, although both are designed to predict potential rather than an appraisal of current performance (Dulewicz, 1989).

As individuals undergo the various exercises, they are observed by a trained team of assessors. Participants' performances on the exercises are rated against a number of predetermined, job-related dimensions.

It is important to identify which characteristics or strengths are to be assessed. The competence approach underlies many development centre designs, focusing on inputs and/or outputs. Many companies appear to focus on inputs to assess, for example:

- Reasoning
- Strategic awareness
- Customer orientation
- Interpersonal skills
- Leadership
- Flexibility
- Creativity and innovation.

They tend only to be used for managers, due to the high cost and perception of investment in potential. There is an increasing concentration on outputs following the MCI standards. Performance data are subsequently pooled and discussed in order to reach as objective an assessment of an individual as possible. Development centres seek to identify individuals who most closely fit the job requirements (usually of higher office), and to build up a list of individual training and development needs. Example 7.4 provides an example.

Example 7.4: The use of development centres

In 1999, a large bank in the UK ran a series of development centres to assess the potential of their senior managers for higher executive posts. The development centre was designed following a large-scale competence identification exercise where over twelve competencies essential for executive performance were defined.

Several exercises were developed, with key competencies assessed in each. In each exercise the candidate role-played certain scenarios to demonstrate his or her competence. The following exercises are briefly described to give you an idea of the type of exercises used in development centre design.

1 Candidates were given 30 minutes to prepare themselves for a simulated management meeting to close down several branches of the bank. The purpose of the exercise was to assess communication skills, leadership, decision-making, customer orientation and people management.
2 Following a sudden absence of their boss, each candidate was given their manager's in-tray of work. They had 1½ hours to take action on the material by prioritizing, delegating and actioning their decisions. Candidates had to justify the reasons for their actions, and effective responses were agreed beforehand by the senior executive team of the bank.
3 An actor played the part of an experienced and relatively autocratic bank manager who had implemented a new policy of increased charges on customer current accounts. Candidates then had to negotiate effectively with the manager for a reversal or modification of the policy. The candidate had to use available statistical data, together with their own knowledge and experience of the bank, to influence their manager's decision. To be effective, the candidate had to allow the manager to 'keep face' and be seen voluntarily to modify their policy.

4 An actor played the part of an effective bank dealer who was highly valued by bank in terms of his technical skill and success in creating new business opportunities. The candidate had to manage a performance appraisal interview with the dealer, whose people management skills needed to be improved. This involved reinforcement of the successful technical performance of the individual whilst influencing him to accept the need for training in people management skills. This exercise was particularly difficult because the bank wanted to maintain the motivation and commitment of the dealer whilst needing to develop their people management skills.

5 Each candidate was given a report from which they had to recommend consolidation of two different bank sites located in culturally diverse locations. The exercise assessed candidates' ability to assimilate information quickly, to make strategic decisions and to take action whilst showing sensitivity to cultural differences.

6 An actor played the part of a newspaper editor keen to write an article on the bank's current and future business direction. The candidate had to prepare a presentation to influence the focus of this article, and to manage questions attacking the financial viability of the bank's future plans. This exercise assessed presentation and communication skills, awareness of the bank's current and future activities, strategic and commercial awareness, and negotiating skills.

Trained assessors analysed the results of each candidate's behaviour in line with the core competencies identified as essential in higher executive performance.

As with any development centre, the validity and reliability of the process is dependent on evidence to support the necessity of demonstrating the relevant competencies. It is essential to validate any development centre by correlating development centre performance with future behaviour. If this validation is not conducted, there is no real evidence that behaviours assessed are truly necessary for effective executive performance. They may only be part of an executive 'wish list', and not linked to tangible performance.

Often organizations adopt the use of too many competencies, thus making assessment onerous and potentially invalid. With too many competencies to assess, an 'exercise effect' is more likely whereby actual competencies displayed in each exercise are not in fact being assessed. Rather, the exercise itself is being assessed, which demonstrates a number of competencies. There appears to be a paucity of validation of individual development centres. A statistical technique called factor analysis is an essential tool for computing reliability. Any advanced statistics text will explain this and other sophisticated methods of statistical analysis.

The expectations of managers are raised by attending a development centre, and it is therefore important to ensure timely and meaningful feedback to participants. That feedback must also be linked to assistance in developing areas identified as weak. Organizations are making increasing use of mentoring and other forms of organizational support following attendance at development centres. For further information about development centres, see Cockerill (1989), Dulewicz (1995) and Woodruffe (2000). It is important to note that whilst the development centre is used to assess needs and potential, it is also in itself a training intervention.

Self-assessment

As organizations continue to change, analysis of needs closer to the job and jobholder is imperative. Ongoing self-analysis and development is essential. This is central to the concept of the learning organization, which Price (1997: 336) highlights as "the ultimate extension of 'learning on the job'".

Numerous self-assessment tools are useful in continued self-assessment, and largely focus on individual style and orientation. We have already looked at Honey and Mumford's (1992) learning styles questionnaire (see Chapter 6). Others include Belbin's team-type inventory and Anderson and West's team climate inventory, covered earlier in this chapter. Coaching and mentoring also play a large part in facilitating learning on the job.

Psychometric tests

Psychometric testing has developed enormously over the past 20 years, and its use in clinical and occupational settings is now widespread. 'Psychometric' literally means 'mental measurement', and a psychometric test is a procedure for evaluating psychological functions.

A distinction is often made between tests of *maximum* performance and tests of *habitual* performance. The former refers to tests of intellectual ability and the latter to measures of personality. Personality measures are often not referred to as tests, since there are no right or wrong answers. A maximum performance test might indicate certain intellectual abilities. However, these may not be displayed on a day-to-day basis because of other influences, including personality factors.

Many organizations now use hundreds of different tests, ranging from single hand-completed checklists to complex computer-aided audits. Some of these tests have a firm basis in psychological theories and have been well researched and validated, while others are extremely subjective and have limited utility. In order for tests to be considered effective, they must possess the following qualities:

- *Reliability*: this means that the test results consistently measure what they are supposed to measure, assuming the test is measuring a stable aspect of an individual. If a test is not reliable, it cannot, by definition, be valid.

- *Validity*: this is the extent to which the test measures what it purports to measure. There are many different forms of validity, but most importantly there must be *criterion* or *external* validity. This means that there is evidence indicating that the test scores correlate with some other measure of the quality they claim to possess. In a work context, the test would have to indicate a correlation with some external measure of job performance.

- *Objective scoring*: the scoring of tests must in no way be influenced by the subjective assessments of an interpreter. For this reason, answer keys are provided with each test.

- *Standardization*: it is essential that the test instructions, environment, presentation and dealings with the candidate are standardized. If the environment is standardized, then differences in candidate performance can be attributed to differences in candidates as opposed to other factors. For example, giving two job candidates a typing test where one works on a computer and another on a manual typewriter will result in performance differences that are probably due to the equipment used rather than differences in their ability.

- *Appropriate norms*: norms are used to assess how meaningful an individual's results are in relation to the spread of scores obtained by a relevant comparison group. The group norms indicate the average score for the group, and the degrees of deviation below and above it. For example, a school leaver with A levels might get a score of 18 on a critical thinking test, which the norm tables indicate to be within the top 40 per cent of the A-level group.

Many original tests are now extensively used for career counselling purposes and for problem-solving in issues such as team development and conflict resolution. They are also used as a means of identifying training and development needs, either as a discrete activity or in the context of a training and development workshop.

Activity 7.12

Have you ever had to complete a psychometric questionnaire? If you have not, you might like to ask a colleague, a friend or a member of your HR department for their comments on the following questions. First, outline the purpose of taking the questionnaire.

- What were your experiences of taking the questionnaire?
- Did you feel that the questionnaire had relevance to the purpose for which it was being used? List the reasons for your answer.
- Outline ways in which the explanation or administration of the test could have been improved.

Your answer might reveal a range of experiences, some of which are positive and others negative. Psychometric questionnaires are used for a variety of purposes, including job selection, performance appraisal, training and development, and career counselling. Experiences of taking questionnaires vary, and are largely dependent on an individual's beliefs in the validity and meaningfulness of test results. They are also influenced by the treatment received during administration. An individual who is treated with respect and support is more likely to feel comfortable and relaxed, whereas hostile treatment will make an individual feel threatened and exposed.

It is important that the test administrator or using organization indicate the purpose behind the use of the psychometric instrument. It is important for a measure to have face validity which relates to whether a test *appears* to be measuring what it sets out to measure (e.g. a test of numerical reasoning used to select a customer care officer might be seen as irrelevant and lacking face validity).

There are many ways in which test administration can be optimized. The provision of clear instructions, the ability to ask questions about the process and a relaxed and comfortable environment are essential to facilitate individuals completing the questionnaire with ease. Standardization of the environment, the instructions and administration is essential to ensure that questionnaire results are a function of an individual's ability and preferences rather than differences in their environment.

Whether psychometric tests or other methods are used, it is essential that a climate exists wherein individuals believe that their efforts will result in positive outcomes. While performance appraisal, development centres and self-reports appear to be highly participatory methods of training needs assessment, they are only really valuable if there is a climate of trust and respect. Organizational assessment is naturally fraught with political undertones, and the trainer must be aware of such agendas if they are to provide truly effective learning and development events.

Integrating individual and organizational solutions

In an ideal world, the HRD needs of the individual would match the long-term skill requirements of the organization. Unfortunately this does not often happen, so we must resolve any conflict between these two sets of goals.

In progressive companies, attitudes have changed over the past 20 years. Employee mobility is now an accepted fact, together with changes in patterns of working – such as teleworking and portfolio careers. Organizational development and formal project teams now exist in many organizations to ensure flexibility and continuous development. Overall, the expectations and aspirations of the individual are considered alongside the requirements of the organization because they are mutually beneficial. Many organizations are developing effective employee development practices to align their human resource development strategically with business goals, and to manage the development and needs of their changing workforces effectively.

Increasingly, there is movement of managers across different companies. There are also stronger links between universities and organizations, to encourage fresh thinking and analysis of management methods and techniques. Many large organizations are encouraging their staff to take sabbaticals or secondments to different companies or educational providers to facilitate further continuous development and return to the organization. The retail outlet John Lewis in the UK has an established system of 6-month sabbaticals for staff. This offers a means for staff to develop outside of the organization and return with renewed insight and experience.

An organization that encourages individual development will attract the more creative and flexible staff it needs to face the future. On the other hand, this advantage will be wasted if the creativity and value of those same managers is not utilized. This presents the HRD function with three areas to consider:

1 The need for the organization to acquire the skills it requires
2 The satisfaction of the individuals' aspirations
3 Genuine acceptance by management that the second is a prerequisite of the first.

Thus, effective management development and career planning can resolve the potential conflict between individual and organization requirements. An appraisal system that focuses on the future rather than the past will help. On the few occasions where an individual's requirements do not match the organization's plans, the choices for each party will be clear. They can either accept modified career plans or business opportunities, or seek alternative activities.

There are two important points we should not ignore:

1 Individuals are more interested in their own jobs and careers, but need to accept that development will be paid for by the employer
2 The organization will be more interested in its long-term survival, which will ultimately take precedence over the aspirations of individuals.

Senior managers must realize, however, that to ignore individual development needs will not be in the organization's long-term benefit.

Many large organizations throughout the world are currently decentralizing to produce networks of smaller 'businesses'. This means that many junior managers will soon be exposed to commercial success and failure. If decentralization is to benefit the organization, junior managers must be adequately trained and developed so that they gain the skills and appropriate outlook to manage the changes. The alternative is to risk creating a cynical attitude towards the long-term motives and abilities of senior management. First-line managers and supervisors have to communicate with the workforce every day, so they need to be skilled.

Senior managers need to realize that real changes in an organization will not happen unless all managers, including junior managers, are committed to them. This commitment will require that the first-line managers feel respected and developed. In this area, British management lags behind European counterparts that have developed more involvement and active participation in company affairs. For example, the Germans and Swedes have supervisory boards with workplace representatives, and the French have enterprise committees. The British 'lag' may come from a class attitude to management development, whereby middle and senior managers get better treatment and working conditions during training sessions than do junior managers. More democratic organizations no longer have to cope with this 'class' problem, or with the loss of motivation it causes at the front line of management.

In brief, any organization that hopes to achieve the excellence required for substantial growth in the future will depend more on the skills, creativity and flexibility of its staff than on its products.

Summary

Identifying performance shortfalls

Training and development can be an excellent way of achieving effective employment development objectives. However, it is important to ascertain from the outset whether a shortfall in performance is a function of lack of training or learning or due to other influencing factors. Traditional assumptions about learning culminated in the individual model of training (Bramley, 1991). This model assumes that a change within the individual will result in improved job performance and increased organizational effectiveness. However, this is not always the case. When an identified need is solvable through training, many factors influence effective learning and transfer back into the workplace. In learning straightforward skills (e.g. typing or a new computer package), the individual model may be applicable. However, the more sophisticated the needs to be addressed (e.g. leadership skills or customer service excellence), the more the wider context in which learning occurs must be integrated with the wider culture and organizational systems.

The increased effectiveness model (Bramley, 1991) is a useful vehicle for identifying the many factors contributing to effective performance, and developing and managing any effective training interventions. This model mirrors a performance management approach, and is a useful approach within any employee development programme. The annual appraisal interview has traditionally been viewed as an opportunity to discuss any training needs that have been identified by the line manager, along with any development needs identified by the individual. With the shift in emphasis to self-managed learning and development, the individual will become much more responsible for this process and the identification of learning needs and a personal development plan. The most effective way is to include it as part of an integrated performance management system, the essence of which was discussed in Chapters 2 and 3.

Assessing needs

For effective human resource development to occur, it is essential that organizational, departmental, group and individual HRD objectives be closely aligned with business goals. This is the basis of effective human resource development programmes.

HRD needs assessment encompasses the assessment of training, learning and development at individual, departmental and organizational levels. There is a variety of methods that can be used to collect data at each level, and we have considered these in detail in this chapter.

At an organizational level, HRD needs analysis (traditionally referred to as an organization training needs analysis) involves a review of key organizational activities such as long- and short-term business goals, major environmental changes and existing human resource development and performance management systems. Reid and Barrington's (1999) training model offers a useful system process for identifying HRD needs at the organizational level.

At the job level, different approaches have been discussed, including comprehensive analysis, key task analysis, problem-centred analysis and competence approaches. An amalgamation of Reid and Barrington's (1999) and Harrison's (2000) framework for carrying out job training analysis is a useful means of doing this. A number of job training analysis techniques to assess and develop interpersonal relationships and teamwork have been discussed, including Belbin's (1981) team-type inventory and Anderson and West's (1994) team climate inventory.

A wide variety of methods exist to assess individual HRD needs, including performance appraisal, development centres, self-assessment and psychometric testing. Each of these offers a different approach to gathering effective data to determine an individual's HRD needs. However, it is essential to ascertain from the outset the nature of the shortfall in performance. The increased effectiveness model is a useful means to ascertain this shortfall within a performance management context.

References

Adair, J. (1996). *Effective Teambuilding*. Pan Books.

Anderson, N. and West, M. (1994). *Team Climate Inventory*. NFER Nelson Publishing Company Limited.

Armstrong, M. and Baron, A. (1998). *Performance Management: The New Realities*. Institute of Personnel and Development.

Belbin, R.M. (1981). *Management Teams: Why they Succeed or Fail*. Heinemann.

Belbin, R.M. (1993). *Team Roles at Work*. Butterworth-Heinemann.

Boydell, T. and Leary, M. (1996). *Identifying Training Needs*. Institute of Personnel and Development.

Bramley, P. (1991). Training & Development. Unpublished Open Learning Materials. Birkbeck College. University of London.

Buchanan, D.A. and Huczynski, A. (2004). *Organizational Behaviour: An Introductory Text*. Financial Times Management.

Cockerill, T. (1989). The kind of competence for rapid change? *Personnel Management*, **September, 21**.

Craig, M. (1994) *Analysing Learning Needs*. Gower.

Dulewicz, V. (1995). Assessment an development centres – problems and successes. Institute of Personnel and Development. Conference Paper.

Fletcher, C. (2004). *Appraisal and Feedback: Making Performance Review Work*. Chartered Institute of Personnel and Development. UK.

Hackett, P. (1997). *Introduction to Training*. Institute of Personnel and Development.

Harrison, R. (2000). *Employee Development*. Beekman Publishing.

Hayes, C., Fonda, N., Pope, N. *et al.* (1983). Training for skill ownership. Institute of Manpower Studies.

Holbeche, L. (1998). *Motivating People in Lean Organizations*. Butterworth-Heinemann.

Honey, P. and Mumford, A. (1992). *A Manual of Learning Styles*, 3rd edn. Honey.

Mankin, D.P. (2001). A model for human resource development. *Human Resource Development International*, **4(1)**, 65–85.

Mills, G.E., Pace, R. and Peterson, B.D. (1988). *Analysis of Human Resource Training & Organizational Development*. Addison-Wesley.

Morgan, G. (1998). *Images of Organizations*. Sage Publications Inc.

Pearn, M. and Kandola, R. (1990). *Job Analysis: A Practical Guide for Managers*. Institute of Personnel Management.

Price, A.J. (1997) *Human Resource Management in a Business Context.* Thomson Business Press, Business in Context Series.

Reichers, A.E. and Schneider, B. (1990). Climate & culture: an evolution of constructs. In B. Schneider (ed.), *Organizational Climate & Culture.* Jossey-Bass.

Reid, M.A. and Barrington, H. (1999). *Training Interventions: Promoting Learning Opportunities,* 6th edn. Institute of Personnel and Development.

Reynolds, J., Caley, L. and Mason, R. (2002). *How do People Learn?* Research Report, Chartered Institute of Personnel and Development.

Sisson, K. (1995). Organizational structure. In S. Tyson (ed.), *Strategic Prospects for HRM.* Institute of Personnel and Development.

Squires, P. and Adler, S. (1998). *Performance Appraisal: State of the Art in Practice* (ed. J.W. Smither). Jossey-Bass, The Professional Practice Series.

Stewart, J. (1999). *Employee Development Practice.* Financial Times Professional Limited.

Truelove, S. (1997) *Training in Practice.* Blackwell Business.

Vinton, K.L., Clark, A.O. and Sebolt, J.W. (1983). Assessment of training needs for supervisors. *Personnel Administrator,* **28(11),** 49.

Ward, P. (1997). *360 Feedback.* Chartered Institute for Personnel and Development. UK.

Woodruffe, C. (2000). *Development and Assessment Centres (Developing Practice).* Chartered Institute of Personnel and Development. UK.

Chapter 8

Learning and development design

Introduction

We have already established in previous chapters that learning occurs in a variety of situations, some of which are planned and structured and others that are spontaneous and seemingly automatic. In planned learning events, there are key principles that underpin effective learning design. Clearly, both individual and group learning will be most effective if it is planned, organized and supported. However, it is also important for individuals to be aware of these principles so that the quality of informal learning can be maximized. If individuals are more aware of how they learn in conjunction with an understanding of learning design principles, then this knowledge is likely to enhance their ability to identify and build upon the benefits of any accidental or informal learning. In many respects this is a crucial ingredient of self-managed learning, and goes to the very heart of individual employees taking responsibility for their own learning.

Many organizations employ a human resource development specialist to design and manage learning activities. More forward-thinking organizations link their HRD plans directly with their strategic business objectives. Their focus is on developing a culture of learning and development linked to performance management objectives in an integrated system. However, this varies from organization to organization, and highlights the extent to which the HRD specialist's role can differ.

When designing any learning event or activity it is important to remember that it should be learner- rather than trainer-focused. The appropriate learning or training strategy needs to be identified as a result of having agreed clearly defined learning objectives. This should flow naturally from the process of identifying the learning or training needs. It is important to avoid making assumptions about the learners (e.g. that they are motivated to learn). This is why it is so important to devote sufficient time to identifying the entry behaviour of the learners (and involving some learners in the design of the learning event/intervention itself). In this context, the word 'strategy' has a different meaning to that referred to earlier when discussing business and HR strategy. Within the learning design context, a learning strategy can be defined as a particular approach. For instance, Reid and Barrington (1999) have identified the following training strategies:

- Training on the job
- Planned organization experience
- In-house courses
- Planned experiences outside the organization
- External courses
- Self-managed learning.

This chapter examines the key principles of learning design. The principles should be considered when deciding which training or learning strategy to use, and then in the planning and delivery of learning events. Guidelines suggested by various authors are discussed in order to provide a useful framework against which to consider training design. This includes many of the key principles previously mentioned. Specific issues to consider when designing learning events for individuals, groups and organizations are considered. This chapter is pragmatic in orientation rather than being an academic debate of theory. This practical orientation allows the reader to apply this knowledge directly to practical training problems in their organization.

Objectives

By the end of this chapter you will be able to:

- Describe the key principles of learning design and link to the needs of individuals, groups and organizations
- Evaluate the contributions the environment and trainer expertise make to the learning process
- Apply the principles of learning to the delivery of learning events.

Key principles

The key principles to consider in designing learning include:

- Learning objectives
- A well-structured knowledge base
- The learning cycle
- Learning styles and motivation
- Trainer style and expertise
- The learning environment, including resources and equipment
- The time and financial resources available
- Organizational constraints, including the HRD policy
- Age factors and cultural differences
- Other influences.

In addition, pace, rhythm, fun, choice and flexibility are factors to consider. All these are discussed below. Learning design is therefore at best a highly complex and demanding activity.

Activity 8.1

Reflect on a specific learning experience that was arranged for you. This may be a specific training course you attended, or, for example, a structured open learning module.

- What were your overall impressions about its design?
- Were you conscious of it having actually been designed, or did it appear to be constructed at random?
- How systematic was it? Was it obvious that design had not been considered at certain stages?

You will find that most conscious learning activities are designed, even if in a very loose and unsystematic way. Learning designers sometimes avoid being too systematic to allow for the unknown individual requirements of the learners and the resultant group dynamics.

In order to accommodate the different requirements of learners and the trainer's ability, every learning activity should be carefully designed. To be given freedom in terms of time and resources is ideal for a designer. All factors can then be measured and taken into account before running the learning event. More often, however, the trainer is constrained by established company norms for learning activities, finite resources, and limited time. Even in this situation, the trainer should follow a proper design process and make every attempt to construct an effective learning activity. This may mean compromising and working with unsatisfactory resources. It may also mean that some of the original learning objectives have to be changed, reduced or eliminated.

In summary, learning design takes place before a learning activity and continues during it.

Learning objectives

When planning learning events, it is important to have clear objectives. Objectives help to determine whether progress is being made, and make evaluation possible. Objectives should contain the following elements:

- *Terminal behaviour* – a clear statement of what the learner should be able to do at the end of the learning activity
- *Standard of performance* – a clear statement of how well the learner should be able to perform the terminal behaviour
- *Conditions of performance* – a clear statement of the circumstances and conditions under which the learner should be able to perform the behaviour.

The more precise the objectives, the better the ability to evaluate training and ensure that learning has taken place.

When planning and designing learning activities, clear and well-defined objectives are particularly useful if the learning of one thing is used to facilitate the learning of something else – for example, the acquisition of presentation skills for use in lecturing. The skills, knowledge and attitudes required must be clearly defined. Much training in organizations is directly linked to competencies that, as observable behaviours, lend themselves to clear objective setting.

Before you can consider which training or learning methods are appropriate for any job, you must analyse what needs to be learned – i.e. the 'learning needs' from which learning objectives can be derived. HRD specialists or trainers often refer to these as 'training needs', as trainers usually focus on the possible training needed to enable learning to be achieved and to bridge the gap between current and desirable performance. This was considered in Chapter 7.

Learning is the acquisition of new knowledge, skills or attitudes by an individual. All training events should begin with some form of negotiation between the trainer and the participants as to their existing knowledge, skills and attitudes – i.e. their entry behaviour. While the trainer might have precisely defined objectives to describe the outcome of the training, it is unlikely that equal precision has been devoted to describing the input to the process.

It is important that the appropriate people are selected for training. Not only should events be relevant to their work, but their knowledge and experience should also be appropriate, so the training can build effectively on their current situations. Knowledge and skills are important, but arguably less so than learners' attitudes. Their own managers should prepare them to contribute positively to the training in order to gain the most from it. This can be achieved relatively easily through a pre-training event briefing at which the individual and his or her line manager discuss various issues (e.g. the individual's expectations, how any newly acquired or improved knowledge or skill can be applied, how the learning will be evaluated etc.). Unfortunately, in many organizations this process is viewed by many line managers as too time consuming, as a bureaucratic exercise only, or even as something which interferes with their department's work. In some organizations, more time and effort is devoted to the maintenance and well-being of equipment and machinery than to the well-being and development of employees!

Learning objectives can be usefully categorized under the following three headings:

1 *Knowledge*: the internalization, understanding and application of new information and concepts
2 *Skill*: the incorporation through practice of new ways of responding (i.e. mental, physical and social)
3 *Attitude*: the adoption of new values, feelings and psychological orientation.

Analysing objectives in this way is useful in prioritizing objectives, selection of relevant learning activities and specifying appropriate evidence of accomplishment. Knowledge, skills and attitudes (KSAs) are related to competencies, which identify observable behaviours necessary to perform effectively in a job. Such core competencies can easily be used to identify training objectives.

The following activities and material invite you to consider objective setting in finer detail. A trainer would not normally use this degree of detail in defining objectives and agreeing on them with learners. Nevertheless, a defined learning objective is the most important factor in the design process and does need very close attention.

Activity 8.2

Think of a job with which you are familiar. This may be a job you are currently doing, one you have held or one held by a colleague or friend.

- List the main job requirements and tasks necessary to perform the job effectively.
- Under the three headings of knowledge, skill and attitude, separate the requirements you have listed.

The information provided under the three headings of knowledge, skill and attitude will depend on the job you have chosen. Under each of these headings there might be many job requirements (core areas), as shown for the role of training manager in Table 8.1.

Under each core area, your specific requirements should then be listed. The lists for some jobs will be much longer than for others. Generally, the more senior the job, the more sophisticated

Table 8.1

Broad knowledge, skills and attitude requirements for a training manager

Knowledge	Skill	Attitude
Systems	Presentation	Involvement
Technology	Interpersonal	Commitment
Professional	Communication	Participation
Requirements	Managerial	Empowerment
Techniques	Negotiation	Innovation
Environment		Confidence/self-esteem
Legislation		Positivity
Markets		Enthusiasm

the competency needed to do it. For example, an IT manager and her secretary may work very closely together and be involved in similar projects. However, it is likely that the competence needed to perform the manager's job is more complex than that of the secretary. From the listed requirements, learning needs can then be identified; they may be a combination of knowledge, skill and attitude.

However, it is not enough simply to list requirements if you are planning training. You need to map them (in other words, to break them down into smaller linked parts). You also need to identify the desired outcomes – that is, the desired behaviours or skills, knowledge used, situations tackled, etc.

Binsted (1990) suggests that effective course designs actively build in opportunities for reflection, discovery and reception of input in relation to each course objective. This sounds complex, but it can be achieved by referring to the example matrix in Table 8.2. This matrix is obtained by plotting types of learning activity against types of objective.

Table 8.2
Course design matrix

Cycle of learning	Objective		
	Knowledge	**Skill**	**Attitude**
Reflection	New insights Changing perceptions	Choosing new skills Gaining confidence	Understanding feelings and own personal reflections
Discovery	Solving problems Behavioural analysis Analysing data	Role-play with focused feedback 'Homework' involving action	Experiencing feelings as a result of an activity
Reception	Listening to a speaker Watching a video	Hearing a description Watching a video demonstration	Receiving feedback on own emotional reactions
Source: adapted from Binsted (1990).			

The learning in each element in the matrix is different, and each requires different types of learning activities. Overlap is possible and may often be desirable – for example, working on skill and attitude objectives simultaneously. The matrix can be used to select learning activities that will match the objectives set.

The learning matrix provides a basis for greater creativity when learning activities are designed, and in particular may encourage you to increase the extent to which you use activities that promote reflection and discovery. In the past, training has too often relied on perception.

Let's pursue the analysis further with a more detailed example. Within the behavioural domain of 'Skills', let's say you can identify four core areas: number, communication, problem-solving and practical factors. Each of these can be broken down into core skill requirement groups, and within these subdivisions there are even finer distinctions you can describe with key words.

This approach enables you to describe precisely the skills needed to perform a job. This is a necessary step in setting precise training objectives and selecting appropriate training methods. In Table 8.3, which shows the entire taxonomy of these four core areas, you can see the core areas broken down into their core skill group subdivisions and then into key words.

Using taxonomy like this, you can identify specific learning needs and therefore set very precise training objectives, although the specific training which would follow will inevitably improve other related skills. For example, if, under Core skill group 8 (Working with people), you see that a learner has difficulty asking for assistance, you can focus training on that specific activity. You might consider the following training methods:

- Videotapes to show right and wrong approaches
- Talks to describe when and how to ask for information and who to go to
- Discussions of difficulties, different approaches, etc.
- Role-plays to allow the trainee to practise in a safe environment.

Take another look at Table 8.3. You will note that the items are listed according to the level of difficulty, starting with number 1. The simpler, earlier items contribute to the more complex ones later in the list.

It was stated earlier that a trainer would not normally use this degree of detail in defining objectives. However, the degree of

Table 8.3
Core skill breakdown

Core areas	Number	Core skills groups	Key words
Number	1	Operating with numbers	Count, work out, check and correct
	2	Interpreting numerical and related information	Interpret
	3	Estimating	Estimate
	4	Measuring and marking out	Measure, mark out
	5	Recognizing cost and value	Compare, recognize value
Communication	6	Finding out information and interpreting instructions	Find out, recognize value
	7	Providing information	Provide information
	8	Working with people	Notice, ask for assistance, offer assistance, react, discuss, converse
Problem-solving	9	Planning: determining and revising courses of action	Plan, diagnose
	10	Decision-making: choosing between alternatives	Decide
	11	Monitoring: keeping track of progress and checking	Check, monitor, notice
Practical factors	12	Preparing for a practical activity	Locate, identify, handle, lift or transport, adjust, arrange, carry out procedures, check
	13	Carrying out a practical activity	Adopt safe practices, lift or transport, manipulate, operate, set up, assemble, dismantle
	14	Finishing off a practical activity	Carry out procedures, check, restock

complexity shown has indicated the detail with which objectives can be set.

Activity 8.3

Reflect on the learning event that you considered in Activity 8.1.

- How well defined were the learning objectives?
- Reflect on whether they were all achieved, and if not, what aspects of the learning design were at fault. If they were achieved, what aspects of the learning design were particularly effective?

Allocating insufficient time and resources to meet the necessary objectives is very often a problem with formal training events. However, you may have identified other reasons why objectives were not met. These may well have related to wider organizational issues – for example, organizational culture, management style or politics. Insufficient account may have been taken of the individuals attending the learning event in terms of their age, training needs, existing level of expertise or commitment. This issue is considered further when we discuss evaluation.

Well-structured knowledge base

Without existing concepts, it is very difficult (if not impossible) to make sense of new concepts. It is essential that learners' existing knowledge and experience be brought to bear in learning. The subject matter being learnt must also be well structured and integrated. The structure of knowledge is more visible and useful to learners where it is clearly displayed, where content is taught in an integrated whole rather than in small separate pieces, and where knowledge is related to other knowledge rather than learned in isolation.

An example of this is project work. Project work almost always involves the application of prior knowledge to problems; it emphasizes the role of a sound knowledge base. In the case of a degree course, for example, the requirements might be to submit a dissertation based on the experiences of an industrial placement. Project work can be highly motivating for students, capturing a significantly greater proportion of students' time and energy than taught courses of equivalent assessment value. The level of motivation seems to depend on the extent of students' responsibility for choosing and managing the project. Group project work can be particularly motivating.

The learning cycle

You have already seen the Kolb's experiential learning cycle described by Honey and Mumford (1989). It is reproduced in Figure 8.1 for ease of reference.

Let us review the four stages in terms of their relevance to learning design.

Stage 1: carrying out an activity (concrete activity)

In order to learn, learners have to do or experience something. This may be an exercise, a video, a lecture, a practical task or an observation. In design terms, the choice of the activity is important since it must be suitable for the required learning, but it must also be able to generate the interest and motivation of the learners. In longer learning activities, there should also be a reasonable variety of activities to prevent fatigue.

Stage 2: reflecting on the experience (observations and reflections)

Following an activity or experience, learners need to reflect on its implications. This can be achieved by methods such as individual contemplation, paired discussion or counselling, group

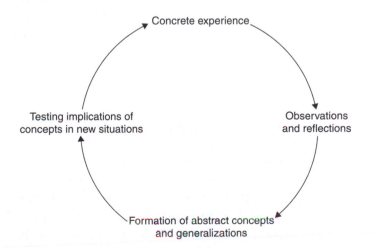

Figure 8.1
Kolb's experiential learning cycle (Kolb *et al.*, 1974: 28).

discussion or formal debate. The designer has to ensure that the form of the reflection is appropriate, and that it takes place in a way that suits the learners' specific needs.

Stage 3: drawing conclusions from the experience (formation of abstract concepts and generalizations)

In some cases this phase can be linked with the previous one, enabling a group discussion to result in a conclusion, or individual reflection to result in the learner coming to clear decisions. This stage is sometimes taken for granted, so the designer should build time into learning sessions for it. This stage could also be exemplified when, after a discussion, the trainer conducts a formal summary.

Stage 4: planning use of the learning (testing implications of concepts in new situations

The final stage of the learning cycle is actually planning what to do with the learning that has taken place. The main issue is how to transfer the learning from the learning situation into the work situation. The designer needs to build a planning session into the activity to identify specific opportunities for using the learning. This stage is often the most under-used. Trainers often assume that learners have identified for themselves how to use the learning. This might be true in some cases, but it should be guaranteed for all learners. Another problem is that the actual learners themselves fail to appreciate the importance of this stage and view techniques such as action plans as paper exercises, which invariably get forgotten about once the training or learning event is over. The use of pre-briefing and post-debriefing sessions between the learner and his or her line manager can help to ensure transfer of learning does take place. This is even more likely if the line manager integrates such sessions with the formal performance appraisal process.

Learning styles and motivation

Each stage of the learning cycle is essential to the design process and should not be omitted. However, if a trainer has sufficient information on the learning style of an individual or a group, then the learning cycle can be refined. Each learner could complete a learning style questionnaire beforehand. This gives the designer valuable information, which can lead to two options: to put more emphasis on (i) the learning stage that reflects the preference of the learning group (if there is a mixture of preferences, different emphases can be placed on activities at different times), or (ii) the learning stage that does not reflect the group's preferences in order to encourage a more challenging and developmental process.

Often you will not have learning style information. Conjecture will have to be used to ascertain preferences of individuals or the group of learners. An experienced trainer might be able to make a calculated guess at an early stage and amend the design accordingly. Otherwise, you will have to try certain activities, assess the reaction and involvement of the learners, and amend subsequent activities. This means that trainers need to be flexible in their approach, able to 'think on their feet' and willing to listen actively to learner feedback.

Even in the workplace it is important that individual employees and line managers have some understanding of learning styles and the learning cycle, given the amount of informal learning that is taking place. It is also highly relevant to anyone who is coaching or helping others in the workplace. Often the coach will need to adapt his or her coaching style to reflect the learning preferences of the learner. Consequently, completion of a learning styles questionnaire on a regular basis (say every 2 years) by all departmental members would be useful best practice for a line manager to introduce. This would also assist with the identification of appropriate learning activities at the annual appraisal.

Whilst learning styles are important to the learner's motivation, it is essential that a learning need is recognized on the part of the learner. If there is any doubt about the learner's wish to learn, the learning designer must build an activity into the early part of the programme which attempts to identify and resolve concerns about commitment. Without commitment, the effectiveness of the entire learning event will be under threat. In an ideal world, it would be nice to believe that these issues could be resolved at an earlier stage (again highlighting the value of pre-activity briefings between the individual and the line manager).

The ongoing motivation of individual learners must be maintained, and action taken to address any lack of commitment. This may mean departing from the original learning design. Deep learning is more likely when the learner's motivation is intrinsic, and when the learner experiences a need to know something. Adults learn best what they need to learn in order to carry out tasks that matter to them. Learners are likely to need to be involved in selecting what is to be learned and in planning how the learning is to take place if they are to experience 'ownership' of it. The motivational context is established by the emotional climate of the learning. While a positive emotional and motivational climate may be a necessary condition for deep learning, anxiety and instrumentalism may be sufficient conditions for surface learning.

When selecting an overall training or learning strategy, Harrison (2000) suggests that the following motivational factors should be considered:

- *Unpredictability*: motivation will vary, often significantly from one group of learners to the next, even with types of learning events that have often been run before
- *Individual differences*: there can be significant individual differences in motivation and expectations within a group of learners
- *Dynamism*: motivation is dynamic, often changing during the course of the learning event.

In addition, social influences, including group norms and consensus issues, may influence the willingness of participants to become immersed in the learning activity.

Activity 8.4

Once again refer to the learning event you identified in Activity 8.1.

- Consider whether the activity you went through took into account, or suited, your own learning style.
- Did you feel comfortable during the process?
- How committed were you to the whole event?

As we have already said, the learning style of individuals is often difficult to ascertain unless the trainer is extremely sensitive. A lack of awareness of individual differences and needs may de-motivate learners and result in loss of commitment to learning.

Trainer style and expertise

The availability of trainers with expertise in the subject matter will affect the learning design, choice of activities or learning media. With insufficient expertise available in-house, the designer may use external resources or alternatives such as open learning, guided reading, e-learning or external courses. Experienced trainers with insufficient subject knowledge are often able to carry through a training programme with no apparent problems. However, learners may become cynical and lose their motivation if they sense a lack of expertise.

In Chapter 12, we explore more fully the role and style of trainers or those responsible for human resource development in organizations. The role as given by the organization or adopted by the individual trainer greatly influences the effectiveness of the learning situation. At this stage, it is sufficient to point out that a learning designer needs to consider the personalities and styles of available trainers. For example, putting a highly methodical and analytical trainer in charge of an experiential learning activity might cause problems for both the trainer and the learners.

The learning environment

An appropriate environment affects both the learning and the learning design. Different activities should be used in a working environment than in an off-the-job situation such as a training room. Space, heat, noise, interruptions and other environmental factors are all-important considerations for the learning designer. In many cases, experienced learners who are relaxed and confident find that this can encourage and foster deep learning.

The designer should also be aware of facilities and equipment. How much space is there for discussion groups? Is there a television monitor available to show videotapes? Is there room for a table? Do learners have to sit in rows? The seating arrangements convey a very important message from the outset. If the learners sit in rows facing the trainer, there is an impression upon entering the training environment that the trainer is in control, and will manage all interactions. Where seats are arranged with participants facing each other as well as the trainer (e.g. a horseshoe arrangement), then the expectation is one of democratic participation. In this way, the learning environment can facilitate the intentions of the trainer and influence learning design. Whilst it might seem trivial to note these issues, attention paid to environmental factors has a facilitating effect on learning. Several factors are discussed here.

Time available

One of the most important factors is the total amount of time available for learning, and whether it is continuous or broken into periods with large gaps between. Time affects the amount of information learners retain, the depth of exploration they can undertake, the pace at which they learn and the amount of personal assistance they may be offered. Time will also have an impact on the possibility of achieving objectives. With less time than expected, a designer may have to alter the learning objectives to make them realizable. There is also a need to let go of some traditional training perspectives, such as participants working long into the night – as was often the case on management development programmes. Tired, fatigued participants do not make good learners. However, many organizational cultures still encourage this although it limits the effectiveness of learning.

Financial resources

Limited finances can override many design decisions. A clearly defined human resource development budget will assist the designer, particularly if learning events are prioritized. If a training event reflects poor financial investment, this may convey important messages regarding the extent to which senior managers are committed to learning and development. However, designers often produce creative and effective learning activities with limited resources. Indeed, designers are often placed in this position because of financial constraints placed upon them, and it is not unusual for them to compromise somewhere.

Organizational restraint

In many large organizations, HRD specialists aim to create learning opportunities, which are directly linked to the strategic objectives of the business. Thus, the development of employees takes place within a strategic human resource development context (see Chapters 1 and 3). However, in other organizations, human resource development may not be closely linked and integrated with other business systems. In this instance, learning designers must contend with powerful pressures from their employers. A company training policy should outline the limits on the timing, expenditure and scope of possible learning activities. Even if such details are not in the policy statement, there may be wider organizational constraints affecting design – such as those related to organizational style, structure, culture, power and resources. Training and learning that is anticipated but is not supported by the structure and culture of the organization makes it difficult (if not impossible) to transfer newly learnt skills and attitudes to the workplace. The transfer of learning will be considered in Chapter 9. In addition, temporary constraints may result from current business difficulties or changes.

The learning designer therefore needs a clear understanding of the strengths and weaknesses of the organization, and the opportunities it does or might offer. This resonates with the need for effective negotiation and influencing skills, as well as for a reasonable level of political acumen.

Age factor

The climate and approach to teaching in traditional education differs from that in industry, and trainers must take this into account when designing learning strategies. An understanding and supportive trainer can do a great deal to help learners who are having difficulty in adjusting to different kinds of learning situation.

Many organizations in the UK appear to favour younger workers, and their recruitment practices reflect this. However, demographic trends indicate the availability of fewer young people in the workforce and an increasing dependence upon the services of older people. This has implications for understanding the specific learning needs of older workers. Studies show that as we become older, speed of performance may decline. However, discrimination and bias may distort the extent to which this is a valid argument for favouring younger workers. Legislation is changing to reflect the value placed on older workers, and a voluntary code regarding the recruitment of older workers was introduced in the UK in early 1999.

In an article in *Personnel Management* in May 1993, Heap argues that trainers should try to create better conditions for learning to take place. These conditions should ideally be similar to those that surround training young people. Heap's argument centres on creating an environment that encourages more support, more learner-centredness, and less detailed instruction. He believes that before we try to teach anything we need to enable learners to release their tensions about learning situations. He states that 'Tense students and tense teachers are not likely to learn well, they will need to learn how to counsel each other'.

Heap's ideas focus on encouraging learners to celebrate their naturally enormous ability to learn and 'crow about their successes'. There needs to be more research into the nature of natural learning processes and play. However, his ideas are a hypothesis based on commonsense observation and require empirical testing. He feels that learning and counselling can be designed to enable positive benefits.

Cultural differences

If training is to be designed effectively, the implications of cultural differences must be considered. The trainer and participants will have their own beliefs, values and assumptions derived from their own cultural backgrounds. To ignore such differences may, at the very least, inhibit learning. At its worst, it will cause offence. Hofstede's (2003) research into the influence of national culture on work attitudes provides a useful description of the main variables in national culture. Hofstede's original research surveyed IBM workers in 40 different countries on their work attitudes. He found that managers and employees vary on five dimensions of national culture:

1 Power distance – the degree to which there is acceptance that the power in organizations is distributed unequally.
2 Individualism vs collectivism – individualism is the degree to which people prefer to act as individuals; collectivism is the degree to which people prefer to act collectively in groups.
3 Quantity of life vs quality of life – quantity of life is the extent to which people value things like assertiveness, acquisition of money and material goods, and where competition prevails; quality of life is the degree to

which relationships are valued and where there is concern for the welfare of others.

4   Uncertainty avoidance – the extent to which people prefer structured to unstructured situations. High anxiety, expressed in greater nervousness, stress and aggression, is a function of high uncertainty avoidance.

5   Long-term vs short-term orientation – long-term orientation is shown by people who look to the future and value thrift and persistence; short-term orientation values both the past and present, and highlights a respect for tradition and fulfilment of social obligations.

Each of these dimensions has implications for training and learning. For example, individualism vs collectivism indicates the extent to which people prefer to act as individuals or in groups. Power distance may influence the extent to which learners feel willing freely to contribute their ideas in the presence of the trainer, who is perceived to be of higher status. Uncertainty avoidance might dictate the preferred learning situations as being structured or unstructured. Long-term vs short-term orientation might indicate the extent to which people welcome risk-taking and various problem-solving approaches. A fuller understanding of cultural differences and mixed cultural groups is necessary to ensure appropriate language, media and encouragement are provided.

Other influences

Learning designers also need to consider the pacing of a learning event, especially if it is relatively long. It is important to keep the momentum going, and maintain the interest and motivation of all learners. Then there is the question of rhythm. The learners can involve themselves in the variety and sequence of events so that anticipation is maintained and a rhythm of learning is sustained.

Many organizational learning events have traditionally been formal and lecture-driven. More recently, the view that learning should be enjoyable has culminated in action learning and problem-solving approaches. Making learning enjoyable and capturing the commitment and creativity of learners is not just a question of trainer personality and style; it is also a function of the culture and style of the organization that offers training. An organization that fosters continuous employee development and growth will facilitate integration of learning both within and beyond the workplace.

It should be obvious to you by now that learning design is a complex task that requires a great deal of attention, ingenuity and intuition. Since no learning activity is perfect, learning design must be a continuous process in the pursuit of excellence.

Activity 8.5

As a design activity, take your learning event from Activity 8.1. Under each of the headings below, check whether, in your view, each one was considered in the design. List details of any evidence you have to justify your views.

- Learning objectives
- Well-structured knowledge base
- Adherence to the learning cycle
- Learning styles and motivation
- Trainer style and expertise
- Learning environment, including resources and equipment
- Time and financial resources available
- Organizational constraints (e.g. organizational structure, culture, politics, training policy)
- Age factors and cultural differences
- Other influences.

It is interesting to evaluate the design of learning events to facilitate effective learning and highlight where improvements are possible. If learning events are to be effectively designed and managed – and valuable – then planning and integration of learning is essential. In addition to these principles, we could also list other important features that may influence design. These include pace, rhythm, fun, choice and flexibility. Learning design, therefore, is at best a highly complex and demanding activity.

Applying principles of learning to the delivery of learning events

We have now considered a number of principles or issues that can usefully be taken into account when designing learning.

These are broadly based, and take into account the wider issues in learning design. However, we also need to consider how the principles of learning can improve the delivery of a learning activity or event.

Harrison (2000) has drawn on the work of Gagne (1977) to identify a set of guidelines for both the design and delivery of training or learning events. We shall consider these from the perspective of delivery.

1   *Design an appropriate structure and culture.* Structure refers to the framework of a learning event – the way it is shaped, and the type of interactions planned to occur within it. Culture is about the prevalent learning climate – i.e. the style and pattern of relationships between the parties, and the values they will be encouraged to share in the learning situation. Do note that culture in this context is different from that discussed in terms of national culture. However, care should be taken to design events that link with local and national cultural expectations.

2   *Stimulate the learners.* The learners should perceive that the purpose and objectives relate directly to their needs. The choice of media and methods should stimulate individuals, and key points must stand out and become memorable. For example, the beginning and end of a learning event are memorable, and therefore the essence of what is to be learnt must be outlined at the start and a summary given at the end. This closes the learning loop.

3   *Help understanding.* Constantly check back on the learners' understanding as the event unfolds. Difficult points should be reiterated and the pace varied to ensure the concepts are thoroughly grasped.

4   *Incorporate appropriate learning activities.* Learning activities must involve an appropriate situation or the use of skills and knowledge that are relevant to their real-life environment and roles. They should carry the learning process forward and build expertise and confidence.

5   *Build on existing learning.* Aim to make past learning and current mindsets an aid to the learning process. It is important to encourage trainees to bring their problems and activities to the learning event. Unlearning and relearning are complex processes that are difficult and

yet essential to acquiring new learning. An atmosphere should be encouraged whereby it is 'safe' to bring up entrenched learning. Views should be evaluated and integrated or discarded. Great skill is needed by the trainer to facilitate learning whilst maintaining the self-esteem and competence of the trainees.

7   *Guide the learners.* Regular feedback and guidance is essential throughout the learning process. Technical competence and interpersonal skills are needed to facilitate learners acquiring new learning (see Chapter 12).

8   *Ensure that learning is retained.* Two major issues should be considered: practice and feedback.

   ■ Practice is essential to reinforce learning; the most critical and/or difficult learning tasks should be given priority.

   ■ Feedback – the tasks themselves should have rewards incorporated into them such as the correct solution to a problem. A smile or word of praise may be enough to reinforce effective behaviour in a learning situation. It is also important to explore with the learner why learning has proved successful, since the correct response might only have been achieved by chance.

9   *Ensure transfer of learning.* Transfer to learning must take place:

   ■ into the learning event
   ■ from the learning event to the job.

   Successful transfer into the workplace will depend on:

   ■ the degree to which the event has been appropriate to the learners' needs in their work situation
   ■ how far the learning tasks have been within the capability of the learners and been mastered by them
   ■ whether the event has achieved stimulation and relevancy of learning throughout its duration
   ■ whether participants will be enabled and encouraged to use their new learning in the workplace.

The exercise should have enabled you to reflect on the importance of planning and preparing learning, and of applying key principles to facilitate learning and development. A practical knowledge of learning theory together with design principles and personal skills go a long way to making a learning event effective, meaningful and enjoyable.

Activity 8.6

As a final design activity, again take your learning event from Activity 8.1. Under Harrison's headings below, check whether, in your view, each one was considered in the design. List details of any evidence you have to justify your views. (Note that this activity is focused on the actual delivery of the learning event.)

- Appropriate structure to the learning event – e.g. type of activities used to facilitate learning
- Climate and culture of learning – e.g. participative, interactive
- Stimulating nature of learning event
- Assistance and help given
- Appropriate learning activities
- Design based on existing learning
- Trainer's facilitation and guidance skills
- Opportunities for practice and feedback
- Successful transfer of learning to learning event – i.e. extent to which learner can use new learning in subsequent activities during the learning event
- Successful transfer of learning beyond the learning event – e.g. into the workplace.

The purpose of training is to create learning situations. A trainer designing a training activity needs to address a number of questions, such as:

- What is this activity required to achieve?
- What content must be present?
- How much time will it take, and how should this time be allocated?
- What methods would be suitable?
- How many trainees will there be, and what do they know already?
- Who should be consulted during the design phase?

The role of trainer is demanding, as discussed in Chapter 12. Nowadays, it is generally recognized that a trainer should be an expert in the process of training as well as in the subject. Trainers' expertise should include an appreciation of the training field, theoretical knowledge of the training process, and the ability to use various methods. Trainers should also offer a range of creative learning activities on different subjects, in different situations and with different kinds of learners.

Learning design for individuals, groups and organizations

Individuals

Designing learning for the individual learner has both advantages and disadvantages. On the positive side, assuming there are sufficient resources available, the designer will be able to tailor the learning activity to the specific needs of one person rather than having to compromise to meet the group needs. This means that, in theory, the learning process should be more effective. The learning activity will often be one-to-one instruction or coaching.

Where expertise to meet the learning need does not exist within the organization, there may be problems. Agreed financial resources may be needed to bring in an 'expert' just for one person's training. If this is out of the question, the learner may have to attend an external course, which may not sufficiently meet his or her needs. Other problems may concern the lack of interaction with other learners. This is particularly important in the area of personal and interpersonal skills, such as working within a team. Although there are options for the learning designer, such as coaching, the usual compromise is an external course.

The advantages, therefore, of designing learning for an individual are that it can be very precise and detailed, relevant to real needs, flexible and responsive. The disadvantages are that it may be time-consuming and expensive. In addition, the 'changed' individual may have to return to an environment and group that remains 'unchanged'.

Groups

Most of the influencing factors we discussed earlier are concerned with group learning design. The main advantage of group learning is that it is far easier to construct reflecting and theorizing activities with a group than it is with an individual. Group activities can, if designed effectively, be more thorough. In fact, the interactive feature of group learning is a key element throughout the learning cycle. For this reason, it is easier to design for a group with members who have interpersonal learning needs than for an individual with similar needs.

The main disadvantages in designing for groups are obvious. It is difficult to reconcile differing needs and learning styles, especially if resources and time are limited. The speed of an individual's learning is another difficult issue in a group situation. It is easier if a high trainer to learner ratio is possible, but this is not often the case. For example, in much of higher education there is often very little discussion due to increasingly large numbers of learners. Interaction can take many forms other than tutorials and seminars. Autonomous learner groups, resource-based learning and peer tutoring can be very effective. Studies have shown that the learner who does the tutoring learns more than the learner who is tutored.

To substantiate this claim, it is useful to see it in practice. Self-managed learning is a term that was defined in the 1970s and has become popular for learners in the workplace. Self-managed learning combines the idea of learners working together in small groups on real-life problems (as in action-learning) with the practice of learners setting their own agenda (or 'contract') and striving to meet targets contained within that.

Example 8.1: J R Phillips and URM Agencies

J R Phillips and URM Agencies are two well-established drink companies that have merged and become part of Hiram Walker Agencies. The senior managers of the two companies recognized a need to change the culture from a patriarchal model that had become common in the 'drinks' industry towards a faster and more entrepreneurial style of organization.

The companies wanted their managers to take responsibility for their own development, while they accepted responsibility to support them in their learning. The core of self-managed learning therefore involved learners meeting in sets with the help of a facilitator. Each individual decided on the goals that he or she wanted to achieve, declared these goals to the group, and signed a learning contract committing to those targets. The aim was for the set to be self-motivated. The facilitator or learning assistant challenged and supported, but did not lead, the sessions. The facilitators were actually senior managers in the company, and this was crucial in order to ensure commitment from top management within the company.

By structuring the sets to include managers from different departments, there was an increased awareness of the activities of other parts of the group. This led to increased cohesion among individual managers, and reduced the sense of departmental barriers at other levels.

Managers on the programme also indicated that the self-managed learning approach produced a range of personal benefits that enabled them to see their own work-life in a broader context. They understood their roles as managers within the company's strategic position and business operations in addition to seeing their place of work within the context of their personal life. Therefore, transfer of learning was assisted by understanding the general principles and concepts rather than by concentration on one narrow application.

The success of this style of learning more than outweighs its cost. Managers, as a result of being responsible for their own learning, became self-sufficient, self-motivated people who could look after themselves as well as others.

Organizations

Designing learning for organizations is a complex process and, as we have seen earlier, in order to be effective and continuous it must be placed within a framework of HRD, performance management and a culture of continuous development. Chapter 1 highlighted the importance of adopting a strategic approach to human resource development, while Chapter 2 outlined the growing importance of concepts such as organizational learning and the learning organization.

Later we will further explore the implications of organizational structure and change on human resource development activities, and consider some of the strategies available for influencing organizational learning.

Summary

When planning specific learning events, it is important to apply some key principles of learning design. Such principles underpin effective learning and facilitate the effectiveness with which people acquire new skills, knowledge or attitudes. It is essential to identify clear learning objectives so that progress can be determined and evaluated. The clearer and more well defined the objectives are, the greater the probability of achieving desirable learning outcomes. Understanding the learning cycle and individual styles and motivation is also important in selecting an appropriate learning context. The learning environment itself influences the effectiveness of the learning event, and issues concerned with time, resourcing and organizational constraints must be considered.

The cultural mix of learners might also influence the tasks or activities chosen, as well as the participants. Inappropriate tasks may be resisted, or prove less valuable due to different cultural expectations and experiences. The style of the trainer will also be crucial in encouraging the participation and motivation of learners. In planning and delivering specific events, Harrison's (2000) guidelines provide a useful way of designing appropriate learning opportunities.

References

Binstead, D.C. (1990). Design for learning in management training and development: a view. *Journal of European Industrial Training*, **4(8)**, 1–32.

Gagne, R.M. (1977). *The Conditions of Learning.* Holt Saunders.

Harrison, R. (2000). *Employee Development.* Beekman Publishing.

Heap, N. (1993). The importance of a learning culture. *Personnel Management,* **May**.

Hofstede, G. (1980). *Culture's Consequences: International Differences in Work-related Values.* Sage.

Hofstede, G. (2003). *Comparing Values, Behaviours, Institutions and Organizations Across Nations.* Sage Publications.

Honey, P. and Mumford, A. (1989). *A Manual of Learning Styles.* Honey.

Kolb, D.A., Rubin, I.M. and McIntyre, J.M. (1974). *Organizational Pyschology: An Experiential Approach.* Prentice Hall.

Reid, M.A. and Barrington, H. (1999). *Training Interventions: Promoting Learning Opportunities,* 6th edn. Chartered Institute of Personnel and Development, UK.

Chapter 9

Learning and development methods, interventions and practices

Introduction

The choice and effectiveness of learning methods are influenced by a variety of factors. To understand these, we need to ask some basic questions about the purpose of learning in specific circumstances. For example, is training the best means of bridging the gap between current and desirable performance? Have the desired outcomes been defined? Is the level of training appropriate for the trainees? Do learners understand the purpose of the learning method and content, and how it relates to their work? Does the environment into which trainees return facilitate transfer of their learning?

Many methods support successful changes, including open and self-managed learning. At a group and individual level, many methods exist to facilitate planning learning opportunities. However, questions will arise regarding the effectiveness of any training intervention. Even if these aspects have been addressed properly, it does not mean that the planned learning opportunities will be effective. Appropriate methods of training must also be selected to gain the maximum benefits from any training event. For example, role-plays and videos can be used for interviewing techniques or appraisal training, whereas some forms of learning (such as first-aid training) may require a practical demonstration.

The first section of this chapter looks more specifically at actual methods used for groups and individuals, largely focusing on planned learning and training events. However, it should be remembered that informal learning in the workplace remains an important factor in developing individual performance. In the second section we will move on to consider open learning, the use of visual aids and some of the limited empirical evidence available on the use of specific learning methods.

Objectives

By the end of this chapter you will be able to:

- Appreciate the value and contribution of different methods used in both individual and group training interventions
- Explain the use of open learning and visual aids
- Describe the key issues that determine the suitability of individual learning methods in specific training situations.

Selection of learning methods

There are many learning methods. To ensure interest and sustained attention, the creative trainer is well advised to adopt a variety of approaches within a single HRD programme. Knowledge of factors influencing learning will also be useful in deciding the combination of training techniques. For instance, an understanding of the different learning styles can be applied to reflect the preferred style of different learners. Likewise, knowledge of personality differences and preferred ways of interacting in the world can be considered. In this section, we review some of the most common methods used for:

- Large groups
- Small groups
- Individuals.

Choosing the most suitable learning methods

Other than personal preference and familiarity, what influences the choice of one learning method over another? Learning theory plays a part, but cost is also a major issue (Tobin, 1998: 17). Media-based training is becoming common, and cost is one reason for its popularity, as it is often cheaper to provide an 'off-the-shelf' video than classroom-based instruction. Frequently, the choice of learning method is made without reference to a key element of HRD strategy: the objectives of the learning experience. Milano (1998: 85) highlights the importance of objectives in designing a training programme:

> ... objectives are the grounding for all good training design and delivery. Many designers have love-hate relationships with objectives, they know objectives are important, but they still feel that writing objectives is an artificial task to be done at the end of the design. In our work, we have learned that objectives are the pot of gold upon which we can design a rainbow.

Milano also points to a number of advantages gained from having clear objectives:

1 Clear objectives help the training designer to distinguish between essential content, and content that 'is nice to know' but not absolutely essential.
2 Objectives are invaluable for making informed choices between different training methods. For example, learning a new computer software package requires skills practice. In this instance, skills practice is an essential learning method.
3 Having clear objectives is necessary for evaluation of the training programme.
4 Taking the objectives of the learning experience into account, and the budget available, trainers can then focus on the most effective combination of learning methods, bearing in mind Meier's (2000: 232) comment that:

> There is a lot of junk food out there in the training world ... Some of it takes the form of highly scripted, linear, hierarchical, and mechanistic learning programs. And some of it takes the form of fluff, hoopla, and so called 'creative' techniques that may be clever and entertaining but produce no deep nourishment and no long-term value.

It is also important to empathize with the needs of the learners in terms of their values, constraints, attitudes and understanding. Material should be presented to learners in such a way that it meets with their understanding and expectations and will motivate and impress them. No matter how well training/learning needs have been assessed, the audience will have differing abilities as far as their knowledge of the material is concerned. It is important not to overestimate their knowledge whilst also not underestimating their intelligence.

Learning methods for large groups

Before we consider the most common learning methods, it will be useful for you to identify some, together with their main aims and advantages.

Activity 9.1

- Reflect on your learning experiences in large groups (greater than 15 people).
- Make a list of the methods that were used to facilitate learning, then identify what their purpose was, and outline the benefits of using the respective methods (e.g. formal lecture; conveying broad ideas; cost effective for large groups).

The answers to Activity 9.1 will depend on your own educational and organizational learning experiences. Some organizations offer a wide range of learning opportunities, whereas others adopt a traditional training approach with lecturing and question and answer sessions being the norm. To a large extent, the method chosen will depend on the actual skills being taught or knowledge being conveyed. However, even when simply conveying information, the innovative trainer will adopt a range of lively and meaningful methods. Next we will discuss a number of methods available for use in large groups. It is important to note that most of these could also be used for smaller groups, but not *vice versa*.

Lectures

The lecture is probably the most common and yet the most heavily criticized of all learning methods (Bligh, 1998). Learners often favour this method because it is almost entirely passive and demands little from them except the appearance of being awake. Trainers (and budget holders) appreciate that information can be thrown at large numbers of people comparatively cheaply. It is also a wonderful opportunity for those with a streak of extraversion to take the stage and expound on their favourite ideas without the intellectual challenge of debate. However, is it an effective method of learning? The didactic nature of the lecture has attracted criticism. For example, in a university context, Barnett (2000: 159) describes the lecture as a:

> refuge for the faint-hearted ... it keeps channels of communication closed, freezes hierarchy between lecturer and students and removes any responsibility on the student to respond ... the students remain as voyeurs; the lecture remains a comfort zone ... the student watches a performance and is not obliged to engage with it.

Nevertheless, the lecture can be a useful medium through which to convey broad ideas about a particular subject. However, the lack of interaction means that misunderstanding may result and clarity on certain issues may not be sought. Success is dependent on a number of factors, including:

- The skill of the speaker
- The extent to which a lecture is appropriate to convey the subject material
- The extent to which the visual support facilitates understanding of the material
- The willingness and ability of the audience to concentrate
- The lecture not being too lengthy.

Saroyan and Snell (1997, cited in Jin, 2000) provide the following framework for evaluating lectures:

1 *Strategy*: appropriateness of level of instructional strategy (synergy between long-term learning plan and student acceptance level)
2 *Organization*:
    - structure: the ways lectures are organized, e.g. in hierarchical form, chaining, or other variations (Bligh, 1998)
    - provision of summary of main points
    - effective use of media.
3 *Clarity*:
    - interaction
    - active involvement of students
    - responsiveness of students
    - communication of expected learning
    - enthusiasm.

Jin (2000) identifies another element that is important in determining the popularity and effectiveness of a lecture: its entertainment value. This is particularly significant with very large groups, especially if there are uncommitted or less able people among the audience. Describing a university situation, Jin observed that:

> Students like to enjoy lectures (so do lecturers, of course). The list of features referring to an entertainment dimension can be very long. For example, good lectures were described as 'interesting, not boring', 'humorous not stern', 'charismatic not weak'. Much less attention was paid to the education aspect. Boring lectures were always the focus of student complaint. They did not like a dull atmosphere in the classroom. They liked jokes and they wanted to be *entertained*. Many groups mentioned the word charismatic. Lecturers are the focal point of the classroom and students expect them to show that they can maintain the audience's attention, by means of good communication skills and the right personality.

Recent opinion has tended to be slightly more favourable toward the lecture as a vehicle of learning. For example, Ward and Lee (2004) found no significant difference in test scores between groups of students randomly allocated to lecture-based and problem-based learning programmes. However, Nadkami (2003) identified more complex mental models being used by learners who had received a mixture of lecture and experiential learning methods than those who had been provided with one of those methods alone. Brookfield and Preskill (1999: 45–6, in Sutherland, 2003) argued that the lecture method can be integrated with discussion techniques:

> One of the traps that advocates of discussion methods often fall into is setting up a false dichotomy between lecturing and discussion ... If you lecture, so their argument goes, you only serve to confirm your authoritarian, demagogic tendencies. This is a disservice to well-intentioned colleagues and a gross misunderstanding of pedagogical dynamics ... We believe this pedagogical bifurcation is wrong. Lectures are not, in and of themselves, oppressive and authoritarian ... Similarly, discussions are not, in and of themselves, liberating and spontaneous ... Instead of reducing questions of pedagogical method to a simplistic dichotomy – discussion good, lecture bad – we see these two methods as complementary ... We want to argue that lectures can provide a wonderful opportunity for teachers to model the ... dispositions they wish to encourage in discussion.

Brookfield and Preskill suggest a number of ways in which lectures can be used to develop discussion, including the following:

1   Pose questions at the beginning of each lecture. These should be questions you intend to answer.

2 End the lecture with a further set of questions consisting of issues raised in the lecture, and questions left unanswered or reformatted in a new, possibly more challenging way.

3 Ask students to write down their own questions about the lecture content. Stop the lecture after every 20 minutes or so and ask students to reflect on the material covered, write down the most important point to them personally, and list further issues raised in their minds.

4 Introduce alternative perspectives. Present the lecture as a debate between two or more different points of view, perhaps delivering each from a different part of the room, or introducing a colleague to give one of the perspectives.

5 Challenge assumptions. Ask students to identify core assumptions in the lecture with questions such as:

   ■ What's the most contentious statement you've heard so far in the lecture today?
   ■ What's the most important point that's been made in the lecture so far?
   ■ What question would you most like to have answered regarding today's lecture?
   ■ What's the most unsupported assertion you've heard in the lecture so far?
   ■ Of all the ideas and points you've heard so far today, which is most obscure or ambiguous to you?

Finally, we should consider the importance of the lecturer's enthusiasm or passion for the subject. Meier (2000: 238) argues that passion is an essential ingredient in a good training programme, holding that 'subjects taught in a mechanical, perfunctory, emotionless way tend to fall flat for the learner'. He adds:

> Books about training and train-the-trainer programs tend to emphasize the trainer's use of methods, techniques, and media and tend to overlook the one thing needful – the trainer's passion for the subject. Any learning program becomes shallow and ineffective when it's all techniques and no heart.

Activity 9.2

Think of a lecture you have attended in the recent past.

• What made it interesting or boring?
• How could it have been improved?

Case studies

Naumes and Naumes (1999: 10) define a case study as 'a factual description of events that actually happened in the past'. Acknowledging that case studies may also be fictional, they consider that the latter 'do not have the intellectual rigour of a case based in factual research'. Case studies comprise a written scenario about an event, situation, individual or problem that requires analysis, interpretation and recommendations for action. The purpose of the case study is to encourage practical application of skills and knowledge. Resolution of the case is often followed by a group discussion facilitated by the trainer.

Alternatively, the trainer can remain outside the group and extract the learning points from group reports at the end. The same case study can be given to different groups so that different solutions and approaches can be compared. In general the approach can be likened to that of action learning, with a step-by-step approach to complex problem-solving being advocated. There appear to be slight differences in the number of steps involved, but the theme is the same. For instance, the following sequence is a classic example:

1 Understanding the situation
2 Diagnosing the problem areas
3 Generating alternative solutions
4 Predicting outcomes
5 Evaluating alternatives
6 Rounding out the analysis and planning for contingencies
7 Communicating the results.

Case studies have been in use since the 1800s, but their use in workplace-related training took off at the Harvard Business School in the early part of the twentieth century (Naumes and Naumes, 1999). Yin (2002: 10) notes some common criticisms of the case study approach:

■ Lack of rigour – case studies vary considerably in quality, length and accuracy. They may be slanted or biased in order to emphasize a particular point.
■ They provide little basis for scientific generalization – the points of learning gained from a case study may be limited to a specific or narrow set of circumstances that have no relevance to a wider range of possibilities.

■ They take too long – some cases may involve a mass of documentation that requires lengthy analysis, possibly obscuring the point of the exercise.

In general, Yin observes that good case studies are difficult to write. Naumes and Naumes (1999: 11) note that learners are often unhappy with the ambiguity of case studies – the fact that there may not be a 'right answer'. However, real-life business problems often have a variety of solutions, and case studies are ideal for developing skills of analysis and group decision-making that are appropriate for the real world. Case studies provide a method of learning by doing, rather than the passive learning provided by lectures.

As with most learning methods – lectures and presentations being the obvious exceptions – the trainer acts as a facilitator. Meier (2000: 232) considers that the facilitator's role is to initiate the learning process and then 'get out of the way', arguing that the facilitator's role is not to 'stand and deliver' or perform in front of the trainees. Rather, the facilitator should 'create a context in which the learners can work with each other to create meaningful learning'.

Case study learning can be combined with brainstorming exercises to produce suggested solutions.

Brainstorming

Brainstorming provides a total contrast to the traditional lecture, being deliberately unstructured in its first stage and demanding activity rather than passivity from learners. Essentially, it is a problem-centred approach to learning. Devised by Osborn in 1938 and publicized in various editions of his book *Applied Imagination* (Osborn, 1953), this technique enables many ideas to be created by a group in a short time. The group is given a topic, a question or an unfinished sentence to focus upon. For a few minutes, members of the group say anything that occurs to them on that topic, and everything that is said is written down – however irrelevant, seemingly foolish or challengeable. During this time there is no discussion, as the purpose is to produce ideas in volume and variety. Nothing is censored or evaluated. At the end of the brainstorm, members have a chance to elaborate on their comments and to challenge and discuss the ideas produced.

Self-censorship is a notable difficulty associated with brain-storming, and is viewed as a major hindrance to the technique's effectiveness (Williams, 2002). Self-censorship may be conscious or subconscious, and difficult to observe in either case. Self-censorship in workplace brainstorming is increased when managers have a critical attitude towards their employees' efforts at being creative. If staff expect to receive a negative or disparaging response, they are likely to keep quiet. Creative brainstorming requires supportive and friendly feedback.

Critical incidents

The critical incident technique (CIT) (Flanagan, 1954) is a method used to elicit key events that, because of their critical or significant impact, are more easily remembered. Associated feelings or reactions can be elicited more easily than life events that are less memorable. For instance, many people are able to remember where they were and what they were doing when they heard about the death of Diana, Princess of Wales, or the 9/11 destruction of the twin towers in New York.

CIT can be used in facilitating ideas and interactions within large groups. In a training context, CIT begins with a brief description of an incident. In discussion, the group then examines the possible feelings and thoughts of the characters involved, various dialogue exchanges and possible outcomes to the episode.

CIT is particularly effective when related to case studies, particularly to those involving a learner's own organization (Stolovich and Keeps, 1999: 703). For example, in a retail training exercise the participants may be asked to consider a situation involving an angry customer with a complaint about a product or service, the interaction with members of the sales staff, and the way that the complaint was resolved. Different groups can exchange findings after separate discussions. In this case, a mere description of the sequence of events is not adequate. For true learning to occur, it is necessary to work through the behaviour and underlying thinking of the staff in achieving the best possible resolution to the complaint. From a strategic perspective, it is also necessary that the choice of critical incident and the behaviours highlighted should fit the organization's policies on dealing with customers.

Discussions and debates

Discussions and debates can be extremely useful for encouraging group members to consider opposing views on particular topics. However, success depends on the willingness of the participants to embrace new ideas, and the skill of the trainer in managing potential conflict. Discussions and debates can be a useful tool for three main reasons:

1 New ideas and perspectives arise which may not have been considered before because of deeply entrenched beliefs or understanding
2 Key interpersonal skills of influencing and substantiating a viewpoint are developed
3 Difficult issues requiring analysis and critique can more readily be attempted.

An experienced and confident group will welcome the opportunity for discussion. A less experienced group will need clear guidelines as to what is expected of them (e.g. a list of written questions to stimulate and direct their discussion, together with some framework on how to proceed). Silberman (1995: 35) suggests that a discussion can be run in the form of a town meeting. First, a topic is outlined and a participant is invited to provide an opinion. That speaker then selects another (willing) participant to follow on, until all members of the group have contributed. Members could be given 2 minutes each to present their individual ideas without interruption. This equal-time technique indicates that everybody's contribution is of value.

Role-plays

A role-play is a simulation requiring trainees to act the roles of individuals in a particular situation or set of circumstances. The scenario employed may be real or imaginary, but should be relevant to the learning needs of the participants. Another way to describe a typical role-play is 'a one-act, unscripted miniplay involving two or more participants taking the parts of different people' (Turner, 1996: 4).

Role-playing is a very useful means of learning and practising new and more appropriate skills in a safe environment. It is the very antithesis of passive learning, requiring active participation, involvement and true action learning. Since most role-play techniques use other members of the group as observers, the 'actors' receive feedback from colleagues or the facilitator.

Drama

Drama takes more structuring and time than role-playing. In a drama, group members perform a scripted piece or devise one for themselves to illustrate a particular learning point. The effectiveness of drama as a learning technique rests mainly on the skill of the trainer and the group in drawing out the learning for themselves in a follow-up processing session.

Exercises

Trainer exercises are a useful way of building on newly presented information, or for identifying the practical application of new topics or skills. An exercise can be any kind of group activity that produces learning about the group itself or the topic or skill. An exercise must have a clearly defined objective, and involve individual and/or group work that is then discussed with the trainer to summarize the learning points.

Games

There are many games available which, although they have an enjoyable aspect, are a valuable means of facilitating interaction and learning. Some may appear relatively simple and straightforward, but are an excellent way of encouraging newly introduced group members to each other in a non-threatening manner. Others are more structured and involve business games with key objectives and criteria applied, against which participants' performance on them can be evaluated. Scannell and Newstrom (1994) outline many of the games trainers play in their book *Even More Games Trainers Play*.

Sugar (1998: xvi) identifies that good training games should be:

1 User friendly, with a game format that is easily explained and quickly understood
2 Easily adaptable, so it accepts your content, can be scaled up or down to any audience, and can be made more or less competitive, depending on the audience
3 Fun to play, evoking a 'smile quotient' among the players
4 Challenging, keeping the players' interest throughout the contest
5 Portable, so it can be taken into any site.

As you can see, a wide variety of methods exists to stimulate and facilitate the learning process. One important issue in choosing methods is the culture in which the trainer is operating. Example 9.1 indicates the difficulty of introducing methods that are unfamiliar to learners.

Example 9.1: Teaching and learning in the Middle East

A large university in the UK has successfully run a number of open learning Business Studies Degree programmes in a Middle Eastern country.

The UK lecturers adopt an action learning approach to teaching during their periodic visits to students. However, resistance to this method is regularly experienced. It appears that mature students prefer tutor-led lectures rather than group exercises to facilitate learning. Where students are open to this mode of experiential learning, it is only after much formal input has provided the context in which they will conduct the exercises. This is contrary to the British higher education teaching methods, where students learn through problem-solving exercises and thus themselves highlight the key issues. The tutor then makes sense of the ideas and places them within an academic framework.

Experience has shown this university that the learning culture is fairly resistant to the notion of experiential learning, and that students would rather receive large amounts of material, which they can learn and apply. To force the students to identify the issues themselves before formal input only raises their anxiety, resistance and lack of co-operation. Thus, the choice of methods and underpinning philosophical assumptions about learning must take into account the culture in which learning takes place.

Outdoor learning

Organizations are increasingly seeking out new and innovative ways to motivate their staff to learn. One example is the range of outdoor training courses available, also known as adventure education or open-air courses (see Example 9.2). They have become an increasingly popular means of facilitating teambuilding and leadership via physically challenging group experiences. They can be tough, especially for unfit and older employees, and the transfer of learning to the workplace may be questionable.

Activity 9.3

- Have you or anyone you know experienced an outdoor or adventure training course? If so, outline the key activities that were undertaken and, under each of these activities outline the main advantages (e.g. increased motivation and co-operation from team members) and disadvantages (e.g. relevance of activities to the workplace were unclear) to arise from this form of learning. If not, outline the main advantages and disadvantages of outdoor training as you see them.

Your answers will depend on whether you have experienced outdoor training firsthand, and whether any experiences you are aware of have been positive or negative. Mark Tuson (1994) gives several reasons for the usefulness of outdoor training programmes. These can be outlined as follows:

- They provide an opportunity to solve real problems for which failure and success have real consequences
- By working in different and unfamiliar environments the behaviour of participants is highlighted, whereas it might pass unnoticed in familiar surroundings
- Participants can try out new ways of operating in a 'safe' arena which has limited financial or business consequences
- Tasks experienced offer the opportunity of developing mutual trust and support amongst participants
- The nature of the exercises provide memorable experiences which, because of their impact, have implications for similar consequent learning opportunities
- Outdoor learning programmes can be highly enjoyable and thus encourage and support a sense of exploration and willingness to try out new options
- Taking into account the factors above, there is a high probability that participants will return to the workplace highly motivated
- Outdoor programmes increase the level of involvement, participation and enthusiasm; this has implications for behavioural changes, learning, problem-solving or organizational and cultural changes which, if properly handled are transferable back to the work environment.

Tuson (1994) outlines a variation of Kolb's learning cycle that explains how outdoor training facilitates learning (see Figure 9.1).

According to Tuson (1994), the team is given tasks to prepare, plan and carry out. After completion, they review their performance, the processes they used, and how their choices and each member's pattern of behaviour affected the outcome. Individual and group behaviour is then adapted to increase effectiveness for use in subsequent tasks.

The argument for using outdoor training is strong, and it is probably more valuable if it is supported by classroom tuition and direct attention is paid to the transferability and maintenance of newly acquired teamworking skills. At present, there is strong criticism in terms of the transfer of learned skills back to

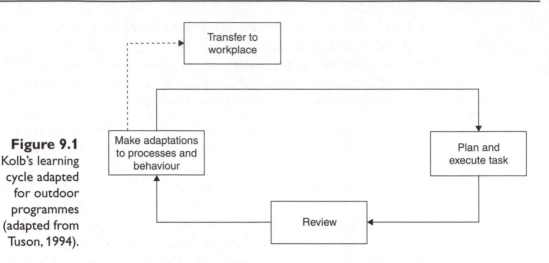

Figure 9.1
Kolb's learning cycle adapted for outdoor programmes (adapted from Tuson, 1994).

the workplace. There are also reports that participants may suffer unnecessary stress and hardship during the training.

Example 9.2: Outdoor training at Ove Arup

The consulting engineering group Ove Arup implemented a competency framework specifying the skills required from employees. Being able to work in and lead effective project teams are specific requirements for new graduates and first-line managers. The training manager, Debra Larkman, said she was looking for demonstrable skills such as planning and organization, decision-making, effective communication, teamworking and leadership. In her opinion, classroom training alone is insufficient for team leader training, which also required an element of experiential learning.

Larkman accepts that there are questions to ask about programmes that send people abseiling or rabbit-skinning, but Ove Arup's real workplace is outdoors, and training in the open can be highly relevant. A number of facilitated exercises are used to develop trust, teamworking and mutual reliance, as well as leadership. One example is the 'trust trail', often used as an initial icebreaker. This involves people working in pairs, where one person is led blindfolded by the other through irregular terrain and sometimes across a rope walkway. They have to maintain total silence throughout this activity, and must agree a method of communication before it begins. The exercise is thought to draw attention to several aspects of trust, communication, leadership and personal relationships.

(Source: adapted from Industrial and Commercial Training, 2002)

Training methods for small groups

In planned training courses or workshops, whether internal or external, trainers can adopt a wide variety of different techniques to stimulate and facilitate interaction and learning. Several possibilities are available in addition to many of those mentioned for large groups, and some of these are outlined below.

Buzz-groups

These are groups of three to eight people. They are useful for energizing group members after spells of inactivity. After listening to a lecture or watching a film, members are asked to turn to a neighbour and share their views or impressions for 5 minutes or so. Alternatively, small, leaderless discussion groups of four to six people can be used. Brief reports from buzz-groups to a general session can be a useful guide to what has been heard, understood, misunderstood or disagreed with.

A carousel

In a carousel, a group sits in a circle of chairs facing outwards. Another group forms a circle around them facing inwards, so that each person is facing someone. The activity takes place with pairs working together for a short time, and then the outer 'wheel' rotates one place so that each person has a new partner. This encourages interaction between all members.

A continuum

In a continuum, an imaginary line is drawn down the room, each end representing opposite viewpoints about a topic. Participants stand on the line, placing themselves according to their points of view. Discussion can take place between people in the same section of the line, or between those at opposite ends.

A horseshoe

For presentations and discussion the group sits in a semi-circle with an open space at one end, in which the trainer can sit or stand, or where there is a chalkboard, flip chart or overhead projector (OHP) screen. This avoids the traditional classroom layout where individuals face the trainer and have to use that person as chairperson. In a horseshoe layout, interaction is increased, although the trainer is directing most of the interactions.

Inter-group competition

Competition is set up between sub-groups engaged in similar tasks. This can develop a feeling of unity within each group, and the rivalry can be very energizing. Sometimes, however, the rivalry can produce division in the larger group, so this may need careful monitoring.

Options groups

A range of activities is outlined, and individuals opt for the one they prefer. Groups then form on the basis of the choices, and undertake their chosen activities simultaneously.

Pairs

Working in pairs is most suitable if the exercise asks for a high level of self-disclosure. Individuals will probably be more willing to be open with information if they are not expected to share it with the rest of the group. After the paired event, the two participants can choose the key learning points to disclose to the wider group without the actual details of the interaction.

Shifting sub-groups

Again, a line is drawn down the room. One side of the line represents one 'position'; the other side represents a different, or opposite position. The group divides according to opinion, forming sub-groups. Buzz or discussion groups can be formed from each sub-group, or a debate can take place between those on opposite sides.

Training methods for individuals

A wide variety of methods exists to facilitate individual learning. Throughout this text, the importance has been placed on organizations creating environments where continuous development is encouraged. It will be difficult for individuals to learn on a daily basis in their roles if the culture and management style do not support it. This is key in individual development and learning. However, in planned learning events there are numerous techniques that facilitate individual understanding and acquisition of new skills, knowledge and attitudes.

On-the-job training

Traditional on-the-job training has been give a variety of names, including: 'sitting by Nellie', 'learning the ropes', 'sink or swim

Activity 9.4

- Make a list of techniques that exist to facilitate individual learning (e.g. learning on one's own without the intended direct input of others).
- Outline the main advantages and disadvantages of each method.

For example:

Methods	Advantages	Disadvantages
e.g. Reading a book	Self-paced	No opportunity to discuss understanding/share ideas
e.g. Information conveyed by company intranet	Expedient	One-sided communication; misunderstandings in intention of message

training' and 'buddy training' (Jacobs, 2003: 23). Sisson (2001: 7) identifies a number of advantages to on-the-job training:

1 *Hands-on approach.* Since any form of training ends with learners performing a real job, on-the-job training is particularly appealing, and especially so for individuals who learn best by doing. Moreover, some degree of on-the-job training is inevitable for most jobs.

2 *Realistic practice.* On-the-job training provides the most realistic context for learning. It does not require the transfer of skills from an external environment such as a classroom. Many people have difficulty in transferring skills from one situation to another.

3 *Simple training approach.* Most changes in the workplace are relatively minor and evolutionary. These small changes require training, but do not justify a major training programme. On-the-job training is a simple mechanism for dealing with this situation.

4 *Ideal informal training system.* Learning is largely an informal process conducted by workers themselves, rather than organized by managers. 'Can you show me how to do this?' and 'How does this work?' are common questions in the workplace. When a fellow employee responds

positively, training is taking place without any formal organization. As Sisson (2001: 8) states: 'No manager asked them to do it. No company program is required. No diploma is offered. And nobody ever thinks twice about it. But this very situation demonstrates one of the most compelling reasons for establishing on-the-job training as a key component in any organization's effort to train employees.'

Sisson (2001: 3) also identifies four characteristic but problematic features of on-the-job training:

1   *Traditional on-the-job training is focused on the work.* Training is a secondary matter to getting the job done. If an instructor is busy, training has to wait.
2   *The work provides the structure for the training.* Learning is unstructured, and follows the flow of the job. According to Sisson, 'a trainee may participate in some incidents that are highly unusual and altogether miss seeing other, more common events. In a very real sense, the traditional on-the-job training instructor is at the mercy of circumstances.'
3   *The instructor relies on job experience to do the training.* The role of instructor is usually given to an experienced employee. However, competence at the job does not mean that he or she is a good instructor. Additionally, the instructor may train the novice to perform a task in his or her own preferred, but unorthodox, way.
4   *The training method is determined by the instructor.* Skills may be taught by showing or telling. Trainees have individual learning styles, and may prefer one method to the other. An instructor may do more telling than showing, or the reverse, without regard for the novice's personal learning style.

Sisson considers that such problems may lead to traditional on-the-job training being inconsistent, inefficient and ineffective.

Checklists and questionnaires

Checklists and questionnaires can be used prior to or during planned learning events. Some questionnaires may identify certain characteristics about individuals (e.g. personality, preferred team roles or interests). They can be used as a framework for understanding one's own and others' behaviour in a larger group or training situation. Whilst they can be useful yardsticks against which to evaluate behaviour, individuals may become typecast by the labels used which limit their real value. Other questionnaires and checklists serve to prepare individuals for later activities or exercises.

Coaching and mentoring

Coaching and mentoring offer an active learning approach to individual workplace learning (see Example 9.3). Typically, mentors are 'established managers who can provide support, help and advice to more junior members of staff' (Price, 2004: 582). Mentors should have an understanding of the employee's job, but should not be his or her direct line manager. Preferably, they should have the same gender and ethnic background, to increase the likelihood of sharing similar life experiences. According to Thomson and Mabey (1994: 60), successful mentors should also be at least 7–10 years older than the people they mentor. Ideally, employees should meet with their mentor on a monthly basis to discuss their progress and career development. The mentor can talk through these issues and suggest appropriate learning objectives.

Coaches may be internal or external mentors who take a more active role than traditional mentoring. Coaching appears in a number of guises, including:

1   *Career coaching.* Chung *et al.* (2003) describe career coaches as 'personal consultants for any work-related concerns such as balancing home and work, learning interviewing skills, developing better managerial skills, executive personal and career development, and even managerial training to help managers become career coaches to their employees'.

2   *Executive coaching.* Often matched with senior executives, executive coaches provide much of the support that more junior employees expect from their managers. Executive coaches may talk through work problems, thus facilitating decisions, or advise on the executive's own motivation and developing his or her managerial skills.

Example 9.3: Coaching survey

A recent CIPD study shows that coaching is increasingly popular as a means of promoting learning and development. The 2004 Training and Development Survey also indicates that coaching is almost universally accepted as a method that delivers tangible business benefits.

Whereas a mere 16 per cent of respondents thought that training courses were the most effective way for people to learn in the workplace, 96 per cent valued coaching as an effective way to promote learning in organizations. Coaching was also viewed as an important way of reducing 'leakage' from training courses, and therefore improved their effectiveness.

The survey also shows that coaching is not viewed entirely through rose-tinted glasses. HR professionals are concerned about the lack of accreditation and regulation of external providers, with only a third of respondents believing that there is sufficient regulation and accreditation of the coaching industry.

More than three-quarters of organizations use coaching, but a mere 6 per cent have written strategies for coaching all of their employees. The study shows that most coaches are line managers, but just 14 per cent of organizations provide compulsory coaching skills for those who manage staff.

'Organizations need to get strategies in place to maximize the impact of coaching for their organization. This will ensure they get the desired business benefits and that employees receive the best learning available,' says Jessica Rolph, CIPD Learning, Training and Development Adviser.

Main findings of the survey:

- More than three-quarters of surveyed organizations used coaching as a training method
- 90 per cent of respondents considered that coaching was a key mechanism for transferring training skills into the workplace
- Virtually all respondents (99 per cent) thought that coaching delivered tangible benefits
- More than 90 per cent of respondents believed that coaching, applied appropriately, could positively influence the bottom line
- Line managers were most likely to deliver coaching, but fewer than 20 per cent of organizations had 'all' or 'a majority' of their line managers trained to carry it out.

Jessica Rolph says:

> Businesses and coaching professionals must join together to push for greater professionalism across the industry. If pressure is exerted to secure minimum expected standards, qualifications and results, the 'cowboy' operators will have no option but to conform.
>
> If coaching is taken seriously and is properly managed, it can increase business competitiveness as well as helping individuals attain their potential. However, a number of issues currently exist that may prevent coaching fulfilling its potential: few organizations are training their managers, there is still confusion about standards and terminology, and little evaluation is taking place.

(Source: www.hrmguide.co.uk, 8 May 2004)

Open learning, visual aids and empirical evidence

First in this section, we discuss the merits of open learning as an increasingly popular and innovative method of individual learning.

Open learning

Open learning constitutes an increasing diverse field of differing terminology and technology. The reader will come across different terms, including open, distance, flexible and resource-based learning.

It is useful to define these terms clearly and to identify what open learning actually constitutes in practice. As a variation of organizationally determined, self-managed learning it has enormous benefits, including increased choice, convenience and flexibility for both the learner and the learning provider. It thus offers a useful medium for continuous development within a learning culture.

It is also important to identify the different assumptions about how and why people learn, as this will influence the different open learning approaches taken. First let us consider these assumptions and their implications for open learning, and we will then look more specifically at what open learning means in practice.

Activity 9.5

- What do you understand by the term 'open learning'? Use key words or phrases to explain your answer (for example, self-managed and self-paced study, increased flexibility), and outline what an open learning system would look like in practice.

Although there is little consensus as to the precise meaning and use of the term 'open learning', your answer will probably have included key words like:

- Resources
- Distance learning
- Flexibility and choice
- Timing and materials
- Support systems.

The following discussion will highlight the nature of open learning, and the different phrases used to explain what it is in practice. Open learning is not the same as 'self study', whereby an individual works alone with materials. However, an open learner will spend a substantial amount of time working alone. Open learning is an organized and planned system of learning that is coupled with support and integrated into the 'learning system' of an organization. It is important to understand what open learning actually comprises in order to design and manage it effectively. Different terms are used to explain different forms of open learning, and include:

- Distance learning, which implies that the learner is in some way physically separated from the learning provider. For instance, a distance learner may not physically visit the providing organization, but study and learn with the use of materials, telephone or electronic communication. This offers opportunities for learners to study at geographically dispersed locations. Much distance learning is now provided through the Internet or corporate intranets. These are discussed in our next chapter on the e-learning revolution.

- Flexible learning, which reflects the gradual transition from traditional education and training as being tutor- or trainer-led within a specified structure and timeframe. It is flexible in terms of content choice, timing, location and the media used. It is often a form of distance learning, and reflects the gradual transition of open learning from a marginal activity in education and training to a key enabler of HRD strategy.

- Resource-based learning (RBL), which is a form of open and flexible learning that highlights the importance and necessity of key resources to support open learning. These resources include new technology (e.g. Internet, e-mail, video conferencing and desktop conferencing) as well as physical and human support systems.

Learning resource centres comprise diverse support materials, and are increasingly being offered within educational establishments and businesses. These will be discussed in greater detail later in Chapter 10. The human support systems offer subject specialist advice, technological support and counselling. Individual differences in the learner, the nature of learning and the learning provider of RBL mean that tailor-made programmes will have a greater opportunity for success than hastily chosen, off-the-shelf packages.

As open learning is becoming an important part of continuous development in the twenty-first century, it deserves greater attention in any text describing HRD methods and techniques.

The benefits and disadvantages of open learning

If open learning is well designed and managed it has many benefits, and forms part of a culture of continuous and self-managed learning. It will be useful at this stage for you to consider what you see to be the main benefits of disadvantages of open learning for both the learner and the learning provider.

Activity 9.6

- Under the two headings below, outline what you consider to be the advantages and disadvantages of open learning for both the learner and the learning provider.

Advantages	**Disadvantages**
Learner	*Learner*
Individuals can learn at their own pace	Individual may feel isolated and lack motivation
Learning provider	*Learning provider*
The range of training can be extended	High initial investment

---

Your answer to Activity 9.6 probably included increased choice, convenience and flexibility for both the learner and the learning provider. Substantial research has been conducted by the MultiPALIO Partnership (1999), which has produced a European-wide open learning package for designing and managing open learning systems. Their research shows that the benefits of open learning can be significant for both organizations and learners.

In organizations:

- Learning can take place when it is required
- Small and large numbers can be served
- Open learning can meet a range of needs and abilities

■ Training becomes standard, and can be offered nationally and internationally
■ Updating can be easier
■ The range of training can be extended
■ Training becomes 'public', thus potentially increasing awareness and ultimately, involvement
■ It contributes towards a learning culture.

Learners, in turn:

■ Are responsible for their learning
■ Can learn at their own pace
■ Can achieve their own objectives
■ Can concentrate on what they need to learn most urgently.

In terms of disadvantages, it is difficult to say when increased choice, convenience and flexibility might not be welcome. However, that is not to say that designing, delivering and managing an open learning system is not without its problems. Problems to be addressed include issues of:

■ Appropriate sustained support
■ Limited financial resources
■ Resistance to change
■ Resistance to new technology
■ Change to power relationships
■ Inappropriate organizational culture and management style.

The commentary has already highlighted a number of advantages to be gained from the use of open learning. The MultiPALIO Partnership (1999) identifies four groups of benefits to be sought from open learning. It is worth examining these because of the increasing use and importance of open learning in employee development. These four categories are:

1 *Cost effectiveness.* There are numerous unpublished reports that indicate the cost effectiveness of open learning. Clearly the cost of designing open learning can be underestimated in terms of the long-term support and updating needed. In addition, 'hidden' costs exist in terms of staff time and support needed to facilitate

effective open learning. In areas such as IT, for example, computer-based learning offers high cost-savings. In other subject or skill areas, cost effectiveness appears to depend on:

- The ability of open learning to deliver proven learning outcomes
- The numbers of learners involved
- The extent of initial and continuing investment.

2 *Improving the supply of learning.* Open learning offers an opportunity to expand the quality and availability of learning, in both corporate training and educational establishments.

3 *Ensuring quality and consistency.* Open learning materials are almost always based on a set of core learning materials which are, to a large extent, standardized. Thus the consistency and quality of the provision for learners studying on a national or international basis can be assured. However, local cultural variations will dictate the need to adapt materials either in content or in language. Terms, phrases or examples used in one local environment may be misinterpreted or meaningless in another location. Whilst standardized materials offer greater opportunity for consistency and quality, the increasing use of new communication technology such as computer conferencing offer learners greater autonomy. This means that individuals have more options for interacting with tutors, trainers and other learners. Other developments in learning technologies and electronic publishing also offer options for individuals to tailor materials more precisely to their own needs (using multimedia resource banks).

4 *Contributing to the learning culture of an organization.* Open learning fits appropriately within the culture of the learning organization – that is, one that consistently facilitates the learning of all its members and consciously transforms itself and its context. Even within organizations that do not fully embrace such a culture, open learning does offer a means of encouraging individual learners to take greater responsibility for their own development. Open learning offers the possibility of improving both the overall availability and access to learning, when and at the time it is needed. Although open learning is a useful

tool in advancing the objectives of the learning organization, the following must be considered:

- How open learning is integrated with other learning methods
- How open learning will be embedded within the organization
- How open learning is assessed as contributing to changes in learning culture.

When might open learning not be appropriate?

There may be occasions when open learning may not offer an appropriate means of facilitating learning – for example:

- When the organizational culture does not support this style of learning
- If there is a shortage of expertise, both technically and idealistically
- If the preferred technology is inaccessible, or outside of budgetary limits
- If the initial investment may be seen as too high
- When support systems do not exist to facilitate this new mode of learning
- If the time spent on the management of training may increase
- When suitable materials do not exist
- If it is difficult to justify it to stakeholders.

The learning of new skills or attitudes may not be possible through the medium of open learning; except where a programme includes workshops or tutorials as part of a totally integrated learning environment. If this is not the case, the development of many interpersonal and counselling skills requiring face-to-face interaction is difficult to achieve. Cunningham (1998) argues that adult learners are best served in groups that include other learners, or in circumstances where learning can take place through interaction with other learners or a subject expert. He also considers that learning methods which make use of workplace problems are best, and that adult learners are particularly keen to direct their own learning.

However, it is possible to use open learning creatively alongside traditional skills development approaches, as Example 9.4 illustrates.

Example 9.4: Interpersonal skills training

At a large university in the UK, a combined method of open learning and face-to-face tuition is regularly used in teaching assertiveness. Open learning materials are given to students, and these provide:

- Definitions of assertiveness, non-assertiveness and aggression
- Examples of typical language associated with these three types of interpersonal interaction.

Students are then given a series of exercises that provide examples of interactions between two people. The student must label these as assertive, non-assertive or aggressive.

Where interactions are deemed non-assertive or aggressive, the student is required to provide more appropriate assertive responses.

Students are then invited in, on a face-to-face basis, for weekend workshops. In developing their assertiveness skills, they are invited to share the results of their activities and act them out. Feedback is given on the appropriate responses and associated non-verbal language. This simple workshop design applies an open learning approach to interpersonal skills training.

Thus, an organization that wants to integrate open learning as a means of realizing its HRD strategies needs to consider flexible ways of designing appropriate systems. The importance of culture has already been highlighted as key in underpinning open learning provision. In addition, key operational issues must be considered – namely, the materials used, the support mechanisms to facilitate this learning, and the choice of media and technology available.

The use of visual aids

When a trainer is presenting information, audio visual aids provide an invaluable means of maintaining an audience's interest and retaining information. Traditionally, overhead slides and flip charts are used to support trainer presentations. However, more sophisticated technologies are now available, including data projectors for use with such applications as Microsoft Power Point. Some other techniques are described here.

Videos

The training video can be a useful means of conveying both simple ideas and information, or of learning vicariously from the mistakes and adoption of more appropriate behaviour by actors. It also provides variety and interest, but there are limitations to its effectiveness.

Table 9.1
The advantages and disadvantages of videos

For	Against
There is a wide choice of generic video training programmes on the market	Learners may assume a passive role – watch rather than do
Learners are usually motivated by video	Difficult to access or branch to particular topics in the linear sequence
Powerful communication tool, since it uses sight and sound in combination	
Very realistic, since it shows the context within which learning points can be made	High standards associated with most broadcast TV programmes can be expensive to emulate
Good for analysing movement	The realism may make a video date quickly
Not dependent on reading skills of learners	Difficult to update
	Playback equipment not easily transportable
	Different national TV standards restricts transferability between countries

Use to:

Illustrate procedures and skills

Provide close-ups of techniques that can usually only be viewed from a distance

Show simulations

Add drama to situations

Convey attitudes and personal views

Demonstrate experience in different locations

Activity 9.7

- List the main advantages (e.g. combines visual and auditory input) and disadvantages (e.g. learners assume a passive role) of using videos in facilitating effective learning.

The advantages and disadvantages of videos are outlined in Table 9.1.

Trigger videos offer short video presentations where a critical incident can be played straight back to the camera and hence to the viewer, who is then invited to react to the incident. Video recordings and feedback of learner behaviours can also be a useful and direct tool in modifying behaviour.

Video-conferencing

Video-conferencing forms an integral part of many open learning programmes. Typically, it involves providing 'tele-lectures' and/or discussions transmitted via telecommunication links or, increasingly, through broadband Internet. This method can be characterized as an attempt to provide a similar style of teaching or training for learners at a distance to that provided in conventional classroom learning. In some uses there is a deliberate strategy of minimizing face-to-face teaching, and a large proportion of a learning programme is delivered in this way. In others, broadcast sessions form one component of a mixed media programme. The model has some specific uses, including:

- Where there is a need to reach scattered groups of staff on a transnational or global basis (e.g. small groups of staff working for multinational companies)
- Where organizations are providing joint learning initiatives across national boundaries
- Where large numbers need to be reached and other options are not viable.

Although there are several successful applications of video-conferencing, it may ultimately have a relatively small number of viable and cost effective uses. It is particularly useful as a means of distance learning where there is a large scattered audience. Access to video-conferencing has increased in recent years, but there are some disadvantages, and the 'balance sheet' of benefits and drawbacks shown in Table 9.2 indicates both the attractions and the serious limitations of the method.

Table 9.2 includes some points you may have thought of in Activity 9.8.

Activity 9.8

- Outline the main advantages (e.g. learners at different sites can communicate) and disadvantages (e.g. requires training of trainers and learners) of video-conferencing as a means of facilitating open learning.

Table 9.2

Benefits and drawbacks of video-conferencing

Benefits	Drawbacks
Allows distance communication by voice and picture with expert tutor/trainer	Need for satellite or telecommunication connections remains a (decreasing) barrier
Heightens motivation to learn	Systems from different producers do not necessarily communicate with each other
Learners at several sites can communicate with each other	
Can form an attractive centrepiece to a distance course – popular with learners	Can be inflexible – learners lose control of time and place
	Often difficult to achieve genuine integration of video-conferencing elements into a course unless they are its core
Can incorporate the transmission of other video material	
Can be cost effective where substantial numbers are involved	May need a substantial number of other components added to make up a course
	Will require tutors and trainers to learn new techniques
Teachers and learners alike can illustrate charts, photographs, computer files and videotapes	Without sufficient use/large numbers, cost may be prohibitive
	Some learners don't like to see themselves on TV
It is easier to get access to external experts/teachers from other countries	Requires teacher training and adaptation of visual training material
Can have the same benefits as traditional classroom teaching	May strengthen cultural misunderstandings by distorting face and body movements
Travel cost savings can be significant	Audio connection may not be good and cause problems, especially in multilingual, international course
Prior planning is often necessary by learners, which contributes to better learning experiences	Delay in transmission of picture and sound can distract learning and teacher/learner interactions

Empirical evidence

What is the empirical evidence for the use and effectiveness of different learning methods? Woods and Perdue (2000) asked a sample of managers in institutions that were members of the National Association of College & University Food Services to rate a number of learning methods on perceived effectiveness. Six criteria were used: acquiring knowledge, changing attitudes, improving problem-solving skills, improving interpersonal skills, participant acceptance and knowledge retention. A summary of their results is given in Table 9.3. Of course this study did not attempt to measure actual effectiveness, and respondents in other industries or circumstances would probably have given different answers.

Table 9.3
Perceived effectiveness of learning methods

Learning method	Comments
1 Case study	Second place for knowledge acquisition, and joint fifth for knowledge retention; otherwise not valued highly
2 Instructional videotapes	Third place for knowledge retention, and fifth for all others except knowledge acquisition (tenth)
3 Lecture	Rated badly for knowledge acquisition, and indifferently to poor for all others
4 One-to-one instruction	Third for knowledge acquisition, and indifferent to poor for all others
5 Role play	Second place for interpersonal skills development and fourth for problem-solving; otherwise, indifferent to poor
6 Games	Rated worst for knowledge acquisition, in but second or third place for all others
7 Computer simulations	Rated worst for problem-solving, and badly for all others
8 Paper and pencil	Fourth for participant acceptance, but poor for all others
9 Audiotapes	Rated badly for knowledge acquisition, and indifferent for all others
10 Self-assessment	Rated badly for all criteria
11 Movies/films	Rated in first place for all categories, except knowledge acquisition and interpersonal skills development (both fourth)
12 Multimedia presentations	Rated badly on all criteria
13 Audio teleconferencing	Rated fifth for knowledge acquisition, and badly on all others
14 Computer conferencing	Rated badly for interpersonal skill development, and indifferently on all others
15 Video teleconferencing	Rated first on knowledge acquisition and interpersonal skill development, and good on all other criteria except problem-solving
16 Sensitivity training	Rated second on changing attitudes and third for problem-solving; indifferent to poor for all others

Summary

A wide choice of methods exists for developing and training groups and individuals. The choice of method will, to a large extent, depend on the personal preference of the trainer, organizational policy, cost, validity and administrative convenience. Cultural differences may also influence the extent to which participants will benefit from the learning opportunity. An effective learning programme will use a combination of approaches to maximize learning, facilitate motivation and encourage transfer of skills back into the workplace. Learning methods are increasingly combined into 'blended learning' programmes, often combined with e-learning methods, as we shall discover in Chapter 10.

References

Barnett, R. (2000). *Realizing the University in an Age of Supercomplexity*. Open University Press.

Bligh, D. (1998). *What's the Use of Lectures?* 2nd edn. Intellect.

Brookfield, S.D. and Preskill, S. (1999). *Discussion as a Way of Teaching*. Jossey-Bass.

Chung, Y.B., Coleman, M. and Gfroerer, A. (2003). Career coaching: practice, training, professional, and ethical issues. *Career Development Quarterly*, **52(2)**, 141.

Cunningham, J. (1998). The workplace: a learning environment. Paper delivered at the First Annual Conference of the Australian Vocational Education and Training Research Association, Sydney. Cited in Smith, P.J. (2003). Workplace learning and flexible delivery. *Review of Educational Research*, **73(1)**, 53.

Flanagan, J.C. (1954). The critical incident technique. *Psychological Bulletin*, **51**, 327–58.

Industrial and Commercial Training (2002). Outdoor learning is not outward bound. Editorial article. *Industrial and Commercial Training*, **34(1)**, 34–5.

Jacobs, R.L. (2003). *Structural On-the-job Training: Unleashing Employee Expertize into the Workplace*. Barrett-Koehlet Publishing.

Jin, Z. (2000). Learning experience from students of Middlesex University Business School: why do they enjoy some modules/lectures and dislike others? *International Journal of Management Education*, **1(1)**, 22–36.

Meier, D. (2000). *The Accelerated Learning Handbook: A Creative Guide to Designing and Delivering Faster, More Effective Training Programs*. McGraw-Hill.

Milano, M. (1998) *Designing Powerful Training: The Sequential Iterative Model (SIM)*. Jossey-Bass/Pfeiffer.

MultiPALIO Partnership (1999). *European Wide Open Learning Materials*. The Open Learning Foundation.

Nadkami, S. (2003). Instructional methods and mental models of students: an empirical investigation. *Academy of Management Learning & Education*, **2(4)**, 335.

Naumes, M.J. and Naumes, W. (1999). *The Art and Craft of Case Writing*. Sage.

Osborn, A.F. (1953). *Applied Imagination*. Creative Education Foundation.

Price, A.J. (2004). *Human Resource Management in a Business Context*, 2nd edn. Thomson Learning.

Saroyan, A. and Snell, L. (1997). Variations in lecturing styles. *Higher Education*, **33**, 85–104.

Scannell, E.E. and Newstrom, J.W. (1994). *Even More Games Trainers Play*. McGraw-Hill.

Silberman, M. (1995). *101 Ways to Make Training Active.* Jossey-Bass/Pfeiffer.

Sisson, G. (2001). *Hands-on Training: A Simple and Effective Method for On-the-Job Training*. Berrett-Koehler.

Smith, P.J. (2003). Workplace learning and flexible delivery. *Review of Educational Research*, **73(1)**, 53.

Stolovich, H.J. and Keeps, E.J. (1999). *Handbook of Human Performance Technology: Improving Individual and Organizational Performance Worldwide*, 2nd edn. Jossey-Bass/Pfeiffer.

Sugar, S. (1998). *Games that Teach: Experiential Activities for Reinforcing Training.* Jossey-Bass/Pfeiffer.

Sutherland, T. (2003). Discussion as a way of teaching (and how lectures can build discussion skills. *Accounting Education News*, **31(1)**, 7–10.

Thomson, R. and Mabey, C. (1994). *Developing Human Resources*. Butterworth-Heinemann.

Tobin, D.R. (1998). *The Knowledge-Enabled Organization: Moving from 'Training' to 'Learning' to Meet Business Goals*. AMACOM.

Turner, O. (1996). *60 Role Plays for Management and Supervisory Training*. McGraw-Hill.

Tuson, S. (1994). *Outdoor Training for Employee Effectiveness*. Institute of Personnel and Development.

Ward, J.D. and Lee, C.L. (2004). Teaching strategies for FCS: student achievement in problem-based learning versus lecture-based instruction. *Journal of Family and Consumer Sciences*, **96(1)**, 73.

Williams, S.D. (2002). Self-esteem and the self-censorship of creative ideas. *Personnel Review*, **31(4)**, 495–54.

Woods, R.H. and Perdue, J. (2000). The effectiveness of alternative training methods in college and university foodservices. *NACUFS Journal*, **22** (online edition accessed 10 May 2004).

Yin, R.K. (2002). *Case Study Research: Design and Methods*, 3rd edn. Sage.

Chapter 10

The e-learning revolution

Introduction

E-learning has followed the pattern of the Internet – a journey from unrealistic 'hype' to a more modest but increasingly important reality. In the late 1990s and early 2000s, e-learning was discussed in dramatic terms as a revolution in learning technology that would become a massive industry in a few years. However, uptake was slow and largely confined to organizations with a strong focus on information technology. Today, e-learning is increasingly seen as one among many possible elements of open learning and workplace training programmes. In the first section of this chapter we examine the nature of e-learning programmes, why and how they have (or have not) been adopted, and their basic methodology. In the second section we go on to discuss the nature of e-learning content, learning management systems and organizational learning centres.

Objectives

By the end of this chapter you will be able to:

- Define and describe the concept of e-learning
- Explain how investment in e-learning can be justified
- Outline the extent of e-learning adoption
- Summarize current opinion on the effectiveness of e-learning
- Describe how learning content can be developed and managed
- Explain the terms 'learning management system' and 'organizational learning centre'.

The nature and methodology of e-learning programmes

Defining e-learning

> … instructional content or learning experiences delivered or enabled by electronic technology.
>
> (Pantazis, 2002)

E-learning is a term used to describe learning through a variety of information technology developments, including the Internet, networking and computers. Some commentators include storage media such as CD-ROMs. Others use a more restrictive definition, for example:

> Learning that is delivered, enabled or mediated by electronic technology, for the explicit purpose of training in organizations. It does not include standalone technology based training, such as the use of CD Rom.
>
> (CIPD, 2002)

Frequently e-learning and related approaches are lumped together under the label of 'new media', along with 'anything that is not either face-to-face or "delivered" from the printed page' (Halkett, 2002). Halkett considers that this vague and often negative haziness about the concept of e-learning arises from a common fear and misunderstanding of technology, which leads to confusion and creates an air of mystery around the whole topic.

Until the late 1990s, e-learning was known under a variety of other labels, including computer-based training (CBT) and web-based learning. Following the fashion of adding the prefix e- (meaning electronic) to a number of common English words – e-mail being the most ubiquitous combination – comparatively longstanding organizations increasingly adopted the new term. For example, The Association for Computer-based Training (TACT), founded in 1987, changed its name to the E-learning Network (ELN).

Computer-based learning is different to other forms of learning in a number of ways, but perhaps most critically in its capacity for interactivity – defined by Clarke (2001: 2) as 'the power of the computer to engage, communicate and adapt to the learner'. Halkett (2002) points out that people have been clicking on web links and icons for years with consequent responses from their Internet browsers or computer software. The 'clever bit', according to Halkett, lies in the teaching and the structure. However, most companies involved with e-learning are focused on techno-logical development, rather than structuring the content and learning processes. This is illustrated by the primary interests of most of the founder members of the European eLearning Industry Group: 3Com, Accenture, Apple, BT, Cisco, Digitalbrain, IBM, Intel, Line Communications, NIIT, Nokia, Online Courseware Factory, Sanoma WSOY, Sun Microsystems, Vivendi Universal Publishing. Lewis and Whitlock (2003: xv) criticize many educa-tors and much training for being too excited about the technology and forgetting to focus on the learners, concluding that:

> E-learning has proved a dispiriting experience for some learners: slogging their way through unattractively presented content on a screen, unsure of where they are going and how long it will take them to get there (if ever they arrive), aware only that it all seems to be taking a lot more time than they ever thought. Trainers using e-learning in this way are providing a one-way experience, focused on the needs of the provider rather than the user.

There are numerous claims that e-learning has been 'over-hyped' (Wilcock, 2002). Effective e-learning requires more than novel technology and attractive presentation. E-learning pro-grammes must take learner motivation, different learning styles, content design and overall management of the learning experience into account. It is essential that content lies at the heart of the learning experience, which also includes:

- Feedback from coaches or mentors
- Interaction with other learners
- The chance to apply new skills and knowledge.

Wilcock (2002) concludes that many online learning providers do not acknowledge this, and that their products are more about instruction than learning and development, being '… fine for showing how to operate a fire extinguisher, tighten the correct nut or even answer the telephone politely but are inadequate for any purpose much more sophisticated than this'.

Activity 10.1

- Define e-learning in your own words.
- What is NOT e-learning?

Justifying e-learning

The justification for investing in e-learning programmes has both strategic and tactical dimensions. Strategic reasons for implementing web-based e-learning include (Driscoll, 2002: 6):

1 *Developing a global workforce.* Web delivery is particularly appropriate for a worldwide audience of learners. Employees simultaneously receive the same basic and updated content material, wherever they are in the world.

2 *Responding to shorter product development cycles.* New product releases and revisions to services are occurring at increasingly shorter intervals. The rapid rate of change requires faster dissemination of product information to sales and support staff.

3 *Managing flat organizations.* The trend towards leaner and flatter organizations has often led to training responsibilities being given to busy line managers. E-learning techniques can be used to develop foundation skills, freeing managers for more advanced skills, coaching and mentoring.

4 *Adjusting to needs of employees.* Increasing flexibility has produced new working arrangements, such as teleworking, virtual offices and flexitime. Employees who are not working in a nine-to-five central location can use e-learning to acquire skills and knowledge at a time and place that suits them.

5 *Enabling a contingent workforce.* Use of contingent employee such as temporary workers, consultants and self-employed contractors has grown substantially in recent years. Web-based techniques provide a convenient way of imparting knowledge to these people.

6 *Retaining valuable workers.* Access to distance learning qualifications up to degree level, vocational certificates and skills acquisition is regarded as a significant benefit by highly motivated employees.

7 *Increasing productivity and profitability.* Acquisition of skills and knowledge by individual workers increases an organization's ability to offer a greater range or more sophisticated selection of products and services. Employees can deal with more complex tasks, faster and with fewer errors.

Strategic reasons for adopting e-learning are more likely to be implemented if they are linked to business goals. However, tactical reasons are easier to understand, according to Driscoll (2002: 8), because of the short-term benefits – such as cost-cutting. Driscoll lists a number of tactical justifications for adopting web-based e-learning:

1   *Reducing travel and related costs.* It is relatively easy to forecast cost savings from travel, overnight accommodation and subsistence payments that are not required when conventional course-based training is replaced by e-learning.
2   *Enabling learning any time and any place.* Theoretically, learners can access web-based programmes from their desks, homes or on the move at times that suit them.
3   *Providing just-in-time learning.* Learners can access material just before they need to know its content, and can refresh their learning at any time.
4   *Leveraging the existing infrastructure.* E-learning can make use of existing technology if an organization has invested in a corporate intranet, dial-in access and personal computers for staff.
5   *Enabling delivery independent of a platform.* This is an advantage for web-based e-learning programmes. Web-based learning is accessible from PCs, Macs and a number of other systems.
6   *Providing tools for tracking and record-keeping.* E-learning programmes can be linked to other organizational systems, including databases and HR records. Progress can be monitored automatically, and recorded on departmental and personal development files.
7   *Making updates easy.* Again, this is an advantage of web-based systems, which do not require new CD-ROMs to be pressed, manuals to be printed or videos to be re-filmed.

Lewis and Whitlock (2003: 37) provide the following list of ancillary benefits from e-learning programmes:

■   *Improvement in skills.* Apart from learning the 'subject matter' of the learning programme, e-learners are also likely to acquire secondary skills in the use of IT, time management and writing that are transferable to workplace situations.

- *Greater participation.* The best e-learning programmes involve answering questions and communicating with tutors and fellow learners. Whitlock and Lewis argue that the lack of face-to-face contact is beneficial because tutors are more likely to treat learners equally when visual cues are absent.
- *Access to resources.* Learners widen their awareness of resources and media, including a range of online websites that have relevant content.
- *Increase in people seeking accreditation.* The availability of e-learning increases the number of people taking up accredited learning programmes, such as those offering certificate or degree qualifications as end goals for study. By using learning management systems (discussed later in this chapter), organizations can match business and individual objectives to meet performance requirements.

Activity 10.2

What are the most likely benefits of an e-learning programme for the following types of business?

- A retailer of family cars
- A large call-centre
- A small company producing specialist food products.

The benefits and disadvantages of e-learning as a method of individual learning are outlined in Table 10.1.

Adoption of e-learning

There's no end to the words surrounding e-learning. 'Revolution', 'evolution', 'hope' and 'hype' are just a few of them. At this moment in time, perhaps a short phrase would provide the most accurate picture: 'mixed bag'.

(Rossett, 2001)

A report by *Screen Digest* in late 2002 stated that both suppliers and commentators had exaggerated the size and short-term growth prospects of e-learning markets (http://hrmguide.net/usa/e-learning_survey.htm). The report valued the US corporate

Table 10.1

E-learning

Benefits	Disadvantages
High degree of interaction between the learner and materials	Requires specific equipment to run the programmes
Understanding can be assessed before the learner moves on	Access to a computer is needed for each learner
Feedback can be tailored to the learner's decisions	Development time can be high
Topics can be accessed in an order which suits the learner	Specialist expertise may be required to design and write the programme
Potential for adapting the learning style to the user's needs	Hardware may be expensive
Relatively easy to update text and graphics	Not good at conveying attitudes or behaviour
Ready means of testing	Some learners find it difficult to read text from a screen
Standardized form of training	Can be inappropriate as a single medium for longer applications
Attractive to many learners	Learner may be unable to comprehend learning material
Learner can use material at his/her own pace	Learning process cannot be followed or modified by tutor following production
Computer aided learning programmes are flexible regarding usage time	Learning programmes may be unreliable
The possibility of using different kinds of material	High-level infrastructure and equipment needed Time spent on studies is reduced, meaning less time spent away from the workplace

When to use:
- Good for simulations
- Procedural training – adds interest and interaction, particularly the ability to check your responses to activities and tasks
- Decision-making 'games' – 'action mazes'
- Keyboard training
- Tutorials for software packages
- Management of learning

market at $3.5 billion, with another $1.5 billion elsewhere – a third of many predictions. However, there is optimism about the longer term, with a forecast of a $50bn market by 2010 (see Example 10.1). According to Kieran Levis of Cortona Consulting, author of the report:

> Companies worldwide currently spend approximately $250bn annually on training. Much of this will shift to e-learning and other ways of networking knowledge. However, the claims made for learning management systems and catalogue content were seriously over-stated, and the market forecasts outlandish.

Whereas many organizations had experimented with e-learning tactically, systematic use of information technology for widespread formal and informal learning was limited to a few early adopters, mainly in the IT, telecommunications, financial services (see Example 10.2) and consulting sectors. The most notable included Cisco, Dell, IBM, Skandia, Merrill Lynch and Shell. IT and knowledge-sharing were seen as being critical to competitive success by these organizations because they were driven by the continuous need to brief large numbers of people on new products and processes. Numerous small-scale samples indicate an increase in awareness of e-learning as a useful learning delivery method.

Example 10.1: E-learning is gaining ground

Classroom-based training and printed books are still the most popular learning delivery methods, but web-delivered learning is gaining ground, according to research by Echelon Learning, a consultancy-led learning publisher. The Echelon study shows that web-delivered learning is the second most popular method of acquiring both skills and knowledge.

Respondents were given five questions to answer:

1 What was their preferred delivery mechanism for acquiring a skill?
2 What was their preferred delivery mechanism for acquiring knowledge?
3 What was their preferred delivery mechanism for resolving an immediate business need?
4 What was the relative importance of certain attributes when acquiring skills, knowledge or resolving a business need?
5 How important were certain delivery mechanisms when implementing a blended learning programme?

Classroom-based training received an average score of 4.29 out of 5 to remain the most popular method of acquiring a skill, but the option of web-delivered learning is increasingly used in self-development and in accessing and referencing knowledge.

Echelon's David Hill commented: 'The richness of classroom based training is being successfully complemented by web-delivered learning, which came second in popularity in both the "acquiring skills" and "acquiring knowledge" polls, and is increasingly being used for self-learning.'

contd

Example 10.1 *contd*

When respondents had to acquire information immediately to meet a business need, online text-based materials were given the highest score (3.55 out of 5), followed by classroom-based learning (3.35) and books (2.81). According to David Hill, this pattern of results is because the Internet has opened up the capability for 'instant research and reference', enabling performance to be supported at the time of need.

When choosing development materials, respondents rated the 'depth of content' (4.06) highest, ahead of 'speed of access' (3.75), 'tutor support' and 'level of interaction with material' (3.73 each). Level of interaction with other learners was rated lowest (3.64).

'Unsurprisingly,' Hill added:

Respondents rated classroom based and web-delivered learning as the key delivery mechanisms of a blended program. This particular combination makes it possible for knowledge to be developed before the training exercise and learning to be accessed after the training sessions on a 'when needed' basis.

It appears a no-brainer means of saving money and making training more effective.

The study was based on questionnaires returned by over 100 training and HR professionals in February 2004.

(Source: www.hrmguide.com, 5 May 2004)

European markets were much less developed. Levis highlights the smaller size of the IT industry in Europe, and lower levels of Internet access and usage. Linguistic and cultural differences also make it difficult to standardize and sell content globally. Up until 2002, the fastest-growing markets were for learning management systems and off-the-shelf content, which, Levis concludes, promised rather more than they actually delivered. The most valuable content was not generic but drawn from companies' own knowledge bases.

Pailing (2002) is similarly unimpressed by the hype:

The entire training industry has been excited almost to the point of exhaustion by the advent of e-learning, the great enabler and the answer to everybody's dream. HR and training managers, training content providers, computer manufacturers, Internet service providers, venture capitalists ... everyone who could conceivably have a stake in it has put a stake in it. The problem is, there are few whose fingers have not been burned.

Pailing attributes the relatively slow uptake (in the UK, at least) to a variety of factors, including:

- *The name.* There remains some confusion over terminology – whether it should be elearning, e-learning, E-learning or eLearning – assuming that it is different from online learning, virtual learning or distance learning.

- *The definition*. How much IT should be included within the term: is it Internet only, or does it include CD-Rom?
- *The expense*. Many businesses have cut their training budget, and the initial investment in e-learning can be expensive. Does it make sense to devote scarce funds to relatively unproven techniques?

Commenting on the relatively slow uptake in Europe, Richard Straub, Chair of the European eLearning Industry Group (eLIG), states:

> There is a reason for this, we have thousands of exciting and interesting experiments, however they are not scalable, and in many cases they are incompatible. The best ideas and practices are not transferable and not reusable in environments other than those where they have been developed.

> (Straub, 2003)

In a survey of US companies, Masie (2001) found that the use of e-learning was constrained by a number of internal organizational factors. According to Masie, successful implementation of corporate e-learning – i.e. where employees were actually using the new techniques – was largely determined by the nature of the organization implementing e-learning, rather than by the characteristics of the programmes themselves. He considers that a number of key motivators affect acceptance of e-learning:

- Good publicizing and championing within the organization
- Provision of time and support during working hours
- Creation of an e-learning culture within the organizations
- Provision of incentives such as career advancement and recognition by fellow employees.

Example 10.2: Financial services get the most from e-learning

Businesses in the financial services sector have been more successful in the implementation of e-learning than firms in any other industry, according to research by e-learning provider SkillSoft.

SkillSoft's qualitative study involved employees in 16 global organizations: AT&T, Deloitte, FedEx, Hilton Group, Intelligent Finance, Lloyds TSB, Nestlé, Norwich Union, Price Waterhouse Coopers, Prudential, Royal Mail, Siemens, Schlumberger, Telewest, Wolters Kluwer and Xerox. The researchers found that 94 per cent of staff in the financial services sector – 10 per cent more than employees working in other

contd

Example 10.2 *contd*

industries – are getting the most from the e-learning opportunities offered to them by actually applying the new skills they have learnt online in the workplace.

Asked about the extent to which they were putting their new knowledge into practice:

- Virtually one-half (49 per cent) of respondents said that they were drawing on what they had learnt online on a daily basis, and improved communications with customers and colleagues were cited as major benefits
- 28 per cent stated that they had applied their new skills to specific presentations and projects
- 11 per cent felt that they had significantly improved their database creation techniques (predominantly Access and Excel)
- 6 per cent considered that they were better at coaching and mentoring.

Additionally:

- 55 per cent of respondents had also passed on their new knowledge to colleagues
- 98 per cent would recommend e-learning to friends and fellow workers.

Praising both businesses and employees within the financial sector for their proactive approach to e-learning, Kevin Young, Managing Director of SkillSoft EMEA, said:

When we asked employees in other industries what they felt the barriers were to e-learning many talked in terms of lack of company support, lack of awareness, unavailability of equipment and the inevitable lack of time and workload. Although lack of time and workload was cited as a barrier by 11 per cent of employees working in the financial sector, more than half of those surveyed (51 per cent) didn't perceive any barriers to online learning at all – suggesting that their organizations had already successfully addressed many of the issues being experienced elsewhere.

The commitment to training is also more pronounced within the financial services industry. Companies operating in the sector are much more likely than those in other industries to have invested in the creation of a dedicated training area for their employees to use (32 per cent as opposed to 10 per cent).

Other findings from the survey were that employees in the financial services industry are:

- More likely to have trained online in the last 3 months (98 per cent against 92 per cent)
- Prepared to learn in their own time if necessary – 26 per cent learn before work, during their lunch breaks or at the end of the working day (10 per cent higher than in other industries), and 5 per cent regularly learn at home (as opposed to 1 per cent of those working in other sectors)
- Able to select which courses they do themselves (100 per cent against 94 per cent in other industries)
- Adept at accessing the learning they need as and when they need it – 62 per cent typically spend just 30 minutes online in any one learning session (in contrast to 33 per cent in other industries).

Kevin Young went on to say:

In view of the sporadic nature of these training patterns we asked employees whether, when learning online, they completed a course in one go. 78% said no but, despite this, 98% of these employees said that they still learned what they needed to – 6% more than employees from other sectors. This proves categorically that organizations which insist on measuring the effectiveness of e-learning against the number of actual course completions are missing the point. Employees don't need to complete a whole course to learn what they need in order to be effective.

(Source: www.hrmguide.co.uk, 30 April 2004)

On the basis of survey evidence, Rossett (2001: 20) lists the following barriers against using e-learning in order of importance:

1 Time employees have available for training/learning
2 Cost versus the value of the learning experience
3 Difficulty in measuring results
4 Quality of learning content
5 Perceived difficulty of using such a system
6 Technology infrastructure
7 Internal resistance to using technology instead of face-to-face learning.

Rossett (2001: 23) highlights four underlying factors that strongly influence organizational approaches to e-learning:

1 Collaboration – technology should provide access to other people as well as content
2 Integration – proven principles of adult learning must be used to provide learning solutions through multiple media
3 Relevance – learning embedded within work processes leads to performance improvement that is significant and sustainable for both individuals and organizations
4 Fundamentals – some organizations forget that the technology is a means of delivering effective learning; it is not the object of the exercise.

The European Commission is committed to a proactive stance on e-learning within the European Union (see Example 10.3). Its 'eLearning initiative [*sic*] is intended to mobilize the educational and cultural communities, as well as the economic and social players in Europe, in order to speed up changes in the education and training systems for Europe's move to a knowledge-based society' (European eLearning Portal, http://elearningeuropa.info).

Example 10.3: eLearning programme: A Programme for the Effective Integration of Information and Communication Technologies (ICT) in Education and Training Systems in Europe (2004–2006)

The eLearning programme is a further step towards realizing the vision of technology serving lifelong learning. It focuses on a set of actions in high priority areas, chosen for their strategic relevance to the modernization of Europe's education and training systems.

contd

Example 10.3 *contd*

There are four action lines of the eLearning programme:

1 *Promoting digital literacy.* This will encourage the acquisition of new skills and knowledge that we all need for personal and professional development and for active participation in an information-driven society. It will also address ICT's contribution to learning, especially for those who, due to their geographical location, socio-economic situation or special needs, do not have easy access to traditional education and training.

2 *European virtual campuses.* The priority here is to add a virtual dimension to European co-operation in higher education by encouraging the development of new organizational models for European universities (virtual campuses) and for European exchange and sharing schemes (virtual mobility). This action line will build on existing co-operation frameworks such as the Erasmus programme, giving them an e-learning component.

3 *e-Twinning of schools in Europe and promotion of teacher training.* The objective here is to strengthen and develop networking among schools. All young Europeans, during their time at secondary school, should have the opportunity to participate, together with their teachers, in an educational project with their counterparts in other European countries. This experience could prove to be decisive in fostering a European dimension in education and awareness among young people of the European model of a multilingual and multicultural society. Internet-based learning communities will contribute to improving intercultural dialogue and mutual understanding. The e-twinning of schools will also help update teachers' and trainers' professional skills in the pedagogical and collaborative use of ICT.

4 *Transversal actions for the promotion of e-learning in Europe.* Building on the eLearning action plan, these actions aim to promote best practice, products and services stemming from the many projects and programmes that have been funded at European or Member State level and strengthen co-operation between all those involved.

Particular emphasis will be placed on disseminating the results of e-learning projects and other relevant information on the support to European networks, specific surveys, studies and events, and on co-operation with existing international projects such as those of the OECD and UNESCO.

DECISION No 2318/2003/EC OF THE EUROPEAN PARLIAMENT AND OF THE COUNCIL.

(Source: European eLearning Portal, at http://elearningeuropa.info)

Activity 10.3

- What factors will influence the extent to which e-learning is adopted over the next decade?

Effective e-learning

Drawing on experience, Wilcock (2002) concludes that there are four essential characteristics required from a successful e-learning programme:

1 *A technically robust delivery platform.* The technology used for delivery, such as a corporate intranet or online web-based

system, must be reliable and offer fast download times. It should also be possible to upgrade the system in response to feedback from its users.

2 *An intuitive user interface.* Navigation should be simple and obvious. The objective is to learn the content – not how to operate the system. As Wilcock observes: 'When is the last time you had to learn how to use a book?'

3 *Online coaching support.* E-learning systems may be most effective as a means of learning support rather than learning delivery. Learners expect much faster feedback from e-learning systems, making proactive coaching support a priority. Wilcock favours online coach facilitation through discussion groups and regular personal contact to provide encouragement and advice. Drawing on considerable experience of traditional open learning methods, Wilcock argues that 'effective support is *the* key factor that makes the difference between success or failure', noting that many e-learning providers, coming from technical rather than educational or training backgrounds, have yet to learn this lesson and are more concerned with technological wizardry.

4 *A high level of interactivity.* Echoing Clarke's views discussed earlier in this chapter, Wilcock considers that one of the strengths of e-learning is the ability to provide instantaneous feedback to learners by means of online tests and quizzes. The motivational effect is considerable, especially for new learners.

E-learning content, learning management systems and organizational learning centres

In this section we consider how e-learning is organized and delivered. E-learning programmes typically use some form of web-based delivery, but there are many options available, ranging from the use of pre-existing websites (including those created by external providers) to customized and sophisticated multimedia presentations. The choice and cost of delivery method and content should be subject to careful strategic decision-making, as the consequences may be irrevocable. This is especially the case with learning management systems that are extremely expensive but have the advantage of providing tracking and feedback mechanisms and can also be used to manage other forms of learning in a 'blended learning' package of e-learning and traditional forms of training.

The Internet and interactivity

Horton (2000: 2) considers that web-based training (WBT) draws on three areas of expertise:

1 Distance-learning (formerly known as 'correspondence courses'), with a long pedigree dating back to Sir Isaac Pitman's shorthand course of the 1840s
2 Computer-conveyed education
3 Internet technologies.

'Learning designers' will differ in their roles, but the most important characteristic is to have an outward looking and experimental approach to learning (Russell *et al.*, 2003). The learning processes depend on a number of issues, such as customer requirements, resource constraints and pedagogic/andragogic principles, and are worked out pragmatically through experimentation and negotiation. One major issue is whether or not to make use of material on the worldwide web.

The Internet is becoming a major repository of information, and is increasingly used for informal learning. A study of American Internet users (Pew Internet & American Life Project, 2001) found that 80 per cent of all users used the Internet to answer specific questions. Moreover, 16 per cent of adult Internet users went online to answer a question. A survey conducted in 2003 by the same project found that just 13 per cent of Internet users had their own websites, with most of these (42 per cent) updating their sites once a month or even less frequently. A mere 10 per cent of website creators updated their sites daily. The survey identified the three most prolific categories of content creators for the worldwide web as:

1 *Power creators.* These are the most enthusiastic about content creation. This group is comparatively young, with an average age of 25 years. They are the people most likely to use instant messaging, play games, download music, and read or write blogs (weblogs). They are the new high-tech generation, making extensive use of broadband.

2   *Older creators.* With an average age of 58, these are experienced users of the worldwide web. They tend to be highly educated, have their own websites and are particularly interested in genealogy and picture-sharing.

3   *Content omnivores.* With an average age of 40, they are the heaviest users of the Internet and tend to be well educated. Mostly employed, they have a wider range of interests on the Internet than older creators, logging on frequently to research, shop and communicate. They are the most likely to create business websites of their own.

Most website creators do not set out to provide professional quality material, many providing content as screens of information – much as a book provides pages of text and illustrations. The worldwide web provides millions of such pages – often containing inadequate and erroneous information. As Descy (2003) states:

> Everything seems to be out there and available to our patrons with just a few keystrokes or clicks. Everything: honest information, dishonest information, biased information, and information that may be just plain inappropriate for the customer because of age or ability to understand.

Considerable care has to be taken in the use of non-professional websites because of variable quality. Creating web-based material for learning programmes requires greater thought and more active planning of objectives and material. Interaction is a key issue.
According to Clarke (2001: 2):

> Learning is an active process, so simply presenting information on a screen is unlikely to be successful. Learners must be able to interact with the content by making choices and receiving feedback.

Clarke (2001: 4) argues that successful learning by means of a computer demands a high level of interaction between learner and material. In this situation, interaction is more than hitting keys and clicking hyperlinks – 'it is about engaging minds'.
Clarke considers that learners must be able to:

■   Consider options
■   Sort information
■   Draw conclusions

- Answer questions
- Take notes
- Reach decisions
- Take action
- Reflect on what they are experiencing
- Make inferences.

Achieving the optimum degree of interaction is not easy, especially for authors whose experience lies in writing text learning material. The relationship between questions and learning outcomes is particularly important, but Whitlock and Lewis (2003: 61) observe:

> A brief inspection of half a dozen packages taken at random suggests that many authors proceed as follows: they begin to write a script and, at a certain point, usually at the end of the page or towards the bottom of the screen because they think that it's about time, they ask a question. At the top of the page when they started writing they had no idea what question they were going to ask. This approach very often results in trivial or irrelevant questions. Technically it may be interactive but it certainly doesn't lead to learning.

Clarke (2001: 5) is of the opinion that interaction is dependent on a motivating and engaging style of presentation, the provision of effective feedback on the learner's progress and performance, offering the largest possible range of choices, and the enhancement of learning through activities such as tests and questions. Table 10.2 shows the range of interaction levels available, from simple to sophisticated computer learning systems.

One example of an interactive Internet method is the WebQuest. This is based on a web page containing a focused and self-contained, enquiry-oriented activity (Descy, 2003). It is designed to lead to information on the Internet and other forms of library resources, including video, DVD and sound. The learner is prompted to visit supplementary web pages designed by the instructor, as well as other websites carrying additional information on the Internet. This information is used to complete a number of defined tasks. The main web page contains a number of elements, including:

- An introduction – this is designed to engage the learner with the activity

Table 10.2
Levels of interaction

Level	Characteristics
1 Foundation level	Linear presentation of material with limited interaction. Could be used for a short tutorial
2 Basic level	Extra choices, back and forward buttons, options for more detail. Sound or video commentary. Effective for browsing through learning material
3 Intermediate level	Questions and answers, feedback and note-taking abilities are added. Considerably more choice and extra options
4 Advanced level	Simulation of real life, with ability to explore environment and test skills to their maximum. Flight simulators and educational computer games are examples

Source: adapted from Clarke (2001).

- A task – this should describe the outcome of the Quest as simply as possible
- A process – this is a list of steps that learners should take (individually or as a group) to achieve the outcome of the Quest
- Evaluation – how the trainee will be assessed or graded
- A conclusion – a summary of the activity
- Resources – links to more projects or topics and other websites with useful content, possibly including the instructor's page.

Activity 10.4

Using a keyword relevant to a topic of interest to you, find five websites on a search engine such as Google.

- To what extent are any of those websites suitable for interactive learning, for example as a WebQuest?
- In what ways would they have to be changed or improved to be made suitable for interactive learning?

Multimedia systems

Multimedia systems extend the range of e-learning programmes, making the fullest use of computers as a communication and information storage medium. Electronic mail (e-mail), discussion forums and online chat are common facilities, but desktop video-conferencing and video-streaming of lectures (live or on-demand) are further features allowed by broadband connections. The latter allow e-learning programmes to fulfil some of the same training objectives as more traditional, classroom-based methods.

The transmission channel is the Internet or one of its variants: intranets or extranets. The intranet refers to an Internet site within a corporate network. An Internet learning model is a platform that is predominantly a learning material store.

Table 10.3 shows the advantages and disadvantages of multimedia systems as a means of facilitating individual learning.

Table 10.3
Benefits and disadvantages of multimedia systems

Benefits	Disadvantages
The variety of learning styles and interactions made possible by interactive video- and computer-based learning may be developed and enhanced	Development may be costly and time consuming
CD/DVD formats provide vast storage capability. This may encourage learning strategies incorporating browsing through large databases of text, graphic and video	Future impact of multimedia via online services is difficult to justify, but may influence the rate of development of new systems
Combines the power of sound and vision with the interaction of computer-based training	Production may be dependent on a team of specialists who may need to master new technologies
Hardware prices are relatively low since they should be based on those acceptable to the consumer market for multimedia systems	Information on Internet is vast, thus confusing learner
Digital storage provides many opportunities for manipulation of still and moving images, giving the learner a chance to examine material in different degrees of detail and presentation	Standards are still in a state of flux and the future leading payers cannot be determined at present

Benefits	Disadvantages
Variable speed of playback provides an analysis of movement or individual frames	Multimedia is an information-rich environment and requires the collection of a great deal of material to fully exploit the medium
Commentary can be added to text, graphics, stills and live action	Desktop access to hardware can be a problem, particularly in corporate networked environments
Can be very motivating and involving for learners	Learner may be unable to open computer files on desktop if attached to email messages
Any frame or sequence of video can be accessed almost instantly	Quality of video-conference communication may be poor
Electronic mail and discussion forums are relatively easy to master and apply	Downloading of documents may be slow
Can communicate and present information in a clear and structured manner whilst retaining flexibility	Learning platforms often require tailored adaptation
Information easy to update and convert to other formats	Although multimedia PCs and broadband connections are increasingly common, access remains variable for home-based learners
Set-up costs are reasonable	Cost of www-based courses is often high
Very flexible – builds on the flexibility of interactive video in that many permutations of still and moving video, graphics, numbers of audio tracks are available within the total capacity of the storage medium used	Desktop video-conferencing requires state of the art processors and well-maintained corporate network

When to use:

- For decision-making process, e.g. management topics, when a number of scenarios can be used
- Simulations
- For learners expecting a sophisticated means of learning
- For training with a high visual content where learners need to explore a process for themselves
- When large amounts of information need to be available to the learner
- Where there is a particular need to gain attention and motivate learners
- As the technology and design expertise develops, many more applications will become available such as: complete courses involving live action, role plays, simulations and access to large amounts of information stored on single discs; courses that at present require access to different media such as text, illustrations and graphics can all be delivered through the same medium; the large storage capacity will accommodate sophisticated programmes which will model the presentations to individual learning styles

Simulations

Flight simulators are impressive machines that give trainee airline pilots an extremely realistic experience of the 'feel' and control of an aircraft in any number of possible situations, varying from a trouble-free take-off to a life-threatening loss of power due to fire in the engines. Each simulator costs millions of pounds, because it is physically built to replicate an aircraft cockpit and rests on a complex system of computer-controlled hydraulic rams.

While only flight simulators can provide 'real' experiences, a microcomputer can simulate aspects of experiences that still exercise necessary motor skills and knowledge. Using the computer as a tool to replicate, control or demonstrate a process is an effective approach to simulation. The learner can view or take part in:

- a production process – for example, in plastic moulding, where a machine operator must understand variables like temperature, speed and pressure
- a business application – for example, in a car rental firm with many vehicles, clients and depots
- problem analysis – for example, where the learner's decisions affect the outcomes
- machine operation – for example, where the learner actually controls the machine in real time to improve motor skills.

In some of these simulations, the learner uses the computer's speed and graphics facilities to accelerate motor responses. In others, a business game can be developed enabling a learner or a team to make decisions which the computer processes, setting the stage for responses to each new situation. A more sophisticated package would enable the actions of the other players in the market to influence the outcomes of all the teams' decisions.

Activity 10.5

- Make a list of ten topics that interest you.
- What forms of multimedia would be suitable for improving your knowledge and skills in each of these topics?

E-learning content

The choice of content for e-learning systems is steadily increasing, with one global directory listing over a thousand providers (Chapman, 2004). Hills (2003a: 30) identifies ten different product types:

1   Courses from universities and other institutions of higher and further education. Often the e-learning material is an extension of existing courses or converted text-based distance-learning content. Most of these courses are supplied as a package, with tutor support, assignment marking and recognized qualifications.
2   Courses and study material from commercial providers of conventional face-to-face training programmes.
3   Converted CD-ROM or text-based material from commercial providers.
4   Original content created for online delivery.
5   Software to allow interactivity between learners – a 'virtual classroom'. Instructors provide learning material through conventional computer applications such as Microsoft Word or PowerPoint.
6   Customized learning websites including discussion forums, chatrooms and e-mail contact between instructors and learners. These are similar to virtual classrooms in many ways, and may incorporate licensed content from other providers.
7   Learning management systems with varying degrees of functionality.
8   Integration services provided by outside consultants and specialist providers.
9   External hosts who will provide all content and a learning management system.
10 Bespoke e-learning packages specially created for individual organizations.

In comparison to traditional learning methods, it is clear that e-learning content is not as distinct from the system and the medium of provision. Hills also points to the international nature of e-learning, with many providers located in the USA. However, a survey of 200 users of e-learning content found that most providers were selected by word of mouth and geographical proximity (Chapman, 2004). Whitlock and Lewis (2003: 119) suggest the following as ways of locating materials:

- Searching the Internet
- Asking librarians/skilled searchers for help
- Publicizing requirements within relevant networks
- Attending relevant conferences or seminars
- Joining relevant user groups
- Searching directories
- Looking more widely, such as not confining oneself to a single medium.

They also identify a number of common issues with e-learning content:

1 Integrating sound and video within web-delivered material is problematic.
2 Material that is designed to look good in one browser may be unattractive on another. The same issue applies to different computer screen sizes. There are several ways of dealing with such problems but none are perfect and they may not be possible for 'off-the-shelf' purchased content.
3 Underestimating the time required to complete a project. Customized or 'bespoke' content requires an amount of time that may be difficult to predict, and there is a natural tendency for both purchaser and creator to be optimistic rather than pessimistic about the time required to do a good (as opposed to an adequate) job.
4 Linking a learning programme into a learning management system. Learning management systems are discussed in more detail later in this section, but it is worth mentioning here that the sales literature for such systems tends to be generous about their ease of use. As with any other systems, they require training and practice to use them speedily and effectively.
5 Reliable provision of support is not easy to organize and provide. In fact, learning support is a recognized deficiency in many e-learning programmes.

Example 10.4: Blended learning produces maximum business benefit

A recent survey of 35 major learning organizations shows that multi-pronged learning initiatives – an approach commonly known as blended learning – produces the greatest business benefit. The 2004 e-Learning Trends survey was conducted by THINQ Learning Solutions, Inc.

Of respondents, 92 per cent rated e-learning programmes as the most effective element in their learning activities, followed by instructor-led training courses at 86 per cent. Most organizations surveyed also included programmes such as virtual classrooms and on-the-job training into their blended learning initiatives – far more frequently than face-to-face tutoring and mentoring.

Along with a range of delivery methods, organizations surveyed were also making the most of varied content offerings. This included commercial off-the-shelf content (COTS) from major vendors such as Thomson NETg and SkillSoft. Virtually all respondents said that their organizations had more than 100 e-learning course titles in circulation or available to their trainees.

However, COTS is not adequate for most organizations – 80 per cent of respondents said that they used custom content created specifically for their own needs. Over 90 per cent of the organizations using custom content designed it in-house, using authoring tools such as Macromedia's Flash and Dreamweaver technologies.

'There is no one size fits all in a progressive learning organization,' said Ray Maskell, CEO of THINQ Learning Solutions. 'To optimize the return on investment in training initiatives, organizations are integrating a variety of programs thereby catering to a broader portion of their workforce. E-learning may be beneficial to one group of employees whereas live instructor-led sessions may be more conducive to the learning habits of others. Blended learning allows industry-leading learning organizations to accommodate individual learning styles while ensuring that critical content is delivered and understood.'

Other significant findings included:

- Standards – 75 per cent of respondents said they were SCORM (Sharable Object Reference Model) 1.2 compliant, and 66 per cent complied with AICC HACP (Aviation Industry CBT Committee HTTP AICC Communications Protocol)
- Mobility – this is a hot topic in the learning industry, but fewer than 15 per cent of surveyed organizations were currently using wireless technology in the training environment
- Learning Content Management Systems (LCMS) – 34 per cent of respondents were currently using an LCMS, and a further 28 per cent expected to adopt or implement an LCMS in the next 2 years.

(Source: www.hrmguide.com, 29 April 2004)

As can be seen from Example 10.4, there is a strong argument for using e-learning within a 'blended learning' programme. As Oakes and Green (2003) state:

> The term blended learning has been the most overused buzzword in the learning industry over the past couple of years, but it has, in fact, always been the way that training has been provided. Technically speaking, any combination of delivery methods is a blended learning solution, such as an instructor-led session coupled with take-home workbooks.

They suggest the following best practices in blended learning:

1   Create a structured core curriculum of learning activities transferred via different delivery methods. Most people need to experience an item of learning content more than once in order to absorb its significance. Effective learning is more likely to take place if the experiences are gained through different learning delivery methods. For example, a classroom lecture can cover a range of content items that are then made available on a web-based system and followed up by a group discussion.

2   Support an environment in which people can learn in small chunks. Workplace learners do best when content is presented in manageable chunks rather than lengthy sessions.

3   Create a system through which people can learn informally. In Chapter 9 we observed that a great deal of learning takes place through informal contact between work colleagues. A carefully designed blended learning programme should provide opportunities and time for this to happen by encouraging networking, e-mail, online forums and small discussion groups.

4   Provide an information management repository – a place to store documents, notes, supporting and reference material that can be read and re-read when needed.

5   Provide your development team with a comprehensive set of tools. Developers of learning content need appropriate software and hardware to create and manage a range of materials and activities, including publishing of web-based and printed courseware; modifying and redesigning existing content; providing support for instructor-led training; and providing live synchronous events.

6   Build a shared development environment. Instead of duplicating content available elsewhere in an organization, development should be cooperative and materials made available for adoption or modification by different groups.

As we shall see in the next part of this chapter, learning management systems offer a means of making the best of the blended learning approach.

Learning management systems

Learning management systems, as the title suggests, are intended to manage a range of learning activities, including those that are not delivered online (see Example 10.5). Learning management systems (LMSs) are expensive, and a major source of income for the principal vendors in the e-learning industry. In the USA, just three vendors – Blackboard, Docent and Saba – have a total turnover of US$116 million (Hill, 2003b). Consequently, an LMS is a major investment for a learning organization.

Example 10.5: Lotus Learning Management System

IBM's Lotus Learning Management System package includes:

- an authoring tool, allowing content creation without the need for programming skills
- the learning management system
- content delivery server
- offline learning client.

The system allows scheduling of classes and optimization of materials for different kinds of learner, tracks enrolments, and provides a catalogue of learning materials – among many useful features.

Third-party content vendors are encouraged to prepare their materials so that they are fully compatible with the LMS. This entitles them to display 'Ready for IBM Lotus Learning software' on their wares. When launched in 2003, the Lotus Learning Management System was marketed through IBM's Lotus Passport Advantage distribution channel at $60 per user, Suggested Volume Price at Passport Advantage Level.

Hill (2003b) considers that 'for the individual an LMS is about access, planning and feedback about progress'. Learners can use the catalogue feature to select courses, possibly with advice from a tutor, coach or line manager. Courses consist of modules, blocks of learning material, and traditional or non-traditional elements such as video lectures, chat discussions and so on. These can be scheduled into a learning plan in which individuals allocate themselves to timetable slots that fit their own working pattern. The LMS may incorporate estimated times for completing elements of the course, and also be able to initiate sending of printed material at appropriate dates.

The LMS should also have tracking and reporting facilities so that learners have feedback on their progress while managers can monitor this on an individual, department or organization basis along with the time and other costs to the business.

Learning can be linked to performance assessment with appropriate courses/learning materials identified to match the knowledge or skills to be developed. Managers can also receive reports showing that employees have completed the requirements and the level of attainment.

> ### Activity 10.6
>
> - What features would you wish to see in a learning management system to be used by the corporate training department of a large public sector organization such as a City Council?

Organizational learning centres

The growth of learning centres has been one of the most significant features within the overall development of organizational learning. To an extent, these developments have been paralleled in both corporate and educational sectors, although there are considerable variations from country to country.

Learning centres have a wide range of titles – learning resource centre, learning centre and open learning centre being the most common in-company terms; with learning workshops, resource centre and open access centre amongst others in further and higher education. However, until comparatively recently most learning centres fulfilled two functions; the provision of learning resources, and a place in which to study and learn. E-learning has reduced the need for a physical space, but learning centres are becoming increasingly popular, with many organizations seeing them as pivotal to integrating a learning culture (see Example 10.6).

Example 10.6: NHS learning centre in Orkney 29 August 2003

A new learning centre has opened for NHS staff in Orkney. Deputy First Minister Jim Wallace officially opened the Hofn (meaning Harbour) Learning Centre, at the Balfour Hospital in Kirkwall.

The centre is equipped with £44 000 of funding from the Capital Modernisation Fund. It includes nine laptop computers, and access via the Internet to the NHS e-library.

Mr Wallace said:

The Executive is committed to supporting lifelong learning, and providing opportunities for people across Scotland, including NHS staff, to benefit from this.

   The Executive's lifelong learning strategy – 'Life through learning, Learning through life' – looks for increased collaboration to give more opportunity for people in Scotland to learn. This partnership between learndirect scotland and NHS Orkney is an excellent demonstration of the benefit that such co-operation can bring.

   I would urge staff in NHS Orkney to take the opportunity to use these excellent in-house learning centres and see the value in continuing to learn throughout their lives.

Anne Earley, NHS Orkney's training manager, added:

In the past we were spending quite a bit of money on outside training that did not always suit us. Having this new Learning Centre means we can fix training to suit staff and their shift patterns.

   As a result, we will be increasing the numbers who are studying. We are offering this training for some of the GP practices and we are looking at partnerships with the community social services.

NHS Orkney has been approved as a branded learndirect scotland learning centre for a period of 3 years. Frank Pignatelli, Chief Executive of learndirect scotland, said:

This achievement is the latest development in our strategic partnership with NHS Scotland, which provides online training for staff at all levels, and helps them to get the most out of technology through web-linked training.

(Source: Scottish Executive)

Activity 10.7

- Make a list of the benefits (e.g. provides learning space and facilities for individuals) and disadvantages (e.g. can involve high set-up costs) of creating and managing an organizationally based learning centre.

Although learning centres are proving an important part of the learning infrastructure in many organizations, they do have disadvantages. Table 10.4 summarizes both advantages and disadvantages.

   As we have seen, the role of learning centres is already changing with the impact of technology (see Example 10.7). Increased access to networks at the place of work is reducing the need for physical centres. Over the next few years, learning centres are likely to take on additional functions such as:

   ■ Being more fully integrated with corporate learning strategies

Table 10.4
Advantages and disadvantages of learning centres

Advantages	Disadvantages
Provides learning space and facilities for individuals	Requires accommodation unless 'virtual'
High visibility for promoting training	Can involve high initial costs
Practical method of managing technology and resources	May be inappropriate for dispersed workforces
Provides a secure place to study and store materials/facilities	Can lock organizations into one route – may use a high percentage of training budget
Provides contact point for support, guidance etc. Can help simplify management of flexible learning Reinforces a culture of continuous learning Reinforces the management message that learning is taken seriously by the organization	May require additional staffing
Source: adapted from MultiPALIO Partnership (1999).	

- Providing a base for facilities such as desktop conferencing, video-conferencing and Internet access
- Changing in structure with more networking of centres within organizations, and more use of small-scale or 'satellite' centres to spread resources throughout an enterprise.

Example 10.7: Grant Thornton University

In 2002, Grant Thornton, then the fifth largest accountancy firm in the USA, started the Grant Thornton University (GTU). This is a continuous learning environment that 3000 employees can access from their computers. GTU provides streaming audio and video webcasts as well as conventional web pages on the company's intranet. Learners have to register for courses, but they are provided free.

GTU offers learning paths at a number of career levels, each with recommended core courses. Every employee is assigned a coach who acts as a 'bridge' between the employee and Grant Thornton's performance management and competency programmes. Employers can check with their coaches that they are following appropriate courses at GTU.

Summary

E-learning is not proving to be as revolutionary as once thought, but is currently showing steady progress as improved technology and content provision becomes available. The uptake of e-learning has been slower in Europe than in North America, but EU initiatives aim to redress the balance. The term 'e-learning' encompasses a wide range of activities and delivery options, ranging from the simple and comparatively cheap to complex and expensive learning management systems. Leading vendors have tended to focus on technology at the expense of content, although there are signs of improvement as more 'off-the-shelf' packages and specialist producers of bespoke learning materials come into the market.

E-learning is increasingly offered as part of wider systems and programmes. The blended learning approach has been fashionable of late, and simply means a combination of different training or learning methods. In this context, e-learning is one delivery method in a programme combining web-based learning with more traditional methods such as classroom or 'face-to-face' learning, coaching, or printed open learning texts. Learning management systems can provide registration, tracking, assessment, and feedback mechanisms for e-learning and other learning methods. They can also take input from performance assessments and be used to tailor learning objectives and material to fit the needs of individual learners and their organizations. Organizational learning centres are likely to provide e-learning as one element of their facilities.

References

Chapman, B. (2004). Customer Content Developers. Brandon-Hall.com.

CIPD (2002). Training and Development 2002 Survey Report. Chartered Institute of Personnel and Development.

Clarke, A. (2001). *Designing Computer-based Learning Materials*. Gower Publishing.

Descy, D.E. (2003). Web-based organizational tools and techniques in support of learning. *Library Trends*, **52(2)**, 362–7.

Driscoll, M. (2002). *Web-Based Training: Designing e-Learning Experiences*. Jossey-Bass/Pfeiffer.

Halkett, R. (2002). E-learning and how to survive it. *Industrial and Commercial Training*, **34(2)**, 80–82.

Hills, H. (2003a). *Individual Preferences in e-Learning*. Gower Publishing.

Hills, H. (2003b). Learning management systems: why buy one? *Training Journal*, **January (Focus on E-learning, special issue)**, 12–15.

Horton, W. (2000). *Designing Web-based Training: How to Teach Anyone Anything Anytime.* Wiley.

Lewis, R. and Whitlock, Q. (2003). *How to Plan and Manage an E-learning Programme.* Gower Publishing.

Masie, E. (2001). *E-Learning: If We Build It, Will They Come?* American Society for Training and Development.

MultiPALIO Partnership (1999). *European Wide Open Learning Materials.* The Open Learning Foundation.

Oakes, K. and Green, D. (2003). E-learning. *Training and Development*, **57(10),** 17.

Pailing, M. (2002). E-learning: is it really the best thing since sliced bread? *Industrial and Commercial Training*, **34(4/5),** 151–6.

Pantazis, C. (2002). Maximizing e-learning to train the 21st century workforce. *Public Personnel Management*, **31(1),** 21–7.

Pew Internet & American Life Project (2001). *The Internet and Education: Findings of the Pew Internet & American Life Project.* 1 September 2001, www.pewinternet.org.

Rossett, A. (2001). *The ASTD e-Learning Handbook: Best Practices, Strategies, and Case Studies for an Emerging Field.* American Society for Training and Development.

Russell, D., Calvey, D. and Banks, M. (2003). Creating new learning communities: Towards effective e-learning production. *Journal of Workplace Learning*, **15(1),** 34–45.

Straub, R. (2003). *Why Isn't e-Learning Taking off in a Big Way in our Daily Lives?* 15 January 2003, http://elearningeuropa.info.

Wilcock, L. (2002). E learning – promises and pitfalls. *Open Learning Today, British Association for Open Learning*, **52 (www.baol.org.uk)**.

Chapter 11

Evaluation of strategic human resource development

Introduction

Imagine this scenario: a medium-sized multinational software development firm has, for the first time, invested in a first-line manager development programme. This investment was made due to the fact that past experiences have taught the senior management team that they employed brilliant analysts and programmers but the firm had lost some key employees and had not completed critical projects because of poor first-line management. The senior management team was very clear that they wanted their first-line managers to be exposed to superior thought leadership and experiences from other industries. This meant that the investment in development was high, and several of their managers were taken out of the business on development days. At the end of the first 12-month modular programme the Finance Director was keen to evaluate his return on investment, and had several meetings with the HR Director and the training and development manager. The Finance Director was left with a conclusion that the development programme 'promised to change the world and now it is impossible to evaluate whether it had any impact at all'. This conclusion no doubt had an impact on future training investments, as well as the relationship between the Finance and HR Directors.

This scenario is not unusual, and is indicative of the challenges involved in evaluating training and development. It is often difficult to evaluate the impact of SHRD due to the complex causal links that form part of the organizational reality. How can you tell that the improved customer service or cost reduction was simply down to the training investment? This means that it is difficult to measure causal relationships between firm performance and formal training and development investments. This challenge of causality is made even more difficult where informal learning is concerned. That is, both the cost and the benefits can be hidden and difficult to evaluate.

In this chapter we aim to address these challenges by asking a set of pertinent questions. First, we ask: '*Why* evaluate?' If we know that 85 per cent of organizations fail to evaluate training (Gibb, 2002) and the difficulties are evident, why is it deemed to be important? We will then go on to learn that different stakeholders would be involved in and interested in the evaluation process for different reasons. This addresses the '*who?*' of the evaluation process. The second and indeed critical question that we address is that of the focus of the evaluation – that is, *what* needs to be evaluated? Here we will refer back to the framework that was presented in Chapter 3 – that is, we use the criteria of SHRD to guide the evaluation criteria.

The 'what' of evaluation is closely linked to the timing of the evaluation process, that is the '*when*' of evaluation. Here we refer specifically to whether it is feasible to evaluate before during or after the delivery of a training or development programme. The transfer of learning and the learning environment are important issues to consider in the post-delivery phases. This would also serve as an indicator of the success of the informal learning processes in the organization. In other words, an organizational environment that is conducive to the transfer of learning is likely to facilitate informal learning as well.

The next question that we consider is the '*how*' of evaluation. This sits in the domain of the evaluation toolkits, and although the aim of the chapter is not to construct such a toolkit we provide a brief overview of the possible ways in which an organization can evaluate the role of SHRD. Finally, we interweave all the different aspects of the evaluation process into a single summative table.

Upon completion of the evaluation framework, directed by the why, who, what, when and how questions, we review the inherent value of the evaluation process itself. Here we ask specifically how an organization may benefit from conducting evaluation. This highlights the realization that evaluation can be a learning process in itself.

> **Objectives**
>
> By the end of the chapter you will be able to:
>
> - Define the concept of evaluation of training and development
> - Understand why it is important to evaluate
> - Identify who should be involved in the evaluation process
> - Explain when evaluation can take place
> - Identify the specific behaviours and contexts that can be evaluated
> - Link the focus of the evaluation process (the what) to the criteria for SHRD
> - Describe how SHRD can be evaluated
> - Draw together the different strands of the evaluation process into a single framework.

Why evaluate?

The purpose of evaluation: viewpoints and challenges

How well did I/we/they do? These are questions that are often asked as a core part of what makes us human (James, 1890/1950), and we frequently gauge our performance by comparing ourselves to others (Mead, 1934; Festinger, 1954). The social comparison vantage point to measuring our relative success indicates that evaluation is also a core part of what makes us compete, or competitive. This generalized statement shows that evaluation is important from three different perspectives. The first viewpoint of the evaluation process is that of *gauging success,* whilst the second relates to a judgement as to whether a financial and time *investment paid off.* A third viewpoint would be an evaluation of the particular *development design,* which answers the 'did that work?' question.

It is possible to think of these three viewpoints in terms of participation positions. In the former case (gauging success), the person(s) interested in this form of evaluation would be those who took part in the development or learning process itself. In other words, if I have invested a whole working week of my time to improve my presentation skills, I would like to know if

I am now actually better at presenting to large audiences than I was before the training. If we now move on to the second evaluation reason (return on investment), those interested in the results from this evaluation output are likely to be the stakeholders that made the training possible – that is, the decision-makers at an organizational level who secured the training budget. To refer back to our initial case, this would be the Finance Director. The third viewpoint would be that of the designers and facilitators of the training programme or process. Information gleaned from this evaluation output can be used to improve future formal and informal development opportunities. Below, we discuss the reasons for evaluation from each of the vantage points.

The active participant's viewpoint: gauging success

Here, the active participant(s) in the learning process would want to know if they were successful at achieving the learning objectives. It is important to remember that within the SHRD context the learning objectives could relate to the individual, team or organizational levels of competence. In essence, this viewpoint seeks to answer the: 'How well did we do?' question. This form of evaluation can take place in both formal and informal ways.

In this context, we define formal evaluation as external measures of success that are formally recognized by the organization. Examples of formal evaluation are competence assessments, skill tests and peer reviews. Informal evaluation refers to an internally motivated process that takes place either during action or learning, or at intervals after action or learning. The main vehicle for this form of evaluation is reflection. For example, individuals learning a new skill will often reflect on how their performance has improved, and will use their own 'introspective' yardstick to do so. Interestingly, it is often the informal, reflective process of evaluation that truly gets a learner interested in the formal evaluation process – that is, 'I think I have improved in batting this ball, I wonder if my coach thinks so too?'

Another important dimension (see Figure 11.1) of the *gauging success* viewpoint to evaluation is that not only will the evaluation process be formal or informal but the learning intervention itself may also be formal or informal. Our definition of formal learning is a planned programme that takes place over a fixed time

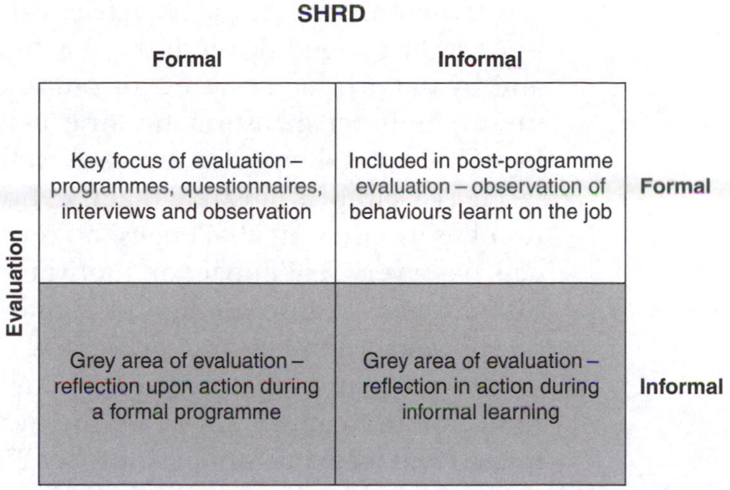

SHRD

Formal   Informal

	Formal	Informal	
Formal	Key focus of evaluation – programmes, questionnaires, interviews and observation	Included in post-programme evaluation – observation of behaviours learnt on the job	Formal
Informal	Grey area of evaluation – reflection upon action during a formal programme	Grey area of evaluation – reflection in action during informal learning	Informal

Evaluation

Figure 11.1
The motivation for
evaluation: gauging
success.

period within a particular context (not normally in the work set-ting). Informal learning is defined (in accordance with Lave and Wenger, 1991) as the process of learning-by-doing, where there is no fixed training programme and skill development is directed through shared practice within a specific work context. The key characteristics are:

- The active nature of the learning process
- The contextual setting of the learning process – i.e. the context within which the skills will be applied
- The behavioural modelling aspect – i.e. learning from the master (Nonaka and Takeuchi, 1995).

Both formal and informal learning approaches present particu-lar challenges to the evaluation process. The first challenge is the absence of formal learning objectives within an informal learn-ing setting. Informal learning processes are, however, extremely valuable to the organization's (and the individual's) success, and these evolving process most definitely do not start with a set of pre-determined learning objectives.

Secondly, even within formal learning programmes the learn-ing objectives are often not measurable – at least not in direct ways. For example, the first-line manager programme that was presented in the scenario at the start of the chapter may have had specific learning objectives that relate to interpersonal skills, performance management and conflict management. However, the achievement of these objectives cannot be directly measured but can be gauged through the reactions of the manager's team and by the productive rates (or outputs) of the team. These are merely indirect measures because it is possible that they have been influenced by other inputs as well.

These examples illustrate that the 'how well did I/we do?' question has its inherent challenges; however, the ability to gauge success has a very real impact on motivation and satisfaction. This is often seen as reason enough to embark on an evaluation of the development and learning processes.

The motivational need to evaluate learning outcomes also raises another important issue: the evaluation process has both formal and informal dimensions (see Figure 11.1). Although the majority of this chapter will be dedicated to the structured and planned evaluation process, it is worth noting that individual- and team-level informal evaluation take place in an informal and continuous way as well. This brings us back to the opening question of this section. The 'how well am I doing' question can be asked continually and in a reflective manner. This is a very important aspect of evaluation, and one that is often overlooked in management texts.

The importance of this evaluation approach lies in its ability to capture the tacit nature of many competencies. In other words, if learning-by-doing is a key method for acquiring particular sets of skills, then a key way in which the acquisition of the skills can be judged is by reflection in action. For example, if I am learning to be a coach I can read instructions, attend a formal training programme, or practise with another experienced coach. It is through this learning-by-doing that I will acquire valuable skills, and, importantly, it is by continuously doing and reflecting on my competence that I can evaluate whether I am more competent than when I started the training. The process of reflecting on my competence is also a natural one, which will be a key indicator for me to disengage from the training. That is, when I know I can do something well I may want to practise as a coach in my own right.

The unplanned and continuous evaluation of informal learning can be described as the grey area of evaluation. It is important, but is often not addressed when designing an evaluation programme (see Figure 11.1). We argue here that because of its inherent value, in terms of motivation and learning, it should be understood better and incorporated in the evaluation framework.

The investor's viewpoint: return on investment

Organizations embark on training programmes because they want to drive up performance outcomes, reduce costs or improve working conditions. It is often the case that substantial investments are made to achieve these ultimate learning outcomes. For example, Bassi and Ahlstrand (2000) found that organizations' investment in training increased from 1.5 per cent of payroll in 1996 to 2 per cent in 1998 – an increase of almost 40 per cent. Added to this investment is often the indirect cost of time lost whilst employees attend training, as well as development cost if the programme is conducted within the organization. More recently, investment in training and development has increased even further because there is a strong belief that organizations that invest in the development of skills in a knowledge economy will be more successful than those who don't.

Having set the scene for the scale of training and development investments, it is not surprising that investors would want to know if the training has 'paid off'. According to Noe (2002), an organization that receives an inadequate return on investment is likely to reduce future investment or look for alternative providers of training external to the organization. In this context, the training evaluation needs to provide data that give a clear indication that the training investment has some benefits for the company.

This viewpoint and the logic behind it seem straightforward. But is this the case? At the start of the chapter we presented the reader with one of the key challenges in evaluation: that of causality. In other words, it is difficult for an organization to ascertain whether a training programme alone has reduced costs or driven up performance (or both). This is because several factors, such as changes in market conditions, increased barriers to entry or even a new recruitment strategy, could impact upon the measures of success at the organizational level.

Again, the case of the challenge is not that simple. This is because there is a direct relationship between the complexity of the training and the measurements used. To illustrate: if an organization were to set out to develop the arithmetic abilities (a concrete skill) of their junior engineers, then a detailed and complicated (but not complex) set of tests could be devised to measure these abilities. On the other hand, a more complex skill such as leadership cannot be measured through tests but needs complex feedback mechanisms as a measurement vehicle. I can gauge my leadership ability from others' reactions as well as my action within a complex set of interpersonal relationships.

Another reason for gathering return on investment evaluation data is to compare the costs and pay-offs of non-training investments with the benefits that result from training investments (Noe, 2002). It is often possible to address strategic performance issues through alternative solutions such as job redesign or performance management. If the true value of a training investment is to be gauged, then adequate measures of alternative solutions are needed as well. Within this context it is also important to compare the cost–benefit analysis of the training investment with the cost of not investing at all. If learning opportunities are continually ignored, what will the impact be on the organizational performance?

Investors may also be interested in comparing different training programmes. The cost of various programmes that address a similar training need may vary tremendously whilst their payoffs might be similar. This would be important evaluation data that would inform future investment decisions. Interestingly, it is not only the investors that would be interested in these data but also the facilitators of learning, who would take a keen interest in the most suitable and effective training method.

Activity 11.1

Imagine that you have designed a training programme for first-line managers.

- What questions would you ask that would help you gain insight into the success of the programme design itself? Compare your questions with your colleague's.
- How do they differ? Why did you arrive at different questions?
- Which questions would you use to guide your future design actions?

(Note: Please do not focus on questions regarding the output of the training.)

The facilitator's viewpoint: development design

The design and impact of a development process falls within the interest field of the learning facilitator. Some of the key questions that the facilitator would want to answer include:

- Did the programme meet the learning objectives that were identified?
- Did the programme design facilitate learning?
- Was the content challenging enough/too challenging for the group of learners?
- Did the administration contribute to successful learning?
- How can the learning environment be enhanced?
- What were the strengths and weaknesses of the programme?
- Which group of trainees found the programme most useful and why?

The key motivation for gathering these evaluation data is to improve future training design and to gain insight into which learning design addresses particular learning needs. In other words, the purpose of evaluation is not only to demonstrate 'what works', but also to improve the 'way it works'. The use of the evaluation data will therefore lead to improved learning opportunities.

At the very least, the evaluation of the training design needs to provide a foundation upon which future learning decisions can be based, and in the long term these evaluation-driven adjustments should lead to improved programme design and, ultimately, increased return on investment, as well as individual performance outcomes. In essence, a refinement of the learning design will often lead to improvements in learning objectives, which are considered to be the focus or the 'what?' of training evaluation. However, Figure 11.1 serves as an indication that evaluation will cover a much wider scope than merely formal training objectives. The following section takes a closer look at the possible foci of an evaluation strategy.

The evaluation process

The focus of the evaluation

This section gets to the heart of the evaluation process and takes a close look at what needs to be evaluated. At a first glance, an easy answer may be: 'learning objectives'; however, closer inspection teaches us that it is first important to understand the parameters of evaluation – that is, which type of learning interventions do we need to evaluate (multi-level and multi-time)? After we have sketched out these parameters we can take a look inside the 'boxes of the parameters'. Here we explore the various learning outcomes that can shape the evaluation process. We use Kirkpatrick's (1975) model to guide the levels of learning outcomes that we identify. This leads us to the conclusion that most of Kirkpatrick's model is focused on formal training programmes. Finally, we will examine how we can evaluate informal learning interventions.

Activity 11.2

Think of the last training programme that you were involved in as a delegate. If you have not attended a training course ask others you know who have attended such a programme.

- What were your impressions of both the enjoyment and the effectiveness of the programme?
- Could you categorize these impressions into various groups of outcomes (such as skills, behaviours or attitudes)?
- Now translate each outcome (e.g. 'made me more effective at presenting to large audiences' or 'kept my interest for four days' or 'couldn't transfer any of the learning to my work environment') into an area that you feel would be important to evaluate.

The parameters of evaluation

Before we can embark on an evaluation process, we need to be very clear about the purpose of the learning intervention. Ultimately this will define 'what' we are trying to evaluate. Research suggests that clear and measurable learning objectives should lay a foundation for sound training evaluation (Coleman and Lim, 2001; D'Andrea, 2001; Guerrero and Sire, 2001; see also arrow 1, Figure 11.2) – that is, the learning objectives are the best indication of the purpose of the learning intervention. Although this statement may seem oversimplified, we have found that several

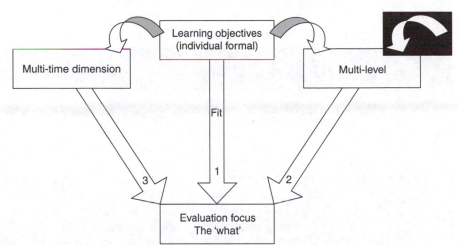

Figure 11.2
The first step in the
evaluation process.

organizations embark on training and development programmes without examining exactly what they want the outcomes to achieve.

Unfortunately, learning objectives are often developed around individual, formal training programmes (Nickols, 1982). This leads to a rather narrow approach to training evaluation, where evaluation outcomes become the sole domain of the HRD function and mainly point to reactive measures. What we are arguing for here is that HRD has a more strategic role to play and that evaluation needs to be adapted accordingly. In this chapter we therefore support the notion of the fit between learning objectives and the evaluation focus (arrow 1, Figure 11.2), but we would like to progress current thinking somewhat. We aim to extend the evaluation focus to include the criteria for SHRD (see Chapter 3). In summary, we considered HRD to be strategic (SHRD) if the intervention was:

1   Multi-level
    ■ individual
    ■ team
    ■ organization
2   Extended across multi-time horizons
    ■ addresses current performance needs
    ■ creates future learning capacity.

Consequently, in the context of SHRD, we would include the evaluation of both formal (planned) and informal (unplanned) learning interventions across several layers and time dimensions (see Table 11.1). This table provides a focus for the evaluation context. It also provides, and stretches, the parameters of the evaluation strategy.

Table 11.1

Evaluation areas of SHRD: drawing parameters

Level and time dimensions	Individual (current and enabling)	Team/department (current and enabling)	Organization (current and enabling)
Formal programme	Focus of conventional evaluation ✔	Some evidence of formal evaluation ✔	Needs development: Kirkpatrick level 4 addresses this to some extent
Informal process	Could be captured in performance appraisal but is often not acknowledged as part of SHRD processes	Could be captured in performance appraisal but is often not acknowledged as part of SHRD processes	Needs development

It is essentially the formal learning interventions at the individual and team levels that have received most attention with regard to the evaluation process. We argue here that both the informal and organizational level interventions have strategic value and are therefore central to SHRD, so need to be included in the evaluation strategy. However, it is much more difficult and complex to evaluate a learning process that does not have clear boundaries (unplanned) and that takes place across different levels. These challenges can be addressed by being clear about the learning outcomes within these parameters. That is, the areas indicated in Table 11.1 could be evaluated more effectively if a typology of learning outcomes were developed that spanned both the ticked and unticked areas.

The next step of the evaluation process would therefore be to identify, for example, behaviours, reactions and changes in abilities that would fit within these parameters. That is, we need to be clear which learning outcomes we need to evaluate in order to address the purpose of evaluation adequately.

Evaluating learning outcomes

The most well-known classification of foci for evaluation is Kirkpatrick's four-level framework for categorizing training outcomes (Kirkpatrick, 1975):

Level 1: Reactions   What does the participant feel about the training?

Level 2: Learning	What facts or information did the participant gain?
Level 3: Behaviour	What skills and competencies did the participant gain, and how are these used in the workplace?
Level 4: Results or effectiveness	What results can be tracked as a result of the participant(s) applying their skills and knowledge?

The first of these learning outcomes refers to the participants' immediate reaction to the training programme. Examples of these measures may include the following:

- The facilities and equipment made it easy to learn
- The administration of the course was efficient
- The material was easy to understand
- The supporting reading was useful
- Overall, I am satisfied with the course.

The second level of Kirkpatrick's (1975) evaluation content model refers to cognitive outcomes. This is mainly used to determine whether participants are familiar with certain facts, information and written procedures. The key question here is, 'do you *know* this as a result of the training?' These cognitive outcomes are mainly tested through knowledge-based tests, such as paper-and-pencil tests.

Activity 11.3

Imagine you were assigned to train newcomers to your motor vehicle manufacturing team how to set up their workstation. You have access to the company policy on workstations, as well as the health and safety manual.

- Design a paper-and-pencil test that will evaluate whether the trainees have acquired the necessary knowledge and information. In this pencil-and-paper test it will be important to ensure that the contents of the company policy are translated into measurable items. For example, a multiple choice question may ask how a certain process would be conducted or what they would do first when arriving in the morning. In essence, knowledge of the flow of events needs to be tested to determine if knowledge was successfully transferred.

The third level of Kirkpatrick's (1975) evaluation model refers to the assessment of skill-based outcomes (Noe, 2002). This level of evaluation is slightly more challenging for two key reasons:

1   The performance environment. Behaviour changes or skill-based outcomes need to be *observed on-the-job*. This form of evaluation therefore relies on a working environment that is conducive to the transfer of learning. That is, this form of evaluation is open to several category mistakes. First, no change in behaviour may be observed. A possible conclusion that could lead from this is that the learning was unsuccessful; however, the fault may lie with the learning environment. Secondly, a change in behaviour may be observed that could lead to a positive evaluation. The change could, however, be due to a wider cultural change in the organization.

2   The actual skills. Evaluated skills often contain a larger proportion of *discretionary elements* (Purcell *et al.*, 2003). The discretionary element will influence observed skills in two main ways:

    ■ The way in which a task is performed. For example, it is possible to observe whether a truck is off-loaded in a certain time after a training programme, but it is more difficult to know (or observe) how conducive the interaction during this task is to teamworking. I can possibly be super-efficient after training, but also so task-orientated that I make my team miserable. I can therefore tick the box of skill development, but I certainly can't tick the 'creating a positive work climate' box. What's more, it is very difficult for an observer to tell the attitudinal outcomes (miserable, task-driven) from my skill-based outcomes (efficient off-loading of the truck).

    ■ The motivation to perform the task. Particular skill sets in organizations have larger discretionary elements than others. For example, mentoring, leading and supervising are often enacted entirely at the discretion of the employee (Purcell *et al.*, 2003). In other words, I can still get my job done whether I am good at mentoring or not. If I am therefore not motivated (by organizational and personal reasons) to illustrate my mentoring skills, you will not be able to tell whether I am a good mentor or not, or indeed whether the training programme was successful.

Activity 11.4

Take a few minutes to discuss the challenges that are presented by level 3 of Kirkpatrick's evaluation model.

• What would you include in the evaluation process to overcome these challenges?

Kirkpatrick (1975) did provide some guidelines as to how we can overcome these challenges. The first step is to conduct a systematic appraisal of the relevant skills before the training programme. This should then be compared with a post-training appraisal using the same method. It is also important to have more than one appraiser involved in the pre- and post-training evaluation. Another key guideline is to give the participant enough time after the training programme to practise the new skill – in other words, the evaluation needs to take into account the learning process. Finally, it could be useful to have a control group's pre- and post-measures to ascertain whether the training resulted in a behavioural change or whether it was another organization-wide intervention.

The final level of evaluation relates to the impact of the development process on the organization as a whole. That is, it determines what the 'pay-offs' of the training investment are. If we relate this back to the first section of this chapter, then it is clear that it is mainly the investors that would be interested in this evaluation data. Direct and indirect measures can be used to gauge the impact of the training and development investment, including:

- Product quality
- Customer service satisfaction
- Sense of teamworking
- Rate of innovation
- Employee turnover
- Absenteeism
- Accidents
- Equipment downtime.

According to Cascio (1991: 269), there are many hidden costs involved in training and development; it is therefore important to take the following issues into account when considering the return on investment (ROI) of the development process:

1   Training development
   ■ analysis time – total staff hours to analyse the job
   ■ design time – total staff hours to design the training programme
   ■ material costs – all material costs incurred from onset through completion of one training programme, including supplies to facilitate training programme development (administrative, graphics, work, travel, duplicating, display boards, training aids, etc.).
2   Training materials (expendable – cost of reproducing copies of developed programmes)
3   Training materials (unexpendable)
   ■ instructional hardware (e.g. video recorder)
   ■ instructional software (e.g. manufacturer's operating manual).
4   Training time
   ■ trainee time – total hours, and resulting salary incurred for trainee to reach a level of competence
   ■ trainer time – total hours, and resulting salary, incurred for trainee to reach a level of competence.
5   Production losses resulting from training
   ■ production rate losses
   ■ material losses.

Although Kirkpatrick's model is extremely useful in shaping the various learning outcomes that form the foundation of the evaluation model, it has as its focus almost exclusively formal training programmes. Earlier in the chapter (Figure 11.1) we stressed the importance of evaluating informal learning. We will now explore this in more detail.

Evaluating informal learning

Activity 11.5

Imagine you are working in a project team that has been tasked with designing an advertisement for a client. You are new to this team, but after a 6-month period you find that you have acquired a great deal of knowledge and skill that you did not have before.

- How would you go about evaluating the success of this informal learning process?
- Linked to this evaluation, in your own experience, what are the success factors for informal learning?
- How can this be replicated to ensure positive evaluation outcomes?

It is often difficult, if not impossible, to 'teach' complex skills such as negotiation, problem-solving or management. These competencies are regularly thought of in a craft-like manner (Nonaka, 1994), and it would be more appropriate for the employee to 'learn from the master'. This method of learning is particularly widespread in Japan. In its extreme form, such as the training of Japanese potters, learning occurs in complete silence – so all attention is consequently focused on observing and practising with the master. In a less strict sense, we have probably all been exposed to this form of informal learning. It is most noticeable when, for example, we join a new organization or have to work on a new project team. The 'expert' soon becomes visible, and we try to learn, in a workplace setting, why a particular individual is 'so much better at this than me'.

Managerial learning is often regarded as most suited to the informal learning sphere. In other words, managers can gain useful guides and mental frameworks from formal managerial training programmes, but it is only by 'doing' and 'copying' others that this form of social learning takes place (Raelin, 1997; Cook and Seely Brown, 1999; Yanow, 1999). It is also this method of learning that leads to competence in an automatic state (Spender, 1996). That is, when I am a competent manager, it is difficult for me to tell you exactly which skills I am using. I almost practise my 'managerial craft' automatically.

It is not only the nature of the competency that dictates the method of learning but particular *situations* could also drive this form of learning. According to McCauley *et al.* (1994), the key influencers here are *change* and *obstacles*. If a transition is made to a new function, or new responsibilities are taken on, or the organization embarks on a major change, then the situation calls for learning-by-doing. Alternatively, challenging projects or problems that have not been encountered before can call for informal learning. Indeed, in the knowledge economy this approach, expressed as, figuring things out by yourself, is regarded as a powerful form of knowledge creation (Swart *et al.*, 2003).

Meggison (1996) referred to this form of managerial learning as emergent learning, which is characterized by retrospective exploration of experience. This definition is extremely useful because it provides a guide to the evaluation process. It indicates that in the first instance, *reflection* would be the key source of evaluation. It is only by looking back over the process of competence development that its success can be judged. This is therefore in essence a retrospective evaluation process, and one that is not without challenge: it is difficult to reflect on how I learnt to negotiate if I didn't set out to learn the skill in the first place. I may be able to recall critical incidents, but on the whole I may miss key indicators of the success of the learning process.

Another approach to evaluating informal learning is to be cognizant of the inputs that will influence the success of the learning process. This will also enable an understanding of the reasons behind the reflective evaluation. In other words, if I am still not able to call myself a master potter, why is that?

The key 'input' criteria for evaluation of the informal learning process can be grouped into:

1   The learning potential of the job context (van der Sluis *et al.*, 2002)
    - Is the work environment conducive to informal learning? (Do I have a supportive manager, do I have a competent leader to learn from, are my colleagues willing to share knowledge?)
    - The variation of subcultures (can I transfer my learning from one environment to the next?)
    - Does my team value learning? (Will they sacrifice time for learning, are they willing to experiment, and is there a belief that continuous improvement is important?)
2   The 'person' characteristics (Guerrero and Sire, 2001)
    - Self-efficacy (the judgement of my capability – I can only learn to be a manager if I believe I have the ability to do so)

■ Instrumentality (the perception that efforts will equal rewards – if I believe I can be a manager I will only be motivated to learn if I believe this is the most suitable context for the acquisition of that skill).

In summary, it is very important to include informal learning processes in the evaluation framework. This is critical because particular skills can only be acquired through this form of learning, and key organizational realities (such as change and challenges) lead to informal learning. The evaluation process can be conducted retrospectively through the reflection of the learner. Alternatively, it can focus on the informal learning 'inputs' or 'facilitators'. These include 'workplace' and 'person' characteristics. An evaluation of these characteristics will provide further insight into the data from the reflective evaluation. Furthermore, it creates a foundation for developing environments that are conducive to informal learning.

In the context of informal learning evaluation it is therefore possible to evaluate either after the learning has occurred (reflective) or before the learning process (inputs/facilitators). This raises the 'when do we evaluate?' question. Next, we explore whether pre-and post-programme evaluation is possible in the event of formal planned learning as well.

The timing of the evaluation

In order to gauge how effective the learning process was at achieving the learning objectives, or to track the changes that have resulted as a result of the learning, it is necessary to conduct evaluation at various stages for different purposes. Table 11.2 provides a useful summary of the various evaluation points and their specific purpose. The first evaluation point is prior to the delivery of the training. This may seem a strange starting point, but very useful evaluation information can be gained at this stage. First, if behavioural changes or skill-based learning outcomes are to be assessed it is useful to estimate the level of competence of the participants before they take part in the training programme. Secondly, it is critical to conduct an evaluation review of the learning objectives. At this stage it is important to review the purpose of the learning process and the intended outcomes. It is during this phase that the measurability of the objectives needs to be reviewed. We regard this as important because

Table 11.2

Evaluation points and their purpose

Evaluation point	Purpose
First point: Prior to training and development	Review purpose of training and provide input into the learning objectives Assess skill level before learning intervention
Second point: During training	Participants and facilitator want to gauge performance improvements (Kirkpatrick level 2) Could use data to feed back into the learning design (in a modular structure, changes can be made)
Third point: Post-programme delivery but prior to workplace transfer	Reactions to the training programme (Kirkpatrick level 1) Perceptions of the facilitator as well the learning process Gain insight into whether the administration and structure of the programme was effective
Fourth point: Post-programme, on-the job approximately 3 months after re-entry	Transfer of learning (Kirkpatrick level 3) Ability to practise skill Information about necessary changes to the workplace can be identified
Fifth point: Post-programme, on-the job approximately 6 months after re-entry	Transfer of learning (Kirkpatrick level 3) Impact on organizational performance as well as individual performance (Kirkpatrick level 4) Identify future training and development needs

Source: adapted from Nickols (2000).

the training investment can be high, and if the purpose and objectives are not revisited it can result it considerable financial losses. A review meeting between an evaluation team (or a facilitator in smaller organizations) and the designers of the learning process is therefore necessary at this stage.

Most critically, learning will be evaluated during the programme. This form of evaluation can serve as a motivator for the participants – that is, they will be able to gauge their performance improvements whilst learning. The facilitator could also make use of these data to make any necessary programme changes. Here, the evaluation serves as a yardstick of initial learning outcomes.

The next evaluation point would be upon completion of the training programme but prior to entry into the workplace. This form of evaluation will mainly be able to gauge whether the participants 'liked' the training programme. These responses are often largely emotive, and reflect on the operation of the training outfit. Once again, the outcome from this evaluation can be used to make administrative changes immediately, and design changes over the longer term.

Often the true test of the effectiveness of the training programme is the evaluation upon return to the workplace. A key issue at this point is the transfer of learning. This will provide an indication as to whether the participant has been able to master the skill that has been taught, and whether the working environment is conducive to the practice of the skill. Very often investments are made in training programmes that do not fit the organizational culture, and participants are left feeling that the training programme was interesting but not useful – mainly because they do not have the opportunity to use and apply their skills. This information can be useful, as it may point to cultural changes that may be necessary.

Finally, evaluation can be conducted after a longer period following the training (often 6 months). This evaluation point provides insight into the 'stickability' of the skills trained, as well as the support in the organization for the knowledge gained. At a higher level, this evaluation point also gives an indication of whether organizational changes have taken place. For example, a 12-month training programme may have as its objective to bring about organization-wide change in how projects are managed. A longer-term evaluation will give an indication of whether the new behaviours have been embedded in the organization – that is, have the routines in the organization changed?

The tools for evaluation

We have discussed *when* we would want to evaluate and *why*. In order for us to complete the evaluation puzzle, we need to understand *how* we can evaluate learning outcomes. Here, we explore the various types of evaluation data together with the particular methods of evaluation.

Activity 11.6

- Identify the key tools that you would use to evaluate the outcome of a management development programme.
- Now list the strengths and weaknesses of each method.

When gauging the success of a training or learning intervention, it is possible to draw on both quantitative and qualitative information. Quantitative information refers to aspects that can be counted and measured. This gives an account of the 'what' of training – the number of people involved, the magnitude of the training investment and the reduction in the number of accidents. This form of evaluation data is gathered by calculating outcomes and by scoring behaviours on a scale from 1 to 5, for example. Qualitative information gives far richer information but may take longer to collect. These data give a feel for the 'how' a programme functions, and the implications that this holds for all of the parties involved. Qualitative information is also much more sensitive to the context, and is related to how people 'feel' and how they have 'experienced' the learning process. The most accessible way of collecting qualitative information is by asking participants questions that allow them to express their opinions, or by observing their behaviour.

Both these types of evaluation data can be gathered through the use of various evaluation tools. The most frequently used instruments or tools include:

- Questionnaires
- Interviews (individual and group)
- Focus groups
- Observations
- Skill tests (written and practical).

Each of these tools has its own theoretical foundation and historical development, which could take up several volumes if discussed in detail. The purpose of the exploration in this chapter is to give an indication of how and when these major tools can be used, and a brief outline of the advantages and disadvantages of each of the evaluation methods.

Questionnaires

According to Gibb (2002), questionnaires are the most commonly used evaluation tool for the measurement of 'reactions' or Kirkpatrick's level 1. On the whole, they are easy to construct (if you know what you want to ask) and administer. Most participants will also be familiar with this tool, and completion rates will therefore be high. Questionnaires that capture quantitative data comprise closed questions where the participant has to indicate answers on a five-point scale – for example:

To what extent would you say has this programme helped you understand the role of the performance management system?

1   2   3   4   5

(1 = to a great extent; 5 = not at all)

Other questionnaires include open-ended questions, which provide an opportunity to express an opinion. These questions therefore provide relatively rich information about a topic. The disadvantages of this method are that people often find it hard to express their opinions in writing, especially if the questionnaires are not anonymous. On the other hand, anonymous questionnaires could result in less useful comments because individuals may not take responsibility for their statements.

When constructing a questionnaire, it is useful to:

1 Give clear instructions as to how to complete the questionnaire and what the data will be used for (i.e. set the scene)
2 Stick to one idea per question
3 Avoid jargon, as this will lead to misinterpretations
4 Use a scale that is easy to identify with and fits the questions (e.g. to what extent do you agree with this statement?)
5 Keep questions short and clear – a very wordy question may confuse the issue that is being evaluated.

Interviews

An interview can be used as an evaluation source in itself, or to validate or cross-check information that has already been gathered. This evaluation tool can be seen as a door-opener that is used once the avenue of interest has been identified. Observation and questionnaires may point to areas that need to be understood better, and this is where the interview technique is most helpful. In other words, interviews are best at answering the 'why?' question.

If the HRD function wants to gain clearer insight into 'why' a particular training design worked especially well (from data already gathered) to facilitate the learning of project management skills, they may wish to conduct in-depth interviews with participants. These interviews will uncover stories, experiences and hard-to-measure concepts that could be valuable to future programme design.

Although an interview provides a rich source of evaluation information and is a powerful validation tool, its key weakness is that it is open to subjective interpretation – so two interviewers may draw different conclusions from conducting the same interview with the same participant. Furthermore, interviews are often time-consuming and expensive to conduct because of their resource intensity.

Focus groups

The resources dedicated to the interviewing process could be used more efficiently when conducting group interviews, or focus groups. In a focus group session, participants are asked to respond to a series of predetermined questions (*Kellogg Foundation Handbook for Evaluation*, 1998). The aim of the focus group is not to gain consensus, but to elicit as many rich views on a particular topic as possible. Gibb (2002) indicates that these focus groups are useful to obtain judgements about quality.

Observations

An even richer, but unfortunately more subjective, evaluation tool is the observation process. This tool is particularly useful in the pre- and post-training assessment situation of complex skills. It may be necessary to observe behaviour closely in order to design a training programme or to understand how a skill unfolds in a group context. These data can be stored and used for post-training comparisons.

Although observations provide a rich source of evaluation data, they have their drawbacks in so far as people may alter their behaviour when observed. This may lead to incorrect data. Being observed may also change the group dynamics and therefore the context of the skill. Finally, the observation process is both time and resource intensive. Nonetheless, this evaluation tool may uncover data about the work environment as well as the behaviours observed. This may usefully lead to the identification of future learning opportunities.

It is important to remember that observing and evaluating behaviour is a skilled task in itself. Observers may therefore need to be trained to conduct systematic observations. Furthermore, a coherent observation and assessment structure needs to be designed and agreed upon beforehand. If this is not done, it is almost impossible to compare observations, report behaviours and code data for future use.

Skills tests

Skill-based tests provide exact measures of the level of ability, and can be used effectively in the pre- and post-training scenarios. These tools give direct access to information required at Kirkpatrick's levels 2 and 3 (although observations are often preferred to assess the level 3 behaviours). Designing a skill-based test involves:

- A detailed task analysis – breaking a job or role down into its building blocks
- Creating a competency matrix for each of the tasks – indicating the knowledge, skills and behaviours needed to perform each task well
- Designing questions that measure each of the high performance tasks
- Developing a rating scale for each question
- Cross-referencing each rating scale to the job or role.

Although extremely useful because of its specific nature, it is necessary to note that not all skills can be assessed by using this evaluation tool. This relates more to abilities than capabilities. For example, I can easily tick-complete a questionnaire that reflects my arithmetic ability. This reflects the skill that I have developed, and it will be pretty obvious what my level of competence is. The main reason for this is the fact that there are right and wrong answers. On the other hand, I could not take a 'test' that would give you an indication of my 'managerial capability'. I would need to enact this and therefore you would need to observe my behaviour to know whether I am now capable of 'leading a team'.

The impact of evaluation itself

Many organizations that have embarked on evaluation programmes have found that they learn a great deal more than is captured by the evaluation data itself. Evaluation as a process can be a powerful illuminator of organizational interrelationships and the influence of culture on learning and success. It can also point to further learning needs and act as an organizational change catalyst. It is important to remember that evaluation takes into account organization relationships – that is, it does not disconnect performance issues, such as observing competent behaviour, from its context. Evaluation is ultimately rooted in the culture and routines of the organization.

In essence, evaluation uncovers performance issues. It tells us *what* works well and, more importantly, *when* it works well. It is by understanding the performance relationships in an organization that we can gain tremendous insight into the interconnections between management practices and performance outcomes. Previous research (Purcell *et al.*, 2003) found that a key indicator of organizational performance is discretionary behaviour. All the training and learning in the world may not make a difference if I do not have the discretion to enact or practise my skill. A significant influencer in the enactment of discretionary behaviour is, of course, motivation. To return to our earlier example, employees may not want to use their skills if they do not feel motivated to do so. It is also their team or their manager, or indeed the HRD practices, that may have an influence on their motivation.

A pre- or post-programme evaluation may not only highlight the impact of discretionary behaviour but also show how competencies unfold within complex power relationships. It provides a 'reality check' for many of the managerial competency models that were developed in the mid-1980s. These data, gathered through observation and interview methods, could also indicate:

- How the organizational culture influences performance
- Whether there are powerful subcultures that have an impact on learning
- Which managerial styles are more conducive to learning.

Finally, evaluating the performance of a team that works closely with a client or customer may provide an explanation of the impact of relationships external to the organization on performance and interactions within the organization. Understanding and managing these linkages between organizations (Kinnie *et al.*, 2003) can not only contribute to more effective learning designs, but also be used in resource allocation and relationship management.

It is only when the HRD function identifies and moves toward addressing these strategic issues that it can be regarded as critical to the success and the survival of the firm. Furthermore, it is fascinating to think that evaluation could provide a route for the development of SHRD. In a sense, the function that completes the learning process (i.e. evaluation) is also the function that creates several possible new paths for strategic contribution.

Summary

By this point in the chapter we have discussed the main questions that we posed of the evaluation process. We have answered the why, who, what, when and how questions. This puts is in a position to integrate these rich answers into a single theoretical framework.

Now let us try to pull these ideas together. In this final part of the chapter we can draw together the various questions we have asked to inform the evaluation strategy. This integration is illustrated in Table 11.3, which is structured around the first set of questions that we asked – i.e. *why* is evaluation important, and from *whose* perspective? The three main perspectives here included the need to judge performance from the participant's perspective, the evaluation of return on investment from the investor's perspective, and the need to get feedback on the programme design, mainly from the HRD function's perspective.

Each of these perspectives relates to different levels of evaluation as indicated by Kirkpatrick. It is important to note that all the levels of evaluation have some degree of relevance for the HRD function – that is, although SHRD is a developmental tool that can

Table 11.3
The why, who, when, how and what of evaluation

Why?	Who?	What?	When?	How?
Gauging performance improvements – 'How well am I doing?'	Participants, facilitators, HRD function	Kirkpatrick levels 2 and 3	During training programme and upon completion of programme	Skill-based tests, observation, interviews
Return on investment – 'Was it worth it'	Investors, HRD function	Kirkpatrick level 4	Upon return to workplace (long term = 612 months)	Questionnaires, human capital accounting
Programme design – 'What worked?'	HRD function	Kirkpatrick level 1, with some emphasis on levels 2, 3 and 4	Directly upon completion of programme (reactions)	Questionnaires, interviews, focus groups

be usefully applied across the organization, its review and management sits mainly within the parameters of the HRD function.

Each level of evaluation data also provides the HRD function with various platforms to base future decisions upon. For example, level 1 feedback can serve as a foundation for changes to course administration or programme structure as well as choice of training facilitator. On the other hand, levels 2 and 3 get more at the heart of the learning process and provide an indication of the training design is effective and the learning objectives achievable in the light of the organizational setting. Level 4 data provide a foundation for the HRD function to make a more strategic contribution. This is because these data link learning outcomes to organizational performance and give an indication of the impact of the HRD processes across the various levels in the organization. It is therefore multi-level in its data capture. Some measures used, such as rate of innovation, could also provide an indication of future capabilities. That is, it shows that a knowledge creation culture has been cultivated which should, in a knowledge economy, lead to a more successful organization. This level of evaluation data can therefore span several time dimensions as well.

There are optimal time periods within which to gather various forms of evaluation data. For example, the experience of a learning programme is best judged just after the event has been experienced. The 'When?'column of Table 11.3 gives an indication of these optimal times for various forms of evaluation processes.

Finally, each type of evaluation data (which are related to variety of purposes and evaluation roles) can be collected by using specific evaluation tools. The 'How?' column of Table 11.3 serves as a guide to some of these tools, but is by no means restrictive. Many organizations and HRD functions have designed their own tailor-made evaluation tools and can therefore use this table as a framework to structure their own processes.

References

Bassi, L. and Ahlstrand, A. (2000). *The 2000 ASTD Learning Outcomes Report.* ASTD.

Cascio, W.F. (1991). *Costing Human Resources: The Financial Impact of Behaviour in Organizations.* PWS-Kent Publishing Co.

Coleman, P.T. and Lim, Y.Y.J. (2001). Research report: a systematic approach to evaluating the effects of collaborative negotiation training on individuals and groups. *Negotiation Journal,* **October,** 363–91.

Cook, S.D.N. and Seely Brown, J. (1999). Bridging epistemologies: the generative dance between organizational knowledge and organizational knowing. *Organization Science*, **10(4)**, 381–400.

D'Andrea, V.M. (2001). Organizing teaching and learning: outcome-based planning.

Festinger, L. (1954). A theory of social comparison processes. *Human Relations*, **7**, 117–40.

Gibb, S. (2002). *Learning and Development: Processes, Practices and Perspectives at Work*. Palgrave.

Guerrero, S. and Sire, B. (2001). Motivation to train from the worker's perspective: example of French companies. *International Journal of Human Resource Management*, **12(6)**, 988–1004.

James, W. (1890/1950). *The Principles of Psychology*, Vol. 1. MacMillan & Co.

Kirkpatrick, D. (1975). Techniques for evaluating programs. Parts 1, 2 , 3 and 4. *Evaluating Training Programs*. ASTD.

Lave, J. and Wenger, E. (1991). *Situated Learning. Legitimate Peripheral Participation*. Cambridge University Press.

McCauley, C.D., Ruderman, M.N., Ohlott, P.J. and Morrow, J.E. (1994). Assessing the developmental components of managerial jobs. *Journal of Applied Psychology*, **79(4)**, 544–60.

Mead, G. (1934). *Mind, Self and Society*. University of Chicago Press.

Meggison, D. (1996). Planned and emergent learning, *Management Learning*, **27(4)**, 411–28.

Nickols, F.W. (1982). Training: a strategic view. *NSPI Journal*.

Nickols, F.W. (2000). Evaluating training. There is not a 'cookbook' approach (Http://home.att.net/~.nickols/evaluate.htm, accessed 15 March 2003).

Noe, R. (2002). *Employee Training and Development*. McGrawHill.

Nonaka, I. and Takeuchi, H. (1995). *The Knowledge Creating Company*. Oxford University Press.

Purcell, J., Kinnie, N., Hutchinson, S. *et al.* (2003). *People and Performance: Unlocking the Black Box*. Chartered Institute of Personnel and Development.

Raelin, J.A. (1997). A model of work-based learning. *Organization Science*, **8(6)**, 563–78.

Swart, J., Kinnie, N. and Purcell, J. (2003). *People and Performance in Knowledge Intensive Companies*. Chartered Institute of Personnel and Development.

Van der Sluis, L., Williams, R. and Hoeksema, L. (2002). *International Journal of Human Resource Management*, **13(8)**, 1266–78.

Yanow, D. (1999). The languages of 'organizational learning': a palimpsest of terms. *Proceedings from 3rd International Conference on Organizational Learning*, **June**, pp. 1075–86.

Chapter 12

The changing role of the human resource development professional

Introduction

Over the last decade the role of the training professional has changed as the concept of HRD has emerged and evolved. The HRD practitioner may still be involved in training delivery, but is increasingly likely to be operating as an internal consultant devoting much of his or her time to a range of activities, from advising on training needs at an individual level to facilitating strategic level change. The increased emphasis on knowledge is bringing about changes in the organization of work and the nature of the employer-employee relationship (Stewart and Tansley, 2002). It may not be possible any longer to use existing typologies, such as Pettigrew *et al.* (1982), to articulate the role of HRD in this rapidly changing business environment. As discussed earlier, there are several implications for the HRD function. As Stewart and Tansley (2002: 32) state, HRD practitioners:

> need to be involved in disseminating the message throughout the organization that attempts to manage organizational knowledge must be founded on an understanding of how people learn, how they implement what they learn, and how they share their knowledge.

In the twenty-first century, HRD practitioners will need to develop competencies that reflect this emphasis on *learning* – rather than on *training*, as was the case for their predecessors.

Objectives

By the end of this chapter you will be able to:

- Discuss the changing context in which HRD now operates, and the resultant demands on the trainer
- Appraise critically the changing role of the HRD professional from that of training administrator to internal change agent
- Discuss the necessary skills required by the HRD specialist.

The changing world of the HRD specialist

The context of organizational training and development has changed enormously in the past 20 years. Traditionally, trainers were often called 'instructors'. They were usually subject experts, and often went into training towards the end of the their careers. Trainers usually had an accepted place in organizations, believed in the value of training and were willing to invest in it. The traditional trainer was able to pass on a finite body of knowledge and skills, supported by a wealth of experience that could be accepted and relied upon to sustain a trainee's evolving career. This early training provided the basis for a lifelong career, so once individuals were 'trained' they were expected to put training into practice for the rest of their careers. No provision was made for further investment in training.

Change has made these traditional views obsolete. All organizations have to cope with perpetual change, and individuals must now accept that their early training will rapidly become outdated. Many organizations require employees constantly to handle new technology, changes in working practices and a highly competitive business environment. There has also been the reluctant recognition by many that some skills, bodies of knowledge and working practices are no longer relevant, and might even inhibit new practices. If changes are significant – and many of them are – trainers might be faced with the prospect of helping people to *unlearn* redundant knowledge and skills, as well as to 'learn' or 'relearn'. As explained in earlier chapters, HRD has evolved from training and development. However, the role of HRD is changing. Walton (1999) refers to HRD professionals as 'learning architects' who 'will need to demonstrate familiarity with strategic concepts, change management approaches, group facilitation processes and individual counselling techniques as well as to exercise sophisticated negotiation skills and handle the subtleties of power dynamics.' Daunting indeed!

Sloman (1994a) argues that the 'training function' exists to make a significant and distinctive contribution to the process of skills enhancement that all modern organizations require. However, nearly a decade later this is too narrow a definition of the role of the HRD function, as it does not adequately reflect all the constituents of HRD. The need to move away from a traditional specialist instructor role was already being recognized back in the 1970s, as the following quotation from a 1978 report of the Engineering Industry Training Board (EITB) indicates:

> we are really at the point where everybody in an organization has some training role ... Where training professionals are employed, their status should be enhanced by support from senior management and by the establishment of their own credibility based on the relevance of training to the business plan.

We are now seeing an ever-increasing shift away from training to learning due to the evolution of concepts such as organizational learning and the learning organization, and knowledge management. The political dimension of the role has also changed. For instance, Sloman (1994a) highlights the importance of training professionals becoming skilled in political behaviour and able to promote the training culture through influence, rather than relying on achieving results through imposition. Mabey and Salaman (1995) are somewhat more direct and succinct in their verdict that training is indeed a political activity.

However, in terms of describing the role of the HRD professional or HRD function there is no single, right model. Indeed, it is still useful to refer to some existing typologies in order to make sense of this issue, even though they were developed in the 1980s.

A 1999 research project by Darling *et al.* highlighted some real differences in how *training* is perceived. The report outlined major changes that influence the environment in which trainers, or HRD specialists, now have to conduct their role. These are outlined in Table 12.1.

Clearly, these issues have a direct impact on the focus and priorities of HRD specialists in their roles.

The list in Table 12.1 is quite extensive – and necessarily so, because the sample included a wide range of *training* specialists.

Table 12.1
The changing world of the HRD specialist

- Increasing concern with labour market issues, including long-term unemployment, skill shortages and equal opportunities
- Increasing recognition of the importance of training, consistent with the notion that ultimately it is the development of a learning culture and the skills for the workforce that determine the long-term competitive performance of an economy and the enterprises within it
- The emergence of a coherent national training strategy based on investors in People, and National and Scottish Vocational Qualifications
- The development of corporate strategies based on 'core' activities, resulting in the buying in of non-core services, including training and consultancy
- The restructuring of organizations, including decentralization and de-layering, and the consequential increase in the power base of senior operating managers
- The widespread efforts to adopt continuous improvement approaches, with their need for teamwork, flexibility and the development of positive attitudes at all levels of the organization
- Enhanced commitment to training from senior management, and a recognition of its strategic role and integrating function
- Renewed interest in organization development, and considerable interest in the concept of organizational learning
- Increasing expectation that individuals should assume much greater responsibility for identifying their personal training needs and managing their own careers
- Greater involvement of line managers in training, particularly as coaches
- Concern to demonstrate the contribution training makes to corporate strategy and that investment in training pays
- Training has become the central thrust to human resource management activity, resulting in the widespread need for most HR practitioners to be competent in training matters
- A shift in orientation from identifying individual needs towards developing and implementing training strategies for achieving overall organization effectiveness
- A concern with the application and transfer of knowledge and skills rather than merely their acquisition
- The development of competence-based frameworks for many occupations, including managers, which focus on an output rather than input model
- Emphasis on continuous development and lifelong learning
- Through developments in information technology, significant investment in learning media and resources, including CD-ROM and psychometric tests
- Increasing interest in how different people learn
- The increasing emphasis on demonstrating credibility/accountability/added value

Source: Darling *et al.* (1999: 12).

The people in their study included those directly involved in training and development within organizations and external training bodies. In addition, line managers responsible for their staff development were also included. Whilst this list is far-reaching in its aims, it identifies the nature of the trainer's roles and highlights the complexity within which organizational training takes place. More recent work corroborates and/or builds upon these findings.

Stewart and Tansley (2002) observe that more time and effort will be devoted to informal learning processes, to supporting a wider 'client' base and, as discussed above, to supporting knowledge management processes. They argue that this reflects a shift from *training provider* to *learning facilitator*. Other changes in role include:

> a more strategic contribution through more regular and closer contact with senior decision makers and a role as internal consultant in relation to operational managers and employees.
>
> (Stewart and Tansley, 2002: 33)

The changing nature of the training market

The nature of the training market itself is changing, which has a direct effect on HRD practices. Before we look at how exactly this has impacted on HRD, it is worth considering yourself how you see the influence of the training market on organizational training practices.

Activity 12.1

- Make a list of the factors, both external and internal to the organization, that influence the nature of the market for HRD activities. (External factors might include, for example, a more strategic approach to training, and changes in legislation regarding health and safety requirements; internal factors may include more outsourcing to external providers, and increased globalization.)

A number of changes, both internal and external, influence the market for HRD activities. A simple PEST analysis would indicate a number of factors derived from political, economic, social and technological changes. These, in turn, influence the market.

However, again it is worth considering the research of Darling *et al.* (1999), which represents the experiences of actual organizations that have been influenced by these changes. Their research outlines the key issues stated by respondents:

- A reduction in direct training with a great emphasis on facilitation and
- Advisory/consultancy work
- The move towards organizational development as a more strategic approach to training
- The organization's need to improve performance of valuable people
- The line manager's need to take responsibility through coaching and mentoring
- More cross-department working, and working in multidisciplinary teams
- More customer-focused training delivery
- More outsourcing to externals
- Increased globalization, where management responsibility extends to people they may never see
- Changing nature of organizations with increased emphasis on flexibility and knowledge.

As traditional forms of employment change, managers must focus on their own development as well as that of their employees. Amin and Van Eupen (1998: 18) argue that 'tomorrow's people' will have to take on the self-employed mindset, and be keen to retain their customer's business and continually to develop their skills to maintain their own employability. Therefore, the HRD specialist's role is now is increasingly as an adviser regarding change.

These changes in the training market clearly influence the demands made on the trainer and the HRD specialist, and represent another factor to be considered in this continually changing function.

The diversity of HRD roles

Pettigrew *et al.* (1982) identified the following roles that training staff were involved in across different organizational settings, namely:

- *Change agent*, whose focus is on the culture change needed to resolve organizational problems. Traditionally, the change agent is a marginal figure who, as an organizational development specialist, was concerned with problem-solving, was client-orientated and politically neutral.

■ *Provider*, who offers training systems and holds an operational delivery role to maintain the current system. This is primarily directed towards maintaining and improving organizational performance rather than changing the organization. This person has a fairly high level of influence, but operates within a fairly stable environment.

■ *Passive provider*, who is a low-key organizational maintainer who works only reactively and not proactively. This low-influence role might be adopted because a trainer is perceived to have a lower power base, whose maintenance role responded rather than initiated action.

■ *Trainer manager*, whose role involves planning, organizing, directing and controlling training operations

■ *Role in transition*, where the role is changing from that of provider to change agent and thus involves a variety of the above roles.

However, as argued above, the organizational context within which HRD specialists operate has increased in complexity. The concept of HRD has replaced that of training, or training and development. Consequently, new typologies are required in order better to understand the role(s) of HRD specialists. Harrison (1998) has extended Pettigrew *et al.*'s (1982) typology to include Sloman's (1994a) twofold typology of roles for training professionals, namely:

1   *The internal consultant*, who provides a service to internal customers and works alongside them to ensure the service is relevant and of high quality. The role is one of the professional who produces targets, costs, key activities to be carried out and the means of evaluating them. Unfortunately, internal consultants *usually* hold no core strategic role, and so their activities may not be linked directly with the strategic direction of the company. As well as holding no real strategic role, they are also in competition with external consultants.

2   *The strategic facilitator*, whose role necessarily involves expressing and ensuring the implementation of a 'clear training strategy with clear targets, control and clear accountability' (Sloman, 1994a: 26). It also requires the

need to develop and manage an appropriate learning culture in the organization. The skills required in this role, according to Sloman (1994a), include:

■ strategic awareness
■ diagnostic capability
■ influencing skills.

It is the role of the strategic facilitator that is essential in facilitating the strategic aspect of HRD, including the awareness that employee development enhances competitive capability. However, Harrison (1998) points out that this real strategic intervention is limited because there is little real evidence that HRD professionals are being represented (or indeed have influence) in board-level decisions.

Thus, Harrison (1998) combines the typologies of Pettigrew *et al.* (1984) and Sloman (1994a) to formulate the following roles of the trainer of the twenty-first century as:

■ Strategic facilitator
■ Organizational change agent
■ Internal consultant
■ Manager of HRD
■ The role in transition
■ Passive provider.

However, as argued by Mankin (2000), it is important to remember that in using terms such as change agent (or similar) the HRD manager needs to be very cautious. The role of change agent can only be truly proactive if the manager is helping to *create* change. This entails adopting a highly innovative stance, and HRD specialists will need to consider very carefully whether they have the competencies to handle the demands it will generate. It can be very difficult to work effectively in a highly ambiguous environment. A new trend emerging is the perceived need for both HRM and HRD functions to foster an entrepreneurial stance within their organizations (Coulson-Thomas, 1999). However, in a survey of 69 organizations, Coulson-Thomas concluded that not one of the training and development teams had investigated plans to take action in this area. What does this suggest? An innate conservatism in HRD functions? A possible fear of outsourcing, which is a logical extension of Coulson-Thomas' argument? Or does it simply mean that the idea is still ahead of its time, or maybe unrealistic? Or that organizations are simply lagging behind changes and trends in their external environment? Of course the implications of this view are significant, as Coulson-Thomas concedes. He claims that corporate cultures need to be turned upside down to embrace an entrepreneurial attitude, rather than encouraging corporate clones to conform to the *status quo*.

Another of the terms often used to describe the changing HRD role is that of 'internal consultant'. However, a problem with this perspective is that the HRD manager cannot disengage from a project in the same way as an external consultant. Indeed, Sloman (1994b) argues that the consultancy model is not an appropriate paradigm for the delivery of effective organizational training.

It has been suggested that someone operating at senior management level holds the role of *strategic trainer*. In a similar vein, Sloman (1994b) argues the case for a *strategic-facilitator* role (see above). So, how are roles likely to change in the future? Whilst we do not possess a crystal ball, the changes in the organization's external environment referred to earlier give us some clues. Bridges (1995) argues that the concept of a 'job' will not exist in the future and that, as the pace of change further quickens, the traditional organizational structure will be replaced by a new organizational form incorporating a core of key workers, supplemented by external workers, temporary workers and customers. This reflects the notion of the flexible organization. These 'workers' will operate on a project-by-project basis and, consequently, will also move in, out and through the organization according to demand. If you consider such ideas, along with those of the 'knowledge' and 'virtual' organizations, HRD specialists have what could be interpreted as an exciting and refreshing future to look forward to – one in which they will have to be sufficiently adaptable to change their way of working and in which the ability to operate in an ambiguous environment will be critical. Indeed, Bridges (1995) suggests that 'training professionals' should begin to think of themselves as independent professionals developing products and services that can be marketed and sold to organizations. The demand for skilled facilitators will be high.

A more recent typology is offered by Stewart and Tansley (2002):

- E-moderator
- Learning facilitator
- Strategic partner

   ■ Internal consultant
   ■ Network co-ordinator.

This reflects the increasing emphasis on knowledge, learning and ICT that characterizes the organization of the twenty-first century. As the authors argue (Stewart and Tansley, 2002: 33):

> Fulfilling these roles will require specialists to have an in-depth understanding of the nature of the knowledge economy, as well as of the particular applications of ICT in training practice. Related to this, they will require knowledge and understanding of advances in learning theories.

In order to facilitate change within organizations, HRD specialists will need to embrace change at a personal level to meet the demands of these roles. Indeed, change is a recurring theme in this chapter. Changes, both internal and external to the organization, greatly influence the nature and scope of the HRD specialist's role. These changes are ongoing, and represent an even greater need for trainers to keep pace with and manage change effectively. It is therefore worth considering the actual qualities of such change agents in organizations today.

Activity 12.2

- Make a list of the qualities that you think are essential in an individual initiating, monitoring and managing change effectively within an organization (such as the ability to communicate effectively and listen to others' opinions).

The role of change agent is a complex one, which requires an individual to have in-depth knowledge of organizational functioning whilst remaining detached, observant to social process and politically neutral. The role has been likened to that of a catalyst, which facilitates change without itself being changed in the process.

One of the key elements of trainers as organizational change agents is their ability to focus on organizational development activities. Haynes (1992), quoted in Darling *et al.* (1999), identified the qualities of change agents as follows:

   ■ The confidence and ability to lead
   ■ Trust and respect for others

- The ability to communicate clearly and listen effectively
- The ability to make decisions
- The possession of planning and organizing skills, including delegation, guiding and co-ordinating
- The ability to maintain control in different situations and knowledge of the field in which one is leader
- The energy and ability to stick to the task in hand
- Presence and consideration for the needs of others.

Let us consider the role of change agent in more depth, since it is crucial in understanding the demands now placed on the HRD specialist.

The HRD specialist as a change agent

Organizations have to face ever-changing environments. In order to survive and evolve, organizations must adapt to the environmental forces within which they operate. These changes might take any of the following forms:

- Developing from a simpler to a more complex form
- Adapting to both and internal and external changes
- Expanding or growing
- Shrinking or downsizing
- Developing new ways of conducting business.

Changes that may improve an organization's ability to adapt can be grouped into three main areas:

1 Technological factors include new products, services and use of automated equipment
2 Structural factors include changes to formal policies, practices and procedures
3 Human resource factors include the expectations and responses of employees.

Since HRD can contribute to all three areas, it plays a significant part in facilitating organizational change, especially if the HRD manager's role is one of change agent. Before we consider this in more detail, let us consider typical human responses to organizational change.

Human reactions to change

Reactions to change vary widely. Many people welcome change, whereas others actively resist it. No doubt there are many personal factors contributing to these responses. Although somewhat dated, Moss-Kanter's (1989) research into American companies produced 10 factors that inhibit progress and still appear to be of relevance now:

1   Loss of control – people are threatened by imposed change, but excited by being able to control the direction of change
2   Excess uncertainty – fear of the unknown brings fear of incompetence, and concerns for future prospects
3   Surprise – change without warning causes resentment or hostility
4   The difference effect – it can be uncomfortable to question old habits
5   Loss of face – some people may perceive change as criticism
6   Concern about future competence – a new job description may cause worry about future effectiveness
7   Ripple effect – change at work can cause change to other plans, family etc.
8   More work – more work and effort are required to make the changes effective, and this can be perceived to be beyond the call of duty
9   Past resentments – previous bad feelings may resurface
10 Sometimes the threat is real – the rise in status of one might mean a loss of power for others, so early communication is needed.

In general terms, the ability or willingness of individuals to change depends upon the level of security they feel. When a person is presented with new information or a new situation after a relatively stable period, the equilibrium is upset and that person does one of two things:

1   Rejects, suppresses and distorts the new information or situation
2   Integrates it and learns from it.

Individuals who feel insecure are more likely to reject the potential change, become defensive and avoid confronting the new situation. On the other hand, individuals with a high sense of security are also likely to take this option, since they will see no reason to change – there will be no incentive or justification for doing anything differently from before. Thus people in both positions reject and distort the situation, even though they have opposing reasons for doing so.

The organization therefore has continually to face change from outside and implement changes within. The issue to be addressed is whether people are actively being trained to accept these changes.

The contribution of HRD to change

Providing rational reasons for change is often insufficient to encourage people to embrace change. Communication becomes increasingly important as a vehicle for persuasion and rapid change because people's fears and feelings can influence the direction of the change. There must be a strong management commitment to change and a management style that is willing to listen, encourage people to take risks and allow people to participate in the pace or nature of the change. As a change agent, careful attention needs to be paid to people's reactions to change, and assistance provided to help them in overcoming any feelings of loss, insecurity, powerlessness, anger or resentment. On the other hand, there should be a focus on why people accept and even welcome change, and the major positive reasons (Moss-Kanter, 1984), have been identified as follows:

- They achieve some personal gain
- They like and are offered a new challenge
- They approve of the source of the change
- They like the manner in which the change was introduced
- They think the change will reduce boredom
- Some of the ideas they contributed were considered
- They feel that change is needed
- They think change will bring more opportunities
- They believe it to be good timing
- They have an overall positive attitude
- They are strongly influenced by their peers.

It is clear from these reasons that HRD has a large role to play in motivating and encouraging people to change. HRD initiatives should include skills development related to future as well as current performance. It should also focus on having and developing transferable skills, such as leadership, decision-making and interpersonal skills. Where appropriate, it can include opportunities to discuss the changes introduced and encourage suggestions and modifications.

The HRD specialist as change agent

HRD specialists are often in a better position to take a broad perspective across an organization and see the need for change that individual line managers cannot. They may notice things such as misunderstandings and poor communications across departmental or functional boundaries. They may see problems arising that could be avoided, and training needs that are not being met.

The extent to which HRD specialists adopt the role of change depends on the organization and the philosophy and mission of the organization. Whatever role they take, they can greatly influence the organization's readiness for change by careful choice of change strategies and by building personal credibility and reputation.

We saw earlier how Pettigrew *et al.* (1982) identified five trainer roles, namely provider, training manager, change agent, passive provider and role in transition. Whilst most of these roles respond to the needs of the organization, it is likely that the most effective 'trainer' role for the future will be that of change agent. Since the goal of the change agent is to challenge and change the organization's culture, this role will push the boundaries of legitimacy; consequently, many HRD specialists may not be willing to take on this role since it demands self-awareness, a strong power base, and risk-taking.

It is therefore apparent that the change agent is a person requiring a certain level of power and respect in the organization. Credibility becomes an imperative if HRD specialists are to maintain an effective power base, as well as being able to develop influencing skills. HRD specialists will need to develop certain skills in particular, such as alliance and coalition building, communication and listening skills, and influencing skills. They will need to appreciate the importance of understanding the organization's culture, the current commercial climate and the business strategy, and of building credibility in the eyes of key stakeholders.

However, is this such a new phenomenon after all? It has always been interesting to note how many HRD specialists admit to having a level of influence that far outweighs their position on the organization chart. This is not something that is given to the HRD specialist; he or she has to earn it through hard work, persistence and determination, and often via difficult and stressful circumstances. Alongside the development of these political skills, the HRD specialist needs to develop commercial acumen and strategic understanding.

Reid and Barrington (1999) say that three conditions must be satisfied if training and development is to achieve a secure status in the organization. These are:

1 The involvement of line managers
2 An appropriate structure in which training and development takes place
3 Specialist staff being viewed as professionals.

These three conditions have implications at an operational level. Thus the responsibility of training should be accepted by line managers, and a structure must exist within which the training roles are seen to be relevant to such aspects as:

- Boundary management
- Organizational culture
- Operational strategy
- Management style
- Organization's geography.

Training specialists must have clearly defined roles and be effectively trained in order to perform effectively and be perceived as competent professionals.

In addition to the above three conditions, Reid and Barrington (1999) highlight the importance of professionals' political and ethical roles. The EOSC (1995) standards, which established the basis for NVQs in training, do not mention these except within a core unit at top level. The term 'comply with professional and ethical requirements' is used. Reid and Barrington (1999), however, highlight the crucial importance of political and ethical judgement, especially if the HRD specialist is to be seen as competent by colleagues and others.

It is also debatable whether the change agent should be internal or external to the organization. The internal agent will have greater in-depth knowledge of the industry and workings of the company; on the other hand, he or she is part of the culture and organizational processes, which deflects from the role of objective observer. On the other hand, the external agent is often a specialist in organizational development, has a detached observer role, and is often better able to identify issues that need addressing before real change can occur.

Different stakeholders within the organization may also be more willing to accept the external agent's direction and offer them more accurate information because of less political comeback. Whilst it is desirable to manage change effectively, some writers are critical of the real ability to do this. King and Anderson (1995), for example, suggest there is an illusion of manageability where change agents or managers merely constantly adapt their styles and interventions to respond to iterative change rather than anticipating such change in a controllable manner.

Key HRD activities

Darling *et al.*'s (1999) research identified that 'trainers' were involved in four main areas or activities:

1 Development activities, including training needs analyses, coaching, evaluation etc.
2 Training delivery
3 Administration, particularly when subcontracting
4 Marketing the training function internally and responding to demand from line managers and senior management.

It is interesting that the areas in which trainers appear to be involved are largely operational activities, despite the general belief in HR circles that the role is becoming increasingly strategic in nature. The fourth area that trainers appear to be increasingly involved in is marketing of the training function and responding to management demands for training. Although this might indicate some strategic component, it appears to be a largely reactive role, and perhaps confirms Harrison's (2000) view that HRD will not be considered a sufficiently powerful tool for change unless it is seen as pivotal to business success and represented at board-level decision-making.

However, the above research has highlighted the too often neglected feature of HRD functions – that of marketing, which Mankin (2000) has argued is (and has to be) a strategic level activity. HRD managers should not be reticent about developing a marketing strategy for their function, or about communicating this to others. Indeed, the HRD function without such a strategy is unlikely to be maximizing its potential. From a pragmatic perspective, the role of marketing should be given a high profile by HRD professionals. Ultimately, it is an issue of whether you view employees as customers or not. To be an effective HRD function begins with understanding what training's customers hope to achieve, and dedicating HRD policies, processes and activities to the fulfilment of those goals (van Adelsberg and Trolley, 1999). Of course, this perspective may obscure potential conflicts between different stakeholders/customers.

However, much of the above may be criticized as still being too theoretical or aspirational. Consequently, it is worth looking at how this is borne out in practice.

Activity 12.3

- Outline how exactly you think the newly emerging role of trainer will be borne out in practice (e.g. increase in outsourcing of key tasks/linking of training initiatives to competence frameworks).

The practical implications of the changing role of the HRD specialist are far reaching. Darling *et al.*'s (1999) research indicated that there was:

- An increase in outsourcing, particularly in the direct delivery of training
- Increasing use of consultants and taking of external advice
- Greater emphasis on line managers taking responsibility for developing their people
- Greater emphasis on using research data to influence choice of interventions
- Increasing interest in the strategic contribution of training.

There is also an increase in work-based learning approaches, which in turn influence the nature and scope of the trainer's role. Organizations are willing to adopt a more flexible approach to meeting individual and team needs by a variety of approaches, including:

■ Portfolios including personal development plans for development as well as assessment
■ Project and assignments
■ Competence-based approaches linking development with NVQs
■ Demand to measure the transfer of learning
■ Use of learning resource centres, which appear to have mixed success regarding their value and use although support is highlighted as a key issue
■ Importance of supervision as a cornerstone of individual development.

This is a welcome change, which is presumably influenced by the changing nature of work – with increasing numbers of people working from home, telecommuting or adopting different shift patterns. In addition, there is an increasing use of ICT to assess learning and development needs and interventions, with the rapid growth in interest in e-learning being the latest manifestation.

The key trainer roles

Darling *et al.* (1999) ran a number of focus groups from the sample organizations to identify the roles that trainers *actually* played, as opposed to the alleged roles that academics and an increasingly strategically focused profession would like them to be taking. The results outlined the key trainer roles from three very different perspectives, namely:

1 Philosophical
2 Strategic
3 Operational.

These labels emerged from focus groups, and were not names given by the researchers. They highlight the focus that trainers themselves appear to be adopting. The philosopher role is one that embraces a strategic and advisory role, and involves a consultancy perspective. These roles are set out in Table 12.2 and identify the anticipated roles that HRD specialists believe they will be called upon to play, depending on how the organization chooses to embrace their roles.

Table 12.2
Trainer Roles

Philosophical	Strategic	Operational
Modernizer	Facilitator at	Facilitator at personal
Stabilizer of chaos	organizational level	level
Creator/supporter of	Integrator	Direct trainer
an innovative culture	Internal adviser –	Internal adviser –
Leader/supporter of	organizational	personal
the vision/champion	Organizational 'confidante'	development
Surfacer of myths and	Interpreter of people –	Coach/mentor
assumptions	implications of changes	Modeller
Banner carrier (in	in the business	Manager of learning
conjunction with HR)	Change agent (learning	Operational manager,
Gateway to learning	is by definition change)	team leader
Prophet	Influence	
	Manager of expectations	

Source: Darling *et al.* (1999).

This clearly demonstrates the expectations of HRD specialists who, whilst they are working within organizations, are no doubt influenced by external sources regarding their professional growth and development. Darling *et al.*'s (1999) research thus illustrates a move from the trainer as deliverer or provider to change agent. If this survey represents a trend towards HRD specialists adopting the role of the change agent, key questions emerge regarding the feasibility of trainers meeting the resultant demands:

■ Can HRD specialists fulfil the demands of the change agent role, and do they have the necessary skills and competence?
■ What are the implications for HRD specialists in terms of their own development?
■ Do the HRD specialists possess the necessary power to action the requirements placed on them?

The answers to these questions will depend on whether they obtain the necessary organizational support and have the motivation to learn. It is a test of their ability to act as learning role models. Many HRD specialists have links with professional bodies, such as the CIPD, the Institute of Management, universities, local authorities and Learning Skills Councils. These all lend support in fulfilling an increasingly complex role. However, for the role to be truly strategic, the status and credibility of strategic HRD as a major contributor to business success will have to be embraced.

The skills of the HRD specialist

The increasing emphasis on change management and strategic issues in the HRD specialist's role calls for a high degree of professionalism and standard practice. Darling *et al.*'s (1999) study, however, indicates a paucity of specifically focused training qualifications held by the respondents to their survey. The most highly educated HRD specialists in their research tended to hold more general management or personnel management qualifications, including MBAs and Diploma in Management Studies qualifications. Where CIPD qualifications are held, it is important to note that professional training does not focus directly on training, but on HRD within strategic HRM.

A wide range of knowledge, skills and abilities is needed to fulfil the different role expectations of the HRD specialist. The requirements will depend, to a large extent, on the specific roles expected in different organizations.

Mankin (2000) identifies the key skills as:

- Communication skills – written; verbal; listening; networking
- Consultancy skills – interviewing; questioning/listening; negotiating; analytical; influencing and persuading; clarifying; summarizing and reviewing; building trust
- Organizational – decision-making and delegation; objective setting
- Political skills
- Marketing and selling skills
- Facilitation
- Counselling
- Coaching
- Information technology
- Analytical – problem-solving; questioning; interpreting
- Design skills
- Psychology skills – especially of learning
- Financial skills

■ Project management
■ Flexibility.

In addition, there has to be an appropriate level of knowledge underpinning these. Knowledge of learning strategies and how to apply them will be crucial. Somerville and Mroz (1997), in discussing new competencies for a new world, believe that the following will be crucial: ways to engage and inspire people, to evolve teams and partnerships, and to acquire and use knowledge.

Darling *et al.*'s (1999) research identified the different skills required by the different categories of trainer. They are quite wide ranging, and before we look at the results of the research it is worth considering the requirements under prescribed headings.

Activity 12.4

Under the following headings, outline the knowledge, skills and abilities required by the HRD specialist:

- Strategic
- Internal consultancy skills
- Operational management skills
- Understanding of HRM and of learning and training
- Communication and interpersonal skills
- Cognitive skills
- Personal attributes.

The knowledge, skills and abilities needed by the HRD specialist, according to Darling *et al.*'s (1999) research, are shown in Table 12.3.

As organizational demands become more complex, so does the pattern of skills required by the HRD specialist. Developing these skills is perhaps the biggest challenge facing the HRD profession in the first decade of the twenty-first century. In order to meet this challenge, Stewart and Tansley (2002) have identified the following methods that HRD specialists could adopt:

■ Gaining knowledge about the services and support available via professional bodies (e.g. CIPD)
■ Being prepared to respond to high job demands and address difficulties in managing their own continuing professional development (CPD)

Table 12.3
Training skills for HR directors

Strategic view
- How to identify key issues; diagnosis, analysis, sifting (how to tease out real issues), understanding the industry and its people
- Good antennae to read situations
- Competitor knowledge
- Understanding of the business and what's important to it (business issues and training implications), showing how training can add value

Internal consultancy skills
- Selling ideas
- Persuasion/negotiation/brokering
- Initiating and innovating
- Managing dilemmas

Operational management skills
- Managing resources and competing for them
- Managing the HR team
- Balancing needs and capacity to deliver on a tight budget, managing budgets
- Project management
- Outsourcing
- Marketing/selling
- Selecting suppliers and contracting

Understanding of HRM and learning, training
- Good industrial relations skills
- What's involved in learning
- Working with line managers (in larger companies – NTO)
- Training design and delivery

Communication, interpersonal skills
- Facilitation of workshops/meetings
- How to operate in formal and informal networks, seeking allies
- Good process, interpersonal, social and communication skills
- Good antennae to read situations
- Acting as a sounding board
- Advising, counselling, coaching, mentoring senior managers, career counselling

Cognitive skills
- Complex problem-solving, critical thinking
- Analytical skills

Personal attributes
- Tact and diplomacy
- Enthusiasm and commitment
- Belief
- Proactive attitude
- Pragmatism
- Robust attitude
- Cultural fit/adaptation

Source: Darling *et al.* (1999).

- Expending effort on using the Internet to support their own CPD
- Forming networks, partnerships or discussion groups to provide informal learning opportunities.

The skills important in teaching and learning

In addition to the knowledge, skills and abilities suggested by the different trainer roles, a number of additional skills are essential in both direct training delivery and internal provider and consultancy roles. They include the following.

1   *Listening and questioning.* This links directly with effective verbal communication and the ability to express oneself clearly and succinctly. These skills underpin all effective management skills, and include the ability to:
    - gain an objective understanding of what another person has said
    - use a range of appropriate open and closed questions to gather information or ensure information is correctly received
    - ask for clarification of what has been said to ensure congruence between what is said and what is understood
    - use paraphrasing and summaries to ensure that understanding occurs and is reinforced at frequent intervals.
2   *Presentation skills.* Effective presentation skills will influence enormously the planning and delivery of training and learning events. They include:
    - directing the material appropriately to the audience
    - providing the listener with sufficient structure on which to digest the points being made
    - providing adequate reinforcement of ideas and summary conclusions
    - handling questions effectively
    - managing body language and voice intonation to enhance credibility
    - providing suitable visual content to support material or ideas being presented
    - managing the environment (e.g. overhead projectors, flipcharts) to ensure credibility and avoid disruption or distraction.

3   *Group facilitation*:
   - understanding the nature of group dynamics and the development of group norms
   - facilitating groups to engage in practical exercises without members being anxious or appearing foolish
   - handling conflict between group members
   - leading and motivating groups towards completion of tasks
   - developing exercises that allow for individual differences in learning style and team roles
   - ensuring that all group members contribute, not just those whose voices are the loudest.

4   *Influencing and negotiation*:
   - carrying out sufficient preparation to respond to unforeseen demands of group members
   - appropriate use of listening and discussion to ensure a win/win solution to conflict
   - the ability to highlight benefits and disadvantages with key options
   - ensuring all members have had an opportunity to present views, evaluate opportunities and agree with 'middle ground' for future activities.

5   *Coaching and mentoring*. An effective coach is supportive, consultative and a risk-taker. He or she encourages the positive and creative analysis of experiences as a basis for learning and growth and uses process techniques to facilitate problem-solving. Skills include:
   - a good understanding of the organization's culture, style, procedures and politics
   - good communication skills
   - a broad perspective of the organization and its activities
   - encouraging and motivating others
   - active listening skills
   - practical experience
   - a network of contacts within the organization
   - managing social process and handling others' emotions
   - providing objective and timely feedback
   - expressing constructive criticism.

6   *Consultancy skills*:
   - being client-centred and understanding clients' organizational and personal issues
   - being proactive

- personal confidence and initiative
- identifying opportunities, taking risks and handing any negative responses
- thinking and acting strategically
- effectively managing change
- being politically sensitive.

It is possible to construct self- and peer-assessment instruments based on the above to assist the HRD specialist in becoming much more aware of his or her own development needs. In order to meet the demands facing the HRD profession, this must be carried out on a continuous basis. As Stewart and Tansley (2002: 34) argue, HRD specialists:

> need to be able to continually investigate what is happening externally in training and development, particularly e-learning aspects, in order to benchmark their own practice.

The message – maybe the mission statement – for all HRD specialists needs to be:

Practice what we preach.

Summary

The environment in which the HRD specialist works has changed considerably as organizations must develop their human assets to remain viable and in order to survive. This chapter has explored the changing role, using different typologies of roles for HRD professionals. The role of the trainer has changed considerably from one of administrative organizer or up-front provider to that of a change agent who facilitates the learning process more widely. In practice, roles vary widely and depend, in part, on the extent to which there is a focus on strategic human resource development (HRD) as opposed to the more narrowly focused delivery of training and development. There have been many influences on the extent to which the role has changed. Some are external, and include economic and social change and technological advance. Others are internal, and are a function of the increasingly strategic focus of HRD. These influences have a direct impact on the expectations of the role, and the skills, expertise and attitudes required to perform the job effectively.

The greater focus on strategic alignment with business goals is apparent as many organizations see HRD specialists as internal change consultants whose role it is to prepare human resources for the twenty-first century.

Recent research indicates diversity in the nature of the trainer's role, but a continuance of an operational rather than a strategic focus. It may be that a strategic focus is the desire of the HRD profession and academic circles, but not something that is borne out in reality.

Recent research has also indicated a range of skills essential for the emerging strategic role, some of which are new and others, particularly interpersonal skills, which have been accepted for some time. It is essential that an organization agrees the role it wishes its in-house employee development specialists or external providers to fulfil. Once this is agreed, it can go about identifying and ensuring that they hold the requisite skills and competence to facilitate the organization growing and surviving.

Not all organizations have responded to the pressure strategically to align their people development with their business goals. The role will thus vary enormously. In some organizations, the focus will be on the trainer as specialist provider or training facilitator. In others, it will seek to align training initiatives with the wider business objectives and performance management systems.

The HRD specialist of the twenty-first century will need to be an internal change agent whose consultancy and facilitative skills are process orientated and operate within a politically sensitive mode. A knowledge of organizational behaviour issues will be essential if the HRD specialist is to initiate and manage change within a turbulent and competitive business environment.

However, whilst the academic and professional bodies constantly point to the importance of the trainer as change agent, recent research into organizations indicates that this may be rhetoric or desire rather than organizational reality. That said, the argument still stands that if organizations are to be fully effective and prepared for the demands of a constantly changing environment, then the HRD specialist will need to be creative and innovative in integrating initiatives that support a culture of learning and development.

References

Amin, R. and Van Eupen, P. (1998). *Tomorrow's People.* CREATE (Scientific Research in Employment and Technology in Europe).

Bridges, W. (1995). *Jobshift: How to Prosper in a Workplace Without Jobs*. Nicholas Brealey Publishing.

Coulson-Thomas, C. (1999). Who dares wins. *People Management*, **2 September,** 44–9.

Darling, J., Darling, P. and Elliott, J. (1999). *The Changing Role of the Trainer*. Institute of Personnel and Development.

Harrison, R. (1998). *Employee Development UK*. Institute of Personnel and Development.

King, N. and Anderson, N. (1995). *Innovation & Change in Organizations*. Thompson.

Mabey, C. and Salaman, G. (1995). *Strategic Human Resource Management*. Blackwell Business.

Mankin, D.P. (2000). *Managing the Training and Development Function*. Thames Valley University (Open learning workbook – internal publication only).

Moss-Kanter, R. (1989). *When Giants Learn to Dance: Mastering the Challenges of Strategy, Management and Careers in the 1990s*. Simon & Schuster.

Pettigrew. A.M., Jones, G.R. and Reason, P.W. (1982). *Training and Development Roles in their Organizational Setting*. Manpower Services Commission Training Studies.

Reid, M.A. and Barrington, H. (1999). *Training Interventions: Promoting Learning*.

Sloman, M. (1994a). Coming in from the old: a new role for trainers. *Personnel Management*, **26(1),** 24–7.

Sloman, M. (1994b). *A Handbook for Training Strategy*. Gower.

Stewart, J. and Tansley, C. (2002). *Training in the Knowledge Economy*. Chartered Institute of Personnel and Development.

Walton, J. (1999) *Strategic Human Resource Development*. Financial Times/ Prentice Hall.

Index